A cyclist's guide to the

PYRENEES

PETER COSSINS

GREAT NORTHERN

To Keith and Pauline for inspiration and being inspirational, and to Joanna 'Jojo' Crabtree, who loved the mountains.

Great Northern Books
PO Box 1380, Bradford,
West Yorkshire, BD5 5FB

www.greatnorthernbooks.co.uk

© Peter Cossins 2020
First published 2021

Every effort has been made to acknowledge correctly and contact the copyright holders of material in this book. Great Northern Books Ltd apologises for any unintentional errors or omissions, which should be notified to the publisher.

All rights reserved. No part of this book may be reproduced in any form or by any means without permission in writing from the publisher, except by a reviewer who may quote brief passages in a review.

ISBN: 978-1-912101-24-5

Design by David Burrill

CIP Data
A catalogue for this book is available from the British Library

CONTENTS

4 Introduction

Pyrénées Orientales

8 Galamus gorge and Cathar masterpieces
10 Tour of the Capcir
12 Tour de Mont Louis
14 A majestic tour of the Cerdagne
16 On the slopes of the magical Canigou
18 Corbières and Roussillon winelands
20 Têt to Tech and return
22 Tour of the cherry orchards
24 Tour of a Vallespir mining valley
26 From Catalogne to Catalunya and back
28 Tour des Monts Albères
30 Dodging the border bargain-hunters
32 Mediterranean coasting
34 Tour de Thuir
36 Tour de Roussillon
38 Prats to Mollo and back again

Girona

40 Catalonia's highest road climb
42 Tour of Garrotxa
44 Tour of the Catalan volcanoes
46 Lost roads of the Ripollès
48 A Catalan pair of Vuelta passes
50 Tour of the Cerdanya
52 A long road to Pal

Barcelona

54 Easy rolling in Barcelona province
56 Beneath the Cadí massif
59 A Catalan wall and a Vuelta summit

Aude

62 Plateau de Sault circuit
64 Tour of Quercorb
66 Close neighbours but so different
68 The Da Vinci Code loop
70 Tour of the upside-down mountain
72 Corbières winelands and a Cathar masterpiece
74 The road to Paradise
76 The joy of the Jau
78 Upper Aude valley back roads

Ariège

80 Ariège leg-warmer
82 One climb, five cols and a grotto

84	To Mur or not?		164	Two Hautes Pyrénées Tour favourites
86	Tour of Cathar castles		166	Tour of Val d'Azun
88	The 2019 Tour's Foix finale		168	Mountain highs at Argelès Gazost
90	In the shadow of Mont Valier			

- 84 To Mur or not?
- 86 Tour of Cathar castles
- 88 The 2019 Tour's Foix finale
- 90 In the shadow of Mont Valier
- 92 The land that time forgot
- 94 The Ariège Alpe d'Huez
- 96 Well off the beaten track
- 98 Tour of the Trois Seigneurs
- 100 2017 Tour stage – with an extra bit!
- 102 High rolling on the Corniches
- 104 Two magical dead-ends
- 106 Exploring the Couserans
- 108 Lost in the Couserans
- 110 In the wheeltracks of Robert Millar
- 112 The Ariège's wild frontier
- 114 Tour du Carlit

Andorra

- 116 Highest pass in the Pyrenees
- 118 Andorran figure of eight
- 120 Andorran high spots and gravel
- 122 Western Andorra highs

Lleida

- 124 Gorgeous Lleida
- 126 South from La Seu d'Urgell
- 128 The Coll de Nargó slalom
- 130 La Seu to Sort and back
- 132 Serene refuge above La Seu
- 134 The beautiful anomaly of Val d'Aran
- 136 A Catalan gem with a big view

Haute Garonne

- 138 A trio of Tour favourites
- 140 The Peyresourde both ways
- 142 The wild and wonderful Balès
- 144 Luchon's twin peaks
- 146 The Haute Garonne valley

Hautes Pyrénées

- 148 The Tourmalet both ways
- 150 Tour of the Bigorre
- 152 The majestic Col de Portet
- 154 Beautiful and endless mountain views
- 156 Tour of the Comminges
- 158 Tour of the Baronnies
- 160 Néouvielle high-rise triptych
- 162 The Majestic Cirques of Gavarnie and Troumouse
- 164 Two Hautes Pyrénées Tour favourites
- 166 Tour of Val d'Azun
- 168 Mountain highs at Argelès Gazost

Huesca

- 170 The trans-Pyrenean bone-breaker
- 174 The wallcreeper and Ordesa National Park
- 176 Vuelta favourites old and new
- 178 In Aneto's shadow
- 180 Huesca's mini Grand Canyon
- 182 High rolling around Jaca
- 184 Huesca's big country

Navarra

- 186 Total tranquillity in Aragón
- 188 Vuelta a Navarra
- 190 Basque Country border hopping
- 192 Inspired by Induráin
- 194 Doubly inspired by Induráin

País Vasco

- 196 Basque ramps and the gorgeous Gorramakil
- 198 A San Sebastián classic day out
- 200 A tour of eastern Euskadi

Pyrénées Atlantiques

- 202 Through the Roncesvalles pass
- 204 The Pays Basque's wild frontier
- 206 Steep walls and ridgeways
- 208 Break for the border
- 210 An historic col and a stunning ridge
- 212 Pays Basque and Euskadi
- 214 Short haul to La Pierre Saint Martin
- 216 Long haul to La Pierre Saint Martin
- 218 My first Pyrenean climb
- 220 The Arette, Aspe and Ossau valleys
- 222 A spicy cross-border loop
- 224 Back country Basque Country
- 226 Tour of the Basque Country
- 228 Green and pleasant Basque lands
- 230 The magnificent Aubisque and Soulor
- 232 In the shadow of Pic d'Orhy

234 Raid Pyrénéen

- 239 **Index**

Introduction

This book is about the Pyrenees, about the mountains, of course, but also about the valleys and hills in between and the roads through and across them. The idea behind it is simple: to provide cyclists with routes to ride no matter where they happen to be in this majestic 430-kilometre-long range, between Cerbère on the Mediterranean and Hendaye on the Atlantic.

I'll readily admit that it's inspired by Alfred Wainwright's iconic guides to walking in the Lake District in north-west England, which are almost as essential to enjoying expeditions on those hills and fells as a well-proofed jacket, trousers and boots. This book is, in essence, a "Wainwright for the Pyrenees", a guide that not only highlights famous cols and passes such as the Tourmalet, Aubisque and Peyresourde, but more than 300 others, all of them connected in a spider's web of 112 routes covering more than 10,000 kilometres of roads in France, Spain and Andorra. They are intended to highlight the riding experience in every part of this beautiful, rugged and ever-changing mountain range, describing the best roads to ride on and the ones to avoid, why one side of a pass might be preferable to the other flank, and reveal new climbs and roads to explore.

The routes have been put together based on three decades of riding, travelling, working and, more recently, living in the Pyrenees. I first visited the range on a bike in 1990, travelling with a friend to watch a mountain stage of the Tour de France. We took the ferry to Santander, crossed northern Spain

and reached the foot of the Port de Larrau. I still well remember wondering how on earth I was going to get my 10-speed Peugeot with its rickety, overladen rack up to the summit. But an hour or so later we were there, looking down on the vultures circling on thermals that had been high above us when we'd started, totally thrilled by the experience and by the breath-taking landscape around us.

In the subsequent decades I've been back numerous times, principally as a journalist covering the Tour, the Vuelta a España and other bike races that run through these mountains. In 2016, I moved with my family to the Ariège in the French Pyrenees, one of the drivers behind that decision being the desire to spend more time riding in the mountain terrain that I've come to love.

Once I'd started to explore more extensively, I realised that there are plenty of books and lots of online information about the climbs in the Pyrenees, particularly the most renowned passes, but very little about the terrain all around them and about other climbs that might be just as challenging or beautiful, but often get missed because they don't ever feature on the Tour route. At the same time, during my own sorties I was reminded again and again that as much pleasure can be gained from climbing a pass in the Pyrenean foothills that may only be a few hundred metres high but presents a startling perspective on the snow-capped main ridge as from topping a high pass that's a regular Tour fixture.

How to use this guide

The order of the routes has been organised running east to west along the chain, placing neighbouring departments, provinces and the country of Andorra next to each. Consequently, the routes begin in Pyrénées Orientales, continue on the Spanish side of the chain in Girona and Barcelona, cross back into France for Aude and Ariège, and so on to finish in Pyrénées Atlantiques in the west. This should make it easier to piece cross-department/province/border routes together.

Ranging from 50-odd kilometres in length to almost 200, these routes have been put together with the aim of providing a wealth of options to riders at all levels. As a whole, they form a web covering the whole range, one route butting up against or overlapping the next, making it easy to increase the distance of a ride by including part of a neighbouring route. Equally, the longer rides feature suggestions on shortcuts where these are possible.

I've endeavoured to include as many circular routes as possible. Unlike Tour riders who tend to ride from place to place each day and can count on team cars and all manner of backroom staff to make this practical, most of the rest of us are limited by where we're staying or where we've parked. Consequently, the start and finish point for every one of these routes is in the same location. Circular routes also have the advantage of allowing you to choose a different start/finish point, one that is convenient to you at any location on almost every one of these routes.

In addition to details on ride distance, vertical gain, the climbs featured, and grading of each ride according to its degree of difficulty, each ride also includes an estimate of the time required to complete it. These times are guidelines and not intended to be prescriptive. A 60km route, for instance, might take most of a day to complete if you want to stop at a mountain-top auberge for lunch and soak in the panorama. Following these stats and details, I then provide an overview of the route, underlining key points, highlighting bits of local history and colour, aiming to give a flavour of what to expect. I also provide a brief insight into what each route is like in the reverse direction, as most are quite different tackled the opposite way, effectively giving you more than 200 routes to explore.

I'm not expecting anyone to carry a book of this size in the rear pocket of their jersey. All of these routes are available for download using individual QR squares or from this guide's associated website (www.roadscolspasses.com) as a GPX file that is compatible with all major brands of GPS bike computer and with apps such as Strava. Each route also includes a detailed itinerary, highlighting key road junctions, towns and villages, and the featured climbs, which I recommend you photograph on your smartphone before setting out. Sticking a printed copy of the itinerary to your bike's top-tube, just as professional racers do, or putting one in a pocket will provide further back-up in case of a battery running down or some other failure.

I've deliberately avoided giving details on cafes, restaurants, hotels and other practical information because businesses of this kind come and go so often and their opening hours can be erratic. I am planning, however, to set up a forum on the guide's associated website where these details can be posted by riders who've completed a route and wish to recommend (or not!) a particular establishment and by business owners who want to highlight their hours and dining/accommodation options for passing cyclists. Ideally, this will develop into an additional resource that riders can reference before setting out on a ride.

The Pyrenees

There are two classical versions of the story of how the Pyrenees got their name. The first derives from Greek mythology, the historian Herodotus recording that Pyrene, the daughter of Gallic king Bebryx, was raped by the drunken Hercules and ran off to the woods, where she gave birth to a snake and was then torn apart by wild animals. After completing his 12 tasks, the repentant Hercules returned to lay Pyrene to rest, pleading remorsefully for her name to be

preserved for the ages. The alternative, and at least slightly believable version, that is described by another Greek historian, Diodorus Siculus, suggests that it comes from the Greek word pyrene, meaning fire, the conflagration started by herders so great that it devastated the whole range.

Providing a natural border between France and Spain, with the tiny country of Andorra nestled in between those nations towards the eastern end, the Pyrenees are a geological marvel, its peaks mainly of highly resistant granite formed by the collision between the Iberian and European plates around 100 million years ago, with the majority of the mountains created between 50 and 75 million years later.

In the millennia since that upheaval, the effects of ice, snow, rain have gradually reshaped the Pyrenees. Some of the most obvious examples of this immense erosive effect can be seen in the Pyrenees-Monte Perdido Natural Park, a UNESCO World Heritage Site towards the middle of the range. On the northern side of the Pyrenean ridge are the four magnificent cirques of Gavarnie, Estaubé, Troumouse and Barroude, their deep hanging valleys created by glacial erosion. On the southern side, the Añisclo canyon, one of the deepest in Europe, has been gouged out over the last few thousand years by the River Bellos. In the current era, climate change, notably global warming, is continuing to change the shape and look of the Pyrenees, and even speeding it up, with most of the glaciers now melted away.

As a result of this tectonic and climatic activity, the range has a number of peculiarities that quickly become evident when exploring the Pyrenees on the bike, to make them, as Italian climber Damiano Cunego once put it, "not like any mountains I've climbed before". On the French side they drop away much more rapidly through parallel river valleys into the plains to the north. The roads up and through them reflect this. Typically, they're steeper with frequent changes in gradient, often described as being like goat tracks that have had tarmac flung down on top of them.

The Spanish side, on the other hand, has far more breadth to its ruggedness. The foothills are more extensive, higher and almost impenetrable in places, the valleys between them deep and often not connected to each other via road because of their inaccessibility and the lack of human settlement. These geological characteristics are highlighted by the number of routes on each side of the chain. There are three times as many in France simply because there are far more roads connecting more towns and villages.

The variations in climate are dramatic too. At the western end of the Pyrenees, the Basque Country is wet and very verdant as a result of its proximity to the Atlantic. On the French side of the range, thanks to the flatness of the Aquitaine plain this greenness extends as far east as the central part of Aude. Even in mid-summer it can and does rain heavily thanks to weather fronts coming off the Bay of Biscay – the most temperate months in the French Pyrenees and, therefore, often the best for riding are September to November. Over in Spain, however, the climate to the east of Navarra is much drier, the terrain parched and even desert-like in some parts during the summer. At the eastern end of the Pyrenees, the climate is different again and archetypally Mediterranean on both sides of the border, the wind off the sea often the most disruptive climatic feature.

Ever since that first ride up the Larrau in 1990 and especially since my move to the Ariège, I've come to realise that the Pyrenees, 430 kilometres long and only 130 kilometres across at its widest point, is a mass of variations. Neighbouring summits and valleys can be subtly to extraordinarily different in terms of landscape and climate. The two ends of the chain may be a frantic buzz of traffic and activity, but almost everywhere in between is tranquil, the roads, cols and passes ripe for discovery by bike. The terrain may be challenging, but the rewards of a wonderful view, slaloming down a thrilling descent and, of course, summiting those passes are all the greater for that. Now let's go and explore…

GALAMUS GORGE AND CATHAR MASTERPIECES

This route may not feature any noted cols, but in less than 50km it packs in more natural and historical splendours than almost every other ride in this guide, and on that basis alone it is very highly recommended to cyclists of all ability levels. It begins in the Corbières wine centre of Maury, but quickly leaves its busy main street, heading south towards Lesquerde. After crossing a single-track railway, the road rises away from the valley floor, with views across Maury towards the high ridge to the north, where the Château de Quéribus can be picked out.

That Cathar monument is for later, though. The elements are likely to be of more concern at the moment. The wind frequently blasts through this valley, often barrelling in off the Mediterranean, in which event it will be providing some substantial support. At the unmarked Coll dal Pourtell, the view opens out to the south, vines on the sun-soaked slopes in the foreground with the Pyrenean high peaks as the backdrop. Keep following signs to Lesquerde, where several *caves* underline that wine is the foundation of the local economy.

The road drops into the Agly Valley and fuses with the D619 just before Saint Paul de Fenouillet. Entering the town, fork left, following the sign to Gorges de Galamus. Head straight over the main road at the crossroads, riding between vineyards across the broad valley and starting to climb again, soon reaching the breath-taking Gorges de Galamus, a deep, narrow cleft carved out by the River Agly. In high summer, this road is often extremely busy, which is testament to its splendour. The narrowest 1.5km section can only accommodate traffic travelling in one direction, which alternates, so a longish pause may be unavoidable.

This tightest part commences with passage via a very low tunnel through a cliff, the road then hanging off or hacked out of the side of the gorge, dozens of metres above the Agly below, rushing in the spring but often no more than a trickle in the summer. It's a wondrous 1,500m, the road continuing beyond it to Cubières sur Cinoble. Turn right in the direction of Soulatgé, ascending to the Col d'en Guilhem. From there, meander gently down to Soulatgé, keeping straight on coming out of the village heading for Duilhac, the road soon following a direct line towards the Château de Peyrepertuse. At a fork, keep right with the immense Cathar fortification still the target.

Passing over the Col de la Croix Dessus and then dropping into Duilhac, there is the option of taking the very steep 4km road up to the castle – it averages almost nine per

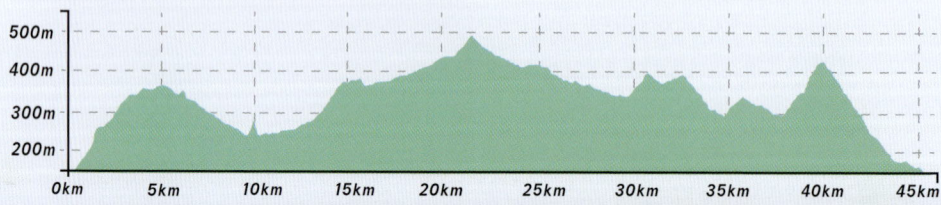

PYRÉNÉES ORIENTALES

The Château de Quéribus with the Château de Peyrepertuse on the ridge in the background

cent and has sections at up to 16. There are staggering views en route, but once the road ends in the car park you'll need to walk for another 15 minutes upwards to reach what is by far the biggest of the Cathar castles, covering the same area as Carcassonne's citadel.

Continuing down from Duilhac, the road drops into a dip, climbs briefly to reach the Col du Tribi, then makes a beeline for Cucugnan. Bear right before this village, then ascend once more to the Grau de Maury, where there's a left turn to the Château de Quéribus. What is believed to be the last stronghold of the Cathars has been beautifully restored. Like Peyrepertuse, though, it's a slog to get there – 1.5km at 14%! – and then there's a 10-minute walk from the car park.

If it's a clear day, the descent back to Maury is sensational, the Pic du Canigou and other towering Pyrenean heights on the horizon beyond a valley that's a patchwork of vineyards. The little town arrives quickly, bringing the curtain down on a short, but unforgettable ride.

Route in reverse
Still a lovely ride, but all of the drama comes in the first half and this diminishes the impact considerably.

Distance: 45.7km
Elevation gain: 992m
Highest point: 498m
Est. moving time: 1.5-3hrs
Degree of difficulty: ●
Climbs: Col d'en Guilhem (498m), Col de Grès (406m), Col de la Croix Dessus (403m), Col du Tribi (344m), Grau de Maury (432m)

Parcours

0km	Maury D19
6km	Lesquerde
9.5km	D19/D619
11km	Saint Paul de Fenouillet D619/D117 ➡ then ⬅ after 200m ①
16km	Gorges de Galamus
20.5km	Cubières D10/D14 ➡ ②
21.5km	Col d'en Guilhem
26km	Soulatgé D14/D10 ➡ ③
30.5km	Col de Grès
32.5km	Col de la Croix Dessus
33.5km	Duilhac
37.5km	Cucugnan D14/D123 ➡
40km	Grau de Maury ④
45.7km	Maury

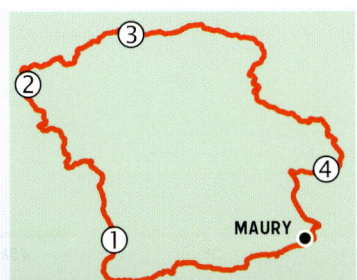

A TOUR OF THE CAPCIR

The high-plateau valleys at the western end of Pyrénées Orientales resemble the landscapes in the Westerns that I'd watch with my dad when I was a kid. On a hot day in the Capcir or the Cerdagne, it's not hard to imagine a lone horseman gradually emerging from the heat haze, cantering towards some dusty little town, where he'll deliver his own form of justice to the villains that are terrorising it.

Even if there's no chance of an Eastwood-like figure slowly becoming apparent in this immense landscape, this terrain does undeniably provide an unforgettable location for two-wheeled exploration, and this ride sees much of the best of the Capcir. It starts in Formiguères, heading out on the main drag and then forking right just on the edge of town towards Les Angles, which soon becomes visible in the distance, the road barely deviating as it hurries towards this ski station, built in the mid-1960s to stem the rapid population drift away from the area.

In common with other winter resorts, Les Angles is now attempting to broaden its appeal to summer visitors, opening up mountain bike trails and hosting the Altriman, reputedly one of the world's hardest Ironman-style triathlons, featuring a 197km bike section that crosses nine passes including the Pailhères, Pradel and Garavel. That event's swim takes place in Lake Matemale, which becomes increasingly apparent climbing away from Les Angles.

After rising steadily through pine woods, the road descends in the same easy fashion towards Mont Louis. When it meets the main D118 highway, turn left towards La Llagonne, starting to ascend very gently once again. Branch off right towards Caudiès de Conflent, a sign immediately indicating the beginning of the climb to the Col de la Llose. On clear days, the panorama from this first stretch of this short ascent are tremendous. The summit and this ride's high point come soon after, next to the Madres Coronat cross-country ski station.

Most of the next 20km are downhill, the landscape changing as the road drops through pine trees to reach rockier and more arid terrain. Keep on towards Caudiès de Conflent, briefly climbing, before weaving down through this village, the narrow road twisting more tightly as it drops out of the pines to a T-junction. Turn right towards Railleu, still descending. Beyond this hamlet, the road ahead can be seen running low down on the opposite mountainside. Keep heading down that way, passing the turn to Sansa.

This is a remote and quite magical section, if a little rough in places. The deeper you get into the valley, the narrower it becomes, the road clinging to the rockface, sweeping this way and that, the peaks of the Canigou massif appearing one moment and then disappearing the next.

After three or four kilometres of descent, a road appears low on the opposite flank of the valley, this the route back up to the Capcir. It begins with a close to 360° turn towards Ayguatebia, the road dropping for a short while to reach a bridge across the River Cabrils, then starting to climb.

Leaving Ayguatebia, switch back hard right, heading towards Railleu once more and, not long after, arriving at the T-junction above that village. This time, turn left towards the Col de Creu, which arrives after ascending through another wonderfully secluded valley and pine woods. It feels like you're in the middle of nowhere, but after swinging down through a couple of corners, the Capcir plateau reappears and the road hurries down

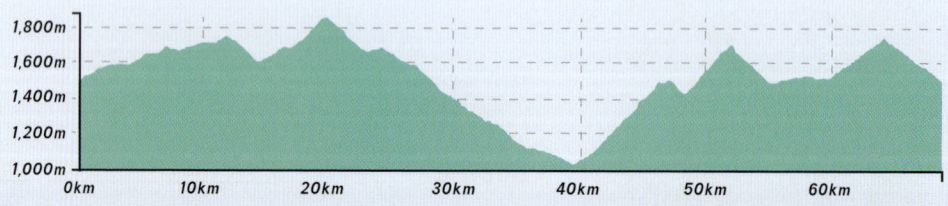

PYRÉNÉES ORIENTALES

The road across the Capcir

into Matemale and on to Formiguères, the ancient capital of the Capcir and the summer residence of the Majorcan kings during the 13th and 14th centuries.

Formiguères is now more renowned for its small ski station, the final summit on this route. Little more than 5km long, the ascent to it may well be the easiest to reach an altitude of 1,800m anywhere in the Pyrenees. Averaging 5.5%, it runs through pine woods to the resort, the view across to the Pic du Canigou making this final bit of effort well worthwhile.

Route in reverse

I'd still leave the climb to the Station de Formiguères till last, but otherwise this circuit is equally enjoyable. The climb from the lowest point of the route is longer, but shallower, which some may prefer.

Distance: 69km
Elevation gain: 1,699m
Highest point: 1,866m
Est. moving time: 2.5-4hrs
Degree of difficulty: ●●◐
Climbs: Col de la Llose (1,866m), Col de Creu (1,712m), Station de Formiguères (1,761m)

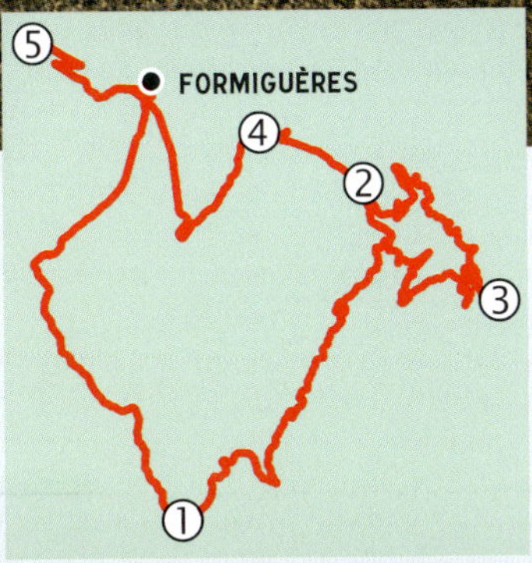

Parcours

0km	Formiguères D118/D32
5km	Les Angles
14.5km	D32/D118 ← ①
16.5km	D118/D4C →
19.5km	Col de la Llose
23km	D4C/D4F ←
29.5km	D4F/D4 → ②
38.5km	D4/D4C → ③
44.5km	Ayguatebia →
48km	D4F/D4 ←
52km	Col de Creu ④
55.5km	Matemale D4/D118 →
60km	Formiguères
64.5km	Station de Formiguères ⑤
69km	Formiguères

TOUR DE MONT LOUIS

The profile of this ride is unusual, boiling down essentially to a 20km descent off the edge of the Cerdagne high plateau followed by a 25km climb back up to it. It begins in Mont Louis, a little town dominated by its fortress that was designed in the 17th century by Sébastien le Prestre de Vauban, Louis XIV's chief military engineer, as a bulwark against invaders from Spain. Now a UNESCO World Heritage Site, it is home to the French army's elite commando training centre. Mont Louis also boasts the world's first solar furnace, which uses energy from the sun to melt metals for industrial use and to create power.

Start by circling the commanding fortress on the N116, which begins to drop as it leaves town, heading down the Têt valley. The road, which is the main route from Perpignan to the Cerdagne and Andorra, is busy and slaloms almost relentlessly, so it should be taken with caution. It runs close to the line of the Train Jaune, the track traversing the road and valley at one point via a stunning viaduct. The line was built in the early 20th century from Villefranche de Conflent up to Mont Louis and on to Latour de Carol to open up the Cerdagne. Its trains in yellow and red Catalan colours are powered by hydroelectricity generated on the Têt.

Coming into Olette, escape from the traffic comes with a left turn towards Évol, this change of direction also bringing a switch from descending to climbing. After a couple of kilometres, the road crosses a bridge over the River Évol and climbs up the opposite side of the valley. Just before this bridge, you can continue straight on to Évol, a medieval hamlet that is one of France's most beautiful villages. Its houses are built with distinctive schist rock and are overlooked by the ruin of a 13th-century castle, just one tower now intact.

The road cuts back to a vantage point above Olette, then begins to track westwards up the Cabrils valley. Underpinned to the mountainside, the road meanders ceaselessly, its higher sections visible one moment, those you've recently left behind apparent the next. Visually, it resembles a climb in the southern Alps much more than an ascent in the Pyrenees, with low, scrubby trees amongst rubbly rock. Above all, though, it's simply a stunning road, and one of many in this region that should be on the radar of many more cyclists.

At a fork after 10km of climbing, dip left on the D4C (see page 10), which crosses to the other side of the V-shaped valley and ascends once more to Ayguatébia, where a gradient that hasn't been wavering much either side of 6% briefly jumps into double figures. The landscape changes too, with birch, pine and oak throwing shadows across the road, the road rising out of the deep valley and onto the edge of the Capcir plateau just below the cross-country ski station at the Col de la Llose, from where it's a 6km breeze back down to Mont Louis.

On the way in, there is the opportunity for an attractive diversion to Lac des Bouillouses, standing at a little over 2,000m in height and the start point for treks up to the Pic Carlit, another 1,000m higher still. It's not a long or particularly hard climb, barely rising at all for 8km as it runs alongside the Têt, which springs from the lake above. The last 4km, above the barrier that keeps the road closed to most vehicles, are much sterner, with 2km at 8% and plenty of ramps noticeably steeper than that. The view from the dam at the top, above the refuge and auberge, fully justify the effort, though, the Carlit and other peaks

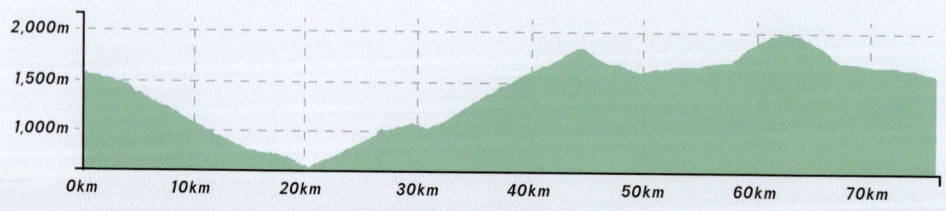

PYRÉNÉES ORIENTALES

Looking down to Évol from its château

close to 3,000m tall providing a wonderful backdrop. At the far end of the dam is the Hotel Bones Hores, which on a warm day has the perfect terrace for lunch and makes for the ideal place to stay for those wanting to combine walking with riding.

Route in reverse

A beautiful ride as far as Olette, but from that point on it could be quite a fraught return to Mont Louis depending on the state of the traffic on the N116. Mixing in parts of the Capcir route on page 10 would provide a more serene and enjoyable alternative.

Distance: 76km
Elevation gain: 1,917m
Highest point: 2,017m
Est. moving time: 2.5-4hrs
Degree of difficulty: ●●◐
Climbs: Col de la Llose (1,866m), Lac des Bouillouses (2,017m)

Parcours

0km	Mont Louis
20km	Olette N116/D4 ← ①
29.5km	D4/D4C ← ②
35.5km	Ayguatébia D4C/D4 ←
44.5km	Col de la Llose ③
47.5km	D4/118 ←
50km	D118/D60 →
62.5km	Lac des Bouillouses ④
75km	D60/D118 →
76km	Mont Louis

A MAJESTIC TOUR OF THE CERDAGNE

Tour de France organisers ASO are always on the search for new climbs that could be used to spice up their race, and in recent years the Pyrenees has provided them with quite a few, including the Port de Balès, the Col de Portet and Prat d'Albis. It has been said that they have also shown an interest in the high point on this circuit, the 2,205m Cime de Coume Mourère, or the Cim de Coma Morera as it is known in Catalan. It lies right on the Franco-Spanish frontier, with the Cadí massif and the resort of La Molina to the west and the 2,910m peak of Puigmal to the east.

The route towards it begins in Font Romeu on the far, northern side of the Cerdagne high plateau. Head westwards out of the resort, turning left about 3km from the centre onto the D33F. Sweeping downwards, there are superb views across the valley floor and to the mountains on its southern side where this route is heading. Just below Estavar, the wiggling descent chutes down on to the high plain, the road arrowing towards the enclave of Llívia, 13 square kilometres of Spain set wholly in France. Under the terms of the Treaty of the Pyrenees in 1659, Spanish villages throughout this mountain region were ceded to France, but Llívia remained part of Spain being a town and the former capital of Cerdanya.

Pass through the centre of town to reach a roundabout in a kilometre-wide corridor of France between Llívia and Puigcerdà, turning left in the direction of Saillagouse, then, a couple of kilometres later, right towards Bourg Madame, which abuts Puigcerdà right across the border. Just after passing beneath the railway bridge, take the left turn to Osséja.

The road streaks across the final stretch of plain to reach this town. Initially, follow the signs to Valcebollère, then to the El Paillès campsite. After crossing a bridge over the river, a sign indicates the Route Forestière d'Osséja. Unlike many ascents to high altitude in this region that saunter upwards, this one takes great strides as it rises through a series of hairpins with frequent ramps in double figures. The road's often broken surface adds to the challenge, particularly around a number of cattle grids.

At 1,660m, the road splits, the shorter route to the left up to the Col de Pradeilles (or Pradelles in Catalan) covering the 340m to the col in 5km, the longer route doing so in 9.5km via an initial false flat and an easier grade thereafter. The surfaces on both are decent, no doubt to accommodate the logging trucks working in the pine woods that rise almost to the Pradeilles.

Above this col, with 2.5km to the summit, the trees begin to give way to open meadows, presenting fabulous views to the north. In the final kilometre, the panorama expands still further to all parts of the compass, a stone marker with 504 on the side indicating the location of the border in a vast open space that would, it is worth noting, give the Tour organisers plenty of room to set up their finish, which would be just 10 metres lower than the Portet, the highest ever in the French Pyrenees.

Caution should be exercised whichever option is taken from the Pradeilles to descend to Osséja as there's often livestock on these roads – the cattle grids are there for a good reason! Once back in Osséja, branch right towards Saillagouse and continue towards this same town when this road meets the N116. At Saillagousse, you can either continue on the main road to return to Font Romeu more quickly, or, as this route does, make a short detour that features some exceptional views across the Cerdagne.

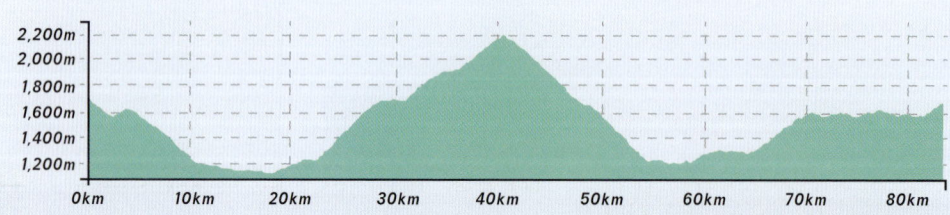

PYRÉNÉES ORIENTALES

Looking across Osséja and the Cerdagne high valley

For this latter option, turn right in Saillagouse towards Llo, climbing steadily towards the border ridge. Half a dozen hairpins lead into and past Llo, the 13th-century Vacaro tower standing sentinel above the village. Climbing away from the last houses, the view opens out marvellously to the north, the road reaching the unusual pipeline/bridge at the Port de Llo soon after. Beyond it is the eLLO, a solar thermodynamic power station opened in 2019 that provides local homes with electricity, almost 100,000 mirrors converting water to vapour to turn a turbine. It's the first in the world able to store power produced during this process.

The road runs along the plateau to Eyne, passing the turn to its quite sizeable ski station, to arrive at a crossroads with the main valley road at the Col de la Perche. Go straight over to Bolquère, the panorama now outstanding to the south, and on to Odeillo, passing the turn to the world's largest solar furnace and its visitor centre, the Héliodyssée, then swinging upwards to the centre of Font Romeu.

Route in reverse

Equally good. The wind may sway your choice of your direction, although almost all of this route is exposed so you won't be able to escape it entirely.

Distance: 83.7km
Elevation gain: 1,974m
Highest point: 2,205m
Est. moving time: 3-5.5hrs
Degree of difficulty: ●●●
Climbs: Col des Pradeilles (1,999m), Cime de Coume Mourère (2,205m), Col de Llo (1,579m), Col de la Perche (1,579m)

Parcours

0km	Font Romeu D618
3.5km	D618/D33F ←
12km	Llívia
14.5km	D68/D30 ←
15.5km	D30/D30C →
17km	D30C/N116 →
17.5km	Bourg Madame ① N116/D70 ←
22km	Osséja → towards Camping El Paillès ②
37km	Col de Pradeilles
40.5km	Cime de Coume Mourère ③
56km	Osséja D70/D30 →
58.5km	D30/N116 →
64.5km	Saillagouse ④ N116/D33 →
70km	Port de Llo
72km	Eyne
75km	Col de la Perche D33/N116/D10 ↑⑤
81.5km	Odeillo D10/D618 →
83.7km	Font Romeu

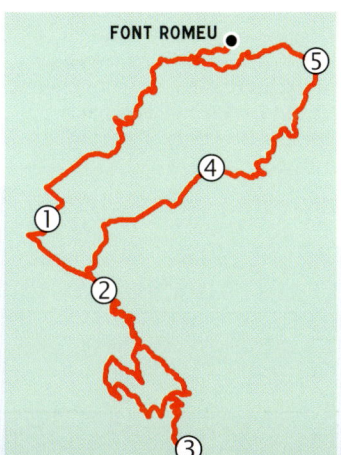

ON THE SLOPES OF THE MAGICAL CANIGOU

The Canigou massif to the south-west of Perpignan is a warren of mountain roads and tracks. Sadly for the organisers of pro races, none of them go anywhere close to the summit of the 2,784m Pic du Canigou, once thought to be the highest peak in the Pyrenean range because it rises so abruptly from the coastal plain and is clearly visible from huge distances. These small roads do, though, offer some wonderful opportunities to explore, exemplified by this route that meanders across the lower slopes of the Canigou before striking out for the Col de Mantet, a beautiful and challenging climb that bears comparison with some Tour regulars such as the Plateau de Beille and Luz Ardiden.

From the centre of Prades, head west towards Villefranche de Conflent, joining the N116. Stay on this main road for half a dozen kilometres until you reach Villefranche's imposing fortress, captured from the Spanish in 1654 and then strengthened by Louis XIV's chief engineer, Marshal Vauban, during the latter part of that century. Passing beneath the viaduct that carries the Train Jaune up the valley, follow the D116 towards Vernet les Bains, turning towards Fillols in the middle of Corneilla de Conflent.

The more direct way to the Mantet is to continue to Vernet, but this diversion on the D47 is both quieter and very attractive. After weaving through Corneilla, this narrow road rises into deciduous woodland. In May, the rich greens of oak and beech are offset by the white flowers of the black locust, also known as the false acacia, which illuminate mountainsides across the Pyrenees at that time of year. In Fillols, swing right at the T-junction, with Vernet once again the goal.

This road soon reaches a crest at the Col Saint Eusèbe, with a long view up the Têt valley and over Vernet, into which it quickly tumbles, the formidable Canigou massif soon appearing as well. With its hot springs, Vernet has long been a popular draw and became very fashionable for wealthy British visitors in the late 19th and early 20th century, novelist Rudyard Kipling among them. He was much taken with the surrounding countryside, describing the Canigou as "a magician among mountains" following one of his three pre-First World War visits.

Go across the junction with D116, chicane left and then right towards Sahorre, climbing before a drop into Rotja valley and to Sahorre itself. In its centre, bear left in the direction of Py and Mantet, the 14.5km ascent to the col starting here.

Almost immediately, this tight lane runs into a spectacular gorge, hugging the eastern side as it climbs at a relatively sedate rate. Even though the valley widens after a few kilometres approaching Py, it's easy to see why the Tour has always bypassed the Mantet. It would look great on TV, but this narrow road is the only access to it and it's too small to cope with the scale of the event, even if limits were imposed on vehicular access. But that doesn't reduce its magnificence and consequent attraction.

At Py, the gradient kicks up seriously for the first time, averaging more than 8%, passing ancient terraces planted with fruit trees. Very soon, Py's red roofs start to look distant, dwarfed by huge peaks, no more than a dot of bright colour in this marvellous landscape. The road narrows to a ribbon of black, the incline easing a little. Take advantage, because the next 5km are hardcore – 2km at 10%, two more at nine. But what views, becoming ever more splendid as you climb, the Canigou indeed looking magical. The summit arrives after a slightly

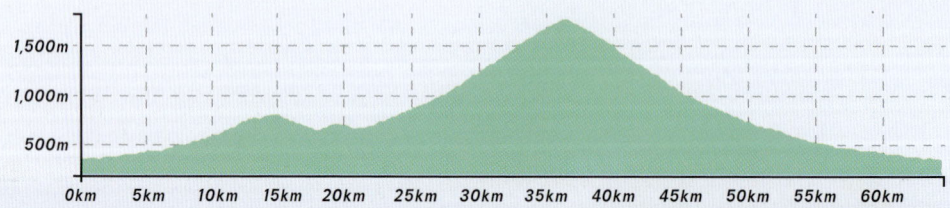

PYRÉNÉES ORIENTALES

Pic du Canigou from the Col de Mantet

more comfortable section. Pass a little beyond it, on the road that drops into Mantet, for the best panorama, looking up to the border ridge, the Spanish resort of Vallter 2000 mere kilometres away on the far side.

After soaking this grandeur in, descend back to Sahorre, keeping straight through the village to Villefranche. From there it's a short return to Prades.

Route in reverse

The Mantet is the highlight and it would come halfway through in this direction, so I'd be against it. But it's a very tough climb and there's a clear benefit to tackling it fresh.

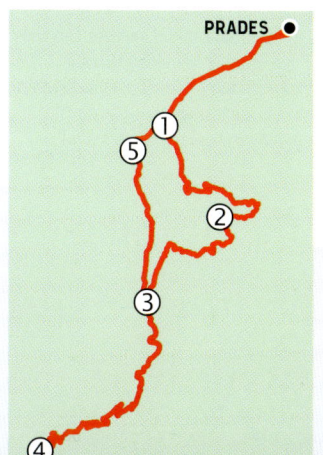

Distance: 64.4km
Elevation gain: 1,756m
Highest point: 1,761m
Est. moving time: 2.5–4.5hrs
Degree of difficulty: ●●◐
Climbs: Col Saint Eusèbe (795m), Col de Mantet (1,761m)

Parcours

0km	Prades
6km	Villefranche de Conflent N116/D116 ← ①
9km	Corneilla de Conflent D116/D47 ←
13km	Fillols D47/D27 →
15km	Col Saint Eusèbe ②
17.5km	Vernet les Bains
21.5km	Sahorre D27/D6 ← ③
36km	Col de Mantet
50.5km	Sahorre D6 ← ④
57km	D6/N116 → ⑤
64.4km	Prades

CORBIÈRES AND ROUSSILLON WINELANDS

This is not so much a rest day, as a rest day from the high mountains. Tracking northwards from Prades, away from the heights of the Pyrenean chain, it doesn't quite reach the 1,000m mark at its apex, but does rollercoaster relentlessly, clocking up more than 1,800m of vertical gain in 80km as it ventures into the Corbières winelands and through some outstanding landscapes.

From Prades town centre, head west towards Perpignan and Molitg les Bains, continuing in the direction of the spa on the D619 from the edge of town. Stay on the D619 when it peels off right soon after climbing away from Catllar, with Sournia the next way point. The Pic du Canigou instantly hogs the attention on these early ramps of the Col de Roque Jalère. The mountain has particular significance for Catalans. On June 23, a flame is lit on top of the summit to celebrate the Nit de Sant Joan, a celebration of the summer solstice and the birth of John the Baptist. Its position and size add to its significance, the mountain standing apart from other peaks almost at the end of the chain, like a Pyrenean Ventoux, but half as big again as "the Giant of Provence", so huge indeed that on clear days at two points in the year it can be seen from Marseille, 250km away, thanks to the refraction of light.

The Roque Jalère, 11km of steady ascent through an arid and rocky Mediterranean landscape, provides plenty of opportunity to gaze at and ponder this distinctive mountain, before, at the summit, the road swings northwards and drops towards Sournia. Like the southern side (see page 76), the northern flank of this col is impressive too, passing through boulder-filled terrain on its shallower opening section, then descending more steeply through stands of pine into the valley bottom.

Stay with the D619 as it climbs through Sournia, branching off left towards Saint Paul de Fenouillet on the way out of the village. As you climb, tree-covered mountain ridges ripple away into the distance. Soon, to the north, the limestone ridge where the Cathar castles of Peyrepertuse and Quéribus are perched emerges, and the road starts to drop into farmland. Just before reaching Le Vivier, turn hard right towards Ansignan, dropping into this village through woods of cedar, oak and acacia, Corbières vines appearing too. Traffic is negligible, even when rejoining the "main" D619 road, heading for Saint Paul once again, vines ever more apparent approaching Ansignan.

In the village, turn right at the towering plane marked as "Arbre de la Liberté 1848" on the D9, staying right towards Trilla soon after, then bearing left in this tiny village to Trévillach. This road is the narrowest of the day, but as this lane climbs the wooded hillside the views are sumptuous. Passing over an unmarked col, they open up to the south, with dozens of summits visible and the Canigou once again unmistakeable. At the last corner before Trévillach, an orientation board reveals exactly what you're looking at.

Turn right in the village on the D2, that rare thing in this area, a road with white lines down the middle. It scampers up to the Col des Auzines. Turn left here, climbing away from the col into the Côtes du Roussillon wine region, the orderliness of the light green vines making them easy to pick out below. Keep with this road beyond Tarerach, then fork right towards Arboussols, climbing for the last time, enjoying expansive views across the Têt valley as the road drops into Marcevol and passes its 12th-century priory.

Having briefly toyed with climbing again,

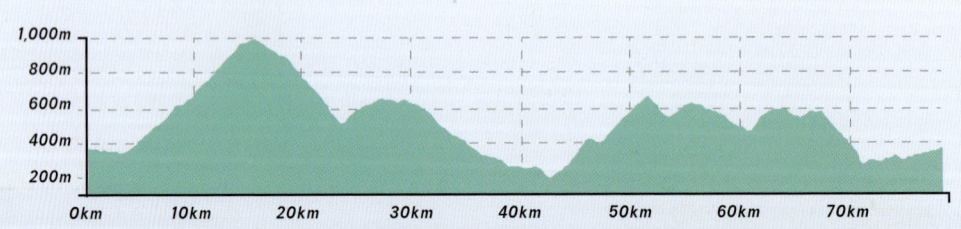

PYRÉNÉES ORIENTALES

the road then swoops exhilaratingly down, overlooking the turquoise waters of the Têt and the farmland beyond to the Canigou massif. Once in the valley, the road darts across the river and makes a beeline back to Prades.

Vines on the road to Arboussols

Route in reverse

Equally enjoyable. There are so many quiet roads asking for exploration around here that there isn't one right way to go, as a glance at the map will reveal. This route came together thanks to Michelin's green "scenic" designation, but could have gone in a different direction at many points.

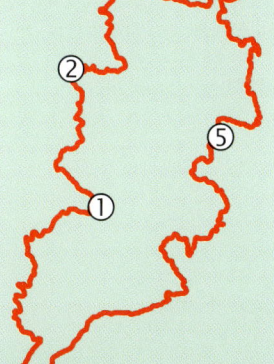

Distance: 78.4km
Elevation gain: 1,809m
Highest point: 991m
Est. moving time: 3.5-5hrs
Degree of difficulty: ●●
Climbs: Col de Roque Jalère (991m), Col des Auzines (603m)

Parcours

0km	Prades D619
15km	Col de Roque Jalère ①
24km	Sournia D619/D7 ← ②
33.5km	D7/D9 → ③
38km	D9/D619 ←
41.5km	Ansignan D9 then D9B → ④
46km	Trilla
53km	Trévillach D9B/D2 → ⑤
54.5km	Col des Auzines D2/D13 ←
67km	Arboussols D13/D35 ←
78.4km	Prades

TÊT TO TECH AND RETURN

The D115, N116 and D117 main arteries that run west from the Mediterranean are often chocker during holiday periods, and are hardly conducive to riding a bike and almost certainly not to enjoying the experience. At the same time, though, many of the roads that run between these major highways along the Agly, Têt and Tech valleys can be almost traffic-free as they weave through dense oak woods and over small- to medium-sized passes. This route on the eastern side of the Massif du Canigou highlights two of these.

From Vinça, it starts to the south on the D13, running between orchards and vineyards, running towards the heart of the Canigou, before veering away to the east as the road kicks up on the opening ramps of the Col de Palomère, more than 20km away but only a modest 700m higher than the floor of the Têt valley.

It's a steady and rather lovely climb, rising through woods of holm oak, the trees packed in so tightly together that few come close to reaching their full height of 30 metres. They blanket the hills and mountainsides throughout this region, often hemming in local roads so that all that can be seen is a corridor of dark green. On the Palomère, however, the hillside onto which the D13 has been pinned is so steep that the trees on the lower side don't block the impressive views up the valley and to the Canigou range. Meandering continually, it's the kind of ascent I love, easy enough that you don't have to devote too much thought to the effort of climbing, each bend revealing a new angle on the landscape. Combined with the all-covering green of the oaks, it can induce a reverie, forward progress being so comfortably made that the action of pedalling is all but forgotten.

Above Valmanya, its name derived from the Latin words meaning "big valley", the road descends for a kilometre or so before making the final approach to the Palomère. The best views, into the Tech valley, can be seen a little way beyond the col as the road starts to drop away towards La Bastide before climbing very gently to the Col Xatard. Turn right here in the direction of Amélie les Bains and into the Vallespir, which was ceded to France by Spain in 1659 under the Treaty of the Pyrenees.

The descent continues to be steppy, the road dropping for a few kilometres, flattening out or climbing a little, then dropping again. Near the bottom, bear left for a backroad route into Céret running on the other side of the River Tech to the D115. Eventually these two roads do meet, but you can opt to stay off the highway at this junction by taking the bike path that runs across the Tech on an old railway, the trail continuing into Céret, where the tree-shaded main square is an ideal spot for a mid-ride break.

Leaving Céret, follow the D115 high across the Tech, parallel to the magnificent Pont du Diable, the world's largest bridge arch when it was completed in the mid-14th century. Turn left just at the end of the bridge towards Llauro, almost instantly leaving the frenetic bustle behind, rising at 6% for 3km before settling down to twos and threes to reach the Col de Llauro and a turn to Oms and then Calmeilles. Above this second village, the gradient returns to 6% for another 3km, then eases off over another three to reach the Col du Fourtou. Join the D618 here towards Ille sur Têt.

For the next 17km, this road serpentines through a forest of oaks. In the same way as the earlier ascent from the Têt, just a few kilometres to the west, slaloming down a corridor of green brings on an almost

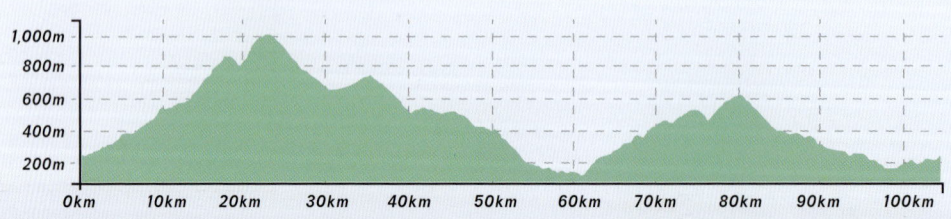

PYRÉNÉES ORIENTALES

Oak-covered hillsides and the Pic du Canigou

hypnotic state. You could press hard, but the constant weaving encourages a brisk rather than a feverish pace, allowing the gradient and gravity to do most of the work while you soak up this reward for your earlier exertion.

For those that fancy a little bit more climbing, the right turn on the D72 towards Casefabre and Saint Michel de Llotes is a super option. Otherwise, keep into Bouleternère, following the signs through the town to the N116 and back to Vinça.

Route in reverse

As so often, it comes down to whether you want to tackle the biggest climb from the off or save it until close to the end. I also think the road up to Valmanya and the Palomère is more attractive when climbing than the ascent from Bouleternère to the Fourtou.

Distance: 104.6km
Elevation gain: 1,894m
Highest point: 1,036m
Est. moving time: 4-6hrs
Degree of difficulty: ●●●
Climbs: Col de Palomère (1,036m), Col Xatard (752m), Col de Llauro (380m), Col du Fourtou (655m)

Parcours

0km	Vinça D13
23km	Col Palomère ①
34.5km	Col Xatard D13/D618 →
52km	D618/D15 ←
58km	D15/bike path ②
60km	Céret D615 ③
68.5km	Col de Llauro D615/D13 ← ④
80km	Col du Fourtou D13/D618 → ⑤
98km	Bouleternère D628/N116 ← ⑥
104.6km	Vinça

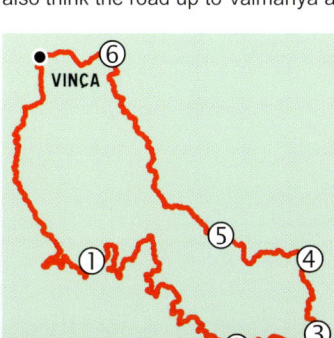

TOUR OF THE CHERRY ORCHARDS

Every April since the 1930s, farmers in Céret have sent the French president a crate of the country's first crop of cherries. The Vallespir's soil, which is light and well-drained, and climate, which tends to be warm and not too windy in the early spring when the trees are in blossom, make it ideal for cultivation of the fruit. On this short route around the attractive and bustling town of Céret, those orchards are much in evidence, but it also highlights how easy it is to escape from the crowds in this last valley before France becomes Spain.

Take the D13F out of the centre of the Céret, following signs to Las Illas. The road weaves through narrow streets and quickly reaches the countryside, running between the first of those orchards, the trees a rich green after the cherries have been harvested. The gradient edges up towards 5% on these first pitches of the 10km-long Col de la Brousse, the cherries soon giving way to the holm oaks that blanket the hillsides in the Vallespir. These trees grow so close together that the demand for light and nutrients means they don't get too high, allowing passing cyclists a view over the top of those on the lower side of the road and across this verdant valley.

After the initial twists, this ribbon of a road starts to run more directly southwards, steepening noticeably, the average gradient between six and seven but some short pitches twice as acute. The steady increase in the incline continues entering thicker woodland approaching the top of the col, boughs of towering sweet chestnuts bending across from both sides to create a shady corridor, the gradient now above 8%. At the summit, a lane runs up to the Pic de Fontfrède, where there's a monument to those who escaped from the Vichy regime during the Second World War by climbing through these woods to the border and into Spain.

Staying left, the road scoots away from the col, occasional breaks in the tree canopy providing views over Céret and out to the Mediterranean. It shoots past the col just below the Pic Mirailles, climbs again for a short time, and drops into the hamlet of Las Illas. At the T-junction, turn left on the D13 heading for Maureillas, a mostly gentle 11km descent away, still through thick woodland. I enjoy roads like this, constantly weaving, completely lost in nature, rarely giving a clue what's around the next bend. Sometimes it's a dark tunnel of green, on other occasions an open section of road with spectacular views. They're for breezing along rather than speeding.

At the crossroads in the middle of Maureillas, turn left on the D618, staying on it for a few hundred metres before heading right to Saint Jean Pla de Corts. At the roundabout intersection with the D115, go straight across towards Vivès and Llauro. Back on the valley floor, the landscape is still very green, but there are cypress and cherries among the oaks, vines as well. Above Vivès, the gradient, relatively imperceptible from Saint Jean, picks up noticeably. The terrain changes too, becoming rockier, the trees not as dense and rather stunted, a very Mediterranean aspect.

A left turn at the junction with the D615 leads up to Llauro, the road continuing to climb beyond the village to reach the col of the same name, whence there's a delicious descent through woods and past orchards back into Céret.

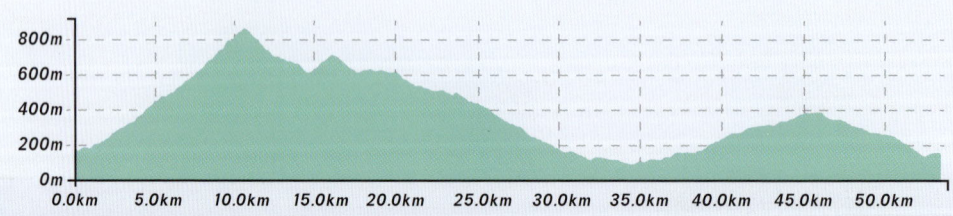

PYRÉNÉES ORIENTALES

Cherry trees in blossom near Céret

Route in reverse

As so often, it comes down to whether you prefer to do most of your climbing early or late on. Riding it anticlockwise makes the Col de la Brousse a good deal easier, although it's not all that fearsome when tackled directly from Céret.

Distance: 53.5km
Elevation gain: 1,273m
Highest point: 860m
Est. moving time: 2-3.5hrs
Degree of difficulty: ●◐
Climbs: Col de la Brousse (860m), Col de Llauro (380m)

Parcours

0km	Céret D13F
10.5km	Col de la Brousse ①
21km	Las Illas D13F/D13 ← ②
31.5km	Maureillas D13/D618/D15 ← ③
32km	D618/D13 →
43km	D13/D615 ←
45km	Col de Llauro ④
53.5km	Céret

TOUR OF A VALLESPIR MINING VALLEY

At this eastern end of the Pyrenees, a lot of the longer and higher climbs tend to be draggy rather than abrupt. The Col de Jau, which connects Pyrénées Orientales to the Aude, is one ascent that bucks that trend, and the Col de Mantet, on the western side of the Massif du Canigou, is another. **This route highlights a third, this time on the southern side of the Canigou, to the long-closed Batère iron mine, which was first exploited two centuries BC and closed in 1999.**

Commencing in Amélie les Bains, follow the D115 towards Spain for a handful of kilometres to Arles sur Tech, turning right just beyond it towards Corsavy and Batère. It's advisable to be well warmed up by this point, because after winding through some houses, the climb takes off in ferocious fashion, soaring away from the Tech valley with a couple of kilometres at 9%. There's respite for a few hundred metres, then another big step up to Corsavy, a beautiful perched village that looks over the Gorges de la Fou. Running for 2km, with the cliffs rising 250m high and in some sections only a metre apart, walking through this awe-inspiring ravine was one of the Vallespir's main tourist draws until a large rockfall in 2019 forced its closure, temporarily local traders hoped.

There's a super view over it from a "balcony" as the D43 passes through Corsavy before switching right on the 13km climb to Batère. For the next 3-4km the road runs along a landing in between the ascent's two big steps. It's heavily wooded, but on several occasions there are longish breaks in the line of trees, and the views across the valley to the east and up into the Massif du Canigou are wonderful.

Approaching the cluster of buildings at La Cazette, with 7km to the top, the gradient begins to steepen. It doesn't get ridiculous, averaging 7% or a tad more most of the way to the summit, and there's considerable pay-off with vertical gain as the views become ever more expansive and glorious, the mine also becoming visible further up the mountainside. The relatively straightforward rate of ascent continues as far as the Coll de la Descarga, which is the prelude to a final kilometre at 10% to reach the summit. A little further beyond the buildings at the summit where the miners lodged lies the Tour de Batère, a signal tower probably built in the early 14th century when the Kingdom of Majorca ruled the Vallespir.

Unless you're on a gravel bike, the only way down from here is via Corsavy. Descend to the T-junction to the west of the village and turn right onto the D44, still heading very gradually downhill. Though the road cuts mostly through trees as it drops to Montferrer, there are a couple more dramatic ledges hewn from the cliff-face. Beyond this village, it winds through woodland, easing down to Le Tech. Turn left here, staying on the main road for a little more than a kilometre, before turning right when the D44 reappears heading for Serralongue.

It winds alongside a small tributary of the Tech for 4km, arriving at a fork. Head to the left here towards Saint Laurent de Cerdans, initially through woods of oak and chestnut, and then open pasture and farmland. In Forge del Mitg – its name highlighting that the local forge was in the middle of something, but no one is now clear exactly what – you will arrive at a T-junction, the sign to the right intriguingly indicating "Figueres", the Catalan city renowned as the home of surrealist Salvador Dalí. That's for another day (see page 26), though. Turn left to sweep steadily down to reach a bridge over the Tech and

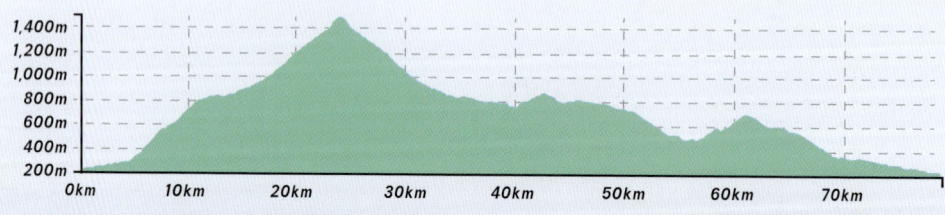

PYRÉNÉES ORIENTALES

a final rendezvous with the D115 for the short drop back into Amélie les Bains.

Route in reverse

There's a little more climbing on the D115 from the start, which might be a drag on busy days. Otherwise this loop works just as well in the other direction. It's worth noting that omitting the climb to the Batère mine turns it into an easy 55km circuit with about 1,200m of vertical gain.

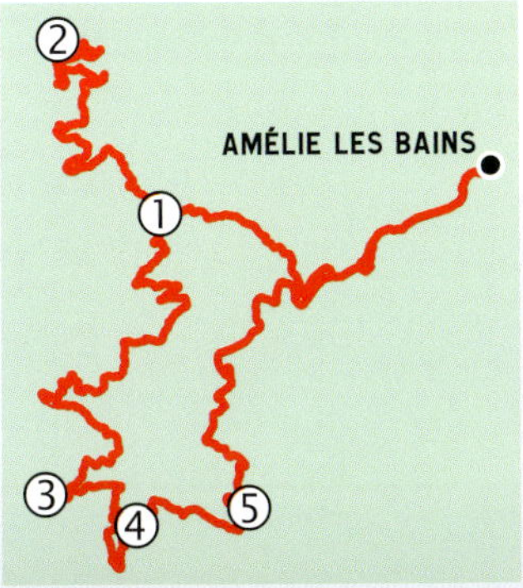

Distance: 79.8km
Elevation gain: 1,942m
Highest point: 1,495m
Est. moving time: 2.5-4.5hrs
Degree of difficulty: ●●○
Climbs: Mine de Batère (1,495m)

Parcours

0km	Amélie les Bains
4.5km	D115/D43 ➡
10.5km	Corsavy ➡ ①
24km	Col de la Batère ➡ ②
37.5km	Corsavy ➡
54km	Le Tech D43/D115 ⬅ ③
55km	D115/D43 ➡
58.5km	D43/D64 ⬅ ④
64km	La Forge del Mitg D64/D3 ⬅ ⑤
70km	D3/D115 ➡
79.8km	Amélie les Bains

FROM CATALOGNE TO CATALUNYA AND BACK

The advent of gravel bikes opens up vast parts of the Pyrenean chain that have hitherto been restricted to mountain bikes. This effect is particularly applicable to the Vallespir, where there are myriad gravel and dirt trails, sometimes linking neighbouring passes like the Col de la Batère and the Col de Palomère that are a considerable distance apart by road, and in many more cases providing access to terrain completely beyond the realm of skinny road tyres. This route, though, includes a short section of *sterrato* – as it's known in Italy and increasingly so elsewhere – on what is in addition a pass with immense historical significance stemming back to the Spanish Civil War.

It begins by climbing up the Tech valley from Amélie les Bains to the D3, following this smaller route on the left towards La Forge del Mitg and Figueres. After dipping over the river, the road winds upwards through dense woodland to pass through La Forge del Mitg, continuing on to Saint Laurent de Cerdans, the gradient increasing on the approach to this pretty little town, once renowned as a hub for contraband and also for the manufacture of espadrilles. Beyond it, the road continues to bump primarily upwards to arrive at the first high point in Coustouges.

The undulations continue, but are now mainly downwards as the road tumbles out of Catalogne Nord, as the French part of Catalonia is known, into the Alt Empordà *comarca* of Girona province. The first thing that stands out is the change in width and quality of the road, the GI503 broad enough to have a shoulder, not that there's much traffic to require cyclists to use it. The landscape changes too. While it's still well wooded, there are long views. The rock is quite different too, a sandstone that's vividly crimson at times.

After winding down to Maçanet de Cabrenys, stay with the GI503 until the left turn to La Vajol. This much narrower road immediately climbs steeply through oak woods, some sections briefly reaching 12%. Nearing La Vajol, the slope eases and then arrives at a crest in this tiny village, which was a hugely significant point at the end of the Spanish Civil War. As Franco's forces closed in, thousands of refugees poured into La Vajol with the aim of crossing the Coll de Lli into France, among them the president of the Spanish republic, Manuel Azaña, the head of the government, Juan Negrín, and the president of the Catalan regional government, Lluís Companys. This brief moment of notoriety is marked with a statue at an impressive look-out point just before the village.

After a brief spell on a rough concrete surface, the lane meets the super smooth GI505, which rises steadily for 3km to the border, then peters out into a gravel car park and picnic area at the Coll de Lli. There's a monument to Companys and members of the Republican government who crossed into France on 5 February 1939 partly hidden in the trees to the right. A gravel track runs out of the far side of the car park and starts to drop towards Maureillas las Illas, France's second-most southerly town after Lamanère, to the west near Prats de Mollo. The route is fairly well used and maintained. After a couple of kilometres on the gravel, tarmac arrives once more at the end of the Impasse de Prat Paillisse.

After descending a little further into Las Illas, turn left towards Céret, climbing through La Selve to a col, then dropping again briefly before the final substantial climb of the day to the Col de Brousse, the ascent steepening

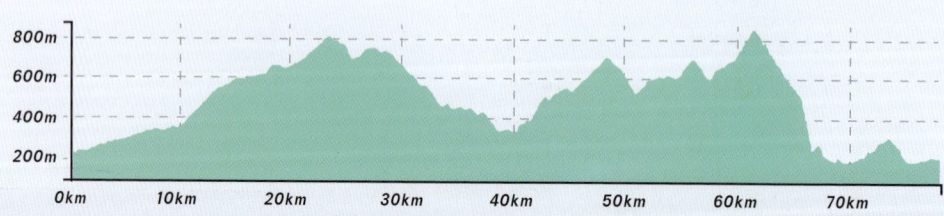

PYRÉNÉES ORIENTALES

Amélie les Bains and the Tech valley

Distance:	80.4km
Elevation gain:	1,976m
Highest point:	860m
Est. moving time:	2.5-5hrs
Degree of difficulty:	●●●
Climbs:	Col de Coustouges (830m), Coll de Manrella (717m), Col de Brousse (860m)

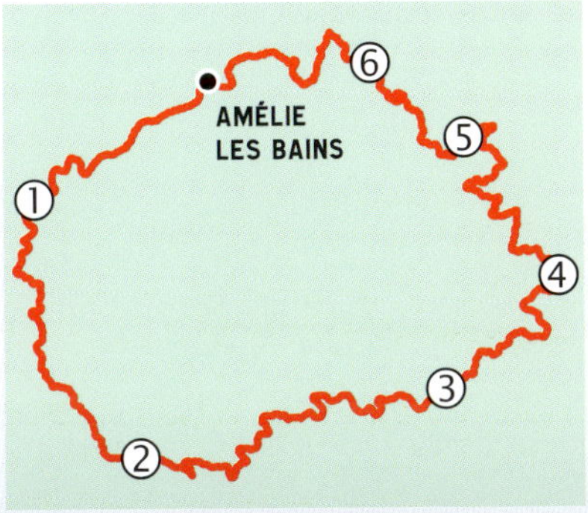

Parcours

0km	Amélie les Bains
9.5km	D115/D3 ← ①
18.5km	Saint Laurent de Cerdans
23km	Col de Coustouges ②
38km	Maçanet de Cabrenys
40km	GI503/unclassified to La Vajol ← ③
45km	La Vajol junction with GI505 ←
48km	Coll de Manrella ④ start of gravel
49.5km	End of gravel Maureillas las Illas
50.5km	D13/D13F ←
61km	Col de Brousse ⑤
69km	D13F/unclassified to Coll de Bouissells ⑥
71.5km	unclassified/D15 to Reynes
80.4km	Amélie les Bains

significantly beyond the Col de Mirailles. From the Brousse, the road races down the hillside towards Céret, but switch hard left on the lane to Coll de Bousseills before reaching its outskirts, continuing past the gîte complex at Baillère to reach the D15, which climbs through Reynès and back into Amélie.

Route in reverse

The climbing begins more abruptly with the ascent of the Col de Brousse, but it's not an overly taxing ascent. Some may also prefer to ride up the gravel section above Las Illas towards the border, and then conclude by running down the D115 into Amélie, spending less time on this busier section.

TOUR DES MONTS ALBÈRES

The eastern end of the Pyrenees come to a dramatic end on the beautiful Côte Vermeille, between Argelès sur Mer and Cap Cerbère on the Spanish border, the mountains tumbling into the Mediterranean, their final vestige a series of towering headlands. Towards the northern end of this spectacular run of coastline lies Collioure, one of my favourite French towns. With its fortress-like château looming over the pebbled beach, which curves gracefully around to the Church of Notre Dame des Anges, its clock tower a lighthouse-like sentinel with the higgledy-piggledy streets of the old town piled up behind it, Collioure has long been a draw for writers and artists, including Derain, Matisse, Braque and Picasso.

However, it tends not to offer so great a pull for cyclists, bar those at one end of their Raid. In summer, the little port is jammed, the roads around it heave with traffic and the Albères massif behind the town appears to offer little opportunity to escape. There are, though, some quiet and quite stunning roads within easy reach of this rugged stretch of coast, as this route highlights.

The first step is upwards from Collioure to join the D114, often busy, but with a decent shoulder and, approaching Argelès, a kerb-protected bike path. From the centre of this popular resort, head inland to Sorède, this road far quieter as it passes between olive groves and orchards, the Albères range visible to the south. This bottom edge of the Roussillon plain is frequently affected by very strong wind, sometimes blowing off the sea, in which case this section through Sorède and Laroque des Albères will literally be a breeze.

Continue from Laroque to Villelongue dels Monts and Montesquieu des Albères, meeting the main D618. Happily, a bike path runs parallel to this highway as far as Le Boulou. When this path meets the D900, turn left for 2km, then right towards Maureillas Las Illas and from there to Las Illas. Weaving through oak woods, the road rises through three very apparent steps, these averaging 5-7% for 2-3km, with far shallower slopes in between.

Nearing Las Illas, after climbing for 10km from Maureillas, fork left, then soon after stay left again on the Route de Manrell. This passes above Las Illas and soon degrades into a rough gravel track that ascends for another kilometre to reach the Coll de Manrella (see page 26). On the Spanish side, the surface couldn't be much more different, smooth tarmac sweeping down to La Vajol and on the GI501 to Agullana, at just about halfway point. Go right here towards Darnius, the road undulating to a T-junction with the GI502. Turn left, travelling for 5km through what in high summer is extremely arid terrain to meet the N11, turning left and northwards on this main trans-frontier route for a kilometre, before branching right to Capmany.

The road passes olive groves and, soon after, vines used to produce what are often very good Empordà wines that are little known outside Catalunya. The rich green plants provide a vivid contrast to the otherwise sun-beaten landscape towards Espolla. Start to circle this town towards Roses, then go into it at the first roundabout, following signs towards the Coll de Banyuls, the road narrow, but in good condition as it begins to climb into the southern edge of the Albères.

The gradient remains quite relaxed until the last couple of kilometres to the pass, when it kicks up, the straightness of the road making this change evident well before it arrives. It's not fearsome, though, and the view from

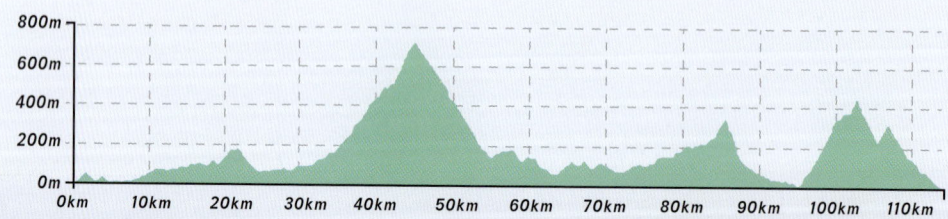

PYRÉNÉES ORIENTALES

the top is gorgeous, Collioure almost in sight through a gap in the hills to the north.

The road down towards Banyuls sur Mer on the French side was resurfaced in 2018, which is doubly good as it plunges away from the pass at more than twice the angle it reached it, some sections at more than 20% in the opening two kilometres. Approaching Banyuls, there's a choice of routes. Continue to the coast for the easier but busier return to Collioure via the D914, or swing left on the D86 for the more scenic – and hillier – finale. This road, the Route des Crêtes, climbs quickly away from Banyuls and soon offers wonderful views over vineyards to the sea. It tops out at 454m, just below the 13th-century Tour de Madeloc, a signalling tower built when this region was part of the kingdom of Majorca.

Caution is advised on the narrow and often twisting descent. The views northwards up the coast can be better taken in too. Pass the turn to Port Vendres, another means of access to this route having recently been resurfaced, climb one final time to the Coll de la Serra and shoot back down into Collioure.

The Route des Crêtes from the Tour Madeloc

Distance: 114km
Elevation gain: 2,224m
Highest point: 732m
Est. moving time: 3.5-6hrs
Degree of difficulty: ●●●
Climbs: Coll de Manrella (732m), Coll de Banyuls (357m), Route des Crêtes (454m), Coll de la Serra (344m)

Route in reverse

The ride will start rather than end with a bang on the Route des Crêtes. But if you want to get most of your climbing done early this is the way to go. Be aware, though, that the eastern approach to the Coll de Banyuls is far steeper, with ramps of more than 20%!

Parcours

0km	Collioure
7km	Argelès sur Mer D114/D2 ← ①
16km	Laroque des Albères D2/D11 ←
22km	Montesquieu des Albères
24.5km	D61/D618 ← ②
28.5km	D618/D900 ←
33km	Maureillas Las Illas D13 ← ③
42km	Fork left and again a kilometre later
45km	End of gravel climb to Coll de Manrella ④
48.5km	La Vajol GI505/GI501 ←
55km	Agullana GI505/GI504 →
59km	GI504/GI502 ←
63.5km	GI502/N11 ← ⑤
64km	N11/GI602 →
75.5km	Espolla ⑥
85.5km	Coll de Banyuls
94.5km	unclassified/D86 ← ⑦
102.5km	Route des Crêtes high point
107km	Coll de la Serra
114km	Collioure

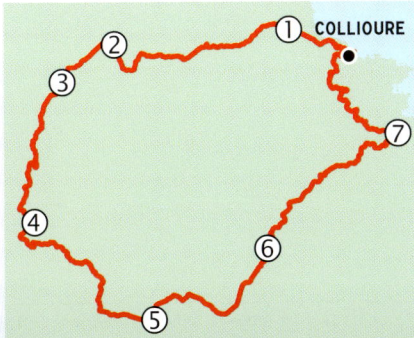

DODGING THE BORDER BARGAIN-HUNTERS

Glance at the map and Le Perthus looks like it might be a good destination for a short, hilly ride. The D900 climbs towards it parallel with the A9 autoroute, which soaks up most of the cross-border traffic that's barrelling into Spain. Despite this, the pass is perhaps the busiest in the Pyrenees because of the cheap booze, cigarettes and other goods available just on the Spanish side of the frontier. As a consequence, Le Perthus has become a downmarket Andorra, its streets lined with shops piled high with bargains, its streets snarled with traffic.

It's not a place that appears conducive to a relaxing ride, but there is a way to sidestep much of its ugliness and, at the same time, explore the highest sealed road in the Monts Albères, climbing to almost a thousand metres at the Col de l'Ouillat. Starting a little to the west of the D900, in this case in Céret, reduces exposure to this road to a minimum. Head first to Maureillas Las Illas. In the town centre, keep straight ahead onto the D13B rather than following the main road as it bends left towards Le Boulou and Le Perthus.

Turn right in Mas d'en Fourcade on a narrow lane towards La Cluse Basse, passing through this village, crossing an old, cobbled bridge and passing beneath the D900 to reach Les Cluses and the right turn onto the D71B. Sandwiched between the two main highways, this minor road climbs steadily to the hamlet of Cluse Haute, its stone buildings extremely well fortified. Although the noise of the autoroute is never far away, there's a feeling of being on a tarmac oasis amidst the hubbub.

Where the backroad finally bobs down to meet the main road after a short descent, keep left on the D71, climbing again. Escape is at hand. Around the next corner, the road passes beneath the motorway and towards the heart of the Albères massif, a corridor of oak trees already shutting out the din. This first section towards the Col de l'Ouillat includes the steepest parts of the 13km ascent, averaging around 7.5% to reach Saint Jean d'Albère. Above this hamlet, there's a short drop, then a flatter section that continues to a T-junction. Go left here for the final handful of kilometres to the col.

It climbs steadily, passes farms, trees dappling the road for the most part, but occasionally thinning to allow glimpses of long views into French and Spanish Catalonia. Higher up, there are majestic pine woods. As these end, the road emerges onto the bare, upper part of the climb, the border with Spain a rickety fence to the right, an immense panorama visible across Roussillon and to the Côte Vermeille, getting ever longer as you approach the telecoms station at the summit, the traffic now no more a hum carried on the breeze.

Returning the way you've just come up, descend to the junction with the D71, this time following the road towards Le Perthus. This is another corridor of green that almost reaches the border town, its proximity indicated by the sight of one of the long viaducts that carry the autoroute up to what has always been a strategically significant gap in the Monts Albères ridge. Soon after passing beneath this highway, the D71 arrives at a T-junction with the D900, thankfully just below Le Perthus. Turn right here to descend back towards Céret, sticking with the main road until the junction with the D618, or taking the right turn back onto the D71 after just a few hundred metres to retrace via the quieter route climbed earlier.

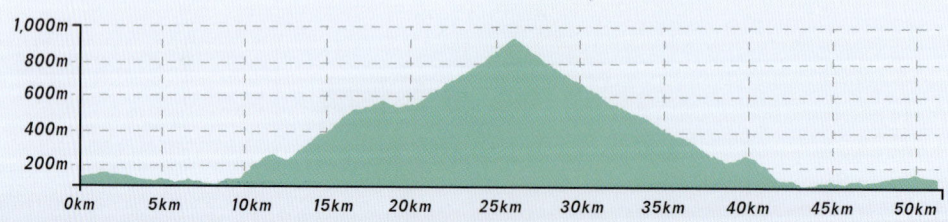

PYRÉNÉES ORIENTALES

Pine forest approaching the Col de l'Ouillat

Distance: 51.3km
Elevation gain: 1,137m
Highest point: 938m
Est. moving time: 2-3.5hrs
Degree of difficulty: ●◐
Climbs: Col de l'Ouillat (938m), Col du Perthus (290m)

Parcours

0km	Céret	
6.5km	Maureillas Las Illas D618/D13B ➡ ①	
8km	Mas d'en Fourcade D13B/unclassified ➡	
9.5km	Les Cluses unclassified/D71B ➡ ②	
12.5km	D71B/D71 ⬅	
20km	D71/D71A ⬅ ③	
26km	Col de l'Ouillat ④	
32km	D71A/D71	
37.5km	Le Perthus D71/D900 ➡	
38.5km	D900/D71 ➡ leading quickly to D71B ⬅ ⑤	
41.5km	Les Cluses D71B/unclassified ⬅	
43km	Mas d'en Fourcade unclassified/D13B ⬅	
45km	Maureillas Las Illas D13B/D618 ⬅	
51.3km	Céret	

Route in reverse

Essentially, this is out and back, but it is of course possible to climb to the Col de l'Ouillat via the upper section of the D71 at Le Perthus. It's very similar and just as enjoyable as the route highlighted.

MEDITERRANEAN COASTING

The profile of the back end of this route reminds me of the finale of Milan-Sanremo, the legendary one-day Classic road race that bumps over a series of headlands and hills running into the Italian Riviera resort. The similarity is provided by the headlands crossed as you travel north along the Mediterranean coast from the Creus peninsula in the north-east corner of Catalunya to Banyuls sur Mer on the Côte Vermeille in the Pays Catalan.

No matter which direction you decide to tackle this route, there's little chance to warm up your climbing legs before they're being called into serious action. Starting by the sea in Banyuls, you either head south into those headlands, or head inland towards the Col de Banyuls. As highlighted on page 29, this unclassified road was treated to some significant improvements in 2018, but those didn't include taking the sting from the goat track-like finale to the summit. It's a breeze as it passes Mas Perotet and Mas Parer, then lifts off like an eagle catching a thermal in the two final kilometres to the summit, which average 11.5% and has pitches almost twice as steep. Once at the top, though, the view back to the Med and the prospect of 30 kilometres that are mostly downhill or flat provide useful compensation.

These begin with a fast schuss into Spain and the Empordà winelands around Espolla. Stay left coming into this town, picking up the GI603 towards Rabós and Roses. These are some of the easiest kilometres all day, this quiet road barely deviating as it skips past Rabós and arrows on south-east through dusty farmland, the hills of the Creus peninsula gradually becoming more prominent ahead. The route skirts Garriguella and hurtles relentlessly towards Roses.

A change comes approaching this resort town, from flat and direct to undulating and meandering. It begins at the intersection with the GI614. Go left here, with Cadaqués now the objective. Initially, the road bores onwards, but those hills are imminent. The road begins to sashay a little, then sways and starts to climb a touch. This isn't a stretch of road that I love, because it's so busy in holiday season, but outside high summer or early in the morning, it's relatively calm and the end goal, Cadaqués, is absolutely worth the fumes you'll have to suck up on this 5km ascent to the Coll de Perafita.

It leads onto a slightly descending plateau, the views to the north already impressive. After dropping for 4km, it reaches a roundabout where you have a choice: swing left towards Llançà to save yourself 10km, or speed down into Cadaqués. This once sleepy fishing village is a true gem, but the only way out is to climb back up the road that drops into it. Similar in its setting and look to Collioure, Cadaqués also has strong links to the art world, most famously to Salvador Dalí, who had a house very close by. If you're wanting lunch, the harbour-side restaurants are hard to beat for their setting.

The road out of Cadaqués isn't steep. It's the traffic that's the drag. Back at the top, turn right (or left if skipping Cadaqués), the road usually quieter in this direction. It sweeps down to the coast at El Port de la Selva. Turn left here to Llançà along a stretch of a coast that remains quite pristine compared to the mess of much of the Spanish Mediterranean, the resorts low-rise and all the better for that. From Llançà there's only the one route north, the N260, heading for Cerbère.

Initially, it runs close to the sea, passing very tempting beaches and bays. For the most part, there's a decent shoulder, which provides refuge when the undulations

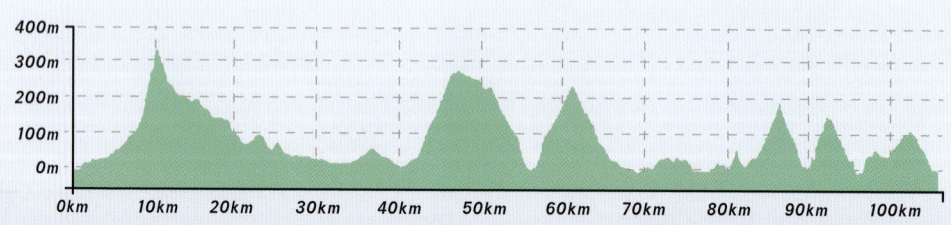

PYRÉNÉES ORIENTALES

commence approaching Colera. Even better, though, north of Colera, the N260 splits, the new road going right and burrowing through the hillside towards the border as the old road weaves upwards, much quieter now, and the views from it quite wonderful.

At the top of this first big headland, the Coll del Frare, the road looks down onto the rail terminal at Portbou, where rolling stock used to be lifted from French bogies onto wider Spanish ones, this process still undertaken for freight trucks running on the old incompatible lines between the two countries. The end of the road tunnel can be seen too, and the two parts of the N260 become one again entering this town. No sooner down in Portbou, the road starts to rear again towards the Coll dels Belitres on the border itself.

Cap Cerbère with Portbou to the left and Cerbère to the right

Again, the views are marvellous and there's also a feeling of déjà vu. From the summit, there is another panorama over the sea and a huge marshalling yard, this time in Cerbère. On the descent towards it, the road goes all the way out to Cap Cerbère, which juts impressively into the Med and has a solar-powered lighthouse at its tip. The climb to the next headland begins at the end of Cerbère's colourful seafront, the road stepping up to Cap Réderis, then easing down into Banyuls, a spectacular day complete.

Route in reverse

There's a good argument for starting this circuit via the coast road as the traffic should be lighter the earlier you begin. This will also take the sting out of Col de Banyuls, which is far easier from the Spanish side. But it does mean being on the landward rather than the seaward side of the D914/N260, which makes the views less impressive.

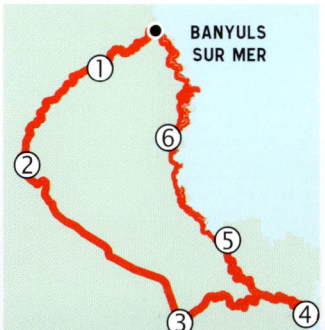

Distance: 106.5km
Elevation gain: 2,100m
Highest point: 357m
Est. moving time: 3.5-6hrs
Degree of difficulty: ●●●
Climbs: Col de Banyuls (357m), Coll de Perafita (246m), Coll del Frare (205m), Coll dels Belitres (165m)

Parcours

0km	Banyuls sur Mer D86
1km	D86/unclassified ←
10km	Col de Banyuls ①
20km	Espolla unclassified/GI603 ②
28.5km	Garriguella GI603/C252 ↑
36km	Palau Saverdera GI610 ↑
40.5km	GI610/GI614 ← ③
51km	Coll de Perafita
56km	Cadaqués ④
61km	Coll de Perafita GI613
69km	El Port de la Selva GI613/GI612 ← ⑤
77km	Llançà GI612/N260 →
86.5km	Coll del Frare ⑥
92.5km	Coll dels Belitres D914
106.5km	Banyuls sur Mer

TOUR DE THUIR

Heading west from Perpignan, the flat coastal plain starts to rise into the *piémont*, or foothills, of the Canigou massif, known as the Aspres, with the Têt valley to the north and the Tech to the south. This circuit explores its eastern edge, and starts in Thuir, nowadays a thriving suburb of Perpignan, but more renowned as the birthplace of Byrrh, a very sweet tonic wine first produced in the early 19th century by brothers Pallade and Simon Violet.

Drapers by trade, they capitalised on the growing popularity of wine by developing a red flavoured with quinine and sweetened with aromatics and mistelle, an alcohol-fortified grape juice. To circumvent the opposition of wine-producers, they marketed it as a health tonic and sold it in pharmacies, its popularity spreading across Europe and into the USA until it fell out of fashion after the Second World War. Pernod-Ricard now owns the Byrrh factory in Thuir, which was partly designed by Gustave Eiffel's engineering company. The brand itself is best remembered thanks to the huge promotional murals painted on the walls of buildings across France, extolling its health-giving properties.

Starting in Thuir's busy centre, a stone's throw from the Byrrh factory, set off westwards on the D48, this road climbing steadily even before leaving the town's outskirts. It soon reaches a viewing point with the Canigou prominent ahead, then dips and rises again into Castelnou, garlanded as one of France's most beautiful villages, its red-roofed stone houses clustered beneath the medieval "new castle". Continuing to climb, long views appear across the Roussillon plain and, soon after, towards the Monts Albères to the south.

At a T-junction, turn right towards Saint Michel de Llotes, climbing a little longer to reach the Col de Fontcouverte. Descending gently along a ridge between scrubby oaks, the views are once again impressive. Rarely more than 7% and averaging just five, this road eases down to Saint Michel. At the junction just beyond a bridge that crosses a stream, turn left in the direction of Casefabre, climbing again.

This ascent to the Col Sainte Marguerite is noticeably steeper, averaging 6.5% for 6km. Hemmed in by trees initially, it soon emerges onto a steep mountainside with views over densely-forested hills that ripple away into the hazy distance like ocean rollers. There's a small shrine at the col, from where it's a quick scamper down to Casefabre and into a series of very tight, gravelly hairpins that draw the eye away from the panorama towards higher ridges in the Canigou's foothills to the west.

This short, but quite technical descent finishes at a junction with the D618, a major highway nearer to the coast, but at this point very much a backroad. It is, though, part of the Route des Cols, an itinerary for cyclists from one end of the Pyrenees to the other, and it's easy to understand why it features, the road ambling gently upwards to this circuit's high point, the Col Fourtou (see page 21), with barely a car to disturb the peace. After twisting through Boule d'Amont, the gradient picks up three or four points, but only to fives and sixes.

At the col, turn left onto the narrow road that follows the contours eastwards, initially to the hamlet of Prunet. This is no one's rat run. Motorised traffic is close to extinct. That alone is good enough reason to wander this way, but add in the tremendous views that emerge as it descends and it really shouldn't be missed.

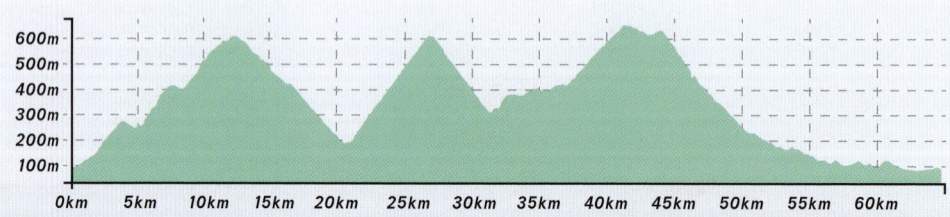

PYRÉNÉES ORIENTALES

Castelnou and the Canigou massif

At the junction with the D2, turn right, the descent now less acute and continuing all the way back to Thuir, swathes of Pyrénées Orientales laid out ahead on the initial drop to Montauriol. Vines appear as the terrain flattens approaching Fourques. Turn left in the centre of this village for the final blast through farmland and the return to Thuir, where a celebratory Byrrh (it is pronounced the same way as beer) is surely in order.

Route in reverse
Equally enjoyable. The choice of direction could depend on where the wind is coming from, although if the Tramontane is howling in from the north and east it's going to have a sapping impact whichever option is selected.

Distance: 65km
Elevation gain: 1,504m
Highest point: 655m
Est. moving time: 2.5-3.5hrs
Degree of difficulty: ●●
Climbs: Col de Fontcouverte (605m), Col Sainte Marguerite (606m), Col Fourtou (655m)

Parcours
0km	Thuir D48
11km	D48/D2 ➡ ①
12.5km	Col de Fontcouverte
20.5km	Saint Michel de Llotes D2/D72 ⬅ ②
27km	Col Sainte Marguerite
31.5km	D72/D618 ⬅ ③
41km	Col Fourtou D618/ unclassified ⬅ ④
47.5km	unclassified/D2 ➡
57km	Fourques D2/D615 ⬅ ⑤
62.5km	Llupia D615/D612 ⬅
65km	Thuir

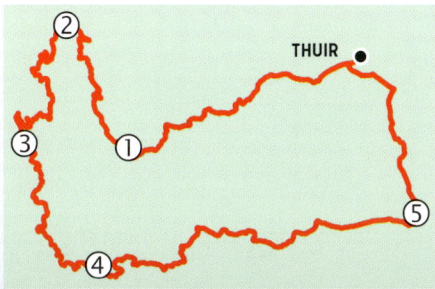

TOUR DE ROUSSILLON

Although this circuit runs away from even the foothills of the Pyrenees, it features in the Força Réal a climb that shouldn't be missed thanks to the wonderful 360° panorama offered from its very prominent summit. Commencing in Ille sur Têt, it tracks east at first to Millas, where a left turn leads over the N116 highway and the River Têt. Turn right at the far end of the bridge towards Corneilla la Rivière.

The Perpignan region is renowned for the frequency and strength of the wind – generally, they're either the Marin blasting in off the Med or the Tramontane howling down from the north and west. If either is blowing, the plane trees bordering this road will provide some measure of shelter, but lots of movement in these trees could well signal a very testing ride to come.

Leaving Corneilla, a well-surfaced bike path runs parallel to the road. Follow this almost to the next town, Pézilla la Rivière, going left at the roundabout just before entering it on the D1, which runs through open farmland, past numerous wind turbines, the Canigou visible to the west, a landmark that is almost always there no matter where you happen to be in the Pyrénées Orientales.

Climbing almost imperceptibly up to this point, the gradient picks up a little more as the road starts to rise off the plain to reach the Col de la Dona. Veer right here towards Baixas, the distinctive conical shape of the Força Réal very evident to the west until the road switches due east and slowly begins to tumble back to the flatlands. This is very much wine country, Corbières to be precise, with the sweet Muscat produced from the grapes in these low hills particularly well rated. But it's too early for a pick-me-up yet.

For now, keep on to Baixas, turning left into this attractive wine-making centre, following your nose through its narrow streets with the aim of passing diagonally through and rejoining the same road, the D18 on its far side, heading towards Espira de l'Agly, then turning left towards Cases de Pène. Turn right and almost immediately left in the centre of this village, crossing the River Agly, the road soon cutting through Corbières vines once more.

This landscape is so open that any small climb reveals a prodigious view, and this section to Tautavel is especially well blessed, the Corbières limestone ridge that's home to the breath-taking Cathar castles at Quéribus and Peyrepertuse standing out. Descending again, the road eases down into a low gorge through which the Verdouble river cuts. Tautavel lies just beyond it. In the late 1960s, the 450,000-year-old bones of a hominid (homo erectus tautavalensis) were found in the Arago cave nearby. These were some of the oldest human remains in Europe. In 2015, volunteers unearthed a tooth 100,000 years older than Tautavel Man.

Turn left in the village centre, crossing the Verdouble towards Estagel, continuing on to this small town, reached via a couple of kilometres on the D117 main road. Turn right here on the D612, which gallops across a vine-covered plain, staying with it for 3km, then go left on the D79 into Montner for a shorter and quieter route into the bottom of the climb to Força Réal. Just 3.7km long, this ascent to the ride's high point is not especially taxing. It's a test for the eyes as much as for the legs, because the vistas are so expansive and far-ranging, especially if you're prepared to push your bike the final few hundred metres to the viewing platform at the summit, the Med and Perpignan off to the east, the Pyrenees to the south, the Corbières to the west, and the Roussillon plain to the north.

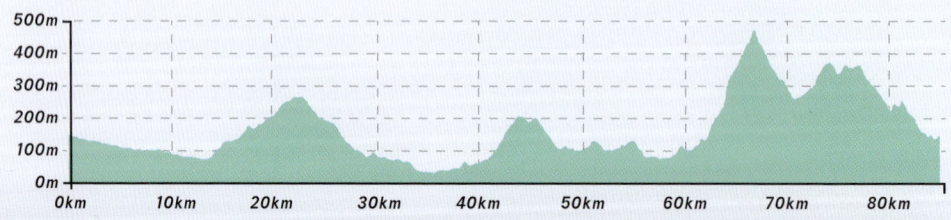

PYRÉNÉES ORIENTALES

Panorama over the Fenouillèdes from Força Réal

Distance: 83.6km
Elevation gain: 1,273m
Highest point: 465m
Est. moving time: 3-5hrs
Degree of difficulty: ●◐
Climbs: Col de la Dona (200m), Col de la Bataille (265m), Col Força Réal (465m)

Descending from this remarkable peak, stay on the D38 as it bisects the D612 at the Col de la Bataille, heading for Bélesta. Savour the views on this section of open plateau, then lap up the breeze of a descent back into Ille sur Têt, where a glass of something nicely chilled is surely called for.

Route in reverse

Riding it clockwise means that the big impact of Força Réal arrives early on rather than near the finale. However, the choice depends to an extent on the wind direction and forecast. It should, for instance, be easier to tackle it clockwise if the wind is going to pick up off the sea during the day.

Parcours

0km	Ille sur Têt	
7km	Millas D916/D612	←
8km	D612/D614	→
13km	Pézilla la Rivière D614/D1	← ①
19.5km	Col de la Dona D1/D18	→ ②
29.5km	Baixas	
31.5km	D18/D18A	← ③
34.5km	Cases de Pène, take D59	
46km	Tautavel D59/D9	← ④
52.5km	D611 (and D9)/D117	
54.5km	Estagel D117/D612	→
57.5km	D612/D79	← ⑤
61.5km	Col de la Bataille D79/D38	←
65km	Col Força Réal	⑥
68.5km	Col de la Bataille	↑
75.5km	Bélesta D38/D21	← ⑦
83.6km	Ille sur Têt	

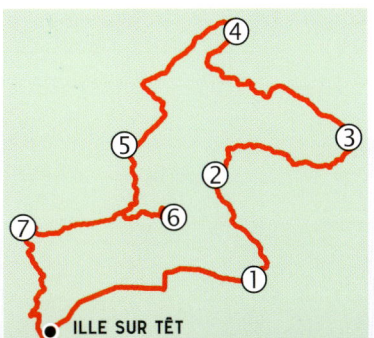

PRATS TO MOLLO AND BACK AGAIN

The far western end of the Vallespir isn't well suited to circular routes, although there are some very enticing gravel options from Prats de Mollo La Preste up to the high ridge that runs south-west from the Pic du Canigou, which lies directly north of this very attractive mountain resort and spa. Given how traffic can clog the D115 up to and beyond this town, I did consider avoiding it completely, but that would be amiss as the town and the Col des Ares high above it are well worthy of exploration, especially if you pick your right moment.

Prats de Mollo translates as "meadows of Molló", denoting the area as once belonging to the Spanish town that lies on the other side of the Col des Ares. In common with large parts of these borderlands, it was ceded by Spain to France under the terms of the Treaty of the Pyrenees in 1659, and considerably fortified under the aegis of Marshal Vauban in the late 17th century. The ride starts in front of the town walls created by Louis XIV's chief military engineer, his chef-d'oeuvre, the Fort Lagarde sitting dominantly above.

Route-finding is simple, at least to start with. Follow the road next to the city walls, which then crosses a ravine and instantly begins to climb towards the border, 13km away. It begins straightforwardly, rising sedately in great, looping bends through lush woodland, birch, beech and oak prominent. As the Col de la Seille nears, though, the gradient becomes more acute, running at close to 10% for a kilometre before easing off just before the col, which merits a stop. With no trees creating a screen, there's a startling 270° panorama, the hulking Canigou easy to pick out to the north if it's clear.

Continuing upwards, the gradient remains benign passing through the Col de la Guille and for another kilometre or so beyond. Then comes a change, comfortable to deal with initially, less so when the road pitches up to 13% nearing a final set of hairpins. There's distraction in the views, though, which are still magical. Coming out of those bends, the Col des Ares is visible and soon reached, what was once the border post now a café.

The Spanish side of the pass is far shallower than the French, sending you coasting into the Camprodon valley. It has a very different look, lusher and more rural, with cattle happily chewing in broad pastures. Its greenness makes it appear more like the Basque Country than Catalunya, where so much of the terrain is parched.

Between Molló and Camprodon, go left towards Rocabruna to start the lasso at the end of this long line of a ride. Stay with this road for two gently rising kilometres, then swing right into Font Rubí, climbing more

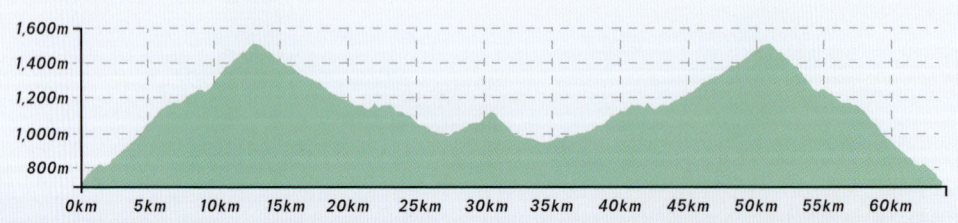

PYRÉNÉES ORIENTALES

Prats de Mollo and the Lagarde fort

steeply through the heart of this holiday village. Beyond it, a straight descent returns to the main C38 coming down from the Ares pass on the edge of the resort town of Camprodon.

It's the length of the western flank of the climb that exacts a toll as much as the gradient, which never exceeds 6% and averages a mere three. However, extending to 18km, it's still going to mean climbing for close to an hour and even more for most riders. There's no rush, though. Find the right gear, let the legs spin, and enjoy this curious corner of Spain. As the altitude rises, the views to the south into Catalunya get longer and longer, the terrain remains strikingly green, a change only coming at the col, where, unusually, it's France that looks drier and more rugged.

That thought quickly disappears, though, thanks to the exhilaration provoked by the sharp drop back towards the Col de la Seille and, from there, the less abrupt return to Prats de Mollo.

Route in reverse

There's much to be said for tackling this ride from the Spanish side of the Col des Ares – the start is far easier, the halfway stop in Prat de Mollo offers more choices for a coffee or lunch, and the most spectacular part of the ride comes towards the end.

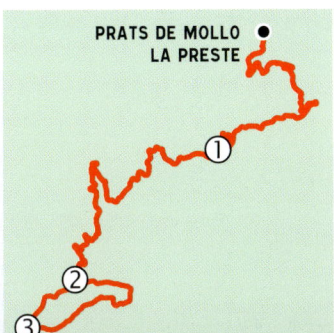

Distance: 64.5km
Elevation gain: 1,758m
Highest point: 1,513m
Est. moving time: 2.5-4.5hrs
Degree of difficulty: ●●◐
Climbs: Col de la Seille (1,185m), Col des Ares (1,513m)

Parcours

0km	Prats de Mollo La Preste
13km	Col des Ares ①
27km	C38/GIV5223 ←②
29km	GIV5223/unclassified to Font Rubí →
34km	unclassified/C38 →③
51.5km	Col des Ares
64.5km	Prats de Mollo La Preste

CATALONIA'S HIGHEST ROAD CLIMB

Vallter 2000 is a name that summons up great climbing feats in the Vuelta a España. The Catalan resort's website mentions its historical link with Spain's national tour, as well as with the Volta a Catalunya, which often has featured it as a summit finish over the last few years. Bizarrely, though, this small ski station tucked away at the top end of the Ter valley (hence Vallter) has actually never hosted the Vuelta. The race has been a regular visitor to Cerler, Pla de Beret, Seu d'Urgell and, of course, the resorts in not too distant Andorra, but hasn't ever followed the Volta's example by heading up this stunning and very testing ascent.

Despite this surprising oversight and, consequently, Vallter's absence from the list of Grand Tour summit finishes, it's well worth the effort. Rather than come straight at it, this route initially takes in some wonderfully quiet rolling roads in the Alta Garrotxa region to the north of Olot. Starting in Camprodon, at the bottom end of the 23km ascent to the resort, it first heads north-east on the main road, then turns eastwards on the GIV5223 a couple of kilometres out of town. Wide to start with, this road narrows considerably not far beyond the turn to Font Rubí, winding down through woodland to Rocabruna, a hamlet of beautiful red sandstone houses.

The Alta Garrotxa is typified by deep valleys with high rock walls and cliffs, as well as the greenness of the terrain, with holm and common oaks proliferating, and the first half of this ride highlights these characteristics. Beyond Rocabruna, the road serpentines downwards, but never viciously. Although there's a nagging thought that what goes down must eventually come back up, it's blissful, the lack of traffic heightening the sensation that you've got this road all to yourself.

It trundles into Beget, a little gem of a village, no more than a cluster of houses around the 12th-century Sant Cristofol church, its tower peeping up out of the trees, an ancient stone bridge spanning the babbling waters of the River Trull. Not far beyond it, the first concerted stretch of ascent commences. Inevitably, it's quite sedate for the most part, long views emerging towards terrain to the south that the route will soon be venturing into. It tops out just beyond the Coll de Pera, the panorama majestic until a sharp drop into Oix grabs the attention. Here the road's demarcation changes, to the GIV5221, and it's wider too as it climbs briefly to the Coll de Camporiol, then drops towards Castellfollit de la Roca. Before reaching it, though, take the right turn towards Vall del Bac just before crossing the Sant Eudald river.

This narrow valley is, if anything, even quieter than the earlier roads. Running steadily upwards through woodland from east to west, there are two or three short and quite severe lumps, notably the 4.5km ascent of the Coll de Carrera. While it certainly winds far more than the main N260 running along the far side of the Serra de Malforat to the south, road riding rarely gets more tranquil than this. It's almost a shock when the terrain opens out, the trees back away and the little lane reaches the main road at Sant Pau de Segúries.

Go right in this largish village, following the C38 road as it arrows north for half a dozen kilometres to Camprodon. At the first roundabout, go left on the road signposted to Vallter 2000. The ascent takes off very gently. It's mainly big ring for the first third, the road hardly wavering from a straight course through the wide valley to reach Vilallonga de Ter. From there, it's threes and fours as far as

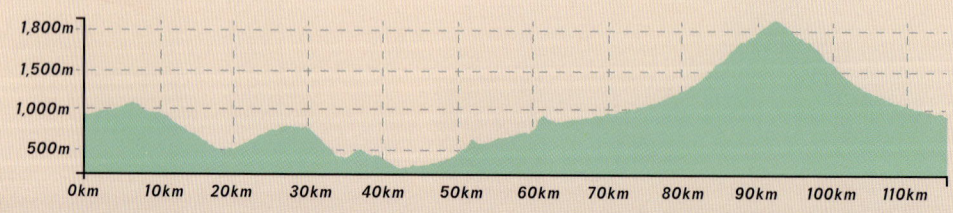

GIRONA

Sunrise at the Vallter 2000 ski station

the busy tourist town of Setcases, its name a tribute to the seven houses that were gifted by a local noble in the 10th century. This is where the climb really begins.

The valley and the road narrow, the gradient picks up a little, then a touch more. Then, approaching the first set of hairpins, wallop! There's a kilometre at 10%, sections of it considerably steeper. The average remains close to double figures as the road makes for the resort more directly again. Four kilometres from the top, the gradient eases off, before picking up again as it passes the first of the car parks, a ladder of eight hairpins providing a final lift into Vallter 2000 and a little beyond. Overlooked by the 2,702m Pic de la Dona, the resort is quite small, its setting beneath a circus of peaks quite stunning.

The return to Camprodon is straightforward and, of course, all downhill, with just a little pedalling required in the final kilometres.

Route in reverse

I'd probably only tackle Vallter 2000 right from the off if I didn't have the time to do the loop into the Alta Garrotxa from Camprodon. As far as that loop goes, tackle it in either direction. I reckon they're equally good.

Distance: 117.1km
Elevation gain: 3,038m
Highest point: 2,140m
Est. moving time: 4-6.5hrs
Degree of difficulty: ●●●●
Climbs: Coll de Pera (794m), Coll de Camporiol (506m), Coll de Carrera (571m), Vallter 2000 (2,140m)

Recorrido

0km	Camprodon
3.5km	C38/GIV5223 ➡
25.5km	Coll de Pera ①
37.5km	Coll de Camporiol ②
43km	GIV5221/unclassified to Vall del Bac ➡ ③
52.5km	Coll de Carrera
63km	unclassified/C153A ➡
64km	Sant Pau de Segúries C153A/C38 ➡ ④
69.5km	Camprodon C38/GI5264 ⬅ ⑤
81km	Setcases
93km	Vallter 2000 ⑥
117.1km	Camprodon

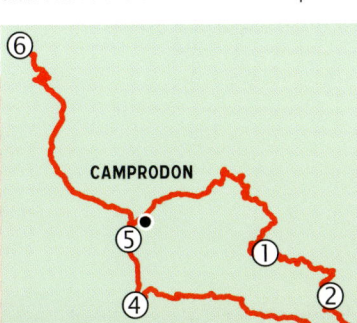

TOUR OF GARROTXA

Spain is, according to its own tourist board, the second most mountainous country in Europe after Austria. I like this fact so much that I'm not going to quibble with its logic by bringing Andorra, San Marino and other mountain territories into the argument. Suffice to say that, although its accuracy is perhaps dubious, it does illustrate perfectly how rugged Spain is and underline how difficult it is to assess where the southern edge of the Pyrenees lies. Unlike France, where the start/end of the range is delineated by a wide plain running parallel, on the Pyrenees' southern edge the mountains run on and on.

There is, though, a geographic dividing line. Topographic maps of the range include the Pre-Pyrenees, or foothills, as part of the chain. On the north side, the Corbières hills are the only significant part of the Pre-Pyrenees, while to the south there are more than 50 mountain massifs classed in this way. In Catalunya, the line runs demarcating them from the Sub-Pyrenees (comprised largely by ranges going north to south) runs east to west a little to the south of Besalú, Olot, Ripoll and Berga.

This route runs through the Pre-Pyrenean massifs between the middle two of those towns, starting in Olot, reputed as the rainiest place in Spain. Don't let that put you off, though, as the capital of the Garrotxa region is renowned for its natural landscape, notably the ancient volcanoes that lie close to the town. It gets under way in the shadow of the Montsacopa, a volcano that's been dormant for 100,000 years and lies just on Olot's northern edge. Head south down the main avenue for 4.5km, then turn right towards El Mallol. Go through this village until the right turn to Vidrà.

This farm lane cuts between fields of pasture and corn, then plunges into woodland hiding the very abrupt start of the Collada de Collfred, a popular test for Girona-based professionals. Its first two kilometres average a tad more than 9%, rising through wonderful beech woods, a copper brown carpet of last season's leaves coating the ground beneath them. These ramps are, though, merely an hors d'oeuvre for the next 2km average 12%, with sections half as steep again as that. When the road starts to emerge from the trees, the slope gradually becomes less acute and startling views to the south provide a welcome distraction.

At Els Plans, the gradient eases back into low single figures. There's still the occasional steeper section, but there's a more bucolic feel, with meadows, livestock and a cattle-grid at the top of the pass. The descent continues in this vein, running steadily down through pasture and beech woods towards Vidrà, and even climbing briefly to reach the village. The valley widens beyond it, the drop getting shallower, the road sauntering into Santa Maria de Besora.

Coming into this, the biggest settlement in this valley, turn 90° right, following the signpost to "Ripoll per Llaers" on a road of concrete slabs, its rippled surface a hand-tingling irritation, but at least in good nick. It judders through woodland for a few kilometres to reach Llaers, then jolts down and northwards through stands of oak and pine for a handful more. A flatter section means the going is a little easier, and when the road begins to climb again it quickly reaches the smooth-surfaced nirvana of the N260a. Turn right onto it in the direction of Vallfogona. This, the western side of the Coll de Canes, is an absolute breeze compared to the earlier ascent of the Collfred. If you're

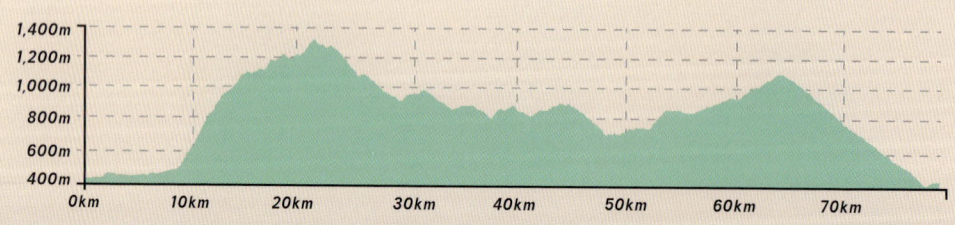

GIRONA

The view over Olot from the Montsacopa volcano

fresh, it's big ring pretty much all the way to Vallfogona, and only 4% for the 4km beyond that to the pass, the road running high on the side of a verdant valley, conical peaks ahead indicating Olot is not too far away.

From the Coll de Canes, the return to the start point is all downhill, the gradient only varying a point or two either side of 5%, a breeze through woodland that runs right to the edge of the town.

Route in reverse

The climbing is certainly easier going at this route anticlockwise. There's not much of a warm-up before starting up the Coll de Canes, but it's not the sternest of uphill tests. There is a little climbing on the concrete road, but it does lead on to the less fearsome side of the Collfred. Of course, that means descending down some pretty hairy ramps on that narrow lane.

Distance: 79.2km
Elevation gain: 1,875m
Highest point: 1,327m
Est. moving time: 3-5hrs
Degree of difficulty: ●●●
Climbs: Collada de Collfred (1,327m), Coll de Canes (1,121m)

Recorrido

0km	Olot	
4.5km	C152/GIP5226	➡
7.5km	GIP5226/unclassified to Vidrà	①
21.5km	Collada de Collfred	②
36.5km	Santa Maria de Besora GIP5227/unclassified to Llaers ➡	③
54km	unclassified/N260a ➡	④
64km	Coll de Canes	⑤
79.2km	Olot	

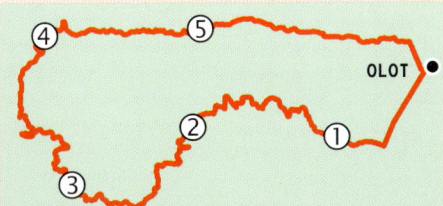

TOUR OF THE CATALAN VOLCANOES

Even though the cycling mecca of Girona lies outside the Pyrenees and Pre-Pyrenees, sitting instead on the edge of a Sub-Pyrenees spur that runs north-south from the chain, I've included this route that brushes the city's western edge and climbs its most celebrated peak because this provincial capital is so well renowned in cycling circles and, particularly, because it enables completion of a fabulous loop that includes the Volcanic Natural Park to the south-east of Olot.

It begins by heading northwards in that town's centre, circling the foot of the long-dormant Montsacopa volcano and picking up the N260. On Olot's outskirts, as this main road swings left towards Ripoll, go right heading for Sant Joan les Fonts, passing through it to reach Castellfollit de la Roca. This town is perched spectacularly on the basalt remains of an ancient lava flow, the crag 50 metres high and almost a kilometre long, although its extraordinary position doesn't become evident until the main road has weaved through the centre and dropped down to cross to River Fluvià, from where there's a good view of its precipitous location.

Continue for a couple more kilometres to a roundabout, going left here to Montagut in order to escape from a parallel course with the A26 motorway. Keep on through Montagut, the route undulating but essentially continuing the gradual downward trajectory from the start. Beyond Montagut, the road narrows considerably and meanders and rolls a little more through farmland to Tortellà. Coming into this small town, keep away from the *autopista* a little longer by going left towards Sales de Llierca and right soon after at a sign indicating the Ajuntament St Martí, taking the right-hand of the two lanes on this corner for a nice interlude through beech, oak and pine woods that ends when rejoining the main road.

With the motorway adjacent, the route contiunues into Besalú, the stronghold of the unforgettably named Wilfred the Hairy, the Count of Besalú, who was credited with unification of Catalonia in the late ninth century. Stay on the main route through the town centre, crossing the Fluvià just downstream of Besalú's magnificent 12th-century Romanesque bridge, with a gate-tower at its mid-point. Follow the C66z out of town towards Banyoles and Girona, this road merging with the main route south. Stay on it for 5km before branching right in the direction of Banyoles. Coming into town, go right towards the Oficina de Turisme, picking up signs for Mieres and Santa Pau, which lie in the volcanic park, and the GI524, which leads out of town. As it starts into open country, there is a left turn towards Pujarnol that is the start of the diversion towards Rocacorba. If for any reason you're not keen, keep straight on here all the way back to Olot through the natural park. For Rocacorba, the main climb of the day, swing left.

The 13km ascent builds up slowly, barely rising initially, picking up more as it swaps farmland for woodland. It climbs a little more approaching Pujarnol, eases back for a kilometre, then takes off with a vengeance at the Collet de Pujarnol. The next 2km are close to 11%, the telecoms masts at the summit occasionally visible through a corridor of oaks. As long views emerge to the north on the right, there is a slight easing, but frequent sections in double figures make this quite imperceptible. A crest does, finally, arrive, leading to the first mast, which signals the start of 1.5km at 10% to reach the summit, the panorama absolutely wonderful as the road hooks back on itself to arrive at the top.

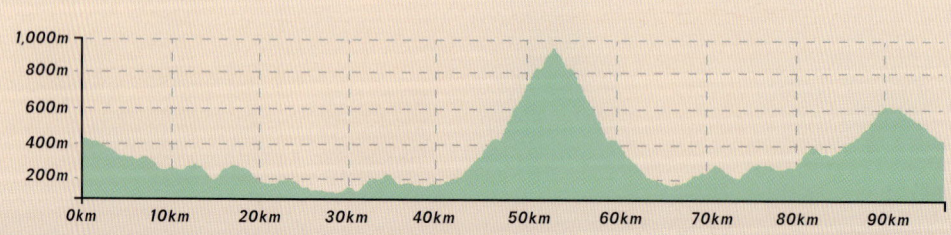

GIRONA

Take it steady when descending off Rocacorba, returning to the junction with the GI524 and going left. Having undulated downwards during its first half, the latter part of this route regains that lost altitude in the same fashion, taking two steps up then a little one down, firstly to reach Sant Miquel de Campmajor, then Mieres, and, soon after, the volcanic park. With oaks cloaking the peaks, it's hard to imagine this area as a Pyrenean ring of fire, the last eruption taking place 11,000 years ago. But walk to the top of many of them and you can look down into the crater from what was once the volcano's rim. Topping the last ridge before the short drop into Olot, there are volcanic cones on all sides, another lasting reminder of the violent forces that created the Pyrenees.

Garrotxa Volcanic Zone Natural Park

Route in reverse
Rather having than the big impact of the volcanoes at the start and the less impressive roads close to the motorway as the conclusion, as would be the case if this loop were tackled anticlockwise, this route could be adapted as a simple out-and-back ride through the natural park to Rocacorba and returning via the same roads to Olot.

Distance: 96.7km
Elevation gain: 1,958m
Highest point: 980m
Est. moving time: 3-5hrs
Degree of difficulty: ●●●
Climbs: Rocacorba (980m)

Recorrido

0km	Olot
3.5km	N260/GI522 ➡
8km	Castellfollit de la Roca
11.5km	N260/GIP5233 ⬅ ①
17.5km	Tortellà GI523/GIV5232 ⬅
18.5km	GIV5232/unclassified ➡
21.5km	unclassified/N260 ⬅
25.5km	Besalú C66z ②
28km	Junction C66z/C66 ➡
33.5km	Junction C66/C150a ➡ ③
38.5km	Banyoles GI524
40km	GI524/GIV5247 ⬅ ④
53km	Rocacorba ⑤
66km	GIV5247/GI524 ⬅
78km	Mieres ⑥
96.7km	Olot

LOST ROADS OF THE RIPOLLÈS

Sitting at the confluence of the Ter and Freser rivers, Ripoll has a rich history as a regional and industrial centre, a town once highly renowned for its armament factories and iron ore mines. As the capital of the Ripollès comarca **within Girona province, it remains a bustling administrative centre as well as being a key communications hub, the N260 climbing into France via the Col des Ares in one direction and via the Cerdanya high plateau in the other.**

This route commences on that latter stretch of the main road across northern Catalunya, leaving the centre of Ripoll and heading north up the tight and sometimes busy Vall de Ribes, climbing steadily but gently for 15km to reach Ribes de Freser. Turn right just after passing under the railway bridge, with Bruguera the next objective. This tranquil lane also marks the beginning of the climb to the little-known Coll de Jou, its initial sections not too acute as it climbs beneath what is in this region the almost ubiquitous canopy of oak, beech and pine.

It steepens a little more for the last 2km into Bruguera, the road emerging onto an open mountainside before dipping down into the village. Take the left fork entering Bruguera, a sign indicating the Coll de Jou and heralding an immediate switch from tarmac to concrete. It comes with a severe change in the gradient too, a typical characteristic of this kind of surface that tends to be laid in jointed blocks and isn't as adaptable as asphalt. Rather than sweeping around a consistently rising bend to take the sting out of a slope, a concrete road tends to go with the gradient more, stepping up hillsides. Bear in mind too that, although longer-lasting than asphalt, roads of this type are also slippery in the wet, which not only makes standing on the pedals a dicey manoeuvre but also, and more worryingly, does the same for descending as well.

On the up side, the views from this cement strip as it clambers up to the Coll de Jou are absolutely tremendous and, assuming it's dry, more than justify the bumpy ride. The gradient does ease too the nearer the summit comes, although the corners are still savagely steep.

The concrete continues for the 10km between the summit and Ogassa, the gradient remaining acute for a large part of this section, especially on the approach to the isolated Sant Martí de Ogassa chapel, located 4km down from the top, and on the last couple of kilometres before Ogassa itself. There are, however, far fewer tight bends, the white surface swaying rather than switching down through the trees. In this final concrete section, the road splits, the route to the right diving sharply to Ogassa and towards Sant Joan de les Abadesses on the main road. The adventurous may want to consider staying left towards Camprodon and looping back to Sant Joan via the C38 and N260.

At Ogassa, the asphalt makes a welcome return, tyres humming rather than rumbling on a surface that's also wide and fast. It shoots down into Sant Joan de les Abadesses, the name recalling the abbesses who ran the monastery established here by Wilfred the Hairy in the ninth century. Bear left in this large village onto the N260 to cross the river on the bridge parallel to the beautiful medieval Pont Vell. Stay with the main road until the right turn to the Collada de Sentigosa.

This climb could hardly be any less like the Jou, the verdant setting apart. Shimmying slowly upwards on a snooker-table-smooth surface, it's a breeze, which continues for another 4km to the Coll de Coubet. Turn hard right here, climbing once more towards the

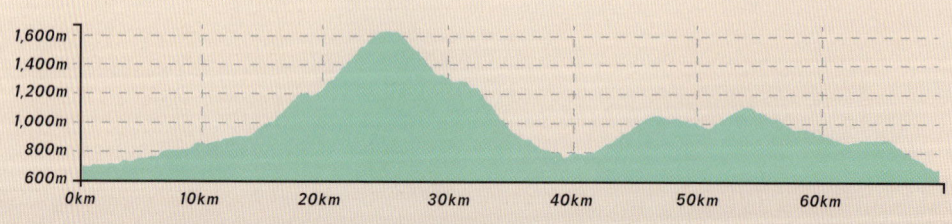

GIRONA

The medieval Pont Vell at Sant Joan de les Abadesses

Coll de Canes (see page 42), 3km distant and very much from the same mould as the Sentigosa. Its 16km of descent average a tad below 3%, offering the option of a high-energy blast back into Ripoll if the Jou hasn't stripped all the vim from your legs, in which you can enjoy a rather more sedate trundle.

Route in reverse

While the serious climbing does come in the second half of the ride, what comes in the opening half isn't overly taxing and should mean you reach Sant Joan de les Abadesses at the bottom of the Jou nicely warmed up rather than running on fumes. Heading this way does also mean travelling downhill on the busy section of the N260 into Ripoll, making it pass more quickly.

> **Distance:** 69.8km
> **Elevation gain:** 1,630m
> **Highest point:** 1,655m
> **Est. moving time:** 2.5-4hrs
> **Degree of difficulty:** ●●◐
> **Climbs:** Coll de Jou (1,637m), Collada de Sentigosa (1,064m), Coll de Canes (1,120m)

Recorrido

0km	Ripoll
13km	Ribes de Freser N260/GIV5263 ➡ ①
25km	Coll de Jou ②
34km	Ogassa
39km	Sant Joan de les Abadesses GIV5211/N260 ⬅ ③
39.5km	N260/GI521 ➡
46.5km	Collada de Sentigosa
50.5km	GI521/N260a ➡ ④
54km	Coll de Canes ⑤
69.8km	Ripoll

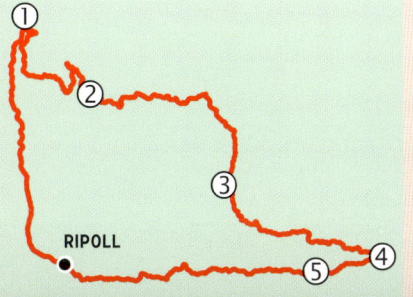

A CATALAN PAIR OF VUELTA PASSES

This route features two big climbs that were regulars on the *recorrido* of the Vuelta a España, but have fallen out of favour in recent years, the Coll de la Creueta and Collada de Toses. They're both lofty tests, but quite different in their topography. The Creueta is extremely long, extending to more than 30km from two directions, while the Toses is consistently steep on its highest sections, with 3km to its summit running at 10%.

Setting out from the centre of Ripoll, head north on the N260 for 4km, turning left coming into Campdevànol. There's no perceptible change in the gradient, the road rising gently through farmland, following the course of the River Merdàs. Carry on past the right turn to Castellar de n'Hug, which will be the route back towards Ripoll much later in the ride, pressing on instead through pine and oak woods to the Coll de Merolla and the start of a steady glide to La Pobla de Lillet, the road wiggling for 8km down to this village, where Antoni Gaudí, the architect of the extraordinary Sagrada Família church in Barcelona, designed a set of gardens for a friend. Restored in the 1990s, the distinctive Jardins de Can Artigas, are now open to the public.

Just before La Pobla de Lillet, turn right towards Castellar de n'Hug and La Molina to start what is from this point a 21km ascent of the Creueta, the slope a little more acute but still far from daunting. There is, though, a sense that you're approaching a more substantial test as towering rock faces and big peaks start to crowd the way ahead, the vistas becoming more impressive. Responding to this, the road kicks up more sharply for a kilometre, then settles down to a consistent 6% as it weaves upwards past the Hostal Les Fonts.

Nearing Castellar, where a statue of a sheep overlooks the road, the gradient rises another notch and the terrain becomes more barren, a seam of red rock appearing that's testimony to this region's violent geological past. A couple of kilometres on, at Castellar, the contrast between this dark crimson and the off-white surrounds is stark. Garlanded as Spain's most beautiful village, it's tucked into a protective fold in the earth's crust between the two strata. Now, every twist of the road presents a startling view, and as it weaves there's also a Ventoux-like trick of the landscape, the summit appearing to come closer, only to become more distant as the road sweeps around a huge cut in the side of the mountain. The Creueta finally arrives, though, at the end of an all but flat final kilometre, the col in the lea of the eponymous peak.

There's a brief drop, then a short climb to a plateau with a large car park and lifts that are part of the La Molina ski station that's a regular finishing point at the Volta a Catalunya. Just below, go right at the T-junction in the direction of Ripoll, soon reaching the Coll de Toses, which is the next climb. But first to get to the bottom of it. Keep straight on to reach the end of the plateau at the junction with the N260. Turn right in front of the hotel and descend smoothly for 17km, the road back up towards the Toses pass often visible way down in the Rigard valley below.

At Planès, turn very sharply right towards Toses, descending a little more before reaching the valley bottom just before Espinosa. The climb back to the Coll de Toses begins there, although it's very benign as the road tracks the Rigard upstream along with the Ripoll-Puigcerdà railway line. Change comes at Toses, where the train disappears

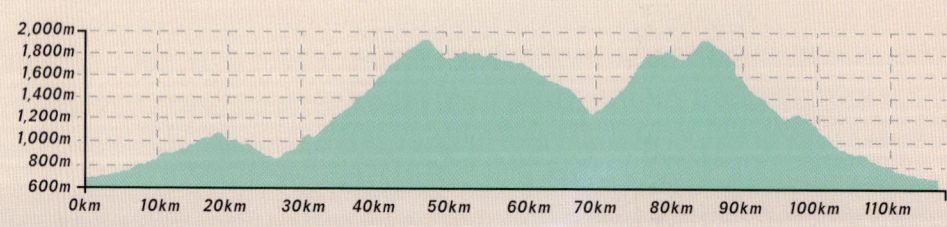

GIRONA

Approaching the top of the Creueta pass

through a very grand tunnel entrance into the mountainside, the road crossing it just beforehand and ascending more quickly. A couple of kilometres later, it steps up again, averaging close to 10% for the next 3km to the summit.

My word, the summit is worth the grind, though. The high ridge of the Pyrenees lies right ahead, snow on the highest peaks all year round. What's more, all of the significant climbing is now complete. Turn left onto the false flat that leads back to the ski car park and lifts passed earlier, passing through the saddle to reach the Coll de la Creueta for the second time and the sweeping descent back to Castellar de n'Hug. Just before its first houses, turn sharp left towards Can Ros and Gombrèn, red rock vivid again as this tight lane slaloms downwards, caution advised due to its narrowness rather than the angle of descent, which is never severe. It arrives back at the GI402 just above Gombrèn, for 15 quite rapid kilometres back to Ripoll.

Route in reverse

This is a superb circuit too, and one that takes the sting from the upper part of the Coll de Toses by descending it. The climb back up from Planès on the N260 is longer but far less challenging. The traffic is significantly heavier, though. Bear in mind, too, that descending from Castellar to La Pobla de Lillet will then demand a return to Ripoll via the Coll de Merolla, normally an easy ascent but far less so when more than 100km have already been clocked up.

Distance: 127.7km
Elevation gain: 2,789m
Highest point: 1,931m
Est. moving time: 4.5-7hrs
Degree of difficulty: ●●●●
Climbs: Coll de Merolla (1,090m), Coll de la Creueta (1,921m), Collada de Toses (1,790m)

Recorrido

0km	Ripoll
3.5km	N260/GI402 ←
18.5km	Coll de Merolla
26.5km	La Pobla de Lillet GI402/BV4031 → ①
47km	Coll de la Creueta ②
52.5km	BV4031/GI400 →
56km	GI400/N260 → ③
73km	Planès N260/GIV4016 → ④
85.5km	Collada de Toses GIV4016/GI400 ← ⑤
88km	GI400/BV4031 ←
93.5km	Coll de la Creueta
103km	Castellar de n'Hug ⑥ BV4031/unclassified to Can Ros ←
113km	unclassified/GI402 ←
124km	GI402/N260 →
127.7km	Ripoll

TOUR OF THE CERDANYA

Split almost equally between France and Spain, the Cerdanya high plateau is one of the most remarkable regions in the Pyrenees, a wonderfully broad valley a thousand metres up running east to west between the Serra del Cadí massif to the south and the high peaks of Catalan Pyrenees to the north. Popular as a base for Spanish pro cyclists, their international colleagues have tended to favour Girona to the east and Andorra to the west. Yet it has an edge on both in terms of the range of riding options and its climate. Warmed by 3,000 hours of sun per year, it's surprisingly temperate considering its altitude. This partly explains its popularity as a venue for the organisers of the Volta a Catalunya, which takes place in late March and regularly features stages in this region, with the resort of La Molina a regular venue for summit finishes.

This shortish loop begins in Puigcerdà, which nestles against the border and the French town of Bourg Madame. Heading out on the N154 and the N260, stay with the latter and begin to climb towards the Collada de Toses. This route skirts past La Molina, and is all the better for that. The climb to the resort from Alp and via Masella is nice enough, but doesn't compare in terms of grandeur with the Toses pass, from which another road runs down to La Molina and back to the plateau.

Compared to its brutal eastern flank, this side of the Toses is far easier. It's 22km long, so it's not a doddle, but the gradient never exceeds 6% and averages just half that figure. As one of the main routes out of the Cerdanya, it can be quite busy, but the 5km tunnel that bores beneath the Cadí massif and onwards towards Barcelona and the rest of Catalunya takes the bulk of the traffic. On the plus side – and this is where it scores heavily over the more direct routes into La Molina – it offers sumptuous views across the high plateau, even from quite low down on the climb. The upper sections of La Molina soon become visible on the ridge way ahead. For now, they are the target, although this route ends up reaching them from above rather than below.

The first sign of the top of the pass is the large Hotel Collada that sits next to the road junction. Turn right here in the direction of La Molina. Running almost level, this road soon passes the top of the brutal ascent from Toses (see page 48) that gives this col its name. Another 3km on is the turn towards the marvellous Coll de la Creueta, which is worth the short diversion for the stunning panorama if it's clear. Otherwise, stay with the GI400 as it drops into the top part of La Molina, a bit of an odd place. It feels much more residential than other ski resorts, covering a vast area as a result of the accommodation being individual houses with gardens rather than the typical high mountain tower blocks. Essentially, it's a town of high-altitude holiday homes.

Keep on the GI400 passing through the heart of it, turning left at one point in the centre, following signs to Masella, which is just a quick scoot down the mountain on the road that the pro racers tend to climb for summit finishes at La Molina. Continue through this lower resort, winding down to Alp on the high plateau. Keep straight here until a crossroads with a no-entry opposite, turning left and staying in that direction to leave Alp and pick up the road across the Cerdanya, the plain Spaghetti Western-like in its vastness, that sense heightened in summer when it's parched.

The road meets the main N260 on the other side of the valley. At the roundabout,

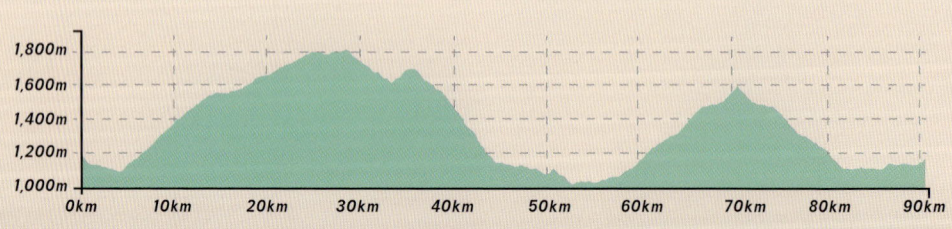

GIRONA

start back towards Puigcerdà, either a direct 14km away or more than twice that distance for those who fancy a diversion recommended largely for aesthetic reasons. Having climbed one side of the valley, there's a nice symmetry to seeing it from the other and the best opportunity comes at the left turn to Meranges, which glides up from the plateau, offering expansive views across to the Cadí massif.

It then begins to turn into a valley running into the heart of the Cerdanya range, the gradient generally very kind and traffic almost non-existent. Above the attractive village of Meranges, the road steepens and narrows, passing through Girul and then pine forest towards a group of lakes nestled beneath the high peaks right on the border. The tarmac runs out halfway there, but I understand the gravel road that carries on is in good condition. However far you get, the return is via the same road to the N260 for the last few kilometres into Puigcerdà.

Puigcerdà viewed across the Cerdanya high valley

Route in reverse

My only gripe with going in the other direction is the ascent up to La Molina via Alp and Masella, which is a pretty humdrum road to a ski resort. The fact that the pros race up this way doesn't make it any more enticing. Even if heading to Meranges first, I'd still advise taking the N260 ascent of the Toses pass and then dropping through La Molina to get back to Puigcerdà.

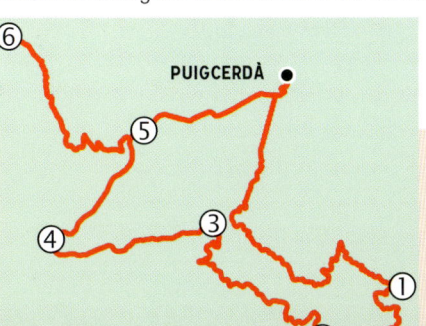

Distance: 90.7km
Elevation gain: 1,662m
Highest point: 1,807m
Est. moving time: 3.5-5hrs
Degree of difficulty: ●●●
Climbs: Collada de Toses (1,790m), Meranges (1,600m)

Recorrido

0km	Puigcerdà
4km	N260/C162 ←
25.5km	Collada de Toses N260/GI400 → ①
31km	La Molina ②
37.5km	Masella
44.5km	Alp ← to LP4033b ③
53km	LP4033b/N260 → ④
59km	N260/GIV4031 ← ⑤
70.5km	Girul ⑥
90.7km	Puigcerdà

51

A LONG ROAD TO PAL

I wanted to include the stunning climb up to Coll de Pal both because it has a significant place in racing history and, just as importantly, it is the only road that ascends into the heart of the Cadí-Moixeró Natural Park. It is not, however, an easy climb to access on a circuit by bike. It could be included in a Tour de Cadí following the roads that run around the edge of the park, but such a route would not only be long at close to 200km, but would also clock up around 8,000m of vertical gain. In other words, it would be a very hard two-day ride. Another option might have been to feature the climb on its own from the small town of Bagà, 20km down the mountain, which was much more appealing. In the end, though, my wish to make every ascent part of a longer route rather than a standalone test resulted in this very challenging expedition via the Creueta pass from Puigcerdà and back again.

It begins by taking the slightly shorter of the two routes from Puigcerdà to the Creueta, via the La Molina ski station. After starting on the N260, branch right towards Alp and then follow signs to La Molina. The climb is steady and not too thrilling, but soon arrives at the bottom edge of the resort. Stay with this road until it passes the Hotel Supermolina, then swing left behind the hotel, rising through the trees to a T-junction with a tunnel a few dozen metres down to the right. Go left, climbing away from the resort, long views now emerging across the Cerdanya peaks to the north. As the road begins to plateau, turn hard right towards Castellar de n'Hug to cross a short but fabulous stretch of terrain to arrive at the Coll de la Creueta, where there is a magnificent panorama.

The descent (see page 48) winds quite majestically down to Castellar and onwards through pine forest to La Pobla de Lillet. Turn right here, following the River Llobregat down the valley for 9km. Don't be tempted to take the main C16 route towards Bagà as it almost immediately enters a lengthy tunnel with no shoulder. Instead, continue for another 250m and turn right into Guardiola de Berguedà, joining the C16 on the far side of this town, but only staying on this main route for a kilometre until it bears right towards the Cadí tunnel toll road. When it peels off, head into and through the centre of Bagà, where the 20km haul up to Pal begins.

The location of Alberto Contador's first major mountain summit win in the 2005 edition of the now extinct Setmana Catalana, Pal is rated by some as one of the toughest climbs in Spain, although the opening three kilometres are straightforward, the Serra de Moixeró at the eastern end of the Cadí massif filling the skyline ahead. That changes, however, when the viaduct carrying the main road towards the tunnel soars overhead, heralding a kilometre at 9%. An easier one follows, then leads into the two toughest kilometres of the climb, averaging nine again.

Try to forget the grind, though, and focus on the view ahead up to a towering 2,500m ridge that overlooks La Molina on the other side. When the road flicks briefly to the south, a glorious circus of rocky peaks appears. As this large loop reaches its most southerly point, there's a stunning panorama across Bagà and down the Llobregat valley, the final ranges of the Pre-Pyrenees to either side of it. Climbing a little higher, the view is eastwards towards Ripoll and Olot, the volcanic cones close to this town easy to pick out on a clear day.

The gradient is still a focus too, but not to the extent it was further down. Running

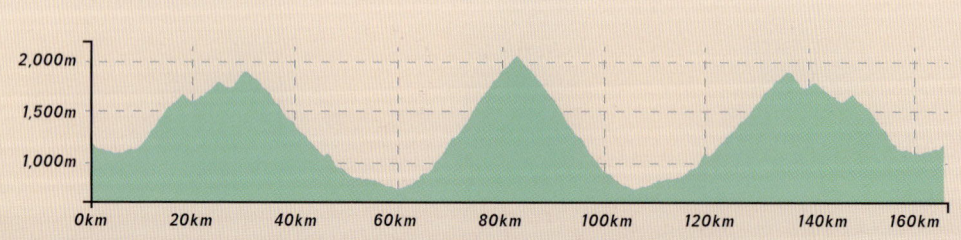

GIRONA

The Cadí Moixeró Natural Park near Bagà

at a touch above 7% for the most part, it does take its toll, but principally because the climb is so long. At the Coll de Pal refuge, the road rises above the tree line, boulders and scree running down to it from the outcrops above. Then the terrain opens out, livestock grazing in the rolling meadows more than 2,000m up. From the high point, the road drops for a couple of kilometres to a cattle grid and a rough track, with the waters of Lago de La Molina visible way below.

The lake gives a clue to this road's existence. In 2005, when Contador took that victory, the authorities in Bagà and La Molina were hoping to create a joint ski area with a lift coming up from the resort to the north. Plans were finally agreed in 2018, with the new lift due to open for the 2019/20 season. The objective is to open Pal up to more visitors, but retaining it as a site of natural beauty with no resort facilities. Hopefully, and bearing in mind its location in the Cadí park, that goal will be achieved because it's a magical upland wilderness.

The return to Puigcerdà is via the outward route. A refuelling stop in Bagà is recommended before commencing the ascent of the Creueta (see page 48). At that summit, the climbing is all but done, the long freewheel back to the start bringing up 100 miles for the day.

Distance: 159.4km
Elevation gain: 4,066m
Highest point: 2,070m
Est. moving time: 5.5-9hrs
Degree of difficulty: ●●●●●
Climbs: La Molina (1,700m), Coll de la Creueta (1,921m), Coll de Pal (2,070m)

Recorrido

0km	Puigcerdà
6km	N260/GIV4033 ➡
17km	La Molina Junction above Hotel SuperMolina ⬅ ①
19km	T-Junction with GI400 ⬅
21km	GI400/BV4031 ➡
27km	Coll de la Creueta ②
47.5km	La Pobla de Lillet BV4031/B402 ➡ ③
56.5km	➡ to Guardiola de Berguedà ④
57.5km	Take slip road onto C16
58.5km	Fork left from C16 into Bagà and pick up BV4024
80km	Coll de Pal ⑤
102.5km	Guardiola de Berguedà ④ junction with B402 ⬅
111.5km	La Pobla de Lillet B402/BV4031 ➡ ③
132km	Coll de la Creueta ②
138km	La Molina ①
159.4km	Puigcerdà

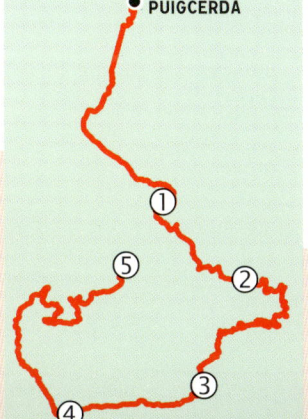

53

EASY ROLLING IN BARCELONA PROVINCE

As is the case on the northern side of the chain, I've included some routes that head away from the mountains with the deliberate intention of providing a more distant perspective on them. Some of my most memorable views of the Pyrenees were from locations well away from the peaks that enabled me to see with stunning clarity the epic scale of this chain, snowy summits visible to the horizon in both directions. This route commencing in the Barcelona province town of Berga fits into this category, although its second half does cover some rugged terrain on the bottom edge of the Pre-Pyrenees, notably the lovely climb of the Coll de Jou and the road that runs back to Berga from that high point.

From the centre of Berga, head south-west, joining the C26 on the edge of the town. Initially, it runs in the shadow of the Serra Queralt on the bottom edge of the Pre-Pyrenees, through which the route will make its return later. To the south is a vast plain running away towards Manresa, Igualada and, beyond them, Barcelona. The road cuts through farmland, undulating a little, then enters pine forest and begins to descend gently to the village of Navès, at a quarter distance. This is the low point, in terms of altitude that is, but there's much to relish in roads like this, where the traffic is local and light, the surface is wonderfully smooth, and there's always something to catch the eye. There are so many roads like this on the Spanish side of the Pyrenees, little known but perfect for riding.

Turn right approaching Solsona, following the signs into it. With 40km covered and most of the climbing still to come, Solsona offers a good opportunity to refuel, the Nucli Antic (old town) clustered around Plaça de Sant Joan its impressive focal point. Once sated, head towards Port del Comte on the LV4241. Heading northwards, progress is now consistently upwards. To begin with, the slope is mild as the road weaves through the trees to Lladurs. Beyond this village, the gradient rears up suddenly, brief sections in double figures over two steeper kilometres as the Pyrenees once again fill the view ahead.

The road steps up onto a gently rising plateau, arrowing unwaveringly through farmland towards the heart of the Serra de Querol and, within it, the Coll de Jou. A flick to the right from this crow's flight leads into some more acute ramps, the road now weaving drunkenly in order to gain height. As it does, the view suddenly opens up to the south and east, and what a panorama to take in as the gradient eases back again, with distant bluffs smudges on the horizon beyond the flatlands recently crossed. A moment later, there's an opening to the north, offering a brief glimpse of precipitous rockfaces, until the road reaches a crest and, that most Pyrenean of features, a descent within a

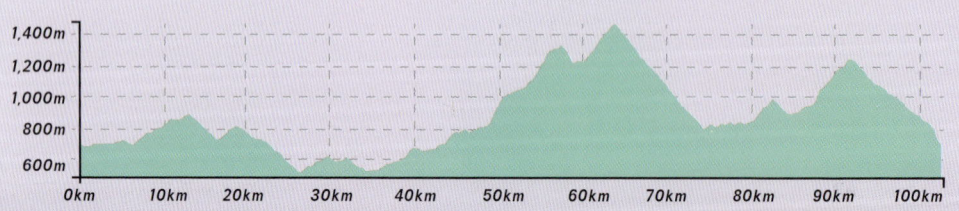

BARCELONA

The road bordering the Llosa del Cavall reservoir

climb. It's not steep and less than 2km long, and launches you into the final 4km up to the Jou pass.

This final section is not overly challenging, rising at sixes and sevens to the dramatic Vilamala observation point on the elbow of the final hairpin, the Coll de Jou just above it with perhaps the most unnecessary roundabout in Spain. Turn right here and start to descend towards Sant Llorenç de Morunys. It's fast to start with, longish straights linked by shallow bends, then reaches a series of sweeping switchbacks that force you to slow and almost encourage contemplation of the view down to the Llosa del Cavall reservoir, hemmed in on all sides by huge rocky outcrops.

The road breezes through the attractive little town of Sant Llorenç and down to the rich blue waters of the reservoir, then bumps along its northern edge for half a dozen kilometres. After wiggling over the river that feeds the lake, it makes a short leap from one pine-clad valley to the next, slightly higher up. Like the other two sections of this triangular route, it's magically serene, climbing through woodland until the two sides of the valley meet and the road squeezes through the unlit, but relatively short, Berga tunnel to reach the ride's final summit, the Coll de Jouet. Beyond it, the final 11km are all downhill into Berga, the road meandering its way back into town at a gentle pace, 100 very agreeable kilometres on the clock.

Route in reverse

Climbs right from the off, although not severely, and does have the advantage of completing all of the most significant ascents when you're fresh. However, the Jou is more impressive from the south than from the east and the road from it towards Berga more picturesque than the bottom end of the triangle from Solsona.

Distance: 102.7km
Elevation gain: 2,305m
Highest point: 1,480m
Est. moving time: 3.5-6hrs
Degree of difficulty: ●●◐
Climbs: Coll de Jou (1,480m), Coll de Jouet (1,232m)

Recorrido

0km	Berga
2km	C149/C26 ↑
39.5km	C26/C55 → ①
41.5km	Solsona C26/LV4241 →
64km	Coll de Jou LV4241/L401 → ②
92km	Coll de Jouet ③
102.7km	Berga

BENEATH THE CADÍ MASSIF

The Cadí massif is so unrelentingly immense that until the construction in 1984 of the road tunnel through its eastern end, it presented a natural north-south barrier that hugely complicated access to the Cerdanya from all points south. Even now, this one main road is the only one to pass through it, albeit underground, and the Cadí national park remains essentially pristine, with barely a village or road encroaching within its limits, essentially only open to exploration by foot.

Its southern edge is particularly impenetrable, huge cliffs formed by folding as a result of the collision of the Iberian and Eurasian plates presenting a façade almost as forbidding as The Wall in *Game of Thrones*. There is, though, one tiny and quite magnificent road that runs along the foot of this barrier, winding and undulating relentlessly for 50km between Tuixent in the west and Collet in the east, access to it from Berga mostly on roads with barely a metre of flat that eventually serve up more than 3,500m of vertical gain.

The route begins easily enough with the steady climb westwards from Berga to the Coll de Jouet on the BV4241 along the southern edge of the Serra de Queralt (see page 54). Rising for 13.5km at an average of 4%, it's by some way the easiest of the four passes on this route, sauntering up to the Berga tunnel at the top. From there, the road drops a little more steeply through pine forest, skips over a hump and runs alongside the Llosa del Cavall reservoir for half a dozen kilometres to reach Sant Llorenç de Morunys. This is the launchpad for the Coll de Jou, but rather than forking left in the town centre towards it, keep straight on with the C462 to take a more direct way northwards that saves a dozen kilometres.

High peaks appear ahead, the road initially undulating as it advances towards them. But, as it narrows leaving the village of La Coma, the road starts to climb consistently and, on occasions, steeply. The landscape is more dramatic too, the valley narrowing, cliffs of crumbling red sandstone pressing in. Rising through a run of hairpins, there are pleasing views down the pass too, back over looping bends towards La Coma.

Passing the turn that gives access to the Port del Comte ski station, there are 4km at a slightly friendlier angle to the Coll de Port, the gradient falling to 6% after 5km almost a couple of points higher than that. The road runs more directly too, although the top of the pass remains out of sight until the very last. And what a view it presents to the north and towards the impassable Serra de Cadí, a wiggling line of tarmac just visible at its foot, the vista a reminder that a pass doesn't necessarily need to be well renowned in order to serve up something quite exceptional.

The descent away to the north from the Port is a little shallower than its southern flank, which is just as well because there's plenty to distract, glimpses of verdant peaks and the village of Tuixent down in the valley appearing in the breaks within a corridor of pines. Circle around Tuixent on the main road and at the T-junction on the far side of it go right to Gósol, starting to climb towards the Coll de Josa, 11km away.

The climb begins gently enough as it winds incessantly up a narrow valley alongside the River Josa. It steepens briefly as it swings around a bend and the village of Josa del Cadí appears, perched on a hill above the river, the Cadí massif's forbidding green wall behind it. The setting is glorious, all the more so because it's so quiet thanks to its remoteness. Beyond the village, there's a dip

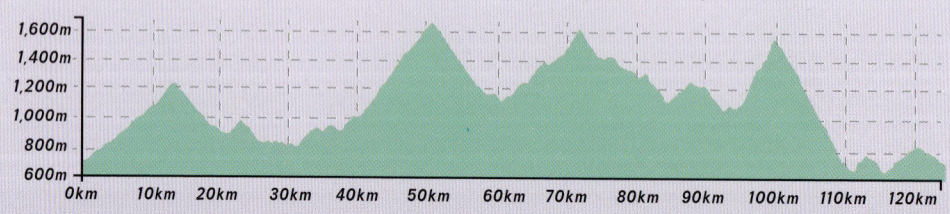

BARCELONA

The emblematic twin summit of Pedraforca

and then four final kilometres to the pass. The first couple are straightforward, but a change comes after the road switches back over the river. There's a short section significantly above double figures, the climb steepening as it enters pine woods, only easing in the last few hundred metres before the summit.

The view into the wider valley ahead is stunning, Gósol and a patchwork of fields encircled by lofty peaks. The drop towards them mirrors the western side of the Josa, quite steep close to the top, but then undulating. Gósol, renowned for its Picasso museum that stems from the artist's extended stay in the village in 1906, arrives quickly, its paved central square a good place for

BENEATH THE CADÍ MASSIF

replenishment for the last third of the ride. This starts through a very green and rural landscape – the valley has its own, very wet, microclimate. It's a little busier too, partly as a consequence of the draw of Pedraforca, the twin-peaked mountain on the other side of the valley, its two soaring parallel ridges joined by a narrow neck. There's so much else to look at too, extraordinary views at every turn.

In order to minimise time on or close to the main C16 between Berga and the Cadí, turn right on the B401 towards Vallcebre, climbing gently, dipping, then climbing again to this village. There's no warning of what follows as the road narrows and rears up to enter the toughest section all day, three kilometres averaging close to 10% heading towards the Coll de Pradell (see page 60). Thankfully, the most severe – and it does get a lot steeper – upper part of this pass is avoided by taking the left turn to Fígols, the gradient easing a bit as the road runs through pine woods and quarry workings to reach the Coll de Fumanya.

The descent eases down to a T-junction. Go left towards Fígols, the gradient becoming more acute, but the road remaining quite wide and well surfaced, with lots of long straights. Further down, it's much more technical, twisting relentlessly, and still steep, impressive views another distraction. It emerges on the C16, just above a very incongruous Cerc power station, which was closed in 2011 and is set to be developed as a centre for renewable energy. Just beyond it, escape is possible from the main route by shooting up the lane to the right into La Rodonella, continuing on Sant Jordi de Cercs, turning 90° left and right coming to take the main route through this village and on down the hill to Cercs and the edge of the Baells reservoir, passing beneath the viaduct carrying the C16.

This diversion does merge with the main route a little further on, but by taking the left fork just before entering the road tunnel that takes the C16 through a hillside and into Berga, you can follow the back route, the C1411z, into Berga, an epic day completed.

Route in reverse

Just as impressive and does have the advantage of covering most of the significant climbing early on, with a long descent in Berga to finish. The most obvious difference is the Fumanya, which is tackled by its longer side with numerous sections where the gradient is well into double figures.

Distance: 123.5km
Elevation gain: 3,542m
Highest point: 1,680m
Est. moving time: 4.5-7hrs
Degree of difficulty: ●●●●◖
Climbs: Coll de Jouet (1,232m), Coll de Port (1,680m), Coll de Josa (1,620m), Coll de Fumanya (1,566m)

Recorrido

0km	Berga
2km	C1411z/BV4241 ←
13.5km	Coll de Jouet ①
31.5km	BV4241/C462 →
33.5km	Sant Llorenç de Morunys C462/LV4241 → ②
50.5km	Coll de Port ③
60.5km	Tuixent C462/C563 →
72km	Coll de Josa ④
92.5km	B400/B401 → ⑤
95.5km	Vallcebre
99.5km	Coll de Fumanya ⑥
100km	B401/BV4025 ←
111km	BV4025/C16 → ⑦
111.5km	C16/unclassified to La Rodonella →
113.5km	Sant Jordi de Cercs
115.5km	Cercs
117km	C1411z/C16 →
117.5km	C16/C1411z ←
122.5km	Junction C1411z/BV4241 ←
125km	Berga

A CATALAN WALL AND A VUELTA SUMMIT

In a similar way to the Coll de Pal, not too far away to the north, the climbs around Berga have been sidelined by the biggest races on the Spanish calendar, no doubt because this most northerly part of Barcelona province doesn't have the population, big resorts and, therefore, the financial resources to attract events like the Vuelta a España or Volta a Catalunya. While that's a shame for fans of racing, there is nothing to stop the rest of us exploring a rugged and spectacular area that has lots of beautiful roads and some very intriguing climbs.

This route illustrates this particularly well. Early on it features the Fumanya and Pradell, both extremely challenging, the latter the type of super-steep ascent that the Vuelta has recently revelled in. Towards the end comes Rasos de Peguera, three times a Vuelta stage finish, although the Spanish national tour's last visit to the little ski station 18km above Berga dates back to 1999.

It begins by heading out of Berga on the C1411z as it winds northwards above the C16. Choosing this undulating backroad serves a double purpose of avoiding that main road and getting the legs warmed up for the first big climb, the quite formidable Coll de Fumanya. It doesn't completely dodge the C16, but it does bypass a tunnel in which there's no shoulder on which to stay out of the way of fast-moving traffic, merging with the main road just beyond that potential hazard, then re-emerging a few hundred metres later heading to Cercs and Sant Jordi de Cercs. Beyond this village, there's another short section on the C16 passing the now-closed Cercs power station before swinging left on the BV4025 and straight onto the Fumanya.

It's rated as one of Catalunya's toughest ascents, averaging 8.5% for 10km before easing off in the last couple of kilometres to the top. Tightly coiled, it gains altitude quickly, long sections at 12 and 13% leading into Sant Corneli. There's no let-up beyond this village, the road running straighter approaching Fígols, but the gradient just as fierce. Once the power station's cooling tower gets swallowed up in the valley, the views are majestic, assuming you can get your teeth off your handlebar for long enough to take them in. It's only in the final kilometre or so that the unremitting grind finally eases off, the last stretch to the summit a gentle roll after following the road right towards Vallcebre.

There's a straight 2km plummet from the Fumanya to reach a T-junction where the route goes left towards Saldes and straight into the toughest segment of the Coll de Pradell, the summit just 3.5km away but 410m higher, giving it a very similar profile to the Mur de Péguère. Like that steepling ascent in the French Pyrenees, the Pradell doesn't bother too much with bends that might take the sting from the vicious slope, preferring to don its crampons and scramble straight up the mountainside. After a kilometre at 11%, the penultimate averages 14. It's a formidable sight, the road running directly towards what appears to be a launch ramp that includes the steepest section at 20%. Further complicating the ordeal, the surface switches from tarmac to cement halfway up, so it's bumpier and tyres don't roll as easily.

The return to tarmac heralds a welcome reduction in the gradient as the road passes the rusting trains and tracks from an old mine. Entering pine woods, the slope eases off even more, moseying to the cattle grid at the top, where there's a superb view of Pedraforca jutting out from the Cadí massif way across the valley ahead. The subsequent descent is, surprisingly, quite benign, allowing a focus on Pedraforca, the perspective on the twin-peaked mountain changing constantly, an effect that continues after joining the B400 towards Saldes and Maçaners (see opposite).

The road drops gently into the Berguedà valley to meet the C16. Turn right onto it, loop around the road tunnel ahead, continuing south for 3km, then turning left to Malanyeu. This narrow lane climbs steeply through woodland set in a cleft in the rockface. At the first junction swing right towards La Nou de Berguedà, still ascending for a short while until the road plateaus, the verdant peaks of the Serra El Catllaràs emerging to the east. The road, now the BV4022, dips towards La Nou. Fork left into the village, where southerly progress is maintained on the BV4023 next to the church.

Bumping along for the next few kilometres, this is a beautiful section of road, passing

A CATALAN WALL AND A VUELTA SUMMIT

through flower-filled meadows and broad pasture, the road then dropping sharply to meet the C26 on the edge of the Baells reservoir. Turn right, heading back to Berga. Just beyond the bridge over the lake's blue waters, bear right towards Sant Llorenç de Morunys. At the junction with the C1411z, there's a choice. Stay left to finish in Berga or bear right again towards Sant Llorenç and pass above Berga to tackle the climb to Rasos de Peguera, soon signposted to the right along with the Santuari de Queralt.

Cutting up through a narrow gorge, the road splits, the right fork veering towards the ski station, 14km away. There are huge outcrops on both sides, testament to the uplift caused by the impact of tectonic plates. There's some significant lift in the gradient too, with a couple of kilometres at 9% before a slight relaxation. The going remains quite comfortable until the road emerges onto open mountainside, with stunning views off to the left. It begins to wind, the gradient touching nine again for a kilometre, then easing until a final steeper drag up to Rasos de Peguera, Catalunya's first ski resort, a tiny set-up that the regional government plans to redevelop. The road continues beyond it, soon reaching a spectacular high point with an amazing panorama, which is definitely a location to pause before the freewheeling 16km descent back to Berga.

Route in reverse

I wouldn't recommend heading up to Rasos de Peguera without your legs well warmed up, but otherwise this route works just as well in the other direction, once again adding the ski station at the end. Overall, the climbing is significantly easier travelling anticlockwise, although caution is advised on the descent away from Pradell, which is steep, straight and extremely quick.

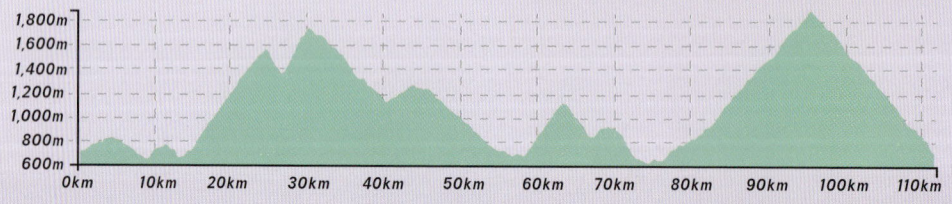

BARCELONA

The Cadí massif looms over Maçaners

Distance: 111.9km
Elevation gain: 3,770m
Highest point: 1,890m
Est. moving time: 4.5-7hrs
Degree of difficulty: ●●●●
Climbs: Coll de Fumanya (1,566m), Coll de Pradell (1,728m), Rasos de Peguera (1,836m)

Recorrido

0km	Berga	
2km	C1411z/BV4241	→
2.5km	C1411z/C16	←
7km	C1411z/C16	→
7.5km	C16/C1411z	→
9km	Cercs	
10.5km	Sant Jordi de Cercs	
13km	unclassified/C16	←
13.5km	C16/BV4025	← ①
24km	BV4025/B401	→
24.5km	Coll de Fumanya	②
27km	B401/unclassified	←
30km	Coll de Pradell	③
37km	unclassified/B400	→ ④
55km	B400/C16	→ ⑤
58.5km	C16/unclassified to Malanyeu	← ⑥
61.5km	unclassified/BV4022 to La Nou	→
66.5km	La Nou de Berguedà BV4022/BV4023	←
73km	BV4023/C26	→ ⑦
77.5km	C26/BP4654	→
78.5km	C1411z/BV4241	→
80.5km	BV4241/BV4242	→
82km	BV4242/BV4243	→ ⑧
95.5km	Rasos de Peguera	⑨
111.9km	Berga	

PLATEAU DE SAULT CIRCUIT

Easy to bypass because of its isolation and lack of renowned climbs, the Plateau de Sault is well worth exploring precisely because it is off the beaten track and, as a consequence, extremely quiet. Its varying landscapes are also surprisingly dramatic, as this route based on the little Audois town of Quillan amply highlights.

The majority of the climbing comes in the ride's first third, starting right from the start on the winding ascent of the Col du Portel, which looms over Quillan and looks quite daunting from the bottom but never gets much above 6%. Although it's one of the main roads out of the town, it's not especially busy, so take advantage of its smooth surface and warm your legs gently. Impressive views to the east across Quillan and up the Pierre-Lys gorge carved out by the River Aude also encourage early dallying. At the summit, switch back left on the road towards Ax-les-Thermes, the gradient sharpening a little beyond the junction, but rapidly easing on the very comfortable 4km approach to the Col de Coudons, the road flattening out as it enters a hanging valley beyond this pass.

It arrows through fertile farmland to Espezel (a significant short-cut towards Niort-de-Sault is an option in this village) and then Belcaire, where there's a small supermarket, and then climbs very steadily again for half a dozen kilometres to the oddly-titled Col des Sept Frères. It's been suggested that it's actually misnamed, and once referenced seven local ash trees or *frênes* – an Audois Sevenoaks, if you like. I much prefer the alternative version that describes how seven brothers perished here in a winter storm, each one venturing out to save the others when the previous brother didn't return.

Here, the route cuts sharply eastwards on a narrow road that rises and dives through thick pine forests for a dozen kilometres. At the little junction (see page 92), turn left to sweep down through Niort-de-Sault. Three kilometres beyond, a right turn to Rodome provides another shortcut, but means missing the gorge below Belfort-sur-Rebenty and the impressive Défilé d'Able and, a little further on, the even more striking Défilé de Joucou. To reach them continue for a kilometre or so past the right-hand turn onto the D29 and drop through the tight gorge and tunnels that have been hewn from the rock and will have you hooting with delight. After 1,500m or so and the last tunnel, make a U-turn to climb back to the D29 junction and the final climb.

This unnamed ascent has two parts, the first longer, a little steeper, through dense woodland and including a beautifully engineered hairpin nestled on steepling stonework that leads into a narrow ravine. Then, emerging from the trees, it rises far more gently through lush pastureland, the spire on the church in Rodome standing out in that village in a long view across the Sault to the west.

This valley broadens as the road glides up to Aunat, the panorama even more expansive. Take a right here towards Fontanès-de-Sault, climbing briefly to the Col des Aychides, then plunge down towards the upper Aude valley on a narrow road cut into the cliff-face. It's thrilling to ride, though a little nervy because it's so tight and due to the litter of rocks and debris peppered on the road surface. Take it carefully, pausing from time to time to drink in the view over thickly wooded mountainsides and down the Aude gorge. Beyond the hamlet of Fontanès de Sault, the sight of its school always leaving me wondering where the children that attend it come from given its remoteness, a final plunge leads to the main D118 road (see

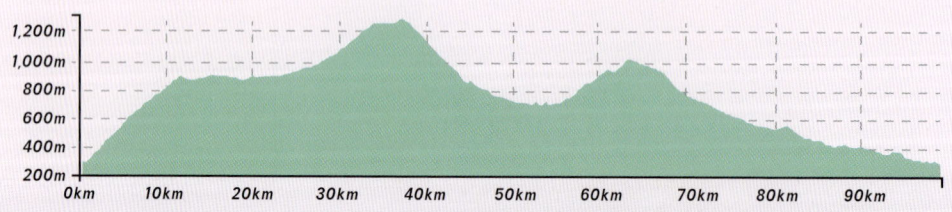

AUDE

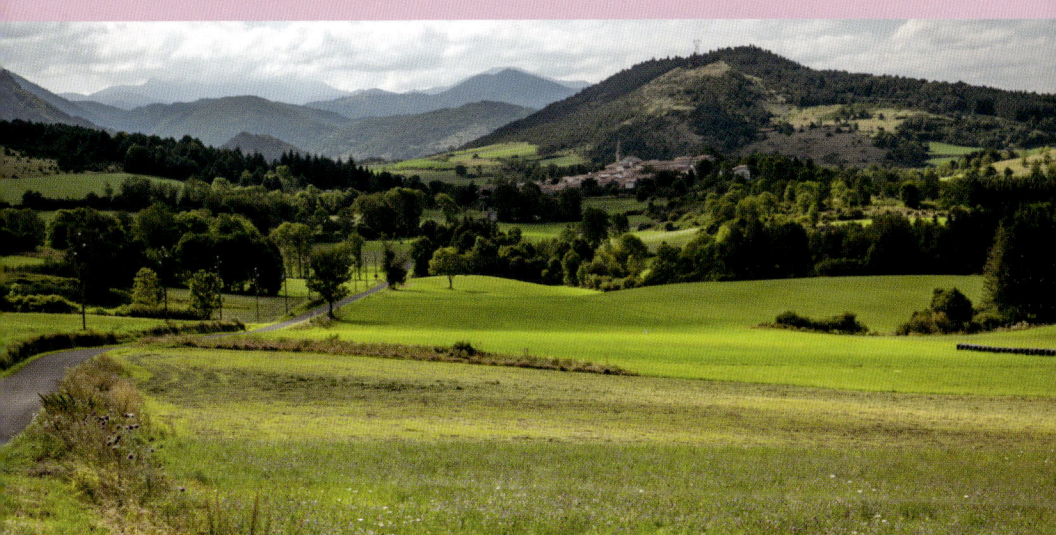

Rodome in the Pays de Sault

page 96).

Turn left towards Axat to enter another spectacular stretch. Although the same issue with debris persists, it's easier to avoid the rubble that's tumbled down from the high cliffs on this wider and better surface as the road slaloms incessantly and delightfully alongside the north bank of the Aude, the valley becoming ever-tighter until, at the Gorges de St-Georges, river and road squeeze through a chasm only a few metres wide just before reaching Axat.

Keep on from here for a couple of kilometres to meet the D117, the principal east-west route close to the mountains. The canyoning return to Quillan continues on this busier road, which weaves through tunnels, beneath overhangs and around endless bends to reach the start point, where a post-ride pick-me-up in a café will be hard to resist.

Route in reverse

Heading up the Aude via Axat means the ride starts with a bang instead of finishing with one. However, some may prefer the clockwise option because some steep and potentially treacherous descents are tackled in the opposite direction. Plus, there's a long, long drop to the finish.

Distance: 99.3km
Elevation gain: 1,760m
Highest point: 1,295m
Est. moving time: 3.5-6hrs
Degree of difficulty: ●●◐
Climbs: Col du Portel (601m), Col de Coudons (883m), Col des Sept Frères (1,253m), Col des Aychides (1,008m)

Parcours

0km	Quillan
5.5km	Col du Portel D117/D59 ←
7km	D59/D613 ←
11.5km	Col de Coudons ①
22.4km	Espezel
28.5km	Belcaire
34km	Col des Sept Frères D613/D20 ← ②
44km	D20/D107 ← ③
46km	Niort de Sault
50km	Belfort sur Rébenty
51km	D107/D29 ← for 2km then return and take D29 ④
60.5km	D29/D20 →
61.5km	Aunat D20/D29 →
70km	D29/D118 ← ⑤
87km	Axat
88.5km	D118/D117 ← ⑥
99.3km	Quillan

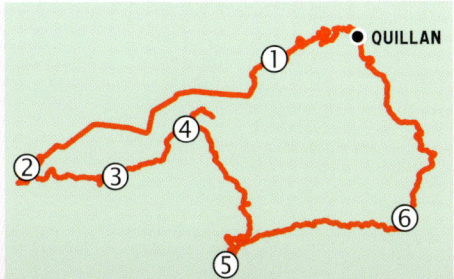

TOUR OF QUERCORB

I got the inspiration for this ride from the 15th stage of the 2019 Tour de France, specifically the first part of it. While that stage that finished on Prat d'Albis above Foix started in Limoux and headed south to climb up to the Plateau de Sault via the Col des Tougnets, I think it makes for a better loop if you begin in Quillan, following the left or west bank of the Aude downstream all the way to Espéraza, where there's a fantastic market on Sundays and the dinosaur museum is home to perhaps the most realistic T-rex model anywhere. It certainly terrified my kids.

The hills east of Lac de Montbel are criss-crossed by small and very quiet roads with numerous passes in the 400-800m range. It's a perfect location for an easier ride or a day when the weather is grim among the higher peaks. This part of the Aude has a much more arid and Mediterranean feel than the Ariège to the west, and from early summer onwards the early section of this ride tends to look very parched.

Rolling through the villages of Fa and Rouvenac, it's hard to imagine the Tour coming along this road almost to nowhere, although the vestiges of road paint on the grippy surface confirm that it did. Beyond Rouvenac, the road begins to climb steadily, but never fiercely, to reach the Col des Tougnets, an unclassified climb for the Tour peloton, but, in spite of that lack of recognition, one that's well worth the effort.

At the crossroads, head left, the road initially arrowing through woodland before the terrain opens out, offering a first view of the very solid-looking castle at Puivert, originally a Cathar fortress, although that building was razed and the relatively well-preserved stronghold that replaced it dates from the 14th century. In the village, once a key centre in the Quercorb region, which was centred on nearby Chalabre, go right on the D117, passing a turn to the Lac de Puivert, one of those French lakes with a beach that's a perfect place to swim and chill out.

The D117 is the main route between Perpignan and Tarbes, a familiar route for those wanting to skirt the high mountains but avoid the *autoroute* much further to the north. This section of it is relatively quiet as it climbs to the Col de la Babourade. This route can be shortened by going left here towards Espezel, but otherwise head straight on, crossing the border into the Ariège on the descent into Bélesta. Turn left in the town centre onto the D9, cross the river, then leave the 2019 Tour route that continued on to Montségur, forking left on the D16 towards Belcaire.

The 6km ascent of the Col de la Croix des Morts begins on a sharp leftward jag, rising for the most part through stands of pine, the buzz of chainsaws often the only sound on this backroad. After flattening out towards the top, the road kicks up a little to the col, where an iron cross once stood. It's said to have been erected in memory of three Catalan merchants who were robbed and murdered at this point during their homeward journey after selling a pack of mules in Laroque d'Olmes.

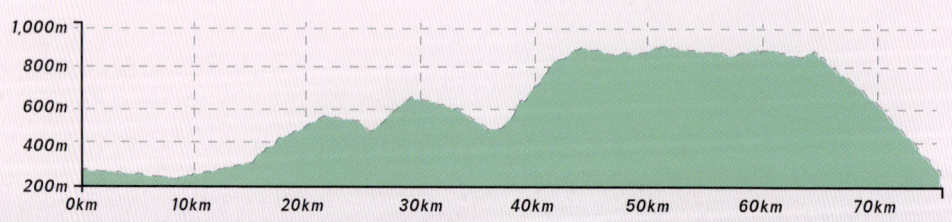

AUDE

The road winds around the château at Puivert

It signals the start of 20km of very gently rolling riding on the Plateau de Sault with the high ridge of the Pyrenees filling the view ahead. Assuming the wind is favourable, progress is rapid to the crossroads with the D613 (see page 62), which bisects the plateau on its journey between Ax les Thermes and Quillan. Turn left for what can be a very fast return to Quillan, the road running in long straights through the Sault farmlands to the Col des Coudons on the northern edge of the plateau. From here, the road drops briskly to the Col de Portel and the start of the sweeping descent back to the start point.

Route in reverse

Much depends on the wind direction, which can be difficult to gauge when down in the Aude valley at Quillan. The prevailing wind comes from the west and if it's blowing hard from this direction the sections across the Plateau de Sault can be a hard grind. But if it's still and especially if it's blowing from the east, a clockwise approach is recommended.

Distance: 75.9km
Elevation gain: 1,197m
Highest point: 916m
Est. moving time: 2.5-4hrs
Degree of difficulty: ●◐
Climbs: Col des Tougnets (558m), Col de la Babourade (655m), Col de la Croix des Morts (898m)

Parcours

0km	Quillan head north on D92
4km	Junction D92/D2 →
8km	Espéraza Junction with D12 ← ①
14.5km	Rouvenac
22km	Col des Tougnets Junction D12/D121 ← ②
25.5km	Puivert Junction D121/D117 →
29.5km	Col de la Babourade
37km	Bélesta Junction D117/D16 ← ③
44km	Col de la Croix des Morts (D16 now D29)
51.5km	Junction D29/D613 ← ④
69km	Junction D613/D59 →
70km	Col du Portel Junction D59/D117 →
75.9km	Quillan

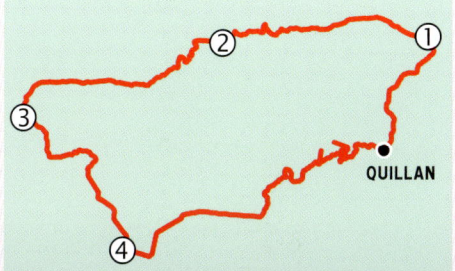

CLOSE NEIGHBOURS BUT SO DIFFERENT

I can't recommend this loop highly enough, but do so with an advisory that it is as challenging as it is beautiful. The Pailhères and Pradel are near neighbours, the latter branching off from the former, but are so different. Between them, they highlight everything that makes riding in the Pyrenees such a magical experience.

There are one or two ways to shorten this circuit, but they require dealing with abrupt climbs out of the Rébenty valley and my experience suggests that the last thing most cyclists will want to contemplate after racking up 2,300m of vertical gain is another ascent at the end, even if it's only 3km long. Consequently, it's best to start in Axat, rising gently up the Aude valley, which is a spectacular gorge in places, high cliffs hemming in the river and road.

The wind can be help or hindrance on the 19km approach to the foot of the Pailhères. Whatever the case, take this section steadily and don't get swept along too fast by a tailwind or battle to keep a big gear turning into a headwind because you'll likely pay for it later.

The climb starts in magnificent fashion, the 11th-century Cathar castle of Usson standing sentinel at the bottom. The road itself offers a ruder introduction to this 16km pass, the opening 2km averaging close to 10% to reach Rouze. There is a mellower option, though, a right turn signposted to Mijanès leading up through a string of more welcoming hairpins to the village.

Above Rouze, swing around the big switchback to the right onto the D116 in the direction of Mijanès. Make sure you've got plenty in your bottles at this point because there's not much available until well after the Pradel. The climbing has been steady up to now, but the gradient becomes more erratic, with some sections at 13 and 14% and not many below seven to recuperate. It's a grind, but in a beautiful setting. The chance to appreciate it a little more finally comes above the little ski station of Mijanès Donézan, but the respite is brief.

The 7km left to the summit compare with anything in the Pyrenees in terms of beauty – and, arguably, difficulty as well. In late spring, before the trees are in full leaf, the summit can just about be picked out, but many of the 20-odd hairpins leading towards it are clearly visible. They're a hugely impressive feat of engineering, huge walls of stone underpinning most of them, but they don't take the sting from the gradient. The straights between them are up to 17%, the road scrambling up rather than easing towards the pass.

The summit arrives, a little surprisingly, soon after a short descent – the old road does still run straight up to the col, but has long been barriered off, with access now via an additional hairpin above this stretch. If you've not paused on the bends below to take in and photograph the views, take the opportunity now. This is, I've been told, Tour de France director Christian Prudhomme's favourite climb, and it's not hard to understand why.

The descent plunges very quickly off the Pailhères in the direction of Ax les Thermes, the road wide and quite straight initially, then slaloming through forest nearer to the turn onto the Col de Pradel at Le Pujal. The road narrows significantly as it climbs through this village and into dense woodland, following the course of a rushing stream. Compared to the openness of the Pailhères, this feels very different, although from the halfway point there are some savage sections that remind that the two climbs have one significant characteristic in common.

The first sign that the top is nearing is

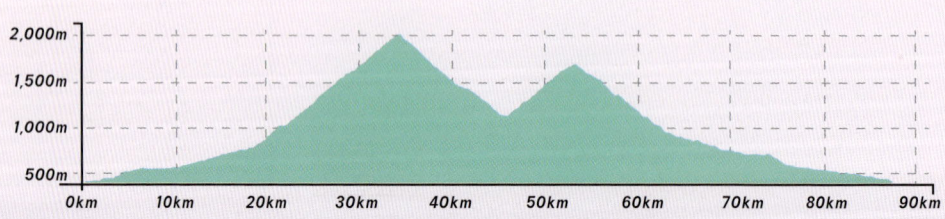

AUDE

often the ringing of cow bells, the summit sitting in a more open area. Once over the cattle grid at the summit, you drop into thick pine forest. Heading northwards, it can be chilly in here even on hot days, the road surface is generally damp, with grit and stones washed on it. This isn't a descent to rush, but demands caution. For those running short on water by this point, there's a *eau potable* tap in La Fajolle at the trough on the left, the hamlet also marking the point where the road starts to run straighter, although it remains quite narrow as it scoots down alongside the effervescent River Rébenty.

Below Niort de Sault there's one final outstanding stretch where the road has been cut under the cliff, and, at the Défilé de Joucou (see page 62), runs through three unlit tunnels, which offer the chance for some final hoots of delight towards the end of a sensational circuit. Another dozen or so kilometres of descent lead to the D118 just below Axat, where refreshments are fully deserved.

Route in reverse

While I wouldn't advise against tackling the Pradel and then the Pailhères, the northern side of the former ascent can be dismal, especially higher up in the damp pine forests. I'm not so keen on the Pailhères from its western flank either. It's arguably not as hard as the eastern side, but the scenery is not in the same league. It's a cracking 35km descent back to Axat from the summit, though!

Hairpins high on the Port de Pailhères

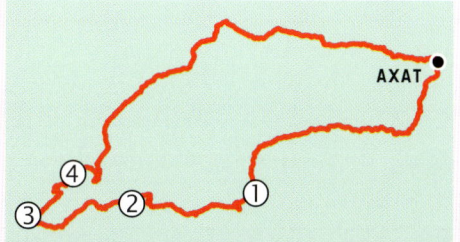

Distance: 91.8km
Elevation gain: 2,366m
Highest point: 2,001m
Est. moving time: 4-6hrs
Degree of difficulty: ●●●●
Climbs: Port de Pailhères (2,001m), Col de Pradel (1,680m)

Parcours

0km	Axat
19km	Usson les Bains D118/D16 ➡ ①
22km	D16/D116 ➡
34km	Port de Pailhères ②
45.5km	D25/D25B ➡ ③
53km	Port de Pradel D107 ④
89.5km	D107/D117 ➡
90.5km	D117/D118 ➡
91.8km	Axat

THE DA VINCI CODE LOOP

One of the biggest attractions for me of riding in the Aude is the quantity of quiet and very attractive roads in the foothills of the Pyrenees. Unlike Pyrénées Orientales to the east and Ariège to the west, these ripple for a substantial distance away from the high mountain peaks before they reach the flatlands around Carcassonne. This loop is typical. It's comparatively short, especially if you decide against the up-and-back ascent to Rennes le Château at the end, and ideal for a warm-up or a quieter day. The views to the Pyrenean peaks are astounding too.

It starts in Couiza, and initially tracks north down the Aude valley for 5km on the main D118 road. This can be busy but there's often a wide verge. The turn towards Véraza arrives quickly and the ride immediately takes on a very different flavour. This narrower and far quieter road immediately climbs away from the valley floor, rising through a corridor of trees, sunlight dappling the road. The gradient is never severe, averaging a little below five per cent for 10km and not varying much either side of that.

Higher up, as the valley narrows, the road is cut into the steep, forest-covered hillside. Passing the hamlet of Terroles, the trees give way to open grazing land and at the same time the Pyrenees begin to emerge. In any period other than high summer, they are snow-capped, but whatever the season they are a breath-taking sight.

The summit of the Col de l'Espinas, next to a farm, is unremarkable. This is a col without much of a view. Beyond it, the road dips into a saddle, meeting the D54 (see page 74) as it climbs again. Turn right towards Arques, climbing a little more to reach the Col de Valmigère, which is altogether more impressive, the mountains stretching away to the east and west, the road arrowing towards the Massif du Canigou. The views are even better just below the stand of pines at the col.

Stay with the D54 all the way to Arques, the unusually shaped Pic de Bugarach (see page 72), the highest mountain in the Corbières, peeking out above the forested ridge to the south as the road descends just as steadily as it climbed earlier. The landscape looks markedly different here, the soil redder, the terrain rockier and more arid. There is a much more Mediterranean feel as the road drops into Arques, sacked in the early 13th century by Simon de Montfort, Earl of Leicester and crusader supreme, because of the locals' adherence to Catharism. The most obvious sign of this is this neat village's solid and partially restored Cathar castle. Turn right in the centre of Arques onto the D613 and this impressive structure soon comes into view on the right.

Passing the junction with the D14, which heads to Bugarach, the ruined Château de Blanchefort becomes visible on an outcrop to the south. Although it was a Cathar stronghold until de Montfort passed this way, it predates this devout Catholic sect having been first established by the Visigoths in the 10th century.

Dropping gently, the road reaches Couiza very briskly to complete a wonderful 33km circuit. For those who want a little more, turn left back onto the D118 for a couple of hundred metres, then left again towards Rennes le Château on the D52. Sitting atop an outcrop high above the Aude valley, this beautiful village has gained international renown thanks to a widespread belief that part of an immense treasure paid as a ransom for French king Louis IX is buried somewhere in the vicinity, the theory stoked by references in Dan Brown's best-selling

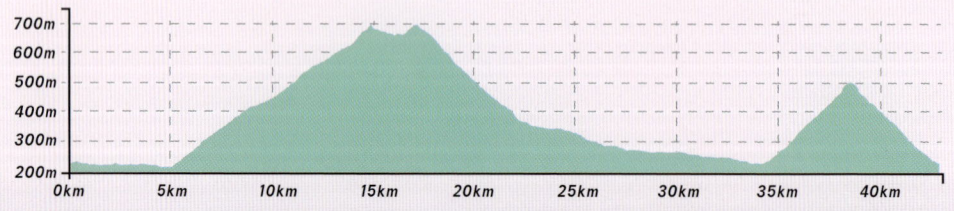

AUDE

often the ringing of cow bells, the summit sitting in a more open area. Once over the cattle grid at the summit, you drop into thick pine forest. Heading northwards, it can be chilly in here even on hot days, the road surface is generally damp, with grit and stones washed on it. This isn't a descent to rush, but demands caution. For those running short on water by this point, there's a *eau potable* tap in La Fajolle at the trough on the left, the hamlet also marking the point where the road starts to run straighter, although it remains quite narrow as it scoots down alongside the effervescent River Rébenty.

Below Niort de Sault there's one final outstanding stretch where the road has been cut under the cliff, and, at the Défilé de Joucou (see page 62), runs through three unlit tunnels, which offer the chance for some final hoots of delight towards the end of a sensational circuit. Another dozen or so kilometres of descent lead to the D118 just below Axat, where refreshments are fully deserved.

Hairpins high on the Port de Pailhères

Route in reverse

While I wouldn't advise against tackling the Pradel and then the Pailhères, the northern side of the former ascent can be dismal, especially higher up in the damp pine forests. I'm not so keen on the Pailhères from its western flank either. It's arguably not as hard as the eastern side, but the scenery is not in the same league. It's a cracking 35km descent back to Axat from the summit, though!

Distance: 91.8km
Elevation gain: 2,366m
Highest point: 2,001m
Est. moving time: 4-6hrs
Degree of difficulty: ●●●●
Climbs: Port de Pailhères (2,001m), Col de Pradel (1,680m)

Parcours

0km	Axat
19km	Usson les Bains D118/D16 ➡ ①
22km	D16/D116 ➡
34km	Port de Pailhères ②
45.5km	D25/D25B ➡ ③
53km	Port de Pradel D107 ④
89.5km	D107/D117 ➡
90.5km	D117/D118 ➡
91.8km	Axat

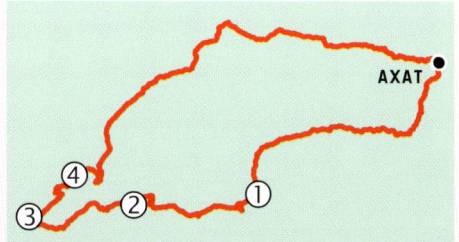

THE DA VINCI CODE LOOP

One of the biggest attractions for me of riding in the Aude is the quantity of quiet and very attractive roads in the foothills of the Pyrenees. Unlike Pyrénées Orientales to the east and Ariège to the west, these ripple for a substantial distance away from the high mountain peaks before they reach the flatlands around Carcassonne. This loop is typical. It's comparatively short, especially if you decide against the up-and-back ascent to Rennes le Château at the end, and ideal for a warm-up or a quieter day. The views to the Pyrenean peaks are astounding too.

It starts in Couiza, and initially tracks north down the Aude valley for 5km on the main D118 road. This can be busy but there's often a wide verge. The turn towards Véraza arrives quickly and the ride immediately takes on a very different flavour. This narrower and far quieter road immediately climbs away from the valley floor, rising through a corridor of trees, sunlight dappling the road. The gradient is never severe, averaging a little below five per cent for 10km and not varying much either side of that.

Higher up, as the valley narrows, the road is cut into the steep, forest-covered hillside. Passing the hamlet of Terroles, the trees give way to open grazing land and at the same time the Pyrenees begin to emerge. In any period other than high summer, they are snow-capped, but whatever the season they are a breath-taking sight.

The summit of the Col de l'Espinas, next to a farm, is unremarkable. This is a col without much of a view. Beyond it, the road dips into a saddle, meeting the D54 (see page 74) as it climbs again. Turn right towards Arques, climbing a little more to reach the Col de Valmigère, which is altogether more impressive, the mountains stretching away to the east and west, the road arrowing towards the Massif du Canigou. The views are even better just below the stand of pines at the col.

Stay with the D54 all the way to Arques, the unusually shaped Pic de Bugarach (see page 72), the highest mountain in the Corbières, peeking out above the forested ridge to the south as the road descends just as steadily as it climbed earlier. The landscape looks markedly different here, the soil redder, the terrain rockier and more arid. There is a much more Mediterranean feel as the road drops into Arques, sacked in the early 13th century by Simon de Montfort, Earl of Leicester and crusader supreme, because of the locals' adherence to Catharism. The most obvious sign of this is this neat village's solid and partially restored Cathar castle. Turn right in the centre of Arques onto the D613 and this impressive structure soon comes into view on the right.

Passing the junction with the D14, which heads to Bugarach, the ruined Château de Blanchefort becomes visible on an outcrop to the south. Although it was a Cathar stronghold until de Montfort passed this way, it predates this devout Catholic sect having been first established by the Visigoths in the 10th century.

Dropping gently, the road reaches Couiza very briskly to complete a wonderful 33km circuit. For those who want a little more, turn left back onto the D118 for a couple of hundred metres, then left again towards Rennes le Château on the D52. Sitting atop an outcrop high above the Aude valley, this beautiful village has gained international renown thanks to a widespread belief that part of an immense treasure paid as a ransom for French king Louis IX is buried somewhere in the vicinity, the theory stoked by references in Dan Brown's best-selling

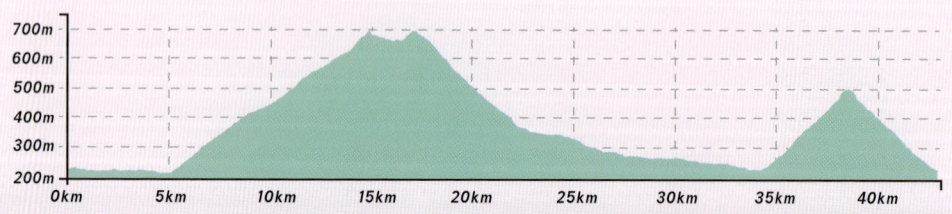

AUDE

Château d'Arques

book, *The Da Vinci Code*.

While that's all hokum, what is undeniable is the spectacular views offered as you climb, on occasions quite abruptly, the handful of kilometres to Rennes le Château, particularly to the east. The village itself remains hidden almost until you reach it. All in all, this is a dead end well worth a diversion.

Route in reverse

I wouldn't advocate climbing to Rennes le Château right from the off, otherwise there's no reason not to tackle this loop counter-clockwise.

Distance: 42.9km
Elevation gain: 847m
Highest point: 705m
Est. moving time: 2-3hrs
Degree of difficulty: ●◐
Climbs: Col de l'Espinas (680m), Col de Valmigère (705m), Rennes le Château (510m)

Parcours

0km	Couiza
5km	D118/D70 ➡ ①
15km	Col de l'Espinas
16km	D70/D54 ➡
17km	Col de Valmigère ②
22.5km	Arques D54/D613 ➡ ③
34km	Couiza D118/D52
38.5km	Rennes le Château ④
42.9km	Couiza

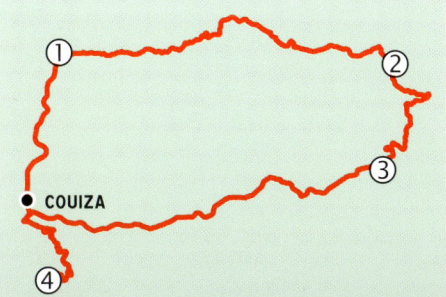

TOUR OF THE UPSIDE-DOWN MOUNTAIN

The profile for this close-to-100km ride looks savage and, even though it barely rises above 700 metres at any point, this is a good day out even for the strongest cyclists. I don't want to give the impression this ride is overly tough, which it certainly isn't compared to one of similar length in the high mountains. Indeed, I've featured it because it merits inclusion. It shouldn't, though, be underestimated.

From Quillan, take the back road down the Aude to Espéraza and Montazels, where you cross the river to Couiza and head east towards Arques (see page 68). A gentle descent to start with, the road now begins to ascend, but almost imperceptibly, to reach the junction with the D14, the crumbling Château de Blanchefort standing sentinel. Turn right here, following the road to Rennes les Bains, a little spa of surprising grandeur. Just beyond it, head left over the River Sals in the direction of Fourtou.

Running through oak, birch and pine woods initially, the road reaches more open terrain above Sougraigne, while the gradient picks up a little too. It's not too taxing, though, until the valley narrows approaching the Col de la Fage through dense woods. For a shorter ride, take the left turn through the Rialsesse Forest towards Arques and back to Couiza. Otherwise, stay with the D74 through Fourtou, passing an impressive waterfall on the other side of this cleft of a valley.

I like roads like this because they appear to be going nowhere, and indeed aren't going anywhere of note, which makes them quiet and perfect for exploring by bike. At Savignan, no more than a cluster of houses, go right towards Soulatgé, and commence climbing again, quickly reaching Auriac and its 11th-century château, with the *mairie* and church tucked up below its pock-marked, decaying walls. The road continues to ascend, cutting through a short gorge, parapets carrying it back and forth over a river to reach the Col de Redoulade, the summit sign claiming an altitude of 752m, although it is at least 50 lower than that.

This pass sits in a shallow bowl, hinting at views that don't quite appear on the drop through beautiful beech woods, all reds and oranges in the autumn, luminous green in spring and summer. At the T-junction with the D10, go right towards Soulatgé, still descending, and chase straight through the centre of the village on what transforms into the D14.

The road begins to rollercoaster, with more ups than downs, to reach Cubières sur Cinoble. A left here leads into the superb Galamus Gorge (see page 8), but that's for another day. Keep straight, the Pic de Bugarach dominating the view ahead. It's an odd-looking rock, described as "the upside-down mountain" because its upper sections are formed by older rock than the lower. From 2011, it drew thousands of New Agers who believed it contained aliens in a spaceship or that it could provide sanctuary from the end of the world. Just beyond the Col du Linas, the terrain opens out and offers the chance to contemplate these peculiarities before the drop towards the village that gives the peak its name.

Just before Bugarach, bear left on the D45, signposted to Quillan. This road runs closer still to the mountain, and the changes of shape and colour constantly draw the eye until a switch to the west puts the mountain behind you. Just before Saint Louis et Parahou, bear right on the D46 towards Saint Just for one last climb – or stay left into the village and the D109 to skip it! Rising through pine forest, it reaches an unnamed col. At

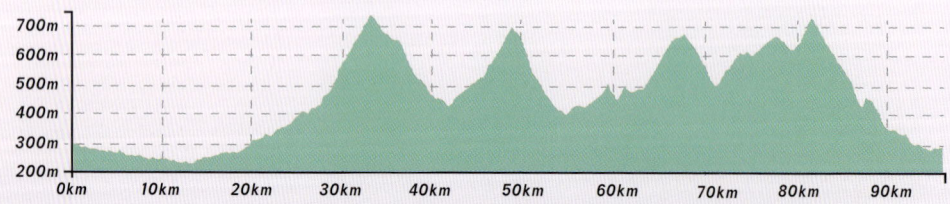

AUDE

Pic de Bugarach

the junction a few kilometres beyond it, stay left to Saint Julia de Bec, where the road runs through what appears to have been a huge barn, with the roof still intact, and continue on to join the D109 arrowing back to the main D118 into Quillan.

Route in reverse

Much to recommend it, particularly the different perspective it gives on the Pic de Bugarach, the undoubted highlight of this route. The majority of the climbing is done earlier, and although the profile makes the start appear tough it's not actually that hard.

Distance: 96.4km
Elevation gain: 1,730m
Highest point: 731m
Est. moving time: 3.5-6hrs
Degree of difficulty: ●●◐
Climbs: Col de la Fage (731m), Col de Redoulade (685m), Col du Linas (667m)

Parcours

0km	Quillan head north on D92
4km	D92/D2 ➡
8km	Espéraza D2/D12 ➡
12.5km	Couiza D12/D118 ⬅
13km	Couiza D118/D613 ➡
18km	D613/D14 ➡ ①
22.5km	D14/D74 ⬅
33km	Col de la Fage ②
41.5km	D74/D212 ➡
48.5km	Col de Redoulade ③
52.5km	D212/D10 ➡
54.5km	Soulatgé D10/D14 ⬆
67.5km	Col du Linas ④
71km	Bugarach D14/D45 ⬅
79km	Saint Louis et Parahou D45/D46 ➡
86km	D46/D609 ⬅
90km	D609/D109 ➡
94km	D109/D118 ⬅
96.4km	Quillan

CORBIÈRES WINELANDS AND A CATHAR MASTERPIECE

There's a real mix of terrain on this route – gorges, vineyards, medium mountains, forest – as well as the almost obligatory over-the-top Cathar castle, in this case the Château de Puylaurens. It begins by heading north on the D118 from Quillan for two kilometres to reach the D109, running south-east through farmland initially, then gaining altitude gradually as woodland takes over.

At the Col de Saint Louis, the road crosses from Aude into Pyrénées Orientales, the D109 becoming the D9 in the process. The terrain becomes a little rougher and looks drier as it begins to descend quite vigorously towards Caudiès. It quickly reaches an unusual piece of road engineering as it crosses over itself via a viaduct over a gorge. When I first looked at the map, I assumed this squiggle was an error and was delighted to find it wasn't. The views from the bridge are impressive, which well describes the section of road below this bridge as well, as it's cut into the mountainside.

The road drops into the wide and fertile Agly valley approaching Caudiès, where it wiggles through a jumble of streets to meet the D118. Turn left and pass along the narrow main street, bearing right just beyond it to pick up the D9 again as it heads for Sournia, climbing away from the valley floor almost immediately, two ruined castles standing out on the opposite hillside as the road makes for the Col del Mas (unmarked).

Not far beyond this summit, there is an opportunity to take a shorter (by 15-20km) route via Vira on the D90 through the Ayguesbonnes forest. Otherwise, keep straight on to reach Le Vivier, the village sitting in the shadow of another tumbled-down fortress, this one dating from the early 17th century. Passing through the village, the D9 merges with the D7, the two roads then splitting just beyond Le Vivier. Fork to the right on the D7 to start 35km of constantly weaving progress.

The road ascends again, passing vineyards and offering long views across the Corbières countryside where many more are evident. I love routes of this kind where the perspective constantly changes, new features appear in the landscape and you become convinced that nothing could be better than exploring by bike. Hypnotised by your surroundings, awareness of the physical effort of pedalling uphill almost disappears, particularly when emerging on to a stretch like the Rue Balcon in Prats de Sournia, the panorama so glorious that you're inevitably enticed into pausing.

Above the village, the towering bulk of the close-to-3,000m Pic du Canigou stands out on clear days, the D7 then sweeping in exhilarating fashion down into Sournia, the ideal refreshment stop prior to a dozen kilometres of ascent to the day's high point, the Col d'Aussières.

Turn right in the village centre in the direction of Rabouillet on the D2. Averaging a mere four per cent, the Aussières is far from severe, particularly approaching this village. It does steepen noticeably above it, but it provides a far easier passage back into the Aude (where the D2 becomes the D22) than the Col de Jau, 20km away to the south-west on the other side of the Serre d'Escales massif. The col arrives after a short descent from the pass's high point a few hundred metres before and sits at a crossroads with a farm track, offering a reminder that they tend to denote a crossing point rather than a high point. Many of those crossing points just happen to be on a ridge.

For most of the next dozen kilometres, the road burrows through forest, initially pine,

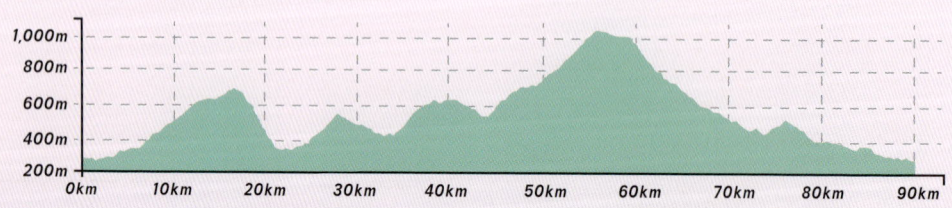

AUDE

then deciduous. Below Gincla, the valley straightens, the road cutting through a tight gorge then opening out and presenting a first glimpse of the Château de Puylaurens, another astounding, precipitously perched Cathar creation, this one relatively well preserved compared to most, some parts of it surviving from that era as it was never captured. Most of the fortress was added later, though, when Puylaurens became one of the "five sons of Carcassonne", a quintet of fortifications that provided a bulwark against any threat from across the border – the other four were Quéribus, Peyrepertuse, Termes and Aguilar.

The road dives down the eastern side of the outcrop on which it stands, reaching Lapradelle, a busy little town. Turn left here onto the D117, climbing initially to the Col Campérié, then descending towards Axat and through the dramatic Défilé de Pierre Lys gorge back to Quillan.

Route in reverse

Just as attractive, although I prefer to ride down the Défilé de Pierre Lys with some speed rather than up it because this section of the D117 can be busy. The drama of the château at Puylaurens gets quite diluted too.

Château de Puylaurens

Distance: 90.4km
Elevation gain: 1,741m
Highest point: 1,020m
Est. moving time: 4.5-6.5hrs
Degree of difficulty: ●●◐
Climbs: Col de Saint Louis (687m), Col del Mas (551m), Col d'Aussières (1,020m), Col Campérié (534m)

Parcours

0km	Quillan
2km	D118/D109 ➡
16.5km	Col de Saint Louis D9 ①
22km	Caudiès de Fenouillèdes D9/D117 ⬅
22.5km	D117/D9 ➡ ②
28km	Col del Mas
34km	Le Vivier D9/D7 ➡
43km	Sournia D7/D2 ➡ ③
56km	Col d'Aussières D22 ④
73.5km	Puylaurens Lapradelle D22/D117 ⬅ ⑤
76km	Col Campérié
90.4km	Quillan

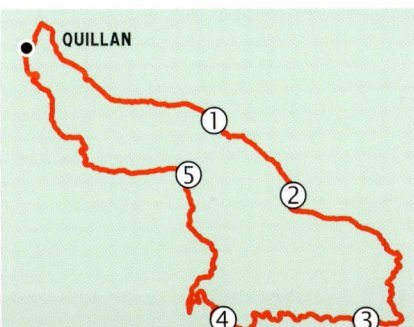

THE ROAD TO PARADISE

I've borrowed this ride from a fabulous map of bike routes that the Aude tourist board produces. This is what they describe as *"une véritable circuit en dent de scie"*, a real saw-tooth circuit, as the profile confirms. Their version is 20km longer, taking a loop over the Col de l'Espinas featured in page 68.

It gets under way in Arques. No matter in which direction it's tackled, it begins right away with a climb, which is rarely a pleasing prospect, although, on the plus side, the way back to the finish is sure to be downhill. From Arques, head north on the D54 towards Valmigère, checking out the striking view across to the Château d'Arques, completed in 1316, its huge keep still quite intact and formidable. With sections up to 12 per cent, the Col de Valmigère has teeth of its own, but the fierceness of the bite is eased by the panorama, which soon includes the Pic de Bugarach and the high Pyrenean chain.

Most of the altitude just gained is lost over the course of the next half dozen kilometres as the road drops into a valley. Just before completing this descent, take a right at the junction with the D129 heading for Caunette, climbing on a lovely section cut into a cliff-face with views across wooded hills to reach Villardebelle and the D529, again to Caunette. Climb out of the village on this road, passing the very sturdy-looking church, before dropping to a T-junction.

Swing right here, and start to ascend once again, initially through woodland, but then the trees give way to wide meadows and a very pleasurable three kilometres to the Col de la Loubière. The descent continues in the same vein, tree cover soon disappearing to reveal long views down the Orbieu Valley, the road finally levelling out in Vignevieille. From there it meanders enjoyably along with the river. Keep straight on at the junction where the D40/D212 part ways, taking the former upwards in the direction of Termes.

Rising into another valley, the Château de Termes comes into view. After a brief foray through woodland, it does again, and quite spectacularly. A bit like the easterly approach to another extraordinary Cathar fortification at Montségur, the road snakes along the side of a gorge, the castle briefly visible then lost again, no more so than when negotiating an unlit though thankfully short tunnel through a cliff-face. Once a frontier bulwark against the Spanish and a base for bandits, which led to it being partly demolished in the 17th century, the fortress withstood a siege by crusader Simon de Montfort for four months in 1210. When their water supply ran out, the Cathars surrendered, only to have a change of heart when sudden rain replenished their cisterns. As the crusaders approached to enforce the surrender, they met them with a volley of arrows. The brutal de Montfort responded by ordering the massacre of most of the survivors when the castle did fall soon after.

The ascent to the Col de Termes steps up via some steep ramps to a ridge with immense views on both sides. Beyond it, the route undulates incessantly. It drops and then climbs briefly to reach the junction with the D613 at the Col de Bedos. Go right, descend fleetingly again, then start upwards again, passing through the village of Laroque de Fa to reach the Col des Fourches.

Now in a high and comparatively tree-free plain, the road arrows into Mouthoumet, then drops back into woodland and coasts down to a crossroads, where the final ascent to the Col de Paradis commences. While it's not nirvana as far as climbing goes, the 6km is very pleasant, cutting up a tight, rocky and wooded valley to begin with, then entering

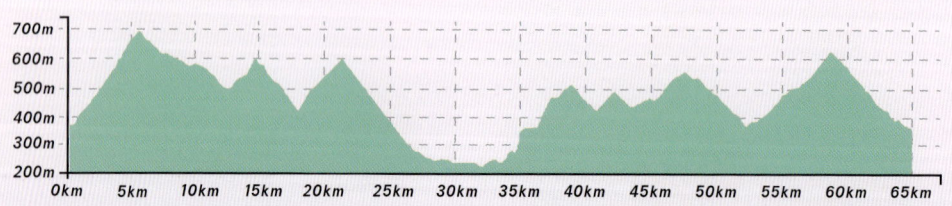

AUDE

Château de Termes

more open pastureland. The col is a tad disappointing, sited at the intersection with a logging trail in stands of pine, but the descent away compensates very nicely, swishing down into Arques with barely any need to touch the brakes.

Route in reverse

While there's something not quite right about starting towards Paradise and riding away from it, this route is just as appealing when tackled anti-clockwise. The Col du Paradis makes for a slightly easier start than the Valmigère, which some may favour.

Distance: 65.2km
Elevation gain: 1,509m
Highest point: 705m
Est. moving time: 2.5-4.5hrs
Degree of difficulty: ●●
Climbs: Col de Valmigère (705m), Col de la Loubière (599m), Col de Termes (520m), Col de Bedos (485m), Col des Fourches (540m), Col du Paradis (622m)

Parcours

0km	Arques
5.5km	Col de Valmigère
12.5km	D54/D129 ➡
13.5km	D129/D40 ⬅ ①
21km	Col de la Loubière
29.5km	Vignevieille
31.5km	D40/D212 ➡ ②
38.5km	Col de Termes ③
42km	Col de Bedos D40/D613 ➡
47.5km	Col des Fourches ④
58.5km	Col du Paradis ⑤
65.2km	Arques

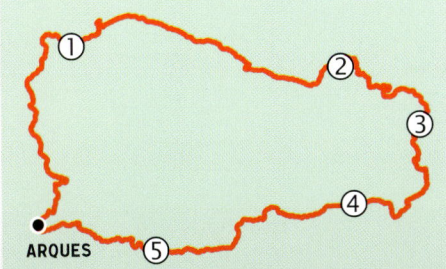

THE JOY OF THE JAU

Although this route starts and finishes in the department of Aude, the terrain it covers is mostly in Pyrénées Orientales. A hundred kilometres long, it features one of my favourite climbs in this chain, the eastern flank of the Col de Jau. There's 60km to cover before reaching that little-renowned gem, the first half dozen or so on the D117 to Lapradelle, the Col Campérié providing a first test of your climbing legs. Take a right here onto the far more tranquil D22, which heads southwards, skirting the foot of the Château de Puylaurens, which is well worth a visit when you're not in cycling shoes.

The road runs up the Boulzane Valley, barely wavering from a straight southerly course as it heads for the Col d'Aussières, the gradient sticking at close to three per cent for the first half of this 15.5km ascent through woods and, higher up, pine forest. Above Gincla, it begins to meander, the road, still running through a corridor of green, built up above the river in a narrow valley.

At Montfort sur Boulzane a large hairpin bend cut out of the rock is the prelude to steeper ramps, some briefly into double figures, but the average is a not too severe six per cent for the next 4km, rising to a much flatter section up to the col, which is very open and has extensive views. Beyond it, the road continues to rise to the apex of the pass, which is hemmed in by stands of pine and is a little disappointing. Much better, though, is the descent, which is never steep and isn't at all technical as it sashays delightfully down through Rabouillet to Sournia with some superb views on the way across wooded hills to the south through which the route will soon be heading.

After winding along Sournia's narrow main street, turn right towards Prades, quickly starting up the Col de Roque Jalère, or Col Roc Jalère in Occitan. From the off, this climb is far harder than the Aussières, averaging close to eight per cent for its opening 5km. The rapid gain in altitude quickly results in long-ranging views across the rocky, scrub-covered landscape. Just beyond Roc Cornut, a huge stone standing upright atop a boulder to the right-hand side, the road reaches a crest where the gradient falls considerably. At the same time, the view extends further to the north and east. While this is impressive, the southerly panorama across the Têt Valley from the summit, which arrives soon after, is staggering. It's dominated by the colossal Pic du Canigou, looming over the towns of Vinça and Prades, with the Catalan Pyrenees stretching away towards to the south-west. More benign than its northern flank and very open, this is a descent to drink in and savour.

It concludes at a T-junction. Turn right here towards Molitg les Bains, a sign immediately signalling the imminence of the Col de Jau. Winding up the Castellane Valley, the tiny spa town of Molitg soon appears, its baths perched above the river, the ruined Château de Paracolls overlooking it. The sudden lushness of the terrain stands out after the arid Roque Jalère.

Approaching Campôme, stay right where the road forks, taking the more direct route towards Mosset, a beautiful *village perché*, terraces cut into the hillside beneath it, its houses piled up along a narrow ridge. The beautiful Jau begins beyond it, gently at first, as it passes beneath the Tour de Mascarda, built in the 13th century to protect it, then gradually ramping up, although never too severely. The pass was both strategically and geographically significant, a key trading route that at one point marked the border

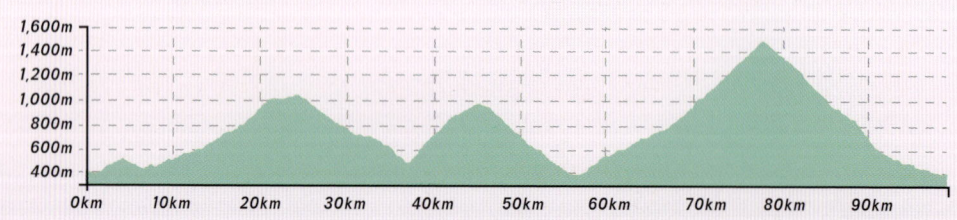

AUDE

between France and Spain. As a link between French Catalonia and the regions to the west in the modern era of autoroutes and trunk roads, it now has little importance, and it's all the more attractive for that.

The final 3km, where deciduous woodland supplants bracken and scrubby trees, are the most consistently testing, averaging 7.5%, and top out at a small plateau, from which the Mediterranean is visible on clear days. Sitting high up between the Mediterranean climate zone to the east and the Pyrenean to the west, this can be a stormy place, the clash of weather systems often producing violent storms. In winter, however, there's no longer enough snow to make the little ski station viable. Said to be the smallest in the world, all that remains are rusting pieces of lift machinery.

Dropping into the Aude, the road cuts through dense forest, which can leave the surface damp in places even on warm days. Apart from occasional steep corners, the gradient is relatively benign until the junction with the D17, a dozen kilometres from Axat. Almost instantly, the road rushes down a narrow valley, cutting through a rock tunnel, hurtling into Ste Colombe sur Guette, then continuing far more sedately into the steep-sided Aude valley to meet the D118 4km above Axat, just above the dramatic Gorges de Saint Georges, where the road is squeezed to a single car-width on a parapet above the river – a fitting finale to a quite wonderful ride.

Mosset

Distance: 99.5km
Elevation gain: 2,604m
Highest point: 1,506m
Est. moving time: 4-6.5hrs
Degree of difficulty: ●●●
Climbs: Col Campérié (534m), Col d'Aussières (1,020m), Col de Roque Jalère (976m), Col de Jau (1,506m)

Route in reverse

Just as enjoyable and highly recommended for the different perspective it offers on some beautiful scenery.

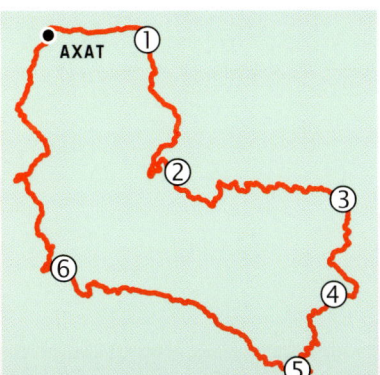

Parcours

00km	Axat
1km	D118/D117 ➡
4.5km	Col Campérié
6.5km	Lapradelle D117/D22 ➡ ①
21.5km	Col d'Aussières ②
36.5km	Sournia D2/D619 ➡ ③
45.5km	Col de Roque Jalère ④
56km	D619/D14 ➡ ⑤
78km	Col de Jau D84 ⑥
88km	Junction D84/D17 ➡
95.5km	Junction D17/D117 ➡
99.5km	Axat

UPPER AUDE VALLEY BACK ROADS

This route exemplifies one of the fundamentals of this guide, as it heads into territory that's close to well-known cycling terrain but almost completely overlooked by most visitors. Starting from Axat, it begins southwards, cutting through the Gorges de Saint Georges with the junction of the D118 and D17 as the first waymark. Bearing left here and climbing, the next is Sainte Colombe sur Guette, the road, often hewn from the cliff-face, steepening beyond this village, which is the start point to the Col de Jau from the west.

After a 2km grind at an average of more than 9%, with a particularly fierce ramp just before it, the road reaches a junction by a bridge, which heads across a river towards the Jau. Stay right here on the D17, the gradient still quite taxing for a kilometre or so until it emerges from the forested valley to enter Roquefort de Sault. For the next few clicks the going is markedly easier, the road rising gently through a broad valley, passing farms and pastureland. At Le Bousquet, the angle of ascent increases again, but not severely, the road switching through two big hairpins to arrive at the Col du Garavel – also known as the Garabeil – an open patch of grazing land with a stone cross just above it and impressive views towards the Pailhères pass and the peaks around it.

After easing down to a junction, where a right to Escouloubre village on the D84 offers a significant shortcut back to Axat, stay with the D17 towards Escouloubre les Bains, the road kicking up for a kilometre to arrive at the telecom masts and farm buildings on the Col des Moulis. From here, there's a steady run down to the D118. Head right on reaching it, dropping to Escouloubre, its thermal baths abandoned in the 1960s but subsequently given a second life as gîtes.

Turn left here towards Quérigut, the road switching very tightly through two hairpins, before scurrying upwards into woodland, making for the Col de Carcanières. The gradient is a good deal more challenging than the earlier climbs, the road averaging 10% through the trees, then around 11% for the first kilometre and a half above them. There's a lull reaching the village of Carcanières, then a couple of hundred metres at 12% to the summit above it. The drop away from it is quite abrupt too, but the road is almost dead straight and thrillingly fast, providing enough momentum to fly up the short rise into Quérigut, the village squashed in around a medieval château that sits on a sandstone outcrop. In front of the church, follow the sign for Le Bousquet, the road swinging northwards to Le Pla, descending all the way.

Stay with the D16 entering Pla, following signs to Rouze, the road still descending through lush meadows and passing the left turn towards Mijanès and the Port de Pailhères (see page 70) heading into the village. Just after crossing the river in Rouze, there's a choice of routes. Go left for a gentler descent back to the Aude valley via some sweeping hairpins and a superb view of the Château d'Usson, or fly down the direct and, therefore, steeper route that passes below the large outcrop on which the castle sits.

Whichever you choose, turn left on the main road towards Axat, following the River Aude through Usson les Bains. Just beyond, there's another decision to be made. Keep straight on for the shortest route back to Axat, or turn left on the D29 towards Fontanès de Sault for something I'd argue is a little better – and I do like the Aude valley road a lot.

Cutting up into the woods, the road loops into the cliff-face above the D118, climbing all

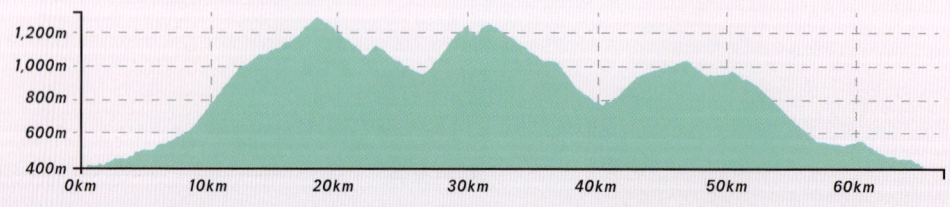

AUDE

View from the Col du Garavel over Escouloubre

the while. It's very narrow, twisting and sometimes fairly steep. Passing through a cleft hacked out of the rock and then two rock tunnels just above, the views are impressive and steadily become more so. Beyond Fontanès de Sault, the road cuts away from the valley and into the hills, climbing gently now to the Col des Aychides, then dropping into a wide, fertile valley on the Plateau de Sault. At Aunat, turn right towards Axat.

After a short section on the flat, the road drops towards Bessède de Sault, then switches back just before the village to shoot down into the Aude Valley, speeding past an oddly sited col, the Castel, which is neither on a ridge nor at an obvious junction, and joining the D118 in time for a second jaunt through the Gorges de Saint Georges before the finish.

Route in reverse

I can't pick between them. Leaving the Garavel till last does mean that the altitude gain is quite evenly staggered across the ride, rather than coming mostly at the front end.

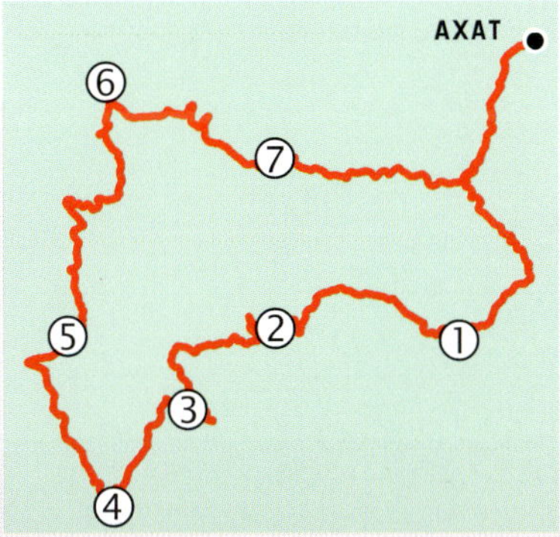

Distance: 66.7km
Elevation gain: 1,755m
Highest point: 1,262m
Est. moving time: 3-5hrs
Degree of difficulty: ●●◖
Climbs: Col de Garavel (1,262m), Col des Moulis (1,099m), Col de Carcanières (1,207m), Col des Aychides (1,007m)

Parcours

0km	Axat
3.5km	D118/D17 ←
11km	D17/D84 → ①
18km	Col de Garavel ②
23km	Col des Moulis
25.5km	D17/D118 →
26.5km	D118/D25 ← ③
29.5km	Col de Carcanières
31km	Quérigut D16 ④
37km	Rouze
39km	D16/D118 ← ⑤
40km	D118/D29 ←
47km	Col des Aychides
48.5km	Aunat D29/D20 → ⑥
57km	D20/D118 ← ⑦
66.7km	Axat

ARIÈGE LEG-WARMER

For those heading into the Pyrénées Ariégeoises from Toulouse and the north, Foix marks the point where the flatlands give way to the first line of peaks, and this ride is designed to offer the chance to acclimatise to that sudden change of terrain. Starting in the shadow of Foix's spectacular 12th-century château on Villote, the main boulevard through the Ariège's administrative centre, the route heads across the river that gives this department its name and initially heads south on the busy main route, before veering left towards Roquefixade and away from the buzz of traffic as the road passes beneath the flyover carrying the *autoroute* towards Andorra.

Climbing gently away from the Pain de Sucre de Montgaillard sugarloaf outcrop just beyond the outskirts of Foix, the road weaves through flower-filled meadows and hamlets, soon offering impressive views across to the mountains of the Pays d'Olmes, through which the route will return. Glancing ahead, the Cathar stronghold of Montségur can easily be picked out atop a conical peak at about one o'clock. On the hillside above the road, limestone pillars stand sentinel beneath the Pic de l'Aspre, the highest point in the Massif du Plantaurel and one of only four sections in France of the Pre-Pyrenees, foothills that run east-west and parallel to the Pyrenean chain, the other being the Corbières. There are, incidentally, more than two dozen such massifs on the Spanish side of the range.

After 16km, and the most testing section of ascent so far, the road flattens to reach Roquefixade, and it is only now that the village's crumbling but dramatic castle is apparent, on an eyrie-like perch up to the left. Although it was a refuge of the Cathars in the 13th century, the ruins date from the 14th to 16th centuries when the castle was used as a stronghold to oversee the domain of the Count of Foix. Its name, incidentally, derives from the Occitan *roca fisada*, denoting the cleft in the rock upon which the castle stands, the structure underpinned by an arch that still supports the crumbling fortification.

Dropping down through woodland, the route briefly follows the main road towards Lavelanet, before switching right to Villeneuve d'Olmes and, after 25km, Montferrier. Here, there are three options: take the right turn towards the Col de la Lauze, continue on for a kilometre and take the right turn towards the ski resort of Mont d'Olmes (see page 86), or keep on ahead for four kilometres to reach the Col de Montségur. For those looking for a leg-warmer rather than a leg-breaker, the first choice is the best. Just after crossing the river, there is a drinking water (*eau potable*) tap set in the wall on the left, just below the turn left up through the village on the D209, which should be followed to the Col de la Lauze. This narrow road soon enters thick woodland, winding tightly through a series of switchbacks to reach open pasture with long views across to the Monts d'Olmes that demand selection of an easier gear and a slowing of the pace. The 5km from Montferrier are blissful and make for one of my favourite climbs anywhere in the Pyrenees. In a nutshell, the Lauze is a little climb that delivers a lot.

At 14km, the descent is far longer and comes in two quite different halves. The first, to Freychenet, bobs either side of the 900m contour line. From the village, there's a rapid slalom through the woods to Celles and the main road again. A detour through Saint Paul de Jarrat allows a temporary escape from the traffic before the right turn towards Foix and a coffee where greater challenges can be studied and discussed.

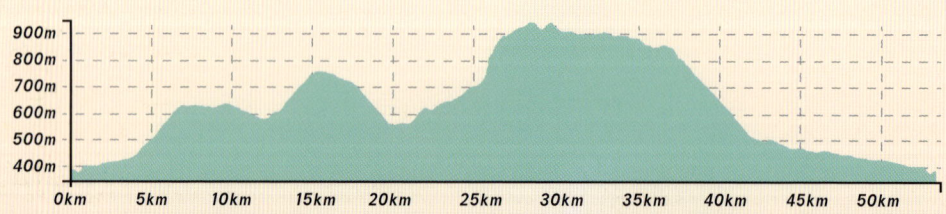

ARIÈGE

The château and village at Roquefixade

Route in reverse

It's very much the same in terms of attractiveness, but a touch harder in terms of difficulty as both climbs are tackled from their harder side. It's hard to choose between them. Give both a try.

Distance: 54.5km
Elevation gain: 1,007m
Highest point: 948m
Est. moving time: 2-3.5hrs
Degree of difficulty: ●
Climbs: Roquefixade (765m), Col de la Lauze (948m)

Parcours

0km	Foix
2km	D117/D9A ←
15.5km	Roquefixade ①
20km	D9A/D117 ←
21km	D117/D509 → ②
22.5km	Villeneuve d'Olmes D509/D9 →
25km	Montferrier Junction D9/D209 → ③
30.5km	Col de la Lauze ④
44km	Celles Junction Junction D209/D117 ← ⑤
45km	Saint Paul de Jarrat D117/D309 ←
47km	D309/D117 ↑
54.5km	Foix

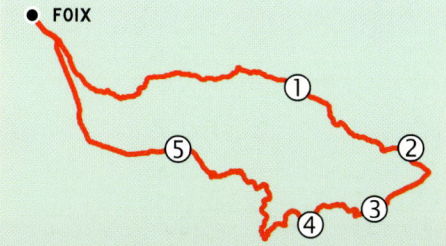

ONE CLIMB, FIVE COLS AND A GROTTO

This ride includes a natural wonder of the Ariège that has become a regular feature in the Tour de France, followed by one of the department's toughest ascents. Beginning in Foix, it winds around the castle, crossing the bridge across the Arget, then follows the western bank of the Ariège beneath high cliffs secured with the ultimate in safety netting to reach Vernajoul. Heading straight through the village, the road rises almost imperceptibly, passing the Grotte de Labouiche, which features Europe's longest navigable underground river that's accessible to the public. Visitors are punted for 1.5km through caverns and tunnels, passing all manner of extraordinary rock formations.

Back above ground, continue through Baulou to a T-junction with the D11, turning right. Another 2km later, at the Resistance memorial to Spanish combatants, swing left to pick up the road that runs on the southern side of the Montagnes du Plantaurel through the hamlets of Aigues-Juntes and Gabre to reach the village of Mas d'Azil. This is one of my stock routes, a backroad that gently rolls and meanders through a tranquil valley. It is, though, what comes next that provides the real pull. Climbing away from the centre of Mas d'Azil on the D119, the road makes for the cliff-face ahead, then enters it, weaving through the spectacular *grotte* alongside the River Arize for more than 400m. As the only cave in Europe passable by bike, it's a unique thrill, especially when the river is in flood and the immense cavern resounds with surging water.

Retrace to Foix from here if the prospect of the tough climbing still to come now appears daunting. Otherwise, press on a couple of kilometres, passing the Église de Reynaude with its stations of the cross scaling the hillside behind, continuing towards Lescure to reach a left turn towards Rimont, the lane to it running through meadows before climbing to this pretty village. Standing out on a ridge, Rimont was almost completely razed by German forces in August 1944 as a reprisal to an attack made by the Ariège maquis Resistance forces.

Take a left here onto the main D117 for 600m, then head right on the D18B in the direction of the Col de la Crouzette. The signs at the next junction indicate the start of the climb and its sister pass, the Col de Portel, although the gradients on them underplay the steepness of much of what lies ahead with the average gradient very close to 9% for the next 8km. Dense deciduous woods on the first few kilometres provide welcome shade on hot days, the road meandering madly as it climbs steeply. Coming out of the trees, it runs truer. Psychologically, I always find these sections harder to cope with. The gradient is no steeper, but the road's straightness makes it appear more relentless and unforgiving. I much prefer a winding road, where bends offer the hope of an easier grade, even if it is so often dashed.

The arrival of the Col de Rillé is the first sign the top is not too distant. Just beyond it, the road emerges onto the ridge on the edge of the Arize massif with views across the Arize valley. Even better, the gradient relents significantly on the final segment up to the Col de la Crouzette, the first of five passes that come in rapid succession. Joined by the steepling route up from Biert, the road weaves up the mountainside, offering captivating views to the south of the peaks rippling into the distance, the loftiest of them snow-capped year-round. A clutch of painted names testifies to the Tour's passage before

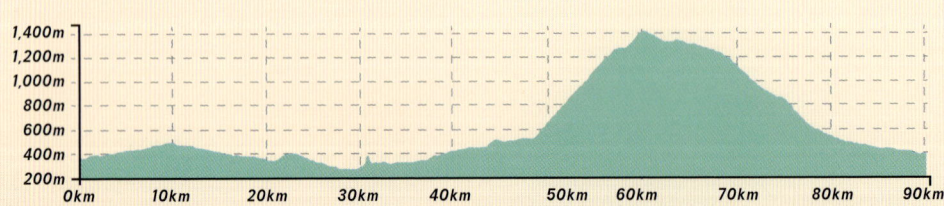

ARIÈGE

Road and river run through the Grotte du Mas d'Azil

two hairpins lead to col number two, the Portel, a narrow saddle with a magnificent 360° panorama.

A brief drop and a short rise leads to the Tour Laffont viewpoint atop the third pass, the Péguère. The brave or foolish can consider the 2.8km plummet down the Mur de Péguère (see page 88) as an add-on, the more circumspect can relish the prospect of 27km of mostly straightforward descending via the Col de Jouels and the Col des Marrous, the final two of the day's cols, back to Foix. Those who still have something in the tank can emulate the riders in the 2019 Tour by turning right by the police station in the town centre and setting their sights on Prat d'Albis. For me, that's for another day, though.

Route in reverse

There's a lot to commend it. The climbing comes earlier and is easier, although the descent of the Crouzette is more technical and hairier. The ride from Mas d'Azil up the Plantaurel is wonderfully serene.

Distance: 90.8km
Elevation gain: 1,655m
Highest point: 1,432m
Est. moving time: 3.5-5.5hrs
Degree of difficulty: ●●●
Climbs: Col de la Crouzette (1,244m), Col de Portel (1,432m), Col de Péguère (1,375m)

Parcours

0km	Foix D117 towards Saint Girons
0.5km	D117/D1 →
11.5km	D1/D11 → ①
13km	D11/D1A ←
28km	D1A/D119 ←
31km	Grotte de Mas d'Azil ②
41km	D119/D18C ← ③
44.5km	Rimont D18C/D117 ←
45km	D117/D18B → ④
56.5km	Col de la Crouzette D18B/D72 ← ⑤
60.5km	Col de Portel
64km	Col de Péguère D72/D17 ← ⑥
90.8km	Foix

TO MUR OR NOT?

Evidently, any circular ride has two options. The direction of choice on this one boils essentially down to a single question: do you want to ride up or down the Mur de Péguère? Averaging 12% for 3km, it's a daunting obstacle in either direction. Living on the Foix side of the pass, I tend to favour rides that head down it, including this one that continues on to the Port de Lers. The Tour de France's preference for tackling these two climbs the opposite way underlines that this route is significantly harder if undertaken clockwise.

Leaving Foix, follow the D17 as it climbs gently to Saint Pierre de Rivière and then Serres sur Arget. The Péguère pass begins just beyond this village, although there's little noticeable change in the comfortable gradient for the first couple of kilometres. That changes as the road switches back sharply over a bridge and starts to step up towards Burret. Beyond this hamlet, the grade remains taxing for a couple of kilometres, then eases again as it approaches the Col des Marrous. The road widens as the gradient rises again, no doubt to accommodate the logging vehicles working in the pine forests, making for a very un-Pyrenean experience, with no views to distract from the grind. There's ample reward, though, at the top of the pass, where a wonderful panorama emerges right at the crest. The Tour Laffont observation point details what you're looking at.

Take care on the plunge down the Mur. It's narrow and gets very noticeably steeper as you go down, the last kilometre below the second and final hairpin particularly acute in angle and technical difficulty. If it's hot, those using carbon rims should also think about lowering the pressure in their tyres to avoid overheating and a blow-out that could cause the whole wheel to fail. In the 2019 Ariégeoise, rims were blowing so frequently in 40°-plus that it sounded like a hunting party was roaming through the dense woodland.

The bottom of the Mur intersects with the D618 at the Col des Caougnous. This is halfway up the western side of the Col de Port (see page 98). Turn left here for a shorter route back to Foix or right towards Massat, a few minutes away down the weaving and wonderful descent. Head into the little square, where at least one café is usually open – there is also a water hydrant a few dozen metres away on the left as the D618 continues out of the square. Once body and bottles are replenished, take the D18 from the top of the triangular *place* to start the 17km climb to the Port de Lers, its name deriving from the old Occitan word for 'steep'.

It commences quite benignly, the narrow road tracking the briskly-flowing Arac upstream, passing through a succession of hamlets, the biggest of them Le Port. Above here, the incline picks up, but remains comfortable until just past the turning to La Ruze, where the road begins to climb more quickly, the weathered pinnacles above the Étang de Lers and nearby Col d'Agnes increasingly prominent. A rise through a run of hairpins leads into the broader upper section of this valley, cattle and horses often grazing freely in this high pasture, a couple of switchbacks sweeping through it to reach a junction adjacent to the Étang, a small lake surrounded by spectacular peaks.

There's a café at the cross-country ski station that sits above the picturesque lake, just to the right at the junction, this road continuing to the Col d'Agnes (see page 98). The Port de Lers is 3.5km away in the other direction, a false flat in between two steeper sections to the summit, above

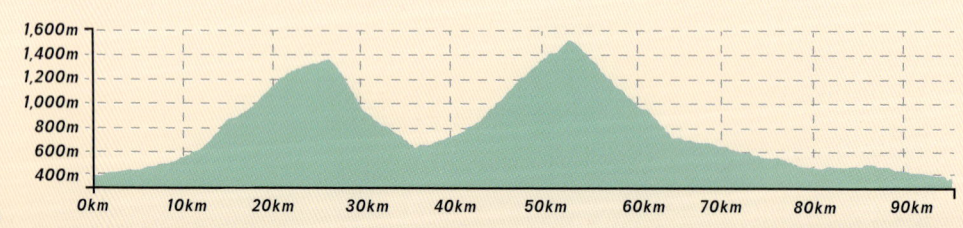

ARIÈGE

which paragliders often soar on the thermals. The landscape evokes Britain's Lake District, the mountainsides mostly bare and grassy, an ancient aspect to the rugged peaks, which include the Pic des Trois Seigneurs, at 2,199 metres comparatively modest in height but so isolated and exposed that it featured a glacier, the Ambans, until the early years of this century.

Mild to be begin with, the drop on the eastern flank of the pass quickly gets more acute, *ers* or *erz* in ancient Occitan, and can be very fast below the hairpins 4km beyond the summit. Hurrying down through thick woodland, the road remains narrow and can often be damp under the trees, so caution is advised. At the bottom, Vicdessos, which has a little supermarket, cafés and a fabulous boulangerie, arrives very quickly. On some profiles, the descent off the Lers continues all the way to Tarascon, another 14km away, but the D8 loses little more than 200m in altitude over this portion. Locals describe it as a *faux plat descendant*, the incline enough to help you breeze along, but not without pedalling.

If, as is often the case in the afternoon, there's a headwind in this valley, don't push too hard as it will almost certainly be blowing with even greater vigour when the road turns north at Tarascon to complete the loop back to Foix. In this event, the road via Arignac and Amplaing is more sheltered than the D618 via Mercus, but does come with a steep dig around a rocky outcrop that results in an almost equal tax on resources being exacted by the time you roll back into Foix.

Looking down the Port de Lers towards Vicdessos

Route in reverse

It's significantly harder, but, aesthetically, I prefer this route up the Port de Lers. An early start often means a tailwind pushing you along from Foix all the way to Vicdessos as well. The descent from the Lers to Massat isn't quite as fast and technical either. When it comes to the Mur, I'm always glad of my 34x30 gear. Don't dismiss the opt-out over the Col de Port if you don't fancy half an hour of hardcore grind. Plenty take it when the Mur feels too daunting, myself included.

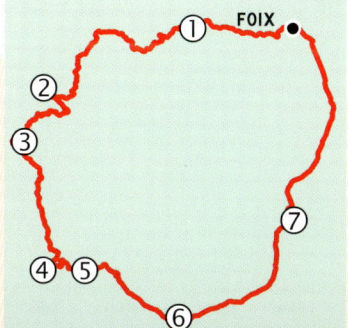

Distance: 95.6km
Elevation gain: 2,067m
Highest point: 1,517m
Est. moving time: 3.5-5.5hrs
Degree of difficulty: ●●●
Climbs: Col de Péguère (1,375m), Port de Lers (1,517m)

Parcours

0km	Foix
0.5km	D117/D17 ←
8.5km	Serres sur Arget ①
27km	Col de Péguère ← down the Mur ②
30km	Col des Caougnous → D17/D618
36.5km	Massat D618/D18 ← ③
49.5km	D18/D8F ← ④
53km	Port de Lers ⑤
64.5km	Vicdessos ⑥
78.5km	Tarascon sur Ariège D8/N20 ← ⑦
79.5km	N20/D618 →
89km	D618/D117 ↑
95.6km	Foix

TOUR OF CATHAR CASTLES

This is a very adaptable route, which can be made shorter by taking out a significant part of the climbing if you bypass Monts d'Olmes and can end by crossing the Col de la Lauze instead of Roquefixade, although that does impact on its Cathar attributes. It begins by heading north on the main road through Foix for a few hundred metres, then forking right towards L'Herm on the D1, which quickly swaps bustle for serenity on what is one of the most popular routes for local riders when the high passes are closed.

Passing Roquefort les Cascades, its spectacular falls offering ideal picnicking territory as well as being the start of several MTB routes, and a short gorge below Rapy, it continues on the D1 through Lieurac to Laroque d'Olmes. Keep straight on to La Bastide sur l'Hers, where a right turn onto the D16 eventually leads onto the main D117 between Foix and Perpignan, which has hitherto been avoided. This section of it is rarely busy, so the next 3km eastwards to Bélesta aren't usually a chore. Just around the 90° bend in the centre of Bélesta, a right turn onto the D9 restores previous levels of tranquillity.

A kilometre after this turn, the Fontaine de Fontestorbes merits a stop. Impressive at any time, it's particularly so in dry periods when the falls become intermittent as a natural reservoir of water within the mountainside fills up over a number of minutes before cascading and revitalising the falls. Continuing through the twin village of Fougax et Barrineuf, the climb towards Montségur commences gently, winding through humid woodland.

The first sight of the castle, perched spectacularly atop an outcrop known locally as the *pog* – from an old word for a hill clearly derived from the same source as the Catalan equivalent, puig – signals an imminent change of gradient, the next section highlighting why I much prefer to climb this side of the mountain. Initially, it appears the road will circle to the right of this immense, conical rock, but it suddenly cuts hard left and begins to climb more steeply, almost encircling the peak to arrive in the village of Montségur, tucked in on the southern side of the *pog*, then rising steeply on switchbacks towards the summit. The last straight drag passes the "burning field" where more than 200 Cathars were killed in 1244 for what the Catholic church considered to be heretical beliefs. Following this siege, the original château was destroyed, the current impregnable-looking ruin being the second fortification to have been built on the site since the 13th century.

After a brief pause at the summit to take in an impressive view over nearby Lavelanet towards Mirepoix and the plains to the north, a very fast and brief descent soon reaches the left turn to the ski resort of Monts d'Olmes. It's an unusual climb, featuring two quite lengthy descents before it reaches the resort that's occasionally hosted stage finishes in pro races, but is best known as the home of 2018 Olympic moguls champion Perrine Laffont. Many dislike this road because of these descents and its route through thick pine forest, but there's something appealing about its weaving, rollercoastering route to the down-at-heel ski station that was established in the late 1960s to boost tourism as the local textile industry began to fail. It's quintessentially Pyrenean, not engineered in the same bulldozing way as a road to an Alpine ski station, dealing instead with the contours as they come, like a Scalextric track on the grandest scale.

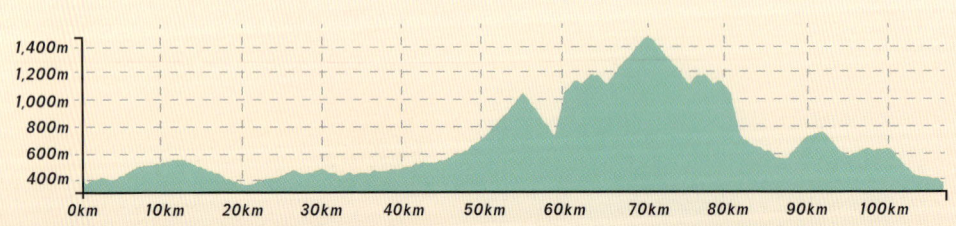

ARIÈGE

View from the château at Montségur over the village and towards Les Monts d'Olmes

Distance: 107km
Elevation gain: 2,399m
Highest point: 1,479m
Est. moving time: 3.5-5.5hrs
Degree of difficulty: ●●●
Climbs: Col de Montségur (1,059m), Mont d'Olmes (1,479m), Roquefixade (765m)

Returning the same way – when those mid-climb descents might start to become a little irritating – there is the option of heading back to Foix via the Col de la Lauze (see page 81). However, to persist with the Cathar theme continue on to Montferrier and then, after another very short stint on the D117, tackle the steep road through shady deciduous woodland to Roquefixade, this village also located below a miraculously perched castle. Beyond it, two fast descents punctuated with a short false flat provide a breezily-quick return to Foix.

Route in reverse
It merits from having all of the toughest climbs in its first half. My only gripe is that it comes at Montségur from the "wrong" side, but even so it still impresses immensely and won't disappoint.

Parcours

0km	Foix
1km	D919/D1 ➡
9km	L'Herm
18km	D1/D10 ➡ ①
21km	Lieurac D1/D12 ➡
27.5km	Laroque d'Olmes D1/D620 ⬆
32km	La Bastide sur L'Hers D620/D16 ➡ ②
37km	L'Aiguillon D16/D117 ⬅
40km	Bélesta D117/D9 ➡ ③
55km	Col Montségur ④
59km	D9/D909 ⬅
70.5km	Monts d'Olmes ⑤
82km	D909/D9 ⬅
84.5km	Villeneuve d'Olmes D9/D509 ⬅ ⑥
86km	D509/D117 ⬅
87km	D117/D9A ➡
92km	Roquefixade ⑦
105km	D9A/D117 ➡
107km	Foix

87

THE 2019 TOUR'S FOIX FINALE

This is one of my favourite routes, largely because the final climb fills the view from my home across the Barguillère valley, but also thanks to significant links with Tour de France history both ancient and recent. It begins by taking the road on the western side of the Ariège valley from Foix, complete with a muscle-rousing little kicker of a hill en route to Tarascon, where it takes a westerly turn towards Saurat and the Col de Port, the tautologically named pass that was the first in the Pyrenees ever to be tackled by the Tour, during the 1910 edition of the race, and from this side too, although the route to the summit has changed a little since then.

The road climbs soon after leaving Tarascon, but there's a significant dip before Saurat, and it's only beyond this village that the ascent towards the Port begins. Unusually regular in its gradient for the Pyrenees, it's also one of the few major passes that is kept open year-round as it's the main obstacle on the route between Tarascon and Saint Girons. In mid-winter, when the road cuts through high banks of snow, it's a wonderful out-and-back ride from the Ariège valley on a sparklingly clear day. Steepest coming into and above the hamlet of Prat Communal, it's the kind of climb that provides a good introduction to riding in the high mountains, testing but not intimidating. Entering the hairpins towards the top, the gradient eases to the extent that some will crest the pass in the big ring if the wind's from the east.

The three-course menu at the summit's auberge is hearty and highly recommended, although a pastry and coffee might be advised bearing in mind what lies ahead. For those who just need a quick refill, about 400 metres beyond the pass, there's an *eau potable* tap on the right, before the road slaloms steadily down to the Col des Caougnous (see page 84), and the first ferocious ramps of the Mur de Péguère. The hard right here is "dead", a turn into which it's impossible to carry any speed from the descent because it's so tight. As a consequence, most riders will need to change down to the inner ring before starting into the Mur's first kilometre, which averages 14% and gets harder as it progresses towards a fearsome jag to the left. If you can keep your momentum going through this hairpin, the gradient does gradually ease, the second kilometre a slightly less savage 12%, the final 1,500 metres rising at a comparatively straightforward 10% until the road emerges from the woods at the col, where the panorama provides ample recompense for the slog if the weather's clear.

Almost 30km of descent follows, the opening third mostly straight and fast to the Col des Marrous, the next third more technical but still quite quick down to Serres sur Arget, the final third into Foix flat for long sections. The route returns almost to the start point, then kicks right and upwards from Villote, Foix's central boulevard, to arrive at the foot of Prat d'Albis, just above the town's outpost of the University of Toulouse.

Deriving its name from meadow or land (*prat* in Occitan) and its former ownership by the Bishop of Albi, Prat d'Albis first hosted a Tour finish in 2019, the riders also coming at it via the Mur. On first sight of its length, height and average gradient, none of which are particularly intimidating, many pros thought the climb wasn't a particularly demanding test. However, when the Tour favourites reconnoitred the stage, they realised it's got Jekyll and Hyde characteristics.

Compared to the Col de Port, it's much more typically Pyrenean, and comes in two halves with a short "landing" in between.

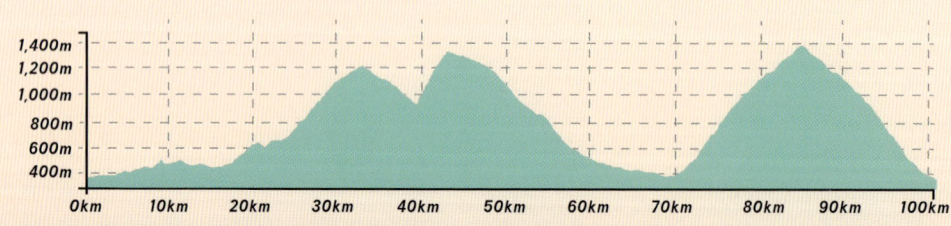

ARIÈGE

The first portion begins straightforwardly, but soon reaches a kilometre worthy of the Mur, winding up through grazing land and woods to the short plateau. Relief is brief, though, as it's immediately followed by a kilometre at 11%, the steepest on the mountain. Just above it, the road climbs out of the woods and into open pasture offering immense views that are initially over the Barguillère, Foix and the flatlands to the north. As the road switches to the east, the 2,000m bulk of Mont Fourcat dominates on the other side of the Ariège valley, with the conical peak of Montségur also easy to pick out. As the road curves past the lower telecoms masts, the vista is southwards up the Ariège valley and into the heart of the Pyrenean range.

The view into the Ariège valley from the Col de Port

The Tour stage ended near the take-off point used by paragliders and is adjacent to a large flat area that was the ideal location for the finish line gantry, podium and broadcast equipment. The road continues upwards, though, for another 3km and another set of masts at the Pla des Peyres, with another spectacular panorama into the high mountains a little beyond and just before the road becomes a rutted track. The return to Foix is via the same road, the views highlighting once again the beauty of this climb, the first high-rise point in the Pyrenees when coming south from Toulouse.

Route in reverse

Saving Prat d'Albis for last, the anticlockwise approach is far easier thanks to its neutering of the Mur, but its descent should be taken with a lot of caution. Although there's very little traffic, the road's very narrow and you don't want to be travelling at high speed if anything is coming up. Snaking almost mesmerically, the western side of the Col de Port is joyous.

Distance: 101.3km
Elevation gain: 2,538m
Highest point: 1,413m
Est. moving time: 3.5-5.5hrs
Degree of difficulty: ●●●●
Climbs: Col de Port (1,249), Col de Péguère (1,375m), Prat d'Albis (1,205), Pla des Peyres (1,389m)

Parcours

0km	Foix
3km	Ferrières via D8H and D8B
7km	D8A/D8B ➡
16km	Tarascon sur Ariège D8B/N20 ➡ ①
17km	N20/D618 to Col de Port ⬆
33km	Col de Port ②
39.5km	Col des Caougnous D618/D17 ➡
43km	Col de Péguère ③
62km	Serres sur Arget ④
69.5km	Foix D17/D117 ➡ then D117/D21 ➡
70.5km	D21/D420 ⬅
81.5km	Prat d'Albis
86km	Pla des Peyres ⑤
101.3km	Foix

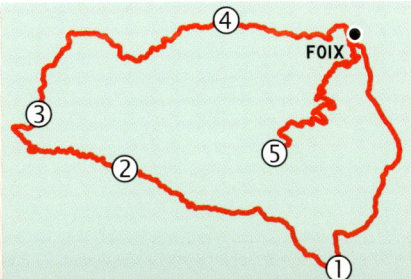

IN THE SHADOW OF MONT VALIER

Sometimes you come across a pass that hasn't figured on your radar before and by the summit you're wondering how that could possibly have been the case. For me, the Col de la Core was one of those places. It's relatively well known, has appeared on the Tour route on several occasions and, more pertinently, is on my home patch in the Pyrénées Ariégeoises, but it was only when researching this book that I realised what a beautiful experience I'd been missing.

Starting in Saint Girons, home of arguably the best market in the Ariège each Saturday, the route initially tracks the east bank of the Salat, then hops across to the west bank to reach the roundabout where the D618 splits, the right fork (see page 100) staying with the Salat towards Oust and Seix, which sits at the foot of the Core, and the left following the Arac, which scurries down from Biert and Massat, 20km upstream. Driving on this road of incessant curves can be sickening in all senses of the word, but on a bike I always relish it, the constant weaving and rushing waters delivering an almost hypnotic experience.

Just before the little triangle of a square in Massat (where there's also a tap on the hydrant on the right just as you reach it), the route jags back sharply on to the Col de Saraillé, a climb that many would bypass with the Lers/Agnes and Port so near. I always enjoy this little gem, firstly for the views it presents back over Massat and then for its continual twists and turns. I suspect that the longest straight is only a few dozen metres long, which some may find infuriating, but chimes with my love of a corner and seeing how fast I can get through it, and also what may be revealed as I round it. Beyond the summit, the road emerges from the woods to display the flank of the high ridge that the route will soon be climbing, the squared-off pinnacle of Mont Valier prominent behind it.

Dropping into the Garbet valley, the route follows the river down to Oust, then switches left towards Seix, an extremely picturesque village overlooked by the Château du Mirabat, which was commissioned by Charlemagne in the 10th century. After crossing the Salat and bumping across the cobbled square, the road towards the Col de la Core rises immediately up a street so narrow that your impulse is to check your route-finding to confirm that you're not riding up a back alley.

To begin with, the climb is steady and not especially remarkable. However, as it switches to the south and climbs with more intent, the views towards the Trois Seigneurs and other heights to the east are amazing, particularly in the spring and autumn when the trees aren't in full leaf. When the road turns west again, the immense bulk of Mont Valier, so distant not so long before, now dominates the way ahead, looming over the ridge on which the col sits, a long hairpin providing the final step up to it. At the top, the road intersects with the Chemin de la Liberté trail, along which Allied airmen and soldiers were smuggled towards Spain during the Second World War, the crossing marked with a monument. On the other side of the road, just above the pass, sextants set into the mountainside allow identification of the surrounding peaks.

The descent to the west towards Saint Girons begins in spectacular fashion, the ridge looking across to the northern side of Mont Valier, the Arcouzan glacier hidden in a cleft on this mostly shaded face. The only one in the Ariège, it's also the most southern, most easterly and lowest of the dwindling number of glaciers in the Pyrenees, extending

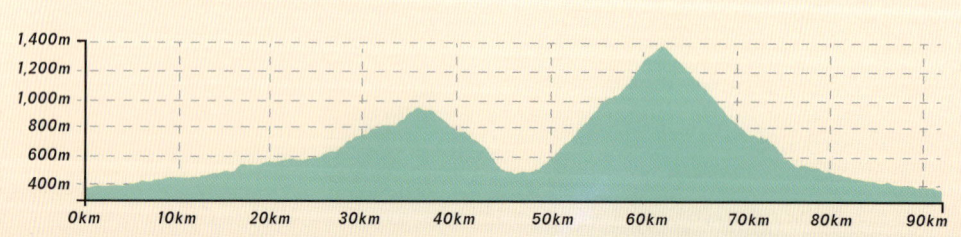

ARIÈGE

to little more than two hectares in 2018. Sweeping around a hairpin, the road hurtles down towards a towering cliff at the end of the ridge dropping northwards from Mont Valier, then veers at the last to dash across the foot of it, the awe-inspiring intersection of rock and road well worth a pause.

After passing the turn to Lac de Bethmale and crossing back to the northern side of the Bethmale valley for three straight and fast kilometres, the gradient eases off considerably before a last dip into Les Bordes sur Lez. The final 16km back to Saint Girons, running slightly downhill through pretty villages, notably Castillon en Couserans, and farmland, is a big gear breeze and a nice end to a super day out.

Route in reverse

Essentially, the choice of direction comes down to whether you want to do most of the climbing early in the ride or later on. The views towards Mont Valier massif on the Core's western flank are very impressive and Seix is a good mid-ride refuelling point. There is an alternative route into Saint Girons following the old rail line on the east bank of the Salat. It's one-way, but lights are required to negotiate several long tunnels.

The squared-off top of Mont Valier stands out from the Col de Saraillé

Distance: 92.1km
Elevation gain: 1,657m
Highest point: 1,395m
Est. moving time: 3.5hrs/4.5hrs/5.5hrs
Degree of difficulty: ●●◐
Climbs: Col du Saraillé (942m), Col de la Core (1,395m)

Parcours

0km	Saint Girons D3
6km	Lacourt D3/D618 ←
12km	D618/D3 ← ①
27km	Massat D618/D17 → ②
36km	Col de Saraillé ③
45km	D17/D32 →
46km	Oust D32/D3 ← ④
48km	Seix D3/D17 →
62km	Col de la Core ⑤
76km	Les Bordes sur Lez D17/D4 → ⑥
79km	Castillon en Couserans D4 merges with D618 ↑
92.1km	Saint Girons

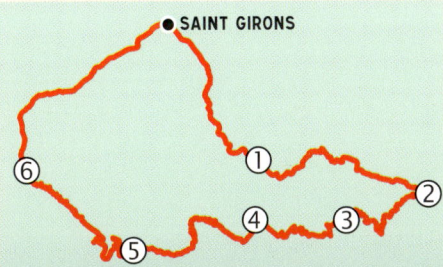

THE LAND THAT TIME FORGOT

There is something of Edgar Rice Burroughs' *The Land That Time Forgot* **about the little-known, mysterious and almost deserted Plateau de Sault that lies across the border between the departments of Ariège and Aude. In parts, it's so quiet and the forest so dense that you could half-imagine a dinosaur emerging from the foliage to shock intrepid adventurers just as described by Burroughs in his lost world of Caprona, and nowhere more so than on the Col du Pradel, a road seemingly to nowhere that cuts through a narrow ravine giving access to the plateau.**

Leaving the spa town of Ax les Thermes, the road ascends immediately beyond the impressive and wonderfully relaxing Bains du Couloubret, switching back and forth to give superb views across the town and towards the ski resort of Ax 3 Domaines nestled in the mountains opposite. Just short of five kilometres up, turn hard left off the main D25 towards the Col du Chioula on the D613.

The gradient is a steady 7% for the most part and never overly demanding, which is just as well given the negligible warm-up. After five hairpins piled closely together, which are a little steeper than hitherto, the 1,431m summit arrives soon after. Appropriately, it's very much a plateau, presenting a gradual rather than a sudden arrival at this first high point with its little cross-country ski station. After a short drop to the Col de Marmare, the start/end of the glorious Route des Corniches (see page 104), the road eases down into one of the Pays de Sault's wide valleys to roll through farmland to reach Camurac, renowned for its Alpine ski station a steep half-dozen kilometres above the village, the little resort the only one in the department of Aude.

Continue on, though, to the junction at the wonderfully titled Col des Sept Frères (see page 62 for the origins of this name). If you need supplies, keep straight on to Belcaire, 3km down the valley where there is a small supermarket, otherwise head right onto the D20, this narrow forest road twisting along a ridge for half a dozen kilometres, before dropping quite rapidly into the Rébenty valley, a steep-sided rift through the centre of the Plateau de Sault. The surface is rough in places and some of the corners tight as the road hares down to a T-junction, where an easily missed sign points right towards the Col du Pradel and the route truly becomes other-worldly.

Rising up a steep-sided and heavily wooded ravine down which the River Rébenty rushes, this quiet road rises gently to the pretty village of Mérial. It's almost a shock to find people living somewhere so remote, especially on dank or wet days when the cloud's right down, which it always seems to be when I pass this way. Beyond the village, a sign marks the start of the Pradel pass and a series of steep ramps provide an early hint of its difficulty, the cliffs pressing in to create three very short but impressive gorges, the first the most spectacular, the chasm so strait that the road has to bore through the bottom of the rockface to remain above the surging river.

Another little hamlet, La Fajolle, then reveals itself, the tidily stacked log piles suggesting that the main occupation is chopping wood to ward off the cold during what must be a long winter. Above it, the gradient becomes more severe, with frequent pitches in double digits and little relief until a sudden and swift drop to cross the Rébenty as the river plunges down the mountainside. When the road kicks up once

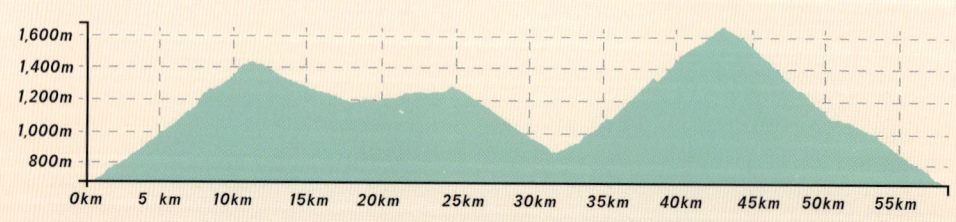

ARIÈGE

The exposed summit of the Chioula

again, the gradient isn't so acute, while dark stands of pine begin to give way to lighter-leafed deciduous woodland. A short run of hairpins signals impending arrival at the summit, with long views into the mountains to the west.

It's downhill all the way now, very steeply for the first 4km, the one-track road rattling down a coil of bends through grazing land and woods, the second half straighter and not as technical, but very quick, plummeting to meet the road that drops from the Port de Pailhères (see page 66). Once they've merged, the descent is more sedate passing the Goulours reservoir and through Ascou to the Chioula junction, the last stretch swooping around curve after curve into Ax, the thermal centre quite frenetic after the extraordinary serenity of the Pradel.

Route in reverse

I like this option too but find that it doesn't provide the same level of tranquillity because the climb towards the Pradel is initially on a busier road and the drop down the Rébenty valley passes so quickly. The approach to the summit of the Pradel is harder, too. On the plus side, almost all of the hard climbing is done when you're fresh.

Distance: 58.7km
Elevation gain: 1,721m
Highest point: 1,680m
Est. moving time: 2.5-4hrs
Degree of difficulty: ●●●◖
Climbs: Col du Chioula (1,431m), Col de Marmare (1,361m), Col des Sept Frères (1,253m), Col du Pradel (1,680m)

Parcours

0km	Ax les Thermes
4.5km	D613/D25 ←
11km	Col du Chioula ①
13km	Col de Marmare
21km	Camurac
22km	Col des Sept Frères D613/D20 → ②
30.5km	D20/unclassified to Espezel → ③
31.5km	D20/107 →
33km	Mérial
43km	Col du Pradel D25B ④
50.5km	D25B/D25 →
54km	D25/D613 ←
58.7km	Ax les Thermes

THE ARIÈGE ALPE D'HUEZ

One of the things I love about living in the Ariège is that there is so much riding terrain to discover beyond the climbs that have become so renowned as a result of the Tour de France. Naturally, though, those celebrated ascents can't be ignored, and this route features one of them, Plateau de Beille, a mountain that is often compared to Alpe d'Huez for its height, length and gradient, although the ski resorts at the two summits could hardly be more different.

The easiest access to Beille is via the N20, the main road that runs along the Ariège valley, but the amount and, especially, the speed of the traffic means it's best avoided. Instead, enjoy one of the region's little-known gems, the Route des Corniches that runs high above it between Bompas and the Col de Marmare. The former arrives quickly on the D618 'back' road from Tarascon towards Foix. Leaving the village, a 180° turn begins to climb alongside the River Arnave towards the village of the same name.

Beyond Arnave, the road steepens suddenly and considerably, eases a little, then steps up more ferociously for the best part of a kilometre to reach Cazenave. It's far gentler from here to the Pas de Soulombrie. However, no sooner has that altitude been gained than it's lost on a fast and technical descent to Barry and then Les Cabannes that should be tackled with a touch of caution.

A switch right and then immediately left in Les Cabannes leads onto Plateau de Beille's opening pitches. Like Alpe d'Huez, some of the steepest sections come early on this 15km climb, the road lifting off quickly to pass the entrance to the 18th-century Château de Gudanes, a very grand neoclassical building which is currently being restored, to reach the first of 14 hairpins. The 8% gradient coming out of it sets the tone, the angle of attack fluctuating a point or so either side of this, but without any steeper sections, at least in the opening half, where an almost unbroken canopy of trees provides very welcome shade on hot days.

Occasional breaks in the greenery do allow you to assess your rate of ascent. Within a few minutes, the floor of the Ariège valley already seems a long way off while the corniche road soon becomes visible on the mountainside opposite. A little longer and harder than Alpe d'Huez, Plateau de Beille is a lot quieter – for a reason that will become apparent at the summit – and more attractive than the legendary Alpine ascent, particularly in its second half. After a dozen kilometres, the road reaches a first plateau, a wide ridge with far-ranging views on both sides. Climbing higher, including a long section close to 11%, this panorama extends to the west above the final two hairpins, the first parking area at the roadside announcing imminent arrival at the tiny cross-country ski station at the top, the "resort" just one low building containing a café.

On the wide, well-surfaced road, the descent to Les Cabannes is one to savour, while the village is the ideal place for a break. To continue, take the N20 towards Ax les Thermes for 2km, then turn left to Vèbre and then Garanou, where a lane leads onto the

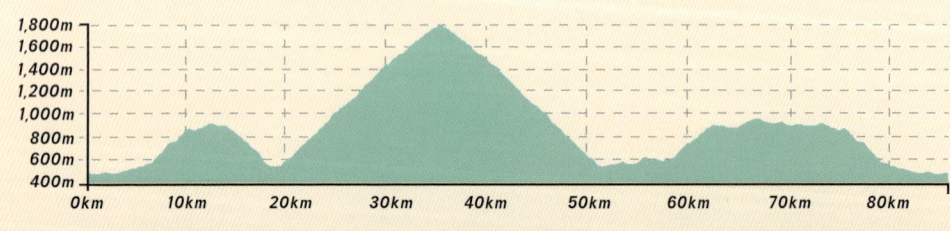

ARIÈGE

Tour fans on the road to Plateau de Beille

D55, which climbs back to the Route des Corniches via Lordat, with its spectacular château, parts of which date from the ninth century. At the crossroads, rather than continue straight on towards the world's biggest talc mine, go left in the direction of Axiat and a longer taste of the corniche road as it bumps through Appy – I always am when I pass through it – and onwards to Arnave and the return to Tarascon.

Distance: 86.1km
Elevation gain: 2,389m
Highest point: 1,790m
Est. moving time: 3.5-5.5hrs
Degree of difficulty: ●●●
Climbs: Pas de Soulombrie (911m), Plateau de Beille (1,790m), Lordat (909m)

Route in reverse

The principal difference is that the descent from the Route des Corniches is not as steep and fast, but the climb back up to it is more taxing, although it's not too long. There's no best option. Both work well.

Parcours

0km	Tarascon sur Ariège D618
3km	Bompas D618/D20 Route des Corniches ➡
12.5km	Pas de Soulombrie ①
14km	D20/D120 ➡
19km	Les Cabannes D120/D522 ➡ ②
35km	Plateau de Beille ③
51km	Les Cabannes D522/D522A ➡
52.5km	D522A/N20 ➡
55km	N20/D420 ⬅ ④
58.5km	D420/D55 ⬅
62.5km	Lordat D55/D20 ⬅ ⑤
83km	Bompas D20/D618 ⬅
86.1km	Tarascon sur Ariège

WELL OFF THE BEATEN TRACK

One of the beauties of riding in the Ariège is the lack of traffic on the roads. The department is half the size of the old county of Yorkshire but with a mere three per cent of its population. In short, large parts of it are completely empty, and even when in the Ariège's biggest towns you don't have to venture far to find these spaces, as this route demonstrates.

Starting in Foix, climb out of the town on the D21 in the direction of Cadirac and Ganac, passing the turn towards the ascent of Prat d'Albis and, after a few kilometres, the landing area for the paragliders who leap off that peak. The road rises through Ganac, weaving through woodland to reach Brassac. Go left at the crossroads in the centre on the D111 towards Cazals, where the gradient briefly kicks up into the village.

Entering the woods above Cazals, the road rears up once again, this time more vigorously, passing a large blueberry farm, beyond which what little traffic there is all but dies away. As the trees give way to open fields, the road rises abruptly again, the last stretch close to 15% to reach the Col de Légrillou, from where a forest track cuts back to the east to Prat d'Albis, the route popular with off-roaders.

For roadies, the only way is straight ahead, the gradient immediately dropping to just two or three per cent as it heads into pine forest. For the next 20km, the road meanders without let up, mostly following the contours for the first half of that distance. Some locals avoid this road because it takes so long to make its way towards the Col de Péguère, its incessant twists and turns making it extremely hard to maintain a fast tempo. But I appreciate the way it forces you to slow your pace, to savour the tranquillity, the trees blocking out all distractions, deer as likely as cars to appear on the road ahead. Starting from the Légrillou, it's also a good road on which to ride with children, the gradient relatively benign leaving the col and ultimately helping them back to it once they start flagging.

The second half is a little more testing, but there's nothing to be too concerned about, at least not until the moment the road briefly emerges onto a ledge cut into a vertiginous rockface, delivering a startling view down the Barguillère valley at the same time. The Col d'Uscla is not too far beyond this nerve-jangling point, the road dropping to meet the main D17 up from Foix. Go left on the D17, which climbs gently past the Col de Jouels (an intersection with a logging road) to the Péguère. The route actually takes a right before this summit, but having come this high I'd recommend pressing on a couple of kilometres to the Péguère, where the view never disappoints if conditions are clear.

Those who do opt to enjoy the panorama should backtrack to the D15, which drops steeply through woodland to reach Sentenac de Sérou and into the upper reaches of the Arize valley. I love this stretch of road, which follows the river very gently downwards, giving the chance to let the legs spin and the chance for a bit more unhurried contemplation.

A couple of kilometres beyond Nescus, take the sharp right turn that climbs through woodland to meet the D21 and continues to rise towards Alzen. High up on the hillside to the right the Alzen waterfall can be seen through the trees, the road passing beneath it and then climbing past it to reach the hilltop village, from which it plunges very quickly into a heavily wooded ravine to reach Serres sur Arget and, just below it, the main D17 route back into Foix.

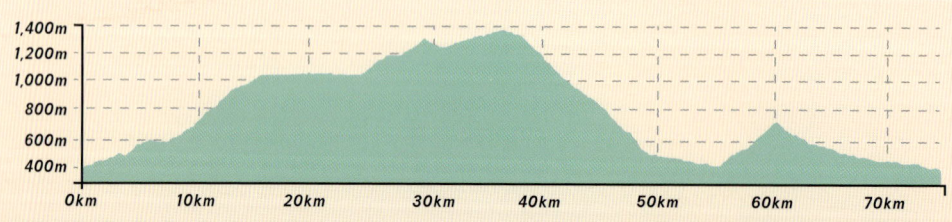

ARIÈGE

Panorama from the Col de Péguère and the top of the Mur

Distance: 74.8km
Elevation gain: 1,432m
Highest point: 1,375m
Est. moving time: 2.5-4.5hrs
Degree of difficulty: ●●◐
Climbs: Col de Légrillou (938m), Col d'Uscla (1,305m), Col de Péguère (1,375m), Alzen (650m)

Route in reverse

A quite different experience. I prefer riding up the Arize valley through Nescus, in the big ring all the way and often with the wind behind. The climb out of it is straightforward until the junction with the D51 above Sentenac, then it's a beast that demands good climbing legs. I'm not so keen on descending back to Foix via the Légrillou, as the road's in the trees and often damp and has debris on it. Don't rush it if you do come this way.

Parcours

0km	Foix D21
8km	Brassac D21/D111 ←
13.5km	Col de Légrillou ①
30km	Col d'Uscla ②
31.5km	D111/D17 ←
36.5km	Col de Péguère ③
38.5km	D17/D15 ←
55.5km	D15/D21 → ④
60.5km	Alzen ⑤
66km	Serres sur Arget D21/D17 ←
74.8km	Foix

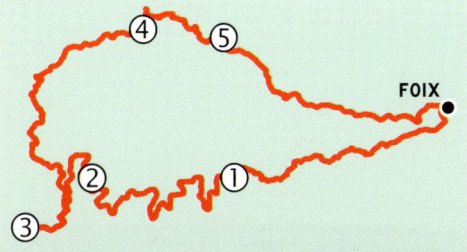

TOUR OF THE TROIS SEIGNEURS

Four of my favourite passes feature on this long and quite challenging loop from Tarascon that completes a full circle around the Pic des Trois Seigneurs, which is reputedly named after a meeting on its summit between the three seigneurs in the Massat, Rabat and Vicdessos valleys to discuss their administration of those remote districts. First up is the Port de Lers, the biggest climb of the quartet in terms of vertical gain in this clockwise direction. The approach to it is just about perfect, the D8 tracking the Vicdessos river on a long false flat that passes Niaux, with its huge caves and famous prehistoric paintings of animals, and rises for 14km to reach the large and attractive village of Vicdessos at the foot of the pass.

The climb begins right on the northern edge of the village, an immediate hairpin slinging traffic towards a kilometre of road at a little more than 10%. Even after the long warm-up from Tarascon, this comes as a bit of a shock, but beyond Suc et Sentenac a crest arrives that leads on to friendlier ramps where racing heart rates can be quelled. For some kilometres, the going through thick and, on hot days, pleasantly cool woodland is comparatively easy.

The Lers, however, doesn't give up its summit easily. It steepens again before two big hairpins and once more passing the waterfall dropping from the Étang d'Arbu on the southern side of the Trois Seigneurs. At the same time, though, the road emerges from the trees and the final run of bends up to the pass present spectacular views.

From the top, a favourite spot for paragliders, a 4km descent leads to the Étang de Lers and a small cross-country ski station and café. Circling the lake, the road climbs again for 3.5km to reach the Col d'Agnes. Although short, this section is extremely sweet in terms of the views, which are long and constantly changing. They continue, too, on the descent away from the Agnes, the peaks of the Montcalm massif running away into the distance towards Andorra. But don't let your eyes wander too long, as this section is steep until it reaches a series of hairpins that take the sting out of the gradient. Below these switchbacks, the road plunges again, determined to reach Aulus les Bains as rapidly as possible.

Leaving Aulus, the road keeps dropping, but more gently, heading down the Garbet valley towards Saint Girons. After 8km it reaches Ercé. Take the small right-hand turn to Cominac, a gentle 5km away. At the T-junction, go right on the D17 heading for the Col de Saraillé (see page 90). I always like this pretty route, which would be a short-cut between the Garbet and Arac valleys if it weren't for the fact that the constant twists and turns demand that you tackle it at quite a sedate pace.

It delivers you to the centre of Massat, a village that's got an equally laidback feel and is renowned for its counter-culture ethos. Turn right and head for the little square, passing a potable water pump on the right, then bear left, dropping past the large church and over the Arac on the first ramps of the Col de Port.

At close to 13km long, the climb is the longest all day, but because it averages less than five per cent and never reaches as much as seven at any point, it's one to be savoured, even though it comes at the end of a long day. It snakes incessantly. For those, like me, who prefer not to see too far ahead when climbing, the Col de Port is absolute bliss, and I'd also recommend it to anyone who has never ascended or descended a major

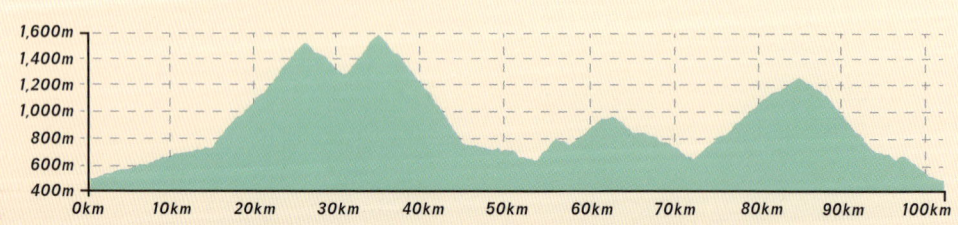

ARIÈGE

The western side of the Agnes pass overlooked by the Pic Rouge de Bassiès

mountain pass as an ideal starting point because there's nothing to fear going up or down.

Just before the summit, on the left, a tap dispenses potable water. The café at the pass provides much more, though, and from it you can contemplate the Monts d'Olmes peaks way over on the other side of the Ariège valley. The drop on this eastern side is steeper than the west, but not intimidating. It hurries down to Saurat, where there's a very short final climb out of a saddle, then on to Tarascon to conclude a fabulous, four-pass day.

Route in reverse

The principal difference is the difficulty of the south/western side of the Col d'Agnes, which averages eight per cent for 10km. Bearing in mind too that the Port is tackled via its tougher flank, and the route is more demanding (●●●●◐), but just as appealing.

Distance: 102.2km
Elevation gain: 2,541m
Highest point: 1,570m
Est. moving time: 4-7hrs
Degree of difficulty: ●●●●
Climbs: Port de Lers (1,517m), Col d'Agnes (1,570m), Col de Saraillé (942m), Col de Port (1,250m)

Parcours

0km	Tarascon sur Ariège N20
1km	N20/D8 ➡
14.5km	Vicdessos D8/D18 ➡ ①
26km	Port de Lers ②
30km	Étang de Lers D8/D8F ⬅
35km	Col d'Agnes ③
45km	Aulus les Bains D8F/D32 ⬆ ④
53.5km	Ercé D32/D132 ➡
58km	Cominac D132/D17 ➡ ⑤
62.5km	Col de Saraillé
71.5km	Massat D17/D618 ➡ ⑥
84.5km	Col de Port ⑦
101km	D618/N20 ⬆
102.2km	Tarascon

2017 TOUR STAGE – WITH AN EXTRA BIT!

This is a replica of the 2017 Tour de France's short stage between Saint Girons and Foix, with a tweak at the end in order to return to the start point, making it a little longer than the course the pros faced and a touch harder too. Head south-east from Saint Girons on the D618 to begin with, following the western bank of the Salat upstream for 14km to reach a roundabout, where you stay right on the D3, the Salat now on the right-hand side in a valley that's much wider than the initial stretch, the mountains looming but still quite distant.

Stay on the D3 towards Seix, the road rising ever so steadily, warming the legs nicely for the huge hurdles that lie ahead. Approaching Seix, the valley begins to narrow, but the D3 continues to arrow through this very fetching little town and beyond. Occasionally, the Salat's rushing increases in volume, signalling a change in gradient, but soon after it's burbling again as the incline drops back to a mere one or two per cent.

An eastward switch through Pont de la Taule appears to herald a change as the valley narrows, but the terrain opens out again in the Ustou valley, the road running towards Aulus les Bains through a series of pretty hamlets for another half dozen kilometres or so. The last of them is Sérac d'Ustou, and, just beyond it, a bright blue Col de Latrape sign finally signals a complete change in topography.

Less than half a dozen kilometres long, the Latrape is a good way to find your climbing legs. There are a few steeper ramps, one briefly touching 16%, but it's mostly in the 6-8% range, the road passing the turn to the Guzet Neige ski station as it works its way steadily towards the pass. The descent away from the col is almost a mirror image of the climb, but the last section is steep and will send you hurtling into Aulus les Bains.

Turn sharp right immediately after the bridge over the river, and a very different type of climb commences. After the sun-dappled and rather friendly Latrape, the western/southern side of the Col d'Agnes is more ferocious from the start, with 2.5km at more than 10%, and barely relents for the rest for 10km haul as it gains 800m in altitude.

For almost half its length, the Agnes is a tunnel of foliage, but coming into a series of hairpins, the vegetation gives way to rock faces that allow breath-taking views to provide a distraction from the hard grind, which does ease a little through these switchbacks. Above the bends, the road breaks out into rough pasture where Pyrenean cattle graze, their bells clanking. Finally, the climbing is far more bearable, until one final kilometre at 10% that reaches almost to the glorious crest of this magnificent pass, its name derived not from a notable woman but from a local word for a water course or torrent.

Dropping down the easier northern flank of the Agnes, the road quickly reaches the Étang de Lers. Go left here on the D18 and cruise down this beautifully wooded valley to reach Massat, the ideal mid-ride stop for refreshments. Bear right in the square onto the D618 to climb the first half-dozen snaking and never too demanding kilometres of the Col de Port to reach the Col des Caougnous, then fork left onto the formidable Mur de Péguère (see page 88). I've never met anyone who's professed to enjoying climbing this viciously steep and narrow road. Those struggling before it should consider the far easier option at Massat of following the D618 back to Saint Girons. Anyone who does venture onto it should hold tight to the fact

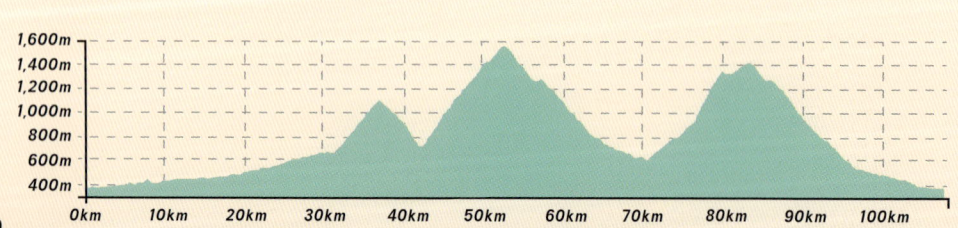

ARIÈGE

Mist in the valleys from the Col de Portel

that the longer it goes on the easier it gets, although that only becomes evident when its opening kilometre at 14% is behind you.

At the top of the Mur, rather than continuing straight on towards Foix, where Frenchman Warren Barguil clinched that Bastille Day stage in 2017 much to the delight of his compatriots, turn hard left for the brief ascent to the Col de Portel, where the 25km drop back to Saint Girons begins. The first section leads down to the Col de Crouzette. Go sharp right here and then, a couple of kilometres below, stay to the left heading for Saint Girons and a helter-skelter drop down a lane with often impressive views across to the Massif de l'Arize. This emerges onto the main road back into Saint Girons just 4km south of the town.

Route in reverse

It's not as severely challenging, though is still a taxing ride. There's much to be said for climbing to the Crouzette first, as this is one of the easier routes up onto the ridge of the Arize massif, especially as it means descending the Mur and coming at the Agnes from its friendlier flank.

Distance: 108.1km
Elevation gain: 2,656m
Highest point: 1,570m
Est. moving time: 4-7hrs
Degree of difficulty: ●●●●○
Climbs: Col de Latrape (1,517m), Col d'Agnes (1,570m), Col de Péguère (1,375m), Col de Portel (1,432m)

Parcours

0km	Saint Girons
14km	D618/D3 ➡
19km	Seix ①
24km	Pont de la Taule D3/D8F ⬅
37km	Col de Latrape ②
42.5km	Aulus les Bains D8F/D32 ➡
52.5km	Col d'Agnes ③
57.5km	Étang de Lers D8F/D18 ➡
70km	Massat D18/D618 ➡ ④
76.5km	D618/D17 ⬅
80km	Col de Péguère D17/D72 ⬅ ⑤
83.5km	Col de Portel
86.5km	Col de Crouzette ⑥ D72/D18B ➡
90km	D18B/D33 ⬅
104.5km	D33/D3 ➡
108.1km	Saint Girons

101

HIGH ROLLING ON THE CORNICHES

There aren't many roads in the Pyrenees that I would advise cyclists to avoid, but the N20 is certainly one of them. Living close to Foix, I drive on it very frequently and often see riders being passed at high speed and very closely by motorists.
In the upper Ariège valley, where there are few alternatives to it, the N20 can especially be difficult to avoid. But there are some fabulous and very quiet roads that can be used in order to steer clear of it and this route is designed to pick some of them out.

From the centre of Ax les Thermes, head north on the old N20 towards Tarascon and Foix for 1.5km to reach the right turn onto the D44 under a very low railway bridge. Be ready for an abrupt start to the day's climbing on the other side of it, the lane rising quickly away from the valley floor for a kilometre, then more gently to reach Vaychis, where a short descent leads on to Tignac. Climbing again, this lovely backroad reaches its steepest section, tracking through a long sweeping bend that presents extensive views along the busy valley, before reaching the junction with the Route des Corniches, the high-rise alternative to the N20 between Tarascon and Ax.

To shorten the route and avoid losing all of the height you've just gained, go right here towards the Col de Marmare. Otherwise, take a left on this road, the D20, contour around to Savenac and jag left in the direction of Luzenac on the D2. This road drops into Unac and then continues to Luzenac with its huge talc factory, the whitened roads testament to its proximity. Reaching a T-junction, turn right on the D55 towards the Château de Lordat, the road wiggling quickly up the mountainside to the village clustered next to the crumbling but spectacular Cathar fortress.

You're now back on the Route des Corniches. Head right to contour on the heights above Luzenac to reach Sevenac and, a couple of kilometres further on, the top of the day's first climb from Ax, continuing past it towards the Marmare pass. Rising quite gradually through thick forest for the 5km, the road reaches open terrain at the pass. Go left and the Plateau de Sault lies ahead, or right, as on this occasion, towards the Col du Chioula, little more than 2km away.

The route returns to the Ariège valley from the Chioula briskly on a wide and well-surfaced road, sweeping past the turn up to Ascou and the Port de Pailhères (see page 114) before the last few wiggling bends send you speeding into Ax, passing the marvellous Couloubret spa baths and continuing down the main street until the left turn to Ax Bonascre, or Ax 3 Domaines as the ski station has rebranded itself.

Zig-zagging sharply up the other side of the Ariège valley, this renowned Tour ascent looks right across to the Route des Corniches initially. Turning more into the mountain, the gradient eases for a kilometre or so, then rises quite severely and persistently. It was in this section that Chris Froome launched his winning attack in the 2013 Tour stage on this mountain, all but winning the race in the process. Battling up through the string of hairpins that follow, shallow corners connected by straights in double digit percentages, it's easy to understand why the Briton chose this point to attack. A little relief arrives above the hairpins, as the gradient eases for a kilometre before a final pitch that's up towards 10% again.

As ski resorts go, Ax is quite attractive, but I'd recommend the quick return to Ax and a post-ride pick-me-up at one of the cafés clustered in the square adjacent to the ski lift

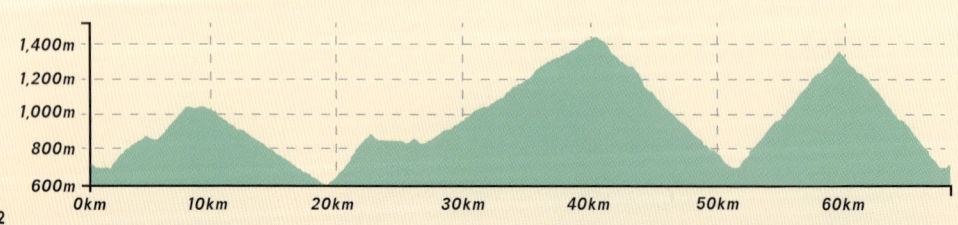

ARIÈGE

Mist in the valleys from the Col de Portel

that the longer it goes on the easier it gets, although that only becomes evident when its opening kilometre at 14% is behind you.

At the top of the Mur, rather than continuing straight on towards Foix, where Frenchman Warren Barguil clinched that Bastille Day stage in 2017 much to the delight of his compatriots, turn hard left for the brief ascent to the Col de Portel, where the 25km drop back to Saint Girons begins. The first section leads down to the Col de Crouzette. Go sharp right here and then, a couple of kilometres below, stay to the left heading for Saint Girons and a helter-skelter drop down a lane with often impressive views across to the Massif de l'Arize. This emerges onto the main road back into Saint Girons just 4km south of the town.

Route in reverse

It's not as severely challenging, though is still a taxing ride. There's much to be said for climbing to the Crouzette first, as this is one of the easier routes up onto the ridge of the Arize massif, especially as it means descending the Mur and coming at the Agnes from its friendlier flank.

Distance: 108.1km
Elevation gain: 2,656m
Highest point: 1,570m
Est. moving time: 4-7hrs
Degree of difficulty: ●●●●◐
Climbs: Col de Latrape (1,517m), Col d'Agnes (1,570m), Col de Péguère (1,375m), Col de Portel (1,432m)

Parcours

0km	Saint Girons
14km	D618/D3 →
19km	Seix ①
24km	Pont de la Taule D3/D8F ←
37km	Col de Latrape ②
42.5km	Aulus les Bains D8F/D32 →
52.5km	Col d'Agnes ③
57.5km	Étang de Lers D8F/D18 ←
70km	Massat D18/D618 → ④
76.5km	D618/D17 ←
80km	Col de Péguère D17/D72 ← ⑤
83.5km	Col de Portel
86.5km	Col de Crouzette ⑥ D72/D18B →
90km	D18B/D33 ←
104.5km	D33/D3 →
108.1km	Saint Girons

HIGH ROLLING ON THE CORNICHES

There aren't many roads in the Pyrenees that I would advise cyclists to avoid, but the N20 is certainly one of them. Living close to Foix, I drive on it very frequently and often see riders being passed at high speed and very closely by motorists. In the upper Ariège valley, where there are few alternatives to it, the N20 can especially be difficult to avoid. But there are some fabulous and very quiet roads that can be used in order to steer clear of it and this route is designed to pick some of them out.

From the centre of Ax les Thermes, head north on the old N20 towards Tarascon and Foix for 1.5km to reach the right turn onto the D44 under a very low railway bridge. Be ready for an abrupt start to the day's climbing on the other side of it, the lane rising quickly away from the valley floor for a kilometre, then more gently to reach Vaychis, where a short descent leads on to Tignac. Climbing again, this lovely backroad reaches its steepest section, tracking through a long sweeping bend that presents extensive views along the busy valley, before reaching the junction with the Route des Corniches, the high-rise alternative to the N20 between Tarascon and Ax.

To shorten the route and avoid losing all of the height you've just gained, go right here towards the Col de Marmare. Otherwise, take a left on this road, the D20, contour around to Savenac and jag left in the direction of Luzenac on the D2. This road drops into Unac and then continues to Luzenac with its huge talc factory, the whitened roads testament to its proximity. Reaching a T-junction, turn right on the D55 towards the Château de Lordat, the road wiggling quickly up the mountainside to the village clustered next to the crumbling but spectacular Cathar fortress.

You're now back on the Route des Corniches. Head right to contour on the heights above Luzenac to reach Sevenac and, a couple of kilometres further on, the top of the day's first climb from Ax, continuing past it towards the Marmare pass. Rising quite gradually through thick forest for the 5km, the road reaches open terrain at the pass. Go left and the Plateau de Sault lies ahead, or right, as on this occasion, towards the Col du Chioula, little more than 2km away.

The route returns to the Ariège valley from the Chioula briskly on a wide and well-surfaced road, sweeping past the turn up to Ascou and the Port de Pailhères (see page 114) before the last few wiggling bends send you speeding into Ax, passing the marvellous Couloubret spa baths and continuing down the main street until the left turn to Ax Bonascre, or Ax 3 Domaines as the ski station has rebranded itself.

Zig-zagging sharply up the other side of the Ariège valley, this renowned Tour ascent looks right across to the Route des Corniches initially. Turning more into the mountain, the gradient eases for a kilometre or so, then rises quite severely and persistently. It was in this section that Chris Froome launched his winning attack in the 2013 Tour stage on this mountain, all but winning the race in the process. Battling up through the string of hairpins that follow, shallow corners connected by straights in double digit percentages, it's easy to understand why the Briton chose this point to attack. A little relief arrives above the hairpins, as the gradient eases for a kilometre before a final pitch that's up towards 10% again.

As ski resorts go, Ax is quite attractive, but I'd recommend the quick return to Ax and a post-ride pick-me-up at one of the cafés clustered in the square adjacent to the ski lift

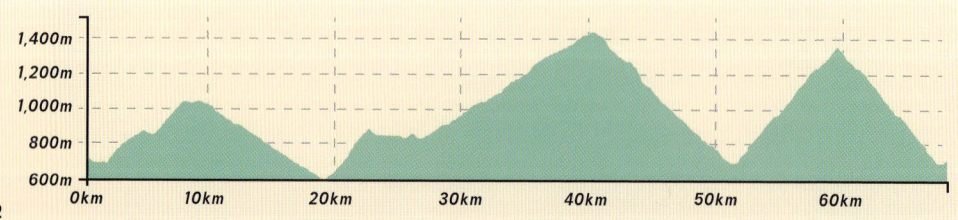

ARIÈGE

Looking over Lordat and Luzenac and along the Route des Corniches

station. Better still, for the perfect finale to a super ride, book in at the Couloubret baths and relieve tired muscles in the Jacuzzis, water jets and steam rooms.

Route in reverse

While I wouldn't advise climbing to Ax 3 Domaines right from the off, riding up to the Chioula and then following the Route des Corniches from the Marmare is just as good a way to start this ride. Take care on the narrow descents, though.

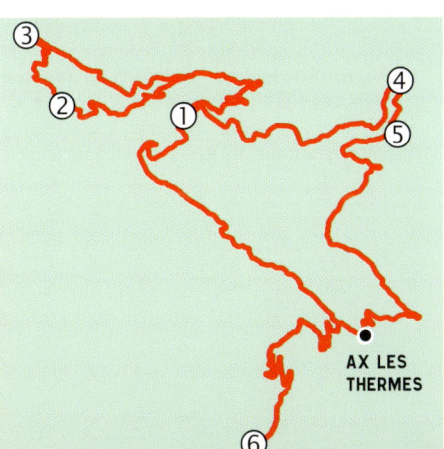

Distance: 68.4km
Elevation gain: 2,081m
Highest point: 1,431m
Est. moving time: 2.5-4.5hrs
Degree of difficulty: ●●●◐
Climbs: Lordat (909m), Col de Marmare (1,361m), Col du Chioula (1,431m), Ax 3 Domaines (1,380m)

Parcours

0km	Ax les Thermes
1.5km	N20/D44 ➡
9km	D44/D20 ⬅ ①
13.5km	D20/D2 ⬅
18.5km	Luzenac D2/D55 ➡ ②
22.5km	Lordat D55/D20 ➡ ③
38.5km	Col de Marmare ④
	D20/D613 ➡
40km	Col du Chioula ⑤
51km	Ax les Thermes
	N20/D82 ⬅
59km	Ax 3 Domaines ⑥
68.4km	Ax les Thermes

TWO MAGICAL DEAD-ENDS

I've tried to avoid including too many out-and-back routes, partly to avoid covering the same section of road twice, but also because circular routes have no set start or end, but numerous possibilities for both, depending on how you want or are able to access them. There are, given the nature of mountain roads, exceptions to that rule, though, and this is one of them.

It has twin peaks, the ski station at Goulier Neige above Vicdessos and the lake above the Soulcem dam, which sits in an awe-inspiring setting. I've put them together because they combine for a magnificent 80km ride, but they can be tackled individually from Tarascon, or even from Vicdessos, and neither will disappoint on its own.

I suspect that most considering these routes will already have ridden over the Port de Lers (see page 98) and will be familiar with the D8 road from Tarascon to Vicdessos and its qualities when it comes to warming up. Rising almost imperceptibly for 14km, it reaches the bridge that sweeps over the Vicdessos river into the village. Yet, rather than taking this well-trodden route, stay left towards Olbier and Sem, passing the blue sign indicating whether the road to Goulier Neige is open or not.

As it's a ski station, it remains open most of the time, although it's north-facing and I wouldn't fancy tackling it on a winter day when the road barely emerges from the immense shadow cast by the Pique d'Endron, its summit a thousand metres above the resort. The road ascends briskly through more than a dozen hairpins to reach the edge of the attractive village of Goulier, before looping up and around it, descending very briefly, and climbing again for the last 4km to the resort, which is now clearly visible.

By some quirk in the landscape – or more likely it's my perception – it still seems a long way off, but arrives sooner than expected. That's not the only surprise either, because as a resort it makes Plateau de Beille's cluster of low buildings seem like Saint Moritz. Established as recently as 1988, it has just 5km of runs and focuses on encouraging families with small children to ski. I remember being staggered by its scale when I first rode up to watch the Ronde de l'Isard under-23 race finish here in 2018.

One of its beauties is the descent, when the wonderful views across to the Pic des Trois Seigneurs and down onto the road rising to the Port de Lers. Further down, the 12th-century castle of Montréal de Sos stands out on a large outcrop towering above Vicdessos and neighbouring Auzat. On a clear day, it's magical.

At the bottom of the descent, cross the river into Vicdessos and follow the signs directly through the village for Auzat, once renowned as a centre for aluminium production but reinventing itself as a sports training and outdoor centre since the factory closed in 2003. With a large hydroelectricity generating plant on its southern edge, it still has an incongruous look in this mountain wonderland, but that blemish is soon forgotten.

This may be a climb, but the mountains in the Montcalm massif are so high, reaching 3,145m on the Pique d'Estats, which lies on the border with Spain, that this is essentially a valley ride, and one of the most impressive in the Pyrenees. The going is straightforward passing through the hamlets of Marc and Carafa, with downs in between the ups. Above Carafa, though, the road runs into a cliff and bounces back off it into a very steep series of bends at the start of a 3km section averaging close to 11 per cent, with pitches

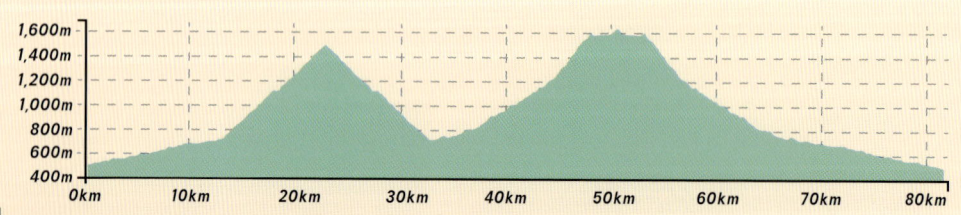

ARIÈGE

The Montcalm massif from the road towards Soulcem

twice that angle to reach the top of the Soulcem dam.

This, though, is where it becomes absolutely jaw-dropping, the road levelling as the valley widens, the deep blue waters of the Étang de Soulcem shimmering beneath huge peaks in this little tongue of France that sticks into Spain to the west and Andorra to the east – remarkably, Arcalís is only a dozen kilometres away as the crow flies and can be reached via the Port de Rat, a gravel road continuing beyond the reservoir. There's no way out, though, on road tyres, so there's no alternative but to turn back for what is essentially 30-odd kilometres of immensely enjoyable descent back to Tarascon.

Route in reverse

While Goulier Neige is a nice ride on its own, it's sure to be an anti-climax if tackled after the ride up to Soulcem, which is undoubtedly the highlight. If you've only got time for one leg of this two-pronged ride, I'd recommend riding to Soulcem first.

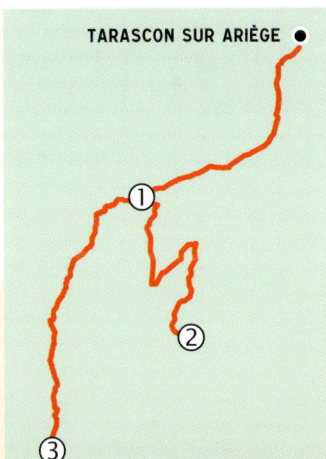

Distance: 81.7km
Elevation gain: 2,163m
Highest point: 1,636m
Est. moving time: 4-6hrs
Degree of difficulty: ●●●
Climbs: Goulier Neige (1,482m), Barrage de Soulcem (1,636m)

Parcours

0km	Tarascon sur Ariège D8
13km	Vicdessos D8/ D208 ←①
23km	Goulier Neige ②
33km	Vicdessos D208/D8 ←①
34.5km	Auzat
50.5km	Étang de Soulcem ③
66.5km	Auzat
69km	Vicdessos
81.7km	Tarascon sur Ariège

EXPLORING THE COUSERANS

Centred on Saint Girons and the neighbouring town of Saint Lizier, the Couserans comprises the western part of the Ariège. Heavily forested and one of France's least populated areas, it has a reputation for a counter-culture ethos, attracting hippies and others who want to enjoy an alternative lifestyle, to live off the grid. For cyclists, it's also a place to get off the beaten track and explore small roads and lanes, to climb little-known cols, and usually in complete tranquillity.

This route delves into that unknown, but also highlights arguably the Couserans' most renowned pass, the Col de Portet d'Aspet, the only east-west route in the mountains between the departments of Ariège and Haute Garonne. Commencing in Saint Girons, it strikes out westwards on the D618 through fertile agricultural land. Although one of the main routes into the southern Couserans, it's not overly busy, and becomes even less so once the D618 turns due west into the idyllic Bellongue valley on the southern side of the eponymously named massif.

The road bobs and weaves through a string of pretty villages, steadily gaining altitude but almost indiscernibly until it reaches Saint Lary and ramps up more vigorously towards the Portet d'Aspet. This is by far the easier side of the pass. There are sections at 10 and 11%, but just as many at two and three, and it doesn't seem too long before you're rounding the hairpins towards the top and standing on the pedals to get up the final steep section to the summit.

The western side is very different. It's consistently steep, sometimes radically so. Hidden beneath the tree canopy, the road surface is often damp in places even on dry days. It's a descent that wants you to rush but requires prudence.

Approaching the bottom, the striking white marble of the Fabio Casartelli memorial is a poignant place to pause. Racing in the 1995 Tour, the young Italian, who was the reigning Olympic road champion, crashed just below this point after a touch of wheels sent several riders crashing to the tarmac. Tragically, Casartelli struck one of the stone barriers on the edge of the road and died at the scene. Local clubs pay tribute to his memory every September with a sportive that runs past this beautiful sculpture.

Stay on the D618 as it sweeps right off the Portet d'Aspet. When this road switches left towards the Col des Ares, keep straight on towards Aspet on the D5. From the centre of the village, take the D34 in the direction of Arbas and the Col de Larrieu, a 6km climb that begins with a descent. It continues in this rather schizophrenic manner, rising gently, rearing up severely, then climbing more sedately again, before another short descent that leads into a kilometre at 10%. This runs up to the Col de Louzet and into an almost flat section up to the Larrieu with views across the low foothills to the plains to the north.

The descent is almost as erratic, the gradient changing regularly, but it is at least all downhill to Barat. There are also long views to the south over the Bellongue range towards the Mont Valier massif. One of the beauties of riding in hills like these is the longer-range perspective they provide on the high mountains, often snow-capped, rippling away into the distance.

In Barat, go left for 4km to reach Castelbiague and from there right for another five to Saleich, forking right in the village centre onto the D60H, which becomes the D133 and drops down to run parallel with main D117 route between Tarbes and Perpignan. Continue on to Prat Bonrepaux,

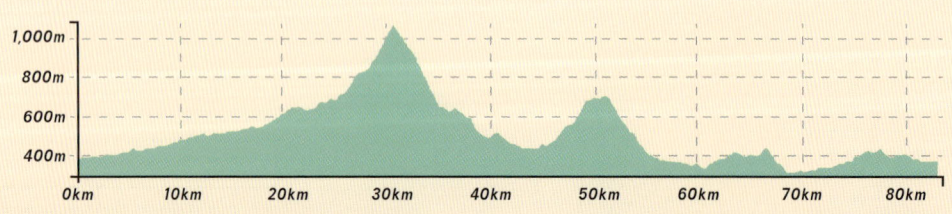

ARIÈGE

The Casartelli memorial on the Portet d'Aspet

where a right turn towards Cazavet and Montgauch returns to peaceful back roads cutting through low hills and farmland for 11km to meet the D117 again on the edge of Saint Girons with almost 1,500m of vertical gain clocked up but in one of the least taxing of ways.

Route in reverse
Essentially the choice of direction comes down to which face of the Portet d'Aspet you fancy, the kind one or the fierce one. I know which I prefer, but the steep side is an excellent judge of fitness.

Distance: 83.6km
Elevation gain: 1,480m
Highest point: 1,069m
Est. moving time: 3.5-5hrs
Degree of difficulty: ●●
Climbs: Col de Portet d'Aspet (1,069m), Col de Larrieu (704m)

Parcours

0km	Saint Girons
12km	D618/D4 ➡ ①
30.5km	Col de Portet d'Aspet ②
40.5km	D618/D5 ➡
45km	Aspet D5/D34 ➡ ③
51km	Col de Larrieu ④
55.5km	Barat D34/D13 ⬅
60km	Castelbiague D13/D60 ➡ ⑤
65km	Saleich D60/D60H ⬆ becoming D133
70.5km	Prat Bonrepaux ⑥ D133/D33A ➡
83.6km	Saint Girons

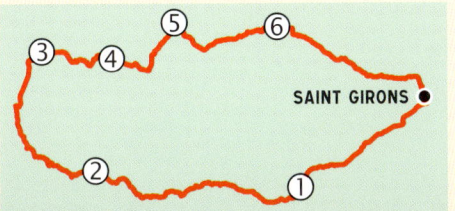

LOST IN THE COUSERANS

The Col de la Core is one of my favourite climbs (see page 90), and this route features the ascent of its western flank followed by two that are far less renowned in the tree-covered hills between its summit and Saint Girons, where the ride begins. It starts to the south-west on the D618, relatively quiet for a main road that runs at a very shallow rise almost all of the way to Castillon en Couserans, branching right just before the village, to which you should continue on the D4.

Two kilometres beyond Castillon, the same road reaches Les Bordes sur Lez, where the climb towards the Col de la Core begins. It's 13.5km long, its opening half quite straightforward in terms of the gradient. I don't usually gauge a climb's difficulty based on the read-out on a computer but on how much time I spend checking out of the view and how much is spent staring fixedly at a point in the road just a few metres ahead, often wishing I was somewhere else. On this basis, the Core can't be too hard because I have very strong memories of the staggering views up to the snowy peaks in the Mont Valier range.

The slope gets more acute after cutting across a bridge 8km up from the Les Bordes, the road passing the entrance to a car park for nearby Lac de Bethmale. But, sweeping around a long right-hand bend, you'll soon put this increase in gradient to the back of your mind as the road emerges beneath a towering mountainside that fills the view ahead. In the spring, snow still covers most of it and it's easy to imagine avalanches barrelling down onto the road in the winter months.

High up at ten o'clock is the summit of the pass. As the road tracks across the top of the valley towards it, there's a majestic view back down towards Les Bordes and Castillon. The gradient picks up a tad more on this section and all the way to the top, but ascending on the other side of the Bethmale valley the views to the square-topped Mont Valier and the peaks nestled around it are so captivating that the effort expended is amply compensated.

From the summit, the panorama is breathtaking, especially in late spring and early summer before the trees are in full leaf. The descent, slightly steeper than the climb, is often one photo stop after another at that time of year, as more peaks appear to the east and the full immensity of Mont Valier can be seen.

At Sentenac d'Oust, take the sharp left turn onto the D37 towards Alos. This narrow lane heralds a change in scenery, from a full-on mountain aspect to something far more agricultural, the road weaving past farms, dropping for half a kilometre or so, then switching back and forth on quite steep inclines for 2km to reach the Col de Catchaudégué. Its viewpoint is almost 360 degrees and quite wonderful.

The road turns north and drops into Alos via open mountainside and occasional woodland stretches, holding its course until right above the village. Follow the signs for Saint Girons, and, at the junction on the hairpin bend below Alos, make sure to sweep around the switchback to track beneath the village and arrive at a T-junction, where there are two routes home. Head straight on to descend almost directly back to Saint Girons on the D37. Alternatively, go left over the bridge onto the D137 to climb another col, the Portech – or Portet on Michelin maps.

The two roads run either side of the Montagne de Sourroque, its high point the 1,252m Sengouagnet. Even tighter than the last one, this road is typical of the more out-

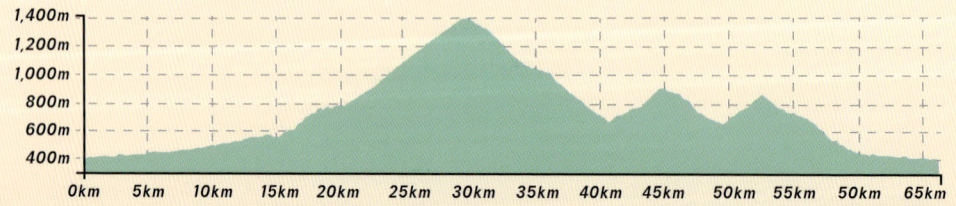

ARIÈGE

Looking across the Col de la Core towards Mont Valier

of-the-way parts of the Couserans. You half expect to find grass growing in the middle of it as it snakes up through thick woods. Nearer the top, which it reaches with a fabulous sweeping bend, its complexion changes. It opens out, bracken replacing trees, giving it a quite British look. The descent is, quite untypically of the Couserans, very open too. It's one of those that, when you get to the bottom, you've got half a mind to climb again so that you can enjoy it a second time.

Towards the bottom, switch right over the river to stay with the D137 into Moulis, where you rejoin the D618 for the final handful of kilometres back to Saint Girons.

Distance: 66.3km
Elevation gain: 1,585m
Highest point: 1,395m
Est. moving time: 2.5-4hrs
Degree of difficulty: ●●◖
Climbs: Col de la Core (1,395m), Col de Catchaudégué (893m), Col de Portech (862m)

Route in reverse

It's just as good a ride. The eastern side of the Col de la Core is the toughest, but thanks to the landscape and views this climb is one of my favourites and I don't hesitate to recommend it.

Parcours

0km	Saint Girons D618
12km	D618/D4 ↑
15.5km	Les Bordes sur Lez D4/D17 ← ①
29.5km	Col de la Core ②
40.5km	Sentenac d'Oust D17/D37 ← ③
45km	Col de Catchaudégué ④
49.5km	D37/D137 ←
52.5km	Col de Portech ⑤
61km	Moulis D137/D618 →
66.3km	Saint Girons

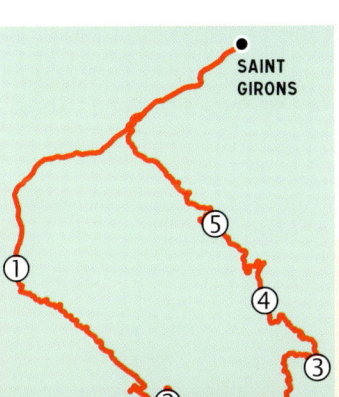

IN THE WHEELTRACKS OF ROBERT MILLAR

As a British fan who came to the sport in the early 1980s, one of my early favourites was climber Robert Millar, who transitioned to Philippa York following her racing career. This ride is a little tribute to her, featuring the attractive Ariège ski station of Guzet Neige, the scene of two of the Scot's most memorable performances. All three of her Tour de France stage wins came in the Pyrenees, the second of them at Guzet in 1984, the year she won the King of the Mountains jersey.

When the Tour returned in 1988, Millar was again at the front, duelling with Frenchman Philippe Bouvatier and Italian Massimo Ghirotto. When Bouvatier accelerated with 300m to the summit, the Scot chased after him, only to follow the Frenchman down the pre-finish diversion used by race vehicles, leaving the flagging Ghirotto to claim the most unexpected of victories as a result of the pair's error.

This ride covers a significant portion of that 1988 stage, reaching Guzet Neige having climbed the Col d'Agnes from Massat and the Latrape from Aulus les Bains. Prior to that section, the ride begins in Seix, not because there's any connection with York but simply as a consequence of my fondness for this very striking village set on the banks of the Salat and tucked in at the foot of the road to the Col de la Core.

Striking out downstream, take the D3 northwards towards Oust, the gentle loss of gradient offering an ideal opportunity to get the legs warmed up well before the majority of the climbing in the second half of the ride. Stay on the D3 beyond Oust and until the junction with the D618. Swing right here, the road climbing towards Biert at much the same easy rate as it's dropped from Oust. As mentioned on page 90, I've got mixed feelings about this road, dreading it in the car, principally because of the sickening effect its constantly weaving course has on any passengers, but always relishing it on the bike, when those bends deliver me into a kind of hypnotic state.

Beyond Biert and the final stamp up into Massat, take the right turn out of the top end of this village's compact square onto the D18 towards the Étang de Lers. After some early meandering, the road begins to climb beyond Le Port, but rather kindly to start with, passing turns to hamlets perched high above, each peeking out towards the sun on the tree-covered mountainside on the western flank of the Pic des Trois Seigneurs. Climbing a touch more steeply, the road begins to rise out of the narrow valley, arriving in the dip between the Agnes and Lers passes after a series of hairpins often frequented by cattle and horses.

Another right turn leads past the Étang de Lers café/cross-country ski station and drops to graze the western side of the small lake that gives this establishment its name, before rising again for the final three kilometres to the Col d'Agnes (see page 98). When it's clear, the views are magnificent on this glorious section of road, which reaches the ride's highest point. The descent away from it is fast and often technical, but exhilarating for those who love a sweeping hairpin.

Aulus les Bains arrives quickly. In the centre, switch left over the river, taking the D8 towards the Col de Latrape. This is not a long climb from the eastern side, but it doesn't give up its summit easily. There are some consistently steep pitches in the two kilometres between the first and second hairpins, above which the gradient does relent quite significantly.

At the point the Latrape flattens out at the

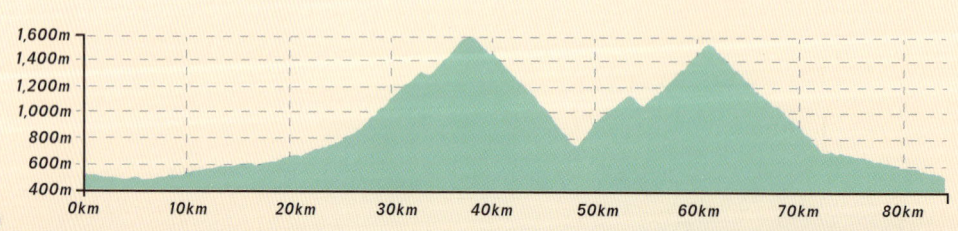

ARIÈGE

Chalets and surrounding peaks at Guzet Neige

top, Guzet Neige is nestled high up in the forest to the left, but the road to it begins 1.5km beyond. Barely 6km long, the climb to the resort is not unlike the first section of the Latrape, with frequent pitches well into double figures as it cuts through thick woodland. Every few hundred metres, the road emerges from this verdant passageway and presents long views to the west, which get more impressive as the road reaches Guzet's first chalets.

For those who like and are equipped for gravel, there's a fabulous ride beyond Guzet to the Col d'Escot and the Chalet de Beauregard. Otherwise, the return route to Seix is via the same road to the D8, heading left for a long, steady and equally enjoyable drop along the beautiful Ustou valley.

Route in reverse

The climbing is packed into the first half of the ride, which some riders may prefer. It's more taxing, too, in this direction, principally because the western approach to the Agnes is much tougher than the eastern. Once conquered, though, the road descends for most of the next 30-odd kilometres.

Distance: 84.3km
Elevation gain: 2,245m
Highest point: 1,570m
Est. moving time: 3.5-5.5hrs
Degree of difficulty: ●●●○
Climbs: Col d'Agnès (1,570m), Col de Latrape (1,111m), Guzet Neige (1,520m)

Parcours

0km	Seix
5.5km	D3/D618 → ①
20km	Massat D618/D18 →
33km	Étang de Lers D18/D8F → ②
37.5km	Col d'Agnès ③
48.5km	Aulus les Bains D8F/D32 ←
53.5km	Col de Latrape ④
54.5km	D8F/D68 ←
61km	Guzet Neige ⑤
67.5km	D88/D8F →
79.5km	D8F/D3 → ⑥
84.3km	Seix

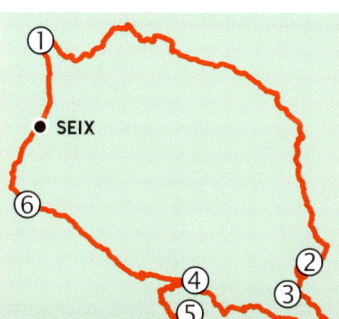

THE ARIÈGE'S WILD FRONTIER

I've purposely avoided out-and-back routes wherever possible because circuits provide more opportunities for start/finish points and, for the most part, don't cover the same sections of road. An exception has been made for this route, however, because the setting for it is so extraordinary, while it can also be linked in with several other rides within the Couserans.

The region is unique within the Pyrenees as being the only one where there isn't a border crossing into Spain, although there have been several plans to build one. In 1813, Napoleon Bonaparte passed a decree calling for the construction of a pass via the Port de Salau, which lies on the border between the two countries. That project met its Waterloo when the French emperor was defeated by Wellington two years later. Prior to the Second World War, the possibility of building a tunnel beneath the Port de Salau was raised, and has been several times since.

Yet, the Col de Pause and, more specifically, the Port d'Aula that sits on the border a few kilometres above it, have become the more likely routing for any new crossing. In 2008, local government members in the Couserans held meetings with counterparts in Spain's Vall del Noguera with a view to establishing a summer-only transfrontier link for light vehicles between the two areas in order to encourage more tourism. If ever built, which still seems unlikely, it would also open up new horizons for cyclists and, of course, bike races. The Aula lies at 2,260m, which would make it the highest road pass in the Pyrenees outside Andorra.

This ride starts in Seix because there are direct links from this exquisite little town to several other routes. Indeed it starts off following one that heads for the Col de Latrape (see page 100), tracking south on the D3. Interestingly, this is the Route d'Espagne, which perhaps hints at a once grand plan to extend it over the border.

It's a lovely stretch of road, which soon reaches Pont de la Taule, where the D8 branches off towards Ustou and the Latrape. The D3 ploughs straight on alongside the Salat, although considerably narrower than before, climbing all the while, but still quite gently. The wall that previously divided river from road disappears too, a humped strip of grass now the barrier. It's idyllic and might well leave you wondering whether opening up this valley to more traffic would be a good thing.

At Couflens, turn right over the river on the D703 heading for Faup. The gradient picks up, but stays at a comfortably manageable 7%. Coming up from the valley floor, the views are tremendous to Mont Rouch (2,858m) on the border to the south, as well as back down and across the Salat Valley. These become more difficult to take in, however, at Faup, where the road gets rougher and the gradient tougher, averaging 10% for the 5km to the col. The surface reminded me of the Col de Portet before it was remade in 2018, some sections of tarmac still intact, but standing proud of the gravel and with rubble around them, so that it's nearly impossible to maintain a straight line.

As on the Portet, there are sections in between the crumbling parts that are in good nick, and it comes as a relief to feel your tyres cruise almost soundlessly across these. Soon, though, these disappear to be replaced by hard-packed gravel for the rest of the climb. This surface is at least consistent and free of holes.

The finale has similarities with the Portet

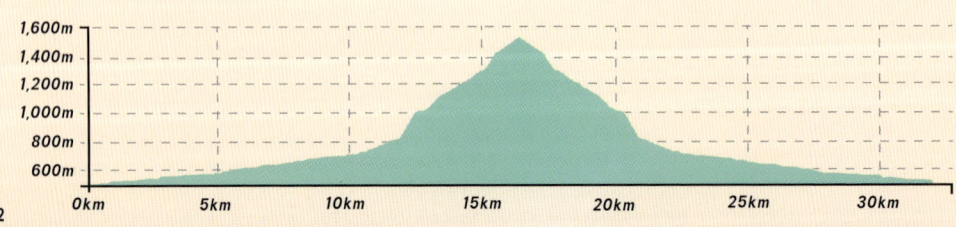

ARIÈGE

The view over Seix and up the Haut Salat valley

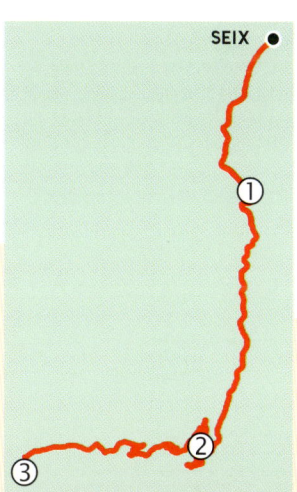

too, the road rising up the right-hand side of a steep valley before scrambling across to the left and making the final big leap to the summit via one final hairpin. It's been hard-earned, but is well worth it, the Pause providing a very seldom-seen perspective of the north side of Mont Valier and a sight of the border, still another 700 vertical metres upwards. In good weather, this is accessible with a gravel or mountain bike, but for those on skinnier tyres it's time to edge back down to Faup and then breeze to Seix, a very memorable escapade completed.

Distance: 35.4km
Elevation gain: 1,039m
Highest point: 1,527m
Est. moving time: 1.5-3hrs
Degree of difficulty: ●●◐
Climbs: Col de Pause (1,527m)

Parcours

0km	Seix
4.5km	D3/D8 ➜ ①
9.5km	Couflens D8/D703 ➜ ②
17.5km	Col de Pause ③
35.4km	Seix

TOUR DU CARLIT

There were two drivers behind this route that encircles the magnificent Pic du Carlit. The first was finding a way to include the N20 in the upper part of the Ariège valley, which I strongly advise should be tackled running downhill from the Col de Puymorens. The second was being passed by a young rider in world champion's kit while climbing the Port de Pailhères. A check later on Strava revealed that it was Britain's Tom Pidcock who'd shot by me as he trained for the 2019 World Road Championships. This is essentially Pidcock's route that day, although he did it in the opposite direction.

Starting from Ax les Thermes, the toughest climbing test of the day commences right away. At more than 18km, the Port de Pailhères is a long pull, and one that becomes gradually steeper, culminating in a 5km stretch up to the summit that averages very close to 10%. The approach to that section is straightforward enough, the road switching back and forth on the mountainside above Ax to escape from the Ariège valley, the grade easing passing through the tight main street in Ascou and then even more for a couple of kilometres beyond it as it runs beside the Goulours reservoir.

A change comes soon after passing the turn to the Col du Pradel, where there's a sudden shift into double figures. Although the slope does relent as the road forges up through the trees, the approach of the car parks at the small Alpine ski resort of Ascou-Pailhères heralds more sustained exertion, with the gradient fluctuating either side of 10% all the way to the summit. It's perhaps no harder than the final few kilometres on the eastern side, but seems more so because it's not as spectacular. Pretty much all you can focus on is the road ahead, until the buildings towards the summit start to emerge, signalling the end is near.

Thankfully, the Pailhères' summit is one that makes this gruelling ascent totally worthwhile. The views are extraordinary and remain so descending towards the little resort of Mijanès, initially through a wonderful series of hairpins. Crossing the river in the village of Mijanès, continue straight on towards Quérigut. Running through lush meadows, this road, the D25, merges with the D16, which soon reaches Quérigut and begins to climb again, cutting through glorious woods of poplar, beech, oak and pine to arrive at the main D118 towards Mont Louis.

This region of high-mountain plateau in Pyrénées Orientales that butts up against Ariège and Aude is the Capcir. Nicknamed "Little Siberia" thanks to its extremely harsh winter climate, it's an ideal place for riding thanks to a surprisingly extensive network of quiet roads with wonderful climbs. Ranging between 1,300-1,700m, it has something of a Wild West feel, with huge vistas across wide expanses of farmland towards high mountains. The road passes the turn to one of the Capcir's three ski stations, Puyvalador, which closed for a couple of seasons due to lack of funds but reopened in the winter of 2019, and then rolls onwards to another, Formiguères, the resorts recently connected by a bike path running alongside the D118.

The route arrows onwards, passing close to another ski station at Les Angles to reach Matemale and its lake. The gradient picks up a little here for a handful of kilometres to reach the Col de la Quillane, where the Capcir meets the Haut Conflent, a line of 3,000m peaks dominating the scene ahead. This high plateau landscape, and specifically Font Romeu, has become a very popular

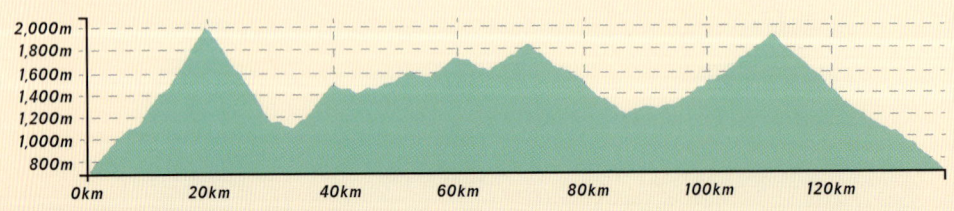

ARIÈGE

high-altitude training destination for elite athletes such as Pidcock, with former marathon star Paula Radcliffe and France's multiple world and Olympic biathlete champion Martin Fourcade among those who have also based themselves here.

Descending through La Llagonne to Mont Louis, the route turns westwards on the D618 towards Font Romeu, reaching it via the intimidatingly named Col du Calvaire, which is actually a bit of a doddle. The rather swanky resort is the ideal place to replenish yourself, not least for its views over the Cerdagne high plateau, which runs west towards Andorra and is one of the lesser-known gems of the Pyrenees, a vast corridor between towering peaks that's a European equivalent of Andean altiplano.

The very gentle 16km drop from the Calvaire to the foot of the Puymorens contines beyond Font Romeu. At Ur, where the D618 is swallowed up by the N20, the downhill coasting ends. A little further on, at Latour de Carol, the 19km yomp up the Puymorens begins. Although this section of the N20 can also be busy, the traffic isn't as heavy as the northern side because there are other, easier routes into Andorra from French and Spanish Catalonia. I find it more impressive, too, especially on the final half dozen kilometres when the tunnel carries off most of the vehicles and you're left with the old road to yourself up to the summit. That only leaves the 28km downhill return to Ax. I don't like it, but at least it passes quickly from this direction.

The western flank of the Puymorens into the Ariège valley

Distance: 137.2km
Elevation gain: 3,230m
Highest point: 2,001m
Est. moving time: 6-9hrs
Degree of difficulty: ●●●●●
Climbs: Port de Pailhères (2,001m), Col de la Quillane (1,713m), Col du Calvaire (1,836m) Col de Puymorens (1,915m)

Route in reverse

I'd advise against climbing up to the Puymorens from Ax because of the traffic issues I've underlined. I also wouldn't be keen on tackling the Pailhères right at the last because it's by far the toughest climb on this route. That said, its eastern flank is one of the great ascents in this chain and should be on everyone's to-do list, even if not today.

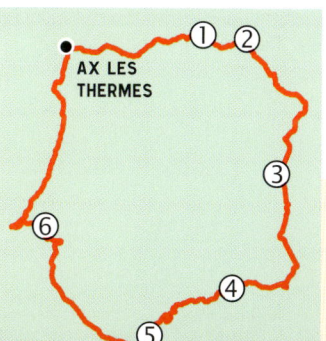

Parcours	
0km	Ax les Thermes D25
19.5km	Port de Pailhères ①
30km	Mijanès D25/D116 ➡ ①
33km	D25/D16 ➡
44km	D16/D118 ➡
49.5km	Formiguères ①
58km	Col de la Quillane
63.5km	D116/D618 ➡
69.5km	Col du Calvaire ①
71km	Font Romeu
85.5km	D618/N20 ➡ ①
109km	Col de Puymorens
137.2km	Ax les Thermes

THE HIGHEST PASS IN THE PYRENEES

There are a handful of roads in the Pyrenean range that I would counsel against cyclists using, the N20 that runs up the Ariège valley and almost all of the way to Andorra being one of them. Lower down the valley, between Foix and Ax les Thermes, it is possible to avoid this often busy and far from bike-friendly route for the most part. Above Ax, however, the N20 is the only route south to the ski resorts and duty-free shops of Andorra, which frequently attract an almost constant flow of vehicles at weekends and holidays – I've seen queues up to 20km long running back from the border crossing. Tight and twisting in many places, it won't be much of a pleasure climbing it when it's that busy.

This is a shame because the Col de Puymorens is hugely impressive. Not far short of 2,000m high, it is a stunning pass that is also, thanks to the road tunnel that bores through the mountain beneath it, comparatively free of traffic. It has a long Tour de France history, first appearing in 1913. I've included one epic circular route that includes it (see page 114) and much of the N20 as well, yet tackled as a descent rather than as a climb, but I much prefer this out-and-back option, starting in Andorra and featuring passage over the highest paved road in the Pyrenean range, the 2,408m Port d'Envalira.

This monumental pass also figures prominently in Tour legend, notably for the Andorra-Toulouse stage in the 1964 race when defending champion Jacques Anquetil was dropped by almost the whole field on the Envalira after overindulging on the rest day 24 hours earlier. The Frenchman managed to recoup his losses firstly with some recuperative swigs of champagne and then by descending like a loon through thick mist on the Envalira's long descent, his daring enabling him to catch up with his rivals and preserve his hopes of overall victory. That stage started in Andorra la Vella, the principality's capital city, which is a little further down the valley that essentially comprises this tiny country than my start point in Encamp. While this makes the ascent of the Envalira 4km shorter, it means you avoid the traffic that often clogs the valley bottom.

In terms of gradient, the Envalira is not especially difficult. There's not a single section that rises into double figures. But its 24km length and 2,408m finale ensure that it shouldn't be taken lightly. It's nice enough to begin with, easing up a narrow V-sided valley to Canillo and El Tarter, both part of the Grandvalira resort area. A couple of kilometres above El Tarter, the valley begins to widen, lofty peaks start to emerge up ahead. Approaching the slip road to the Envalira tunnel, which diverts much of the traffic away from the pass, you go above the 2,000m mark and the point

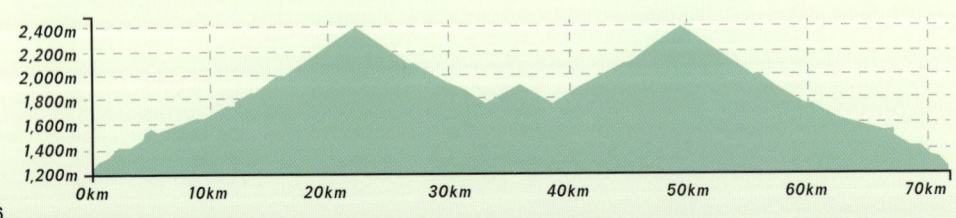

ANDORRA

The Envalira pass and karting circuit

where, aesthetically, the climb really begins. These final half-dozen kilometres are quite wonderful, sweeping switchbacks providing long views back down the valley and across the Grau Roig resort, which is being rapidly expanded and could become the site of the international airport that Andorra has long sought in order to improve connections beyond its mountainous borders. That would certainly blot what is, ski lifts apart, a beautifully pristine landscape.

The top of the pass is a let-down with three petrol stations highlighting one key reason why the French flock to its neighbouring country, but the panorama across to the peaks above the Puymorens more than compensates. Below, the ugly resort of Pas de la Casa appears, with its Lego brick car park and hosts of duty-free shops. Shoot through this and the border (you'll need to carry your passport or ID card as Andorra is not part of the EU) and down to the junction with the N320, turning right towards the Col de Puymorens.

Like the Envalira, it's the climb towards the pass that stands out rather than the summit, where dilapidated buildings and piles of gravel give it an air of a place that has lost its significance since the tunnel was bored beneath it. I prefer its southern approach from the other end of the tunnel entrance, but that's for another day (see page 115). Having crested the pass, make an about-turn towards Andorra and the climb back up to the Envalira, during which the messiness of Pas de la Casa can be truly appreciated and then put to one side as those panoramas fill your view again. On a perfectly surfaced road, the descent back to Encamp is one to be savoured too.

Distance: 71.8km
Elevation gain: 2,161m
Highest point: 2,408m
Est. moving time: 3.5-5.5 hrs
Degree of difficulty: ●●●
Climbs: Puerto de Envalira (2,408m), Col de Puymorens (1,915m)

Parcours

0km	Encamp CG2
22km	Port de Envalira ①
28km	Border crossing CG2/N22
33km	N22/N320 ➡ ②
36km	Col de Puymorens ③
39km	N320/N22 ⬅ ②
44km	Border crossing N22/CG2
50km	Port de Envalira ①
71.8km	Encamp

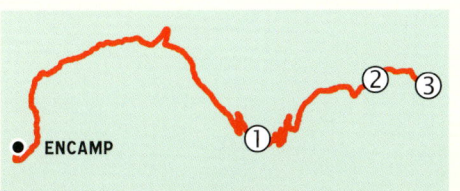

ANDORRAN FIGURE OF EIGHT

Few places divide opinion quite as broadly as Andorra. For some, the principality is an ugly jumble of tax-free shops and ski resorts defiling what would until quite recently have been a very pristine Pyrenean valley. For others, it's a wonderland of ski resorts, spas and shopping centres. I fall somewhere in between. When I first visited in 1985, Andorra was very much a duty-free attraction, pulling in hordes from France and Spain looking for a bargain. It was low rent and a little seedy. More than three decades on and now living nearby, I've become a regular visitor and have seen a considerable change. It's still a shopper's paradise, but it's been smartened up and there's increasing emphasis on other attractions, skiing most obviously, but also cycling, partly thanks to a recent influx of pro riders drawn by the benefits of high-altitude training and low taxation on income.

The Tour de France and Vuelta a España have also become regular visitors, and this ride recommended by my friend and regular riding buddy Keith focuses on three of those races' favourite climbs. It begins in the capital, Andorra la Vella, not "Old Andorra" as many assume based on the French mistranslation of Andorra La Vieille, but "Andorra the Town" to differentiate it from the country's name. Heading south alongside the rushing waters of the Gran Valira, use the slightly downhill run to Sant Julià de Lòria to get well warmed up.

At the main crossroads/roundabout in Sant Julià swing left towards the Juberri and the Naturlandia amusement park, climbing steeply for a kilometre to reach a fork. Bear right, once again heading towards Naturlandia and Juberri, the gradient easing as the road runs on a "balcony" above the main valley before turning into the mountains on the eastern side of the principality. A series of three hairpins leads into another tough section, this one more sustained with 3km at 9.5%. Across the valley, the road up to the Collada de la Gallina can be picked out, assuming you can divert your attention from the tarmac beyond your front wheel on this grind through Juberri, where it eases a couple of points entering pine forest.

Passing beneath Naturlandia's Tobotronc, the world's longest toboggan run, which drops 400m over 5.3km, the angle of attack falls a little more, the road climbing through a series of straights connected by widely spaced hairpins, staying in the pines until it's almost reached the resort of La Rabassa and the upper part of Naturlandia, where there's all manner of diversions for kids and a chance to finally take in a wonderful peak-filled panorama.

The descent begins with a 4km return down the same road to the right turn onto the CS131, this northern flank of La Rabassa very similar to the southern – the gradient not too severe high up, but becoming more so on the final approach to the main Andorra valley. The principal difference is that the forest isn't as dense, which makes it easier to see the views and, more importantly, the traffic ahead when negotiating the many hairpins on the drop through Aixirivall to Sant Julià.

At the foot of the climb, take the CG1 right from the roundabout, travelling north for 1,200m to go left on the CG6 towards Os de Civís, the road quickly leaving the bustle of the central valley behind as it climbs up a narrow ravine alongside the River Os to Bixessari. Cross the small bridge over the river here, following a sign to the Santuari de Canòlich. Already abrupt in parts, the gradient

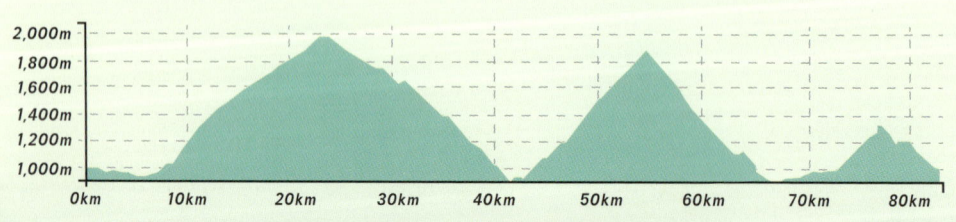

ANDORRA

becomes consistently vertiginous, averaging 9% for the next 8km to the Collada de la Gallina. It's quite unlike most ascents in the principality, less engineered, very quiet and beautiful despite the scarped incline. Above the Canòlich church, the gradient relents a touch and the views become increasingly expansive. The buzz from the valley starts to encroach too, but mercifully it remains hidden from view, even from the summit, from which the panorama is to the south into Spain.

The Gallina's southern flank is even steeper, averaging very close to 10% for its initial half dozen kilometres. Once again, it's narrow and caution should be exercised, especially if you want to take in the majestic views across the valley towards La Rabassa. The gradient does ease off a tad, and there's even a short and shallow climb towards the bottom, but this side is not only a tougher climb than the northern approach, but arguably harder than any other in Andorra.

Heading north from Sant Julià, return almost to the start point in Andorra la Vella, bearing right just before the capital on the CS101 towards La Comella. Only 4km long and averaging 8%, it runs high above the central valley, but is nicely cloaked from it for the most part by trees. The equidistant descent winds down to Escaldes for an easy roll back to Andorra la Vella.

Route in reverse

There is no right or wrong way to tackle what is essentially a figure of eight route. Riding in the opposite direction, the northern flank of Rabassa is more open with better views, but the descent's a little trickier, while the Gallina is a more severe test from Sant Julià, but the descent to the north is a touch easier.

The view down the Collada de la Gallina

Distance: 83.3km
Elevation gain: 2,840m
Highest point: 2,036m
Est. moving time: 3-5hrs
Degree of difficulty: ●●●●
Climbs: Alto de la Rabassa (2,036m), Collada de la Gallina (1,907m), Alto de la Comella (1,344m)

Parcours

0km	Andorra la Vella
6km	Sant Julià de Lòria CG1/Carretera de la Rabassa ←
7km	Carretera de la Rabassa → to Naturalandia ①
23.5km	La Rabassa ②
27.5km	Carretera de la Rabassa/CS131 →
41.5km	Sant Julià de Lòria → on CG1
42.5km	CG1/CG6 ← ③
46km	CG6/Santuari de Canòlich ←
54.5km	Collada de la Gallina ④
67.5km	Sant Julià de Lòria CS140/CG1 ←
73km	Andorra la Vella CG1/CS101 → ⑤
77.5km	Alto de la Comella ⑥
81km	Escaldes CS200/CG1 ←
83.3km	Andorra la Vella

ANDORRAN HIGH SPOTS AND GRAVEL

This route features two legendary Grand Tour finales made famous by two young tyros of the sport. The first is the ski station at Arcalís where 23-year-old Jan Ullrich decimated his rivals and captured the yellow jersey on his way to victory in the 1997 Tour de France. The second is the dirt road between Lake Engolasters and the road to Cortals d'Encamp, where 21-year-old Tadej Pogacar took the first of three stage wins in his 2019 debut in a three-week event. With the Coll d'Ordino as a weighty aperitif, this ride racks up almost 3,500m of vertical gain in little more than 100km.

Heading north-east from Andorra la Vella and through Escaldes, this route rises from the off. Approaching Canillo, turn left at the mini-roundabout just before the main built-up area, a sign pointing towards the Ordino. Cut into the cliff-face to begin with, then switching up through a series of heavily buttressed hairpins, it's an impressive piece of engineering, the relative ease of the gradient (a steady 6%) encouraging appreciation of what has become a Vuelta staple, although it's not appeared on Tour's *parcours* since Ullrich's leap to prominence. The view back down the climb is particularly striking, not only for the stunning perspective on Andorra's main valley, but also because you can see the extent of the terracing that was constructed to support and secure the road.

Further up, the road eases its way up a hanging valley to reach the Roc del Quer observation point, which merits a brief pause, and continues on to the summit, where there's a spectacular panorama towards Arcalís and the 3,000m-high peaks on the French border. Most of the height gained on the eastern flank of the Ordino is lost on the western side, which is just a little steeper and much more wooded as it drops into the town of Ordino. At the little roundabout where it meets the main CG3 road up from the valley, turn right in the direction of Vallnord Arcalís to start the 19km ascent to the resort.

It begins straightforwardly, the gradient rarely going north of 3% during the initial 7km. A change comes as the valley narrows approaching El Serrat. The gradient picks up significantly approaching this village, then even more passing through it. This was, incidentally, where Ullrich launched his winning attack, no doubt aware that this section is the steepest on the climb. The quality of the scenery picks up too, the road winding upwards between precipitous rock walls, the surrounds spectacular and quite pristine, bar a series of avalanche shelters that ensure the road can be kept open throughout the winter. Above these, a longish and unlit tunnel leads into the lower part of the Ordino Arcalís ski station and towards the climb's most renowned feature, a dozen hairpins piled one on the last that ascend well past the 2,000m mark.

Just beyond them is another distinctive feature of this mountain, Italian sculptor Mauro Staccioli's giant 'O', the sculpture designed to make those passing see the landscape in a different way. The road runs for another 1,500m to the upper part of the station, just a handful of discreet buildings encircled by a ring of peaks. Here it turns from tarmac to gravel, climbing to the Port de Rat, a now disused pass into the Ariège (see page 110).

The descent is a breeze, the highlight undoubtedly the drop down the hairpin ladder. At Ordino stay on the CG3 to La Massana and on into the main valley, passing through three tunnels just below this town – they're well lit but a rear light at the very least is

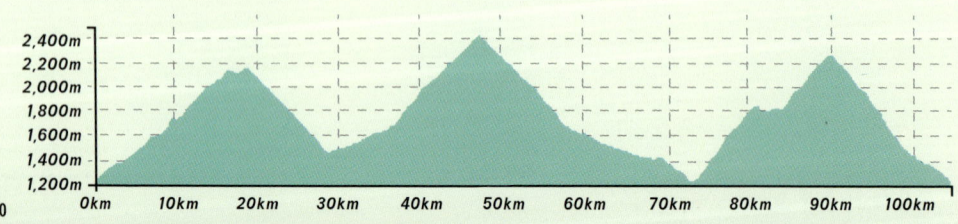

ANDORRA

highly advised. Coming into Escaldes, keep straight on with CG3 to the junction with the CG2, going left and uphill at the roundabout towards France for 500m to reach the right turn to Engolasters.

Relatively benign to begin with, the ascent lifts off above the first hairpin, with occasional ramps in double figures and an average of more than 9% for 3km as it rises through thick woodland. Coming out of the trees at Sant Miquel d'Engolasters, the gradient eases noticeably, then kicks up again to take the final step up to Lake Engolasters, a popular site for walkers and picnickers. Just beyond the car park close at the top, bear left on a road marked as a dead end but accessible to bikes. This narrow lane runs to the lake and onto a gravel path that featured memorably on a mucky day during the 2019 Vuelta. It rolls through pine trees along the water's edge, climbing a little to begin with to reach a restaurant, then following the contours just above 1,600m for another 3km.

The return to tarmac arrives close to the climb to Cortals d'Encamp, and in the midst of its steepest section – 5km at 9.5%! Three of them are below this junction, but two remain. Irish sculptor Michael Warren's standing stones sculpture Lloc Pagà (Pagan Place) signals the imminence of friendlier ramps leading up to the huge ski lift at the summit. The setting isn't as grand as the heights above Arcalís, but it does have a similar feeling of beautiful remoteness, of being away from the hubbub below.

The descent back to the valley is fast, particularly the steep second half of it into Encamp and the junction with the CG2. Go left here for six very easy kilometres back into Andorra la Vella.

Route in reverse

As with most circuits in Andorra, there are plenty of options when it comes to varying this route, particularly by including the climb of the Beixalis. However, climbing from the valley to La Massana via the three tunnels should be avoided. In this instance, ascending via the Beixalis is certainly a better choice.

The Ordino pass rising up from El Canillo

Distance: 104.8km
Elevation gain: 3,433m
Highest point: 2,241m
Est. moving time: 4-6.5hrs
Degree of difficulty: ●●●●●
Climbs: Coll d'Ordino (1,981m), Arcalís (2,241m), Lac d'Engolasters (1,639m), Cortals d'Encamp (2,068m)

Parcours

0km	Andorra la Vella
10km	Canillo CG2/CS240 ← ①
19km	Coll d'Ordino ②
29km	Ordino Carretera Coll d'Ordino/CG3 →
47km	Arcalís ③
65km	Ordino
67.5km	La Massana ④
73.5km	Escaldes CG3/CG2 ←
74km	CG2/CS200 →
81km	Lac d'Engolasters ⑤
83.5km	Carretera de les Pardines/CS220 →
90km	Cortals d'Encamp ⑥
98.5km	Encamp CS220/CG2 ←
104.8km	Andorra la Vella

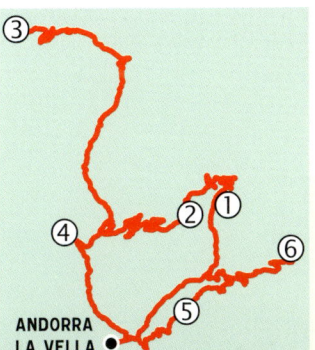

WESTERN ANDORRA HIGHS

I've been told a number of times that a decent rider need only spend a couple of days in Andorra to conquer most of the principality's significant ascents, which leaves me wondering whether I've drifted a long way from being in that class on the climbs or if those insisting on the need for only a 48-hour stay are missing out on some of this little country's highlights. I prefer to think the latter is the case, and put together this circuit with the aim of supporting that argument.

It starts and ends in Canillo at the foot of the Coll d'Ordino, initially heading downhill and away from this pass to Encamp for a much more severe examination. The Collada de Beixalis is a mere 6.6km long, but what it lacks in size it makes up for in gradient – it boasts the principality's highest average at 8.4% and steepest ramp at 16%. At the far end of Encamp, turn right towards Vila, tracking back along the other side of the river to another roundabout with a statue of a farm labourer in the middle, switching back hard left, again towards Vila.

It's not at all frightening to begin with, winding up between houses and fields of tobacco, one of Andorra's main crops. The road all but flattens out at one point, but this little landing is the launchpad for a 13% kilometre which includes the sharpest section, the hairpins zig-zagging up the mountainside directly above. It relents above these tightly stacked bends, although 1.5km at 10% is never easy. This section was only surfaced in 2015, and that work took some of the sting from the higher sections, where there are superb views across the valley towards the dirt road between Lake Engolasters and the climb up to Cortals d'Encamp before pine woods close off the views on the final section up to the summit.

The western flank of the Beixalis is nothing like as fierce, although there are some more abrupt segments when it comes out of the trees above Anyós as well as a smashing view up the Valira del Nord valley towards Arcalís. At the junction approaching the bottom of this valley, go left towards Anyós, continuing through it to meet the CG3 main road, heading right to La Massana, keeping straight through this busy resort town towards the ski stations of Arinsal and Pal on the CG4.

At Erts you can choose to fork left towards Pal and the very lofty Port de Cabús or branch right to Arinsal, a shorter and easier challenge, which is the initial choice on this route. Lined with hotels and apartments until the first hairpin adjacent to a tunnel, which only leads to more blocks of the same type on the other side of the ridge, the road becomes far more picturesque as it bobs back and forth up the mountainside. Towards the ski station, the valley tapers considerably, so that these buildings all but disappear from sight, leaving a view over the hairpins just conquered to mountains rippling away into the distance.

Retrace to Erts to begin the climb to the Port de Cabús via Pal, the most southerly of the Vallnord resort set-up that also includes Arcalís. At 14km, this is a much longer ascent than Arinsal. It's also less cluttered with skiing infrastructure as it climbs quite steadily to Pal. Above this village, the average is at least three points higher as it rises through pine forest. Nearing the Coll de la Botella, the road rises above the tree line, the section to the Port de Cabús easy to pick out on the other side of the bare mountainside as it horseshoes to the border with Spain. It's so wide and well surfaced that you can't avoid the feeling that there must be something substantial at the summit, and, of course, there is, but there's no resort or lifts, simply

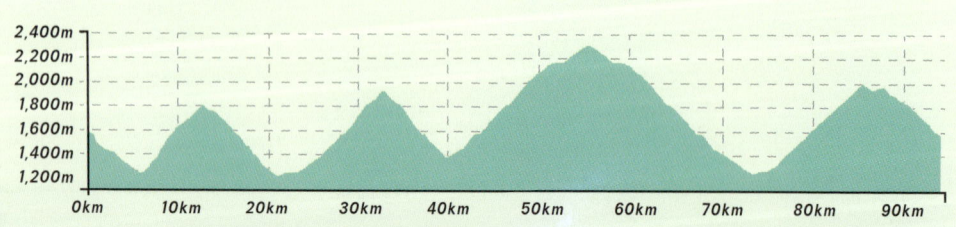

ANDORRA

a panorama that fully justifies the exertion required to ride above 2,300m, on one side sweeping across Andorra and on the other peeping into Spain.

Given the remoteness of the Vall Ferrera on the western side of the Cabús, it's very likely that the track leading away from the pass into Spain will remain rough and restricted to off-road bikes and to walkers. As a consequence, for riders on skinny tyres there's no choice but to descend back to Erts and La Massana, bearing left in the town centre towards Ordino, 3km away, and the day's final obstacle.

Turn right on the CS340 in the centre of Ordino towards Canillo, ascending from the off. At the start of a ride, the Coll d'Ordino's 10km at a touch under 7% wouldn't be too taxing, but with close to 3,000m already in the legs it's quite a haul, albeit with some fine views as a distraction until the pines thicken to envelop you in a corridor of greenery that runs all the way to the summit and the end of serious pedalling for the day. The descent to the finish is glorious, the road open and well surfaced, the scenery wonderful, the sense of achievement sky-high no matter what your level as a rider.

The Coll de la Botella

Distance: 94.2km
Elevation gain: 3,311m
Highest point: 2,328m
Est. moving time: 3.5-6.5hrs
Degree of difficulty: ●●●●○
Climbs: Collada de Beixalis (1,795m), Arinsal (1,905m), Port de Cabús (2,328m), Coll d'Ordino (1,981m)

Route in reverse

I'd be reluctant to start straight up the Ordino without a warm-up, but starting at a different point would make this more palatable, particularly if you'd prefer to tackle the easier side of the Beixalis given the overall difficulty of this ride.

Parcours

0km	Canillo
5.5km	Encamp CG2 ➡ to Vila
6.5km	⬅ to CS210
13km	Collada de Beixalis ①
21.5km	CS210/CG3 ➡
23km	La Massana CG3/CG4 ⬅ ②
25.5km	Erts CG4/CG5 ➡
33km	Arinsal ③
40km	Erts CG5/CG4 ➡
55.5km	Port de Cabús ④
73km	La Massana CG4/CG3 ⬅ ⑤
75.5km	Ordino CG3/CS340 ➡
85.5km	Coll d'Ordino
94.2km	Canillo

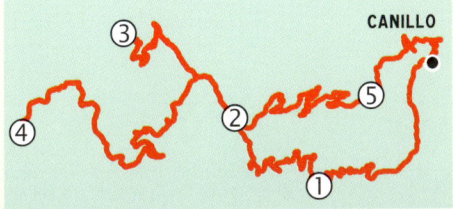

GORGEOUS LLEIDA

Coll de Nargó summons up memories of a huge plate of pasta that I once ploughed my way through on a ride over the Jou and Bóixols passes on a cold June day. The other thing that sticks in my mind about that ride were the beautiful climbs on perfectly surfaced roads that were almost free of traffic.

The Bóixols, to the west of Coll de Nargó, features on page 128, while this circuit heads into the spectacular Serra de Odèn for a rollercoaster ride that clocks up 2,800m of vertical gain. The only significant flat section comes at the start (and again at the very end) rolling out northwards from Coll de Nargó on the C14, one of the main routes between the Catalan coast and Andorra. This highway can be busy – further to the north as it winds constantly into La Seu d'Urgell it's a hazardous place to be on a bike – but acquaintance with it in this instance is brief, extending only as far as the right turn towards Cambrils after a couple of kilometres.

Within moments, the speeding traffic is forgotten as the road starts to ease upwards. The gradient is never severe, even when the valley narrows into a gorge approaching Alinyà. A series of five short and unlit tunnels lead through this photogenic section, with Alinyà just beyond the last of them. Above this village, the road rises out of the pine forest to an open section looking over huge rocky folds in the landscape, the gorge and tunnels visible way down on the other side of the valley. It only gets better after that, the views extending further on the easy run up to reach the Port del Comte.

From there, the road drops sedately past Llinars and Cambrils into the verdant Odèn valley, but doesn't lose too much height before it begins to rise again. Weaving beneath the Serra de Odèn, at one point it cuts through a rock buttress via another (unlit) tunnel and emerges onto a breath-taking balcony with an astonishingly long view to the south, very similar to the one between the Soulor and Aubisque in the French Pyrenees.

The road rolls on, losing a little altitude, regaining it, and consistently wonderful. Just when it seems it couldn't get any better, you swing around a corner to start the final push up to the Coll de Jou to face the magnificent escarpment of the southern edge of the Serra de Querol, its sheer rock-face tinged with different shades of red, white and grey. Winding onwards for another 3km, it reaches the Jou pass, where a right turn leads into a longer descent towards Solsona, that is once you've had the almost obligatory stop at the *mirador* just below the summit to marvel at the canyons below.

This is the kind of descent that encourages every cyclist to let rip. The road is wide, the straights long, the bends not too tight, and the surface very good. It's not technical or steep, and each quicker section is followed by a shallower one or, in the first case, a short climb. After 15km, bear right towards Lladurs, the road flattening out across farmland to arrive at a T-junction on the LV4011. Go right, the road undulating but mainly down through pine forest for 8km to reach Pont del Clop, where the Salada river cascades through a strait in the rock to create deep pools that are

The statue on the Serra Seca marking the Tour's passage

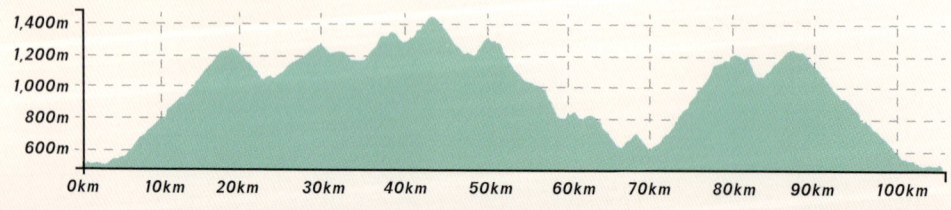

LLEIDA

popular with bathers in summer, the derelict hostel next to the bridge suggesting it was once much more of a draw.

In 2009, Pont del Clop had huge sporting significance as the start point of the first-category climb to the Coll de Serra Seca on that year's Tour de France stage from Barcelona to Andorra. That rating seems misplaced to begin with, the gradient comfortable as the road breezes upwards through pine woods. But, when the terrain opens up, there are long sections well into double figures, carrying the road past the church at Montpol. This pattern is repeated, pines signalling an easing in the incline for 2km, before another couple that are far ruder including 500m at 14% that reaches the plateau where the Serra Seca sits, a sculpture of a cyclist on the roadside just below its spectacular observation point a short walk up the hillside.

Entering a rocky and very open landscape, the road steps up along a ridge, a stunning view across the Coll de Jou and the escarpment close to it emerging before it tumbles down into Cambrils. Here, a left turn leads up the short southern side of the Port del Comte and into the glorious descent past Llinars and Alinyà, the road slaloming exhilaratingly all the way down to the Segre reservoir and the return to Coll de Nargó.

Route in reverse

There's nothing that particularly sets one direction over the other. In fact, it's well worth riding both options as they offer a different perspective on some extraordinary landscapes.

Stunning geological formations near Coll de Nargó

Distance: 106km
Elevation gain: 2,778m
Highest point: 1,480m
Est. moving time: 4-6hrs
Degree of difficulty: ●●●○
Climbs: Port del Comte (1,249m), Coll de Jou (1,480m), Coll de Serra Seca (1,230m)

Recorrido

0km	Coll de Nargó
2.5km	C14/L401 ➡
19km	Port del Comte ①
43km	Coll de Jou L401/LV4241 ➡ ②
58.5km	LV4241/unclassified to Lladurs ➡ ③
61.5km	unclassified/LV4011 ➡
78km	Coll de Serra Seca
84km	Cambrils LV4011/L401 ⬅
87km	Port del Comte ④
103.5km	L401/C14 ⬅
106km	Coll de Nargó

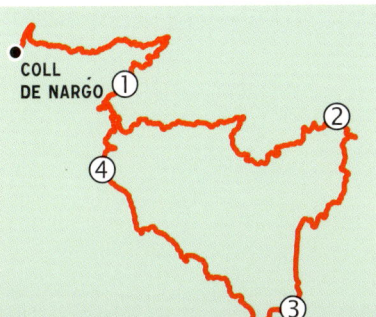

SOUTH FROM LA SEU D'URGELL

With its Olympic canoeing complex and mountains on all sides, La Seu d'Urgell is a very popular outdoor centre, located just to the south of Andorra. Yet if it's two-wheeled action you're after, a gravel or a mountain bike are likely to get a lot more use than a road machine because of the large number of off-road routes and the relative paucity of roads within this extremely rugged area in northern Lleida. Options are further limited by the amount and speed of the traffic travelling on the C14 into Seu and the N145 that continues from the town into Andorra. These are the main routes into the principality from the south and aren't well suited to a relaxing ride.

This route into the mountains to the south of Seu, however, could hardly be any more chilled. Within a minute or two of rolling away from the town centre, you roll across a bridge over the rushing Segre and enter a rural haven, the road running between huge fields of rich green sweetcorn and lush pasture, taking its first gentle steps up to the Coll de Trava, 15km away, woodland taking over from farmland as the climb gets under way.

Just beyond Cerc, turn right towards Tuixent, a small village at the south-west corner of the Cadí massif and natural park. Coming from the north-west, this road heads towards it initially, skirting the edge of the park. The woods, mainly pine, alder and poplar, become thicker as the gradient picks up, although it never gets too arduous, the steepest kilometre a modest 7.5% and the average just five.

Halfway up the climb, the road emerges from the trees, revealing expansive views into the Cadí massif. With a backward glance, it's also possible to see up the valley towards Andorra, the main Pyrenean ridge just beyond the principality. It's quite a sight, but soon lost when the road is swallowed up by the forest again. It does, though, give a flavour of what's ahead. There's much better to come.

Above the cluster of houses that is El Ges, the road enters the Cadí natural park, one of the very few to run within the bounds of this pristine mountain wilderness. The gradient eases too, then kicks back a little more, before a more acute haul up the summit in the final 2.5km. Halfway into this, the road swings out to the west in a long, sweeping loop on open mountainside with a jaw-dropping panorama. La Seu d'Urgell is at the heart of it, nestled in the valley, with Andorra and the central spine of the Pyrenees now clearly visible behind it and extending for a long distance in both directions. There's an observation point on the apex of the loop that's undoubtedly worth a stop, but with the pass now just a few hundred metres away that can perhaps wait until later when descending back to Seu.

In this case, what goes up doesn't come back down. Over the next 10km the road does lose a little bit of altitude, but essentially follows the contours, twisting to pass beneath the outcrop on which the village of Adraén is perched, then running almost flat to arrive at the junction where the 22km loop at this route's far end begins. Keep left on the C462, with wonderful views now to the south to the Serra de Port del Comte and to the east towards the high southern wall of the Cadí. There's a short drop to Fórnols, then another long section of contouring where the vistas are a constant distraction. Passing Cornellana, a more sustained descent commences.

Two-thirds of the way down, take the very acute turn to the right towards Sorribes – some may fancy continuing on to Tuixent to

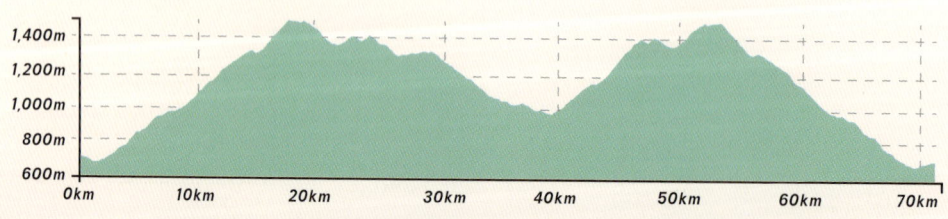

LLEIDA

Climbing away from a stormy La Seu d'Urgell

climb either the Port or the Josa (see page 56) – passing the Moli de Fórnols hotel/restaurant and Montargull. Not far beyond this hamlet, the road begins to climb, soon reaching Sorribes de la Vansa. Turn right here towards Seu d'Urgell, ascending steadily to Sisquer, then with a little more venom to return to the end of the loop at the junction with the C462.

This leaves another half dozen kilometres of easier ascent to reach the Trava and, just past it, that stunning *mirador*. While the descent from there back to La Seu isn't particularly steep, caution should be exercised on a surface that is cracked and uneven.

Distance: 71.7km
Elevation gain: 1,682m
Highest point: 1,491m
Est. moving time: 2.5-4hrs
Degree of difficulty: ●●
Climbs: Coll de Trava (1,491m)

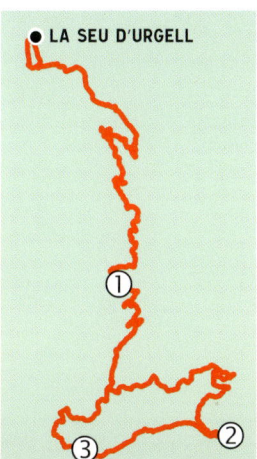

Route in reverse

Not applicable although it is, of course, possible to ride the loop at the far end of this route in the other direction. Neither way is best, although going clockwise does mean being on the outer side of the road when there's a lot to see.

Recorrido

0km	La Seu d'Urgell
1km	Go south from centre to cross river on LV4008 ←
6km	LV4008/C462 →
17.5km	Coll de Trava ①
24km	C462/unclassified to Sisquer ←
35km	C462/unclassified to Sorribes → ②
40.5km	Sorribes de la Vansa → to Sisquer and La Seu d'Urgell ③
47km	unclassified/C462 ←
54km	Coll de Trava ①
71.7km	La Seu d'Urgell

THE COLL DE NARGÓ SLALOM

Having said that I don't like out-and-back routes because they reduce the sense of being on a journey, I'm going to eat my own words here by highlighting a route that does precisely that, although it does feature a short loop as well. The neighbouring Bóixols and Faidella are among the passes that I most remember over many years of riding in the Pyrenees, principally for their descents, which made me shout with glee. I've never been much of a skier, but descending off these two passes has brought out my inner Alberto Tomba, the roads wriggling in slalom-like fashion to such an exhilarating extent that my first thought at the bottom has been to turn around and ride up again to have another go.

The route begins with a straight run away from Coll de Nargó, the road arrowing towards the uplifted peaks of the Serra de Carrasquers for 2km, then starting to rise and running through a short gorge, where the dark green of pine and oak contrast with the red of the crumbling sandstone. Emerging from it, the wiggling begins, one bend only a few dozen metres from the next, the gradient comparatively comfortable. This allows a chance to focus on the landscape, which is remarkable. To the left, the Valladarques river, which runs into the Oliana reservoir just south of Coll de Nargó, is lost in the depths of a canyon, while high up on the right there's a ridge of towering cliffs.

Two-thirds of the way up, there's a sizeable plateau, followed by 2km at 6.5%, above which the gradient eases back and road emerges onto a ridge with views to the north through the Pre-Pyrenees and into the high mountains. You may well still be gawping at this when the top of the pass arrives, indicated as 1,380m but around 50 less than that by most calculations. Look back when a few dozen metres beyond it and you'll realise that it's perched close to a sheer drop, which makes for quite a photo.

Another pause may be required a few hundred metres down the road to take in the view over what is essentially a huge hairpin bend with the rocky ridge of the Serra de Carreu looming over the road towards the Col de Faidella on the other side of the valley. Swooping down and around the switchback, the first slalom begins, the gradient only 3% at most but the bends so close together that it feels like you're flying through them. They lead to a cleft that's been cut through the rock and onto the very short rise to the Faidella, its stature also stacked with a few extra metres of height.

The real fun begins now. On what's a very good surface, a comparatively wide road and a relatively benign gradient, you can channel your inner Tomba or Mikaela Shiffrin, swaying one way and then the other through corner after corner, mostly without needing to touch the brakes. Don't go crazy, simply relish the helter-skelter, which is particularly thrilling lower down before the Faidella fires you out into a vast plain and into Isona to start a loop at the southern end of the Pallars region.

Follow signs for Tremp, the road still descending slightly as it passes through Conques and Figuerola d'Orcau, then heading for Sant Salvador de Toló. Although outside the Pre-Pyrenees, I enjoy roads like this precisely because they are set away from the mountains and, as a consequence, often provide expansive views of the peaks. As this one starts to edge its way gently upwards the views get increasingly impressive, particularly in the spring and early summer when there's still snow on the tops.

Having risen to 1,100m beyond Sant

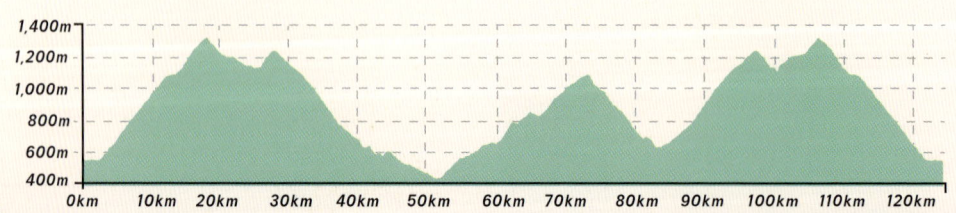

LLEIDA

Salvador, almost all of that gain is lost on the return to Isona from the south. On a clear day, the views over these dozen kilometres of breezy descent underline why it's worth standing back from the Pyrenees on occasions in order to admire their magnitude. At Isona, follow the signs to Coll de Nargó, starting to climb the Faidella from its longer western flank. The 12km rise isn't too taxing and offers the chance to take in some of the views that flashed by so quickly on the way down.

Beyond it, the western side of the Bóixols extends to a mere 6km, two-thirds of it false flat and only slightly steeper on the run up the top. Then the fun starts again. The bends aren't quite as close as on the Faidella, the road weaving rather than slaloming until a section about two-thirds of the way down where the sways turn to wiggles that are sure to return you to Coll de Nargó smiling broadly.

Route in reverse

This is just as good a ride from Isona and the west, especially as it would conclude with the slalom off the Faidella. When it comes to the loop, gauging the wind direction is key, particularly on the more exposed sections at the northern end.

Looking towards Isona and the Pyrenees

Distance: 125.1km
Elevation gain: 2,660m
Highest point: 1,332m
Est. moving time: 4.5-7hrs
Degree of difficulty: ●●●○
Climbs: Coll de Bóixols (1,332m), Coll de Faidella (1,236m)

Recorrido

0km	Coll de Nargó
18km	Coll de Bóixols ①
28km	Coll de Faidella ②
40.5km	Isona L511/C1412bz ➡ ③
47km	C1412bz/C1412b ➡
49.5km	C1412b/L912 ⬅ ④
62km	Sant Salvador de Toló
73km	L912/C1412b ⬅ ⑤
83.5km	Isona C1412b/C1412bz ➡ ③
84.5km	C1412bz/L511 ➡
97km	Coll de Faidella ②
107km	Coll de Bóixols ①
125.1km	Coll de Nargó

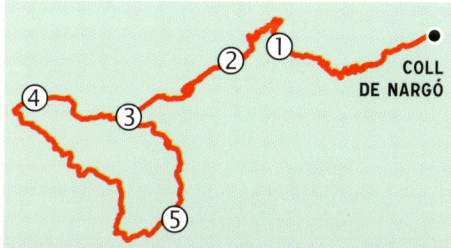

LA SEU TO SORT AND BACK

When I was putting this book together, I read a couple of brief descriptions of the Coll de la Basseta, a pass very close in height to the renowned Port del Cantó and only a dozen or so kilometres to the north. It appeared that the Basseta was passable and could, therefore, form a significant part of a circuit from La Seu d'Urgell in the Segre valley to Sort and the ski station of Port Ainé in Noguera Pallaresa valley to the west. Sadly, further investigation revealed that, although the road is paved on the eastern side to the Basseta refuge near the pass, the route from the west isn't sealed and suitable only to off-road bikes.

Moving inland from the population centres near the Catalan coast, the paucity of east-west routes like the Cantó and, to the south, the Coll de Bóixols often makes piecing together circular routes problematic. Although there's nothing wrong with an out-and-back ride, there's something fundamentally pleasing about moving in one direction all day, even when you do end up back where you started. It feels as if you've made a choice about your direction of travel, perhaps because the wind is coming from a certain direction or the climbing is less or more challenging. From that comes the sense of being on a journey. You've made the decision on where to explore, whereas on an out-and-back route that choice is taken for you.

There are times, though, when out-and-back is the only way. This is one, but because both sides of the Cantó are exceptional I've got no hesitation in including it. It begins by heading west from the centre of La Seu d'Urgell to join the N260, staying on this busy highway for 6km until Adrall, where most of the traffic keeps flying south as the N260 turns to the west, soon starting the 24km ascent to the Cantó. Wide and well-surfaced because it's the main route running parallel to the Pyrenees, the Eje Pirenaico (Pyrenean Axis), it winds up from six to seven to eight to nine per cent over the opening 4km and stays there for a couple more. The road twists frantically, one moment presenting views south down the Segre, the next north towards Seu.

As the bends become less acute and the straights stretch out, the gradient halves, and the Cantó becomes a quite different climb, the principal challenge its length. At 25km, it's a long haul, more than two hours of climbing for many, an ascent not to be rushed. It's so beautifully engineered, surfaced, located and quiet, it almost insists you take your time and enjoy the ride. Above Pallerols, it becomes less of a stroll for 3km as it wiggles through pine forest to reach Guils de Cantó, but from there it's a false flat for the last half dozen kilometres, lovely views to the south all the way to the summit, where a sign marks out the altitude as 1,720.8m precisely.

The western side isn't as long, nor is its gradient as forgiving. Averaging a point more than the eastern flank at 5.4%, it's a steady grind, which perhaps explains why Thomas de Gendt, the king of the long breakaway, was the first to the top when the 2016 Tour came up from Sort on the way to Andorra Arcalís. It makes for a rip-roaring descent, though. It's fast, but not frighteningly so, wide and sweeping bends reducing the momentum built up on its long straights. It hurries down into the centre of Sort, the halfway point and the obvious place to replenish yourself.

There are two options for the return, either head back via the same road or take a slightly different option that climbs most of the way back to the Cantó pass on back roads. For the latter, stay with the N260 through Sort, heading south for 2km to reach the left turn

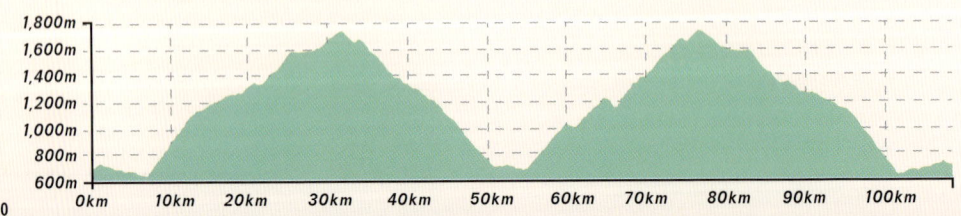

LLEIDA

to Tornafort, the initial stretch shaded by a beautiful line of poplars, before the narrow lane starts to climb up the hillside through a string of hairpins. Above these, the terrain is agricultural and open, presenting long views along the Noguera Pallaresa. Oddly, the road widens too, although the route soon returns to little more than a vehicle's width taking the left turn towards Soriguera.

It dips into pine forest and climbs in the style of a "normal" Pyrenean ascent, the gradient fluctuating between benign and brutal. It drops again to cross the River Cantó, then rises steeply through Soriguera and the hillside above it to rejoin the N260 a little more than halfway up the Cantó pass. It may be a consolation to know that this little diversion also means missing the more arduous sections of this climb, which are towards the bottom. Running at fives for the most part, the road eases up through the huge hairpins negotiated two or three hours earlier, bringing the top of the pass into sight.

Unlike Thomas de Gendt, who had three more climbs on the menu after this point, the hard work ends when you crest the Cantó. There is some pedalling to be done on the two flatter sections and on the final run up the valley to Seu, but essentially this is a descent to savour, the panorama now more easily seen from the outer side of the road, the coiled turns towards the bottom an exhilarating adrenalin rush.

Route in reverse

I'd counsel against descending the sometimes very narrow lane through Soriguera and down to the Noguera Pallaresa valley, which is technical, a little rough in places and, although very quiet, isn't the kind of road where you want to meet something coming the other way on a sharp bend.

Mountain ridges from the Port del Cantó

Distance: 109.5km
Elevation gain: 2,640m
Highest point: 1,721m
Est. moving time: 4-6hrs
Degree of difficulty: ●●●◐
Climbs: Port del Cantó (1,721m)

Recorrido

0km	La Seu d'Urgell
6.5km	Adrall N260/C14 →
31.5km	Port del Cantó ①
51km	Sort ②
53.5km	N260/LV5131 ← ③
59km	LV5131/unclassified to Soriguera ←
68.5km	Soriguera unclassified/N260 →
77.5km	Port del Cantó ①
103km	Adrall N260/C14 ←
109.5km	La Seu d'Urgell

SERENE REFUGE ABOVE LA SEU

Describing the ride over the Cantó pass from La Seu d'Urgell (see page 130), I mention that I'd been hoping to make it into a circuit by including a return over the Coll de la Basseta. I knew the eastern side of this little-known pass was surfaced, but discovered that the western flank via Port Ainé turns to gravel as soon as it leaves the ski station. A second access road via Romadriu is also unsealed beyond that remote village. Ultimately, though, I decided to include the Basseta, simply because it's such an attractive climb.

Beginning in La Seu d'Urgell, head west on the N260 for 3km, then turn right towards Castellbò on the road that also leads to the Andorra-Seu d'Urgell airport, which has been developed in recent years but has only been used by private jets since the summer of 2018, some of these no doubt used by some of the many pro racers who have set up home in the mountain nation. Keep straight at the junction where a road bears right to Aravell, still heading for Castellbò, the road rising a little and then dipping into this village.

At its far end, the road splits, one branch swinging left towards Sant Andreu and the cross-country ski station at Sant Joan de l'Erm, the other keeping towards Seix and Santa Creu. The two roads meet again at Sant Andreu before the final run up to the Basseta refuge at the top of the climb, the route via Seix slightly shorter. It's also narrower and has a rougher surface, therefore it's better suited to climbing than descending. It is also, I think, more scenic too.

Its appearance might suggest a climb that's going to fit the Pyrenean stereotype, with regular changes in gradient. However, it rises quite consistently, averaging between five and six per cent to reach Seix. It starts up a narrow and heavily wooded valley to reach two hairpins, which lift the road into much more open terrain, the pine-covered ridge where the Basseta is located now visible directly ahead. Soon after, it reaches Seix, the hamlet perched above the road, and starts to contour to the south, passing through lush pastureland, with the Serra de Cadí clearly visible in good weather and becoming easier to pick out approaching Sant Andreu.

When the roads meet again, swing hard right towards Sant Joan de l'Erm and into the final 6.5km up to the Basseta. As before, the climb is steady and the view impressive on the initial switchbacks, beyond which the road is cloaked by dense, pine forest. It only emerges at the Basseta, where the Sant Joan de l'Erm ski station and the refuge are set in a broad, grassy clearing that shouts "Picnic!" There is a café, but check on opening times if a lunch stop does appeal rather than assuming that it will be open.

When descending, stay straight on at Sant Andreu, taking the wider road, which barely loses any altitude at all for half a dozen kilometres until it reaches a sequence of switchbacks that lead back into Castellbò. Dropping down through these bends, the Cadí massif often prominent ahead, the gradient isn't at all severe apart from two or three sections in the first couple of turns. Entering Castellbò, turn right through the village and continue back via the outward route to La Seu.

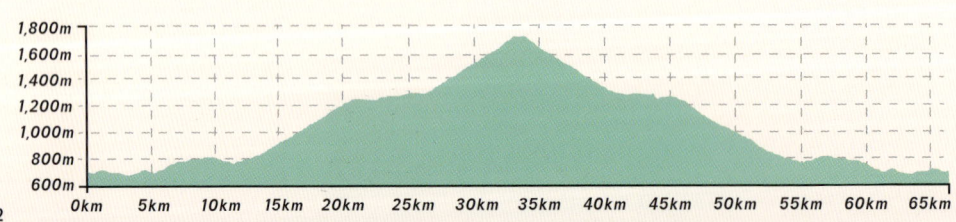

LLEIDA

The Castellciutat fort overlooking La Seu d'Urgell

Route in reverse

As noted, the road via Seix on the northern side of this valley is narrower and not as well maintained as the one that climbs the southern side, so extreme caution should be exercised if descending this way through the blind bends in the woods below Albet.

Distance: 66.3km
Elevation gain: 1,381m
Highest point: 1,728m
Est. moving time: 2.5-4hrs
Degree of difficulty: ●●
Climbs: Coll de la Basseta (1,728m)

Recorrido

0km	La Seu d'Urgell
3km	N260/unclassified to Castellbò ➡
13.5km	Castellbò ➡ to Seix ①
26km	Sant Andreu ➡ to Sant Joan de l'Erm ②
33km	Coll de la Basseta and Sant Joan de l'Erm ③
39.5km	Sant Andreu ➡ to Castellbò ②
52.5km	Castellbò ➡ La Seu d'Urgell ①
63km	unclassified/N260 ⬅
66.3km	La Seu d'Urgell

THE BEAUTIFUL ANOMALY OF VAL D'ARAN

The Val d'Aran is an oddity. It's one of only two areas in Spain that lies on the northern side of the Pyrenees, its southern edge formed by an impenetrable barrier of mountains including the highest in the whole range, the 3,408m Pic d'Aneto. So remote that it used to be completely cut off from the rest of the country in winter until the construction of the Vielha tunnel in 1948, it remains relatively secluded, often more easily accessed by Spaniards via France and the Portillon pass than from the N230 main road that burrows its way through to it from the south.

Although not blessed with many roads, this huge valley does feature some iconic cycling locations, notably the Portillon pass, which crosses the frontier and drops into the French spa town of Bagnères de Luchon, the Port de la Bonaigua, to the east of the Aran's main town, Vielha, and the ski station of Beret, in between the Bonaigua and Vielha. It hosted a stage finish in the 2006 Tour.

Starting in Vielha, head east from the resort town's main square, which climbs from the off towards the Bonaigua pass, 23km away. The first nine, averaging a mere 2.5%, aren't hard going, allowing the legs to get well warmed up before the more exacting second half of the climb. Underlining the distinctiveness of this valley, the river the road is tracking upstream is the Garonne, which is generally associated with Toulouse, Bordeaux and south-west France but rises close to the Puerto de Beret.

At Salardu, 10km into the climb, the gradient picks up, but only to just above 5% and never gets much more acute. It's the amount of ascent more than the angle of attack that will steadily take a toll on the Bonaigua. Above the resort town of Baqueira, where the route will later turn towards Pla de Beret, the terrain becomes more rugged and spectacular, high peaks appearing to block out the end of the long, picture postcard valley, its forested sides curving symmetrically to meet in a perfect 'U'.

A series of big switchbacks brings a change of perspective and, pleasingly, a slight easing in the gradient. Exiting them, the top of the pass comes into sight just a couple of kilometres distant, the summit just beyond the ski lifts and the solid-looking Cap del Port restaurant, half-French chateau, half-railway station. The summit is flat and wide, so the best views don't come until the descent to Esterri d'Àneu begins, and what stands out is the Frenchness of the landscape, scree on the mountainsides, loose rocks littering the grassy slopes, livestock roaming free, the road weaving into a small ski station below, very reminiscent of the Barèges side of the Tourmalet.

The road, though, maintains its engineered feel, the gradient never varying much either side of 5%, its average of 4.9% just one tenth higher than the western flank. It works its way down into the valley through a series of coiled switchbacks, each one a stair to the valley floor. Once down there, and next to the River Bonaigua, it holds close to a straight line, flying past La Bonaigua de Baix and on to a final hairpin. Take the left turn towards Sorpe on its apex, the road tumbling quickly down to edge of the Borén reservoir and then more sedately into Esterri through the beautiful upper section of the Noguera Pallaresa valley.

Just short of halfway, Esterri is an ideal place for a break. From there, weave up to Valencia d'Aneu to join the main route back towards the Bonaigua, which is more impressive from this side. Once again, there are echoes of the Tourmalet, but the hairpins evoke different locations, their almost sheer stone buttresses reminiscent of roads in

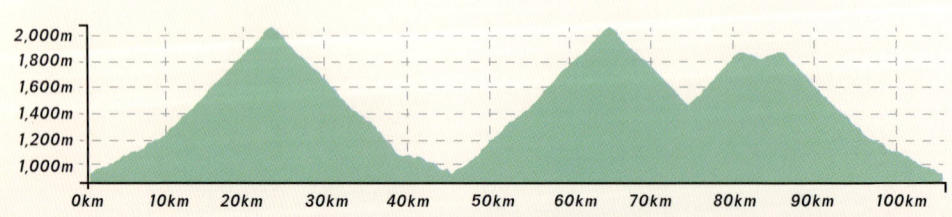

134

LLEIDA

View from the Beret pass over Baqueira towards the Bonaigua

the Italian Alps, an upward glance to the towering crags and scree fields reinforcing the feeling.

By the top, you'll have been climbing for 46km. The question is, can you handle half a dozen more? The mostly straight 10km to Baqueira allows time to ponder whether to take the right turn up to Pla de Beret. I'd encourage it because it's a beautiful diversion and not too hard either. As with the Bonaigua, the gradient is steady at around 6%, with some steeper pitches rounding the initial switchbacks. Above these, a glance up to the right reveals the avalanche protection gallery not far below the summit.

Climbing towards it, the panorama is magnificent, the snow-capped peaks in the Aneto massif visible for the first time. After passing through two shorter galleries, the road reaches the longer one seen a few minutes earlier from below, and just beyond it is the Puerto de Beret, the stream to the right of it the source of the Garonne. Continuing past this high point, the road enters a vast hanging valley, slightly scarred by an immense car park for this upper part of the resort, but otherwise green and quite glorious, the frontier peaks dividing Lleida from the Ariège directly ahead.

The hard work is done. All that remains is to lap up that stunning 180° view from the top of the first hairpin one more time, then swish back down to Baqueira and onwards to Vielha.

Route in reverse

If I were starting from the other side, I'm not sure whether I would divert off to Pla de Beret on the way down to Vielha or on the way back up. I suspect I'd opt to do it before lunch, rather than adding it into the long haul back up to Bonaigua, giving 30km of climbing broken up only by the short descent into Baqueira.

Distance: 105.9km
Elevation gain: 2,830m
Highest point: 2,072m
Est. moving time: 4.5-7hrs
Degree of difficulty: ●●●●◐
Climbs: Port de la Bonaigua (2,072m), Pla de Beret (1,830m)

Recorrido

0km	Vielha
13km	Baqueira
23km	Port de la Bonaigua ①
36km	C28/C147 ⬅②
45km	Esterri d'Àneu C147/C28z ➡③
48.5km	C28z/C28 ➡
64.5km	Port de la Bonaigua ①
74.5km	Baqueira C28/C142B ➡
81km	Puerto de Beret
83km	Pla de Beret ④
92.5km	Baqueira C142B/C28 ➡
105.9km	Vielha

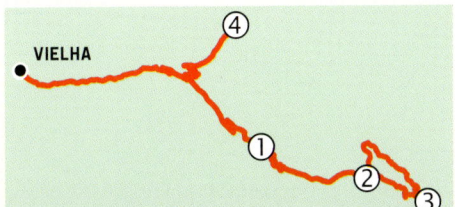

135

A CATALAN GEM WITH A BIG VIEW

Although there isn't yet a practicable road passage from the Noguera Pallaresa valley to the east via the Coll de la Basseta, the picturesque climb up to the Port Ainé ski station is still well worth a look. It's the highlight of this loop that features two smaller climbs on the western side of the valley above Sort.

Setting off southwards from the middle of this little town on the N260, the route darts up into these hills within the opening kilometre towards Enviny. Rising fairly evenly, the gradient 6% or a tad more, a fine view quickly emerges along the valley to the south and keeps stretching passing Montardit de Dalt and Llarvén. There's better to come, though. Switching northwards to Enviny, the road runs along open mountainside with the Cantó pass easy to pick out to the east, a pale line of rock and tarmac cutting upwards through the trees, while to the north and high above it Port Ainé is also visible.

The Vuelta a España passed this way in 2008 on a stage between Andorra and Pla de Beret that went over the Bonaigua pass, which isn't too far away to the north as the crow flies. Pausing at the viewpoint on the Alto de Enviny, it's easy to understand why the Vuelta organisers were tempted here.

A flattish 5km follows, allowing further contemplation of that view and, in the far distance, higher peaks close to the French frontier. It's a glorious stretch of road, that feeling heightened because it's so unexpected. Nearing Olp, it tumbles down towards the valley, where the small town of Rialp appears to be waiting for its arrival. However, the route kicks up and away from Rialp at the last, ascending gradually towards the Llessui valley. Once again, after just a little bit of altitude gain, the views are delightful.

This road peters out in the pretty village of Llessui, which had a little ski station until the late 1980s, but rather than continue up as far as that, bear right to Caregue on the apex of a hairpin to start the descent back to the Noguera Pallaresa. It's a bit rough in places, but the surface improves after branching right towards Escàs, beyond which it follows a thrilling trajectory along a ledge cut into the hillside and scooting down the main road again.

Go left, heading towards Vielha for a kilometre to reach the right turn up to Port Ainé, 18km and 1,200 vertical metres away. The climb is a favourite with the organisers of the Volta a Catalunya, Ireland's Dan Martin winning there in 2013 and Belgium's Thomas de Gendt doing so in 2016 on a stage that also featured the Cantó and Enviny passes.

The first 3km are the toughest, averaging 8.5%, as the road climbs through woodland initially before switching back towards Roní, where there's a long view up the valley towards lofty peaks to the east of the Bonaigua pass. The gradient gradually becomes more comfortable and the vista ahead more impressive, the Pic d'Aneto and the summits around it visible on the clearest days.

Climbing higher, the road becomes enclosed in pine forest, the gradient steady at around 7%, but emerges into more open terrain again at Port Ainé 1650, the lower part of the ski station. The 180° view to the west and north is quite staggering, the highest mountains in the Pyrenean chain easier to pick out now and dozens more on the skyline. A significant easing in the angle of ascent for a kilometre makes this easier to take in before the forest returns and the road rears up to make the final 4km run to the summit, a hard kilometre followed by an easier one, the

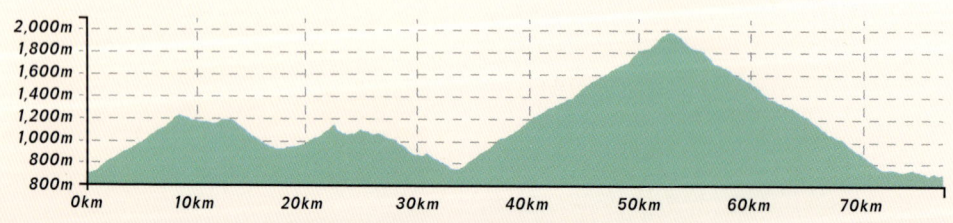

LLEIDA

Llessui at sunrise

pattern then repeated.

The resort only comes into sight in the final kilometre, just before a dirt road branches to the right towards the Coll de la Basseta (see page 132). It's no more than a single building, a handful of lifts and the inevitable large car park, but what a jaw-dropping outlook they have, the valley leading towards the Bonaigua pass at the centre, myriad peaks on either side, the quality of the view far exceeding the degree of effort required to appreciate it.

The return is straightforward, initially to the foot of the climb, and from there a left turn for half a dozen gently descending kilometres through Rialp and back to Sort.

Route in reverse

This ride has to build towards Port Ainé and, as a consequence the loop towards it doesn't really work the other way around. It's best to stick with the course usually taken by the Volta, with the Enviny climb as the leg-warmer.

Distance: 77.4km
Elevation gain: 2,250m
Highest point: 1,967m
Est. moving time: 3-4.5hrs
Degree of difficulty: ●●●
Climbs: Alto de Enviny (1,209m), Port Ainé (1,967m)

Recorrido

0km	Sort
0.5km	N260/LV5222 ➡
8.5km	Alto de Enviny ①
14km	Olp
17.5km	LV5224/LV5223 ⬅ ②
22.5km	LV5223/unclassified to Caregue ➡
25km	unclassified to Escàs ➡ ③
33km	unclassified/C13 ⬅
34km	C13/unclassified to Port Ainé ➡
52.5km	Port Ainé ④
71km	unclassified/C13 ⬅
77.4km	Sort

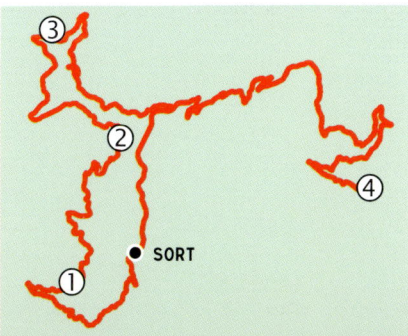

137

A TRIO OF TOUR FAVOURITES

This is one of my favourite loops anywhere in the Pyrenees, although it does feature five kilometres of climbing that I always dread. It begins in the little town of Saint Béat, famed for its white marble, which was used for many of the sculptures and statues that decorate the Palace of Versailles. We'll come back to the marble quarrying at the end…

To begin with, head north on the N125 and then fork right towards Chaum. Although there are other routes down this valley, this one offers the kindest of introductions to the Col des Ares, a Tour regular that's perfect for finding your climbing legs. It begins with a big step up to Antichan de Frontignes, then sweeps around a huge hairpin where there's a useful information board picking out the peaks and other details in the surrounding panorama. From there, the road climbs gently through woodland for the next 5km. Topping out at a little less than 800m, it's a blissful way to the ride, the feeling heightened by a descent that's never severe and can be tackled with barely a touch on the brakes.

For the next few kilometres, the road weaves through thick forest, passing the occasional village, bumping over the Col de Buret, a smaller version of the Ares. Just before Sengouagnet, the D618 cuts back hard on itself, drops into a valley, then slowly begins to climb for 5km to reach a T-junction beneath a towering cliff-face. Here you have a choice, go left to climb the harder western side of the Col de Portet d'Aspet or head right towards the Col de Menté and the most direct route back to Saint Béat.

The plaque marking where Luis Ocaña crashed out of the 1971 Tour

For the full Tour experience, I'd recommend going left, although you might spend a good deal of the next 4.5km wondering why you'd followed that advice. Climbing very steeply through a tight ravine, the tree-shrouded Portet d'Aspet is one of the most tranquil of passes. It is also home to arguably the most beautiful of cycling monuments.

Little more than 500m up the climb, just beyond a gently curving bend to the right, the brilliant white and grey marble *Flight of Light* sculpture by Bruno Luzzani commemorates Italy's 1992 Olympic road race champion Fabio Casartelli, who crashed and died a few dozen metres further down the road during the 1995 Tour – this spot is marked with a plaque and, usually, flowers. It's as breath-taking as the climb that passes it and demands a stop to appreciate the many details highlighting Casartelli's life and career.

Back in the saddle again, there is no let-up in the gradient all the way to the top of the pass (see page 106), the 4km above the memorial averaging only a shade below 10%, this pass very similar in this respect and its final altitude to the Col de Marie Blanque (see page 220), much further to the west. This short, but memorable detour concludes with the high-speed drop back to the T-junction and the approach to the Col de Menté.

This pass is idiosyncratic, typically Pyrenean and, I believe, one of the most attractive in the chain. It begins straightforwardly enough, the road rising right away from the foot of the Portet d'Aspet, then drops into a hamlet, from which it ascends again, more steeply and a little further this time, only to descend

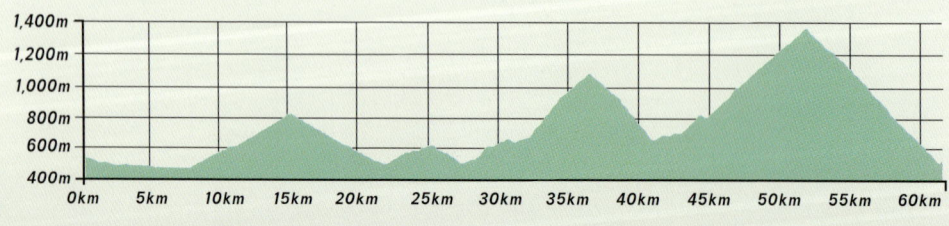

HAUTE GARONNE

The eastern side of the Col de Menté

a second time into the village of Soulan, where the ascent of the Menté truly begins.

Climbing through almost a score of hairpins, divided between two separate "ladders" where the bends are heaped tightly on each other, it rises through open mountainside with far-ranging views. But it's the coil of bends that tends to draw the eye as they wriggle down into the valley behind you. There are some steep sections but none as formidable as those on the Portet d'Aspet, before it enters dense forest towards the humped summit, where a road heads left to the Le Mourtis ski station.

The descent is fast from the off, rattling down another string of hairpins, a long straight leading into two final switchbacks. Coming into the first of these, there's a plaque on the rock wall ahead that recounts the tale of Luis Ocaña's loss of the yellow jersey at this point in the 1971 Tour. Chasing Eddy Merckx down a descent made treacherous by a sudden squall that washed rocks onto the road, the Spaniard crashed, tried to stand, only to be hit by two more riders who were out of control. His race was over. Unfortunately, he was just one bend away from the mostly straight and far less technical run down into Saint Béat.

The last section of the descent passes disused marble quarries, where a quirky mural pays tribute to those who once worked here. Prized by French kings, who used it in preference to Carrara marble from Italy, Saint Béat still has nine working marble quarries, one of them underground. It's a fine end to a relatively short but captivating ride.

Route in reverse

The ride is just as impressive in the anti-clockwise direction, but the climbing is full on from the start as the Menté is a far harder test from the west than it is from the east. Warming up by riding on the D618 to Ore and back is highly advised. The Ares is harder in this direction too, but remains a relatively easy ascent.

Distance: 61.7km
Elevation gain: 1,855m
Highest point: 1,349m
Est. moving time: 2-4hrs
Degree of difficulty: ●●●
Climbs: Col des Ares (797m), Col de Portet d'Aspet (1,069m), Col de Menté (1,349m)

Parcours

0km	Saint Béat N125
3km	N125/D825A ➡ becoming D618
10.5km	Antichan de Frontignes
15km	Col des Ares ①
26.5km	Sengouagnet D618/D5 ➡ ②
32km	D618/D85 ⬅
36.5km	Col de Portet d'Aspet ③
40.5km	D618/D85 ⬅
51.5km	Col de Menté ④
61.7km	Saint Béat

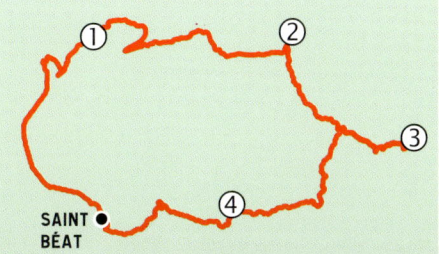

THE PEYRESOURDE BOTH WAYS

I have a bit of mental block when it comes to the Col de Peyresourde, or at least its eastern flank that rises from the edge of Bagnères de Luchon. I always find it a real grind. It's partly to do with the nature of the road. Compared to the Pyrenean ascents I particularly enjoy, it's wider and straighter. It may once have been laid on a goat track, but it no longer evokes that feeling of intrepidness and roughness, of a journey into the unknown. It is a motorway of a climb that strides up to 1,500m with barely a stutter.

I'm being picky, I know, especially as this is one of the Tour's classic climbs that should be on everyone's to-do list, this circuit offering that possibility as well as immediate comparison of the Peyresourde's two flanks. It commences as soon as the D618 reaches Luchon's outskirts, rearing up suddenly, so be sure to be well warmed up. It quickly reaches a run of three hairpins. On the corner of the third, the D51 heads off to the right towards the Port de Balès (see page 142), a climb that's definitely still in touch with its inner goat track.

Meanwhile, the Peyresourde streaks upwards through a series of small villages, the gradient a steady eight per cent or so. At Garin, a smaller and often much steeper road, the D76, follows a parallel course towards the summit, meeting the main route within a series of spectacular hairpins just before the top that offer sensational views back into the Pique valley.

Descending past the turn for the ski station and altiport at Peyragudes, the panorama is even more magnificent. Straight ahead across the Louron valley is the next high point, the Col d'Azet, beyond it the Col de Portet, which was discovered by the Tour in 2018, and the peaks of the Néouvielle massif. Straight and extremely fast, the road flies down the open mountainside. At the junction with the D25, turn hard left towards Loudenvielle, which arrives after much weaving through little hamlets where it's easy to mistake a driveway for the road.

Circle around Lac Génos-Loudenvielle to Génos, where the climb to the Azet pass begins just as abruptly as the Peyresourde. Heavily wooded on its lower slopes, its opening half averages more than nine per cent as it snakes upwards. The slope eases, though, as the trees give way to more open pasture, the views once again justifying the hard effort. It tops out close to the tiny ski station at Val Louron, then follows a much straighter course into the Aure valley, passing through the village of Azet on the way down to Saint Lary Soulan, which is a good diversion for lunch.

Rather than head into the town, the route bears right before it at Sailhan and Bourisp to join the D115, which climbs into woodland at Grailhen as it tracks northwards towards Lançon. There are alternative routes northwards in the bottom of the valley, but I prefer the tranquillity of this one, even though it does add 150 or so vertical metres to the total.

Ride past the pretty church that dominates Lançon, the road climbing steeply through open fields and then into woodland before cresting this beautiful and often bypassed little pass to drop to Ilhan and back into the Louron valley to join the D618 that returns to Luchon. This section can be busy, but most of the traffic is left behind when the road splits, the left fork heading for the western side of the Peyresourde. At seven per cent, this flank is almost exactly the same gradient as the eastern, but I always find it easier, the dread removed I suspect by the fact I'm as warmed

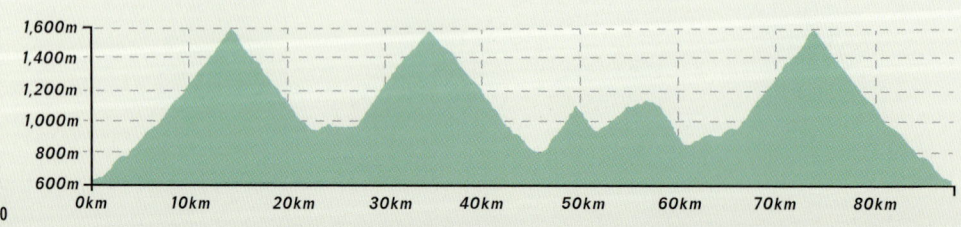

HAUTE GARONNE

View from the Peyresourde pass to the Col d'Azet

up as I'm going to be and the incredible views, with the earlier ascent of the Azet very prominent.

Cresting the pass, the descent back to Luchon is a joy. The surface is good and when the conditions are the same it's rip-roaringly fast. Every climb delivers a reward in the descent that follows, but rarely a bigger one than here.

Route in reverse

It's not hugely different. If pushed, I'd say I just about prefer climbing the Azet from the east, primarily because there are some very steep ramps early on the western side.

Distance: 85.6km
Elevation gain: 3,014m
Highest point: 1,580m
Est. moving time: 3.5-5.5hrs
Degree of difficulty: ●●●●
Climbs: Col de Peyresourde (1,569m), Col d'Azet (1,580m), Col de Lançon (1,120m), Col de Peyresourde (1,569m)

Parcours

0km	Bagnères de Luchon D618
14km	Col de Peyresourde ①
21.5km	D618/D25 ←
25.5km	Loudenvielle D25/D725 → ②
27km	Génos D25/D225 ←
34.5km	Col d'Azet ③
42km	D225/D25 →
44.5km	D25/D115 →
49km	D115/D25 →
54.5km	Col de Lançon ④
58.5km	D25/D618 →
71.5km	Col de Peyresourde ①
85.6km	Bagnères de Luchon

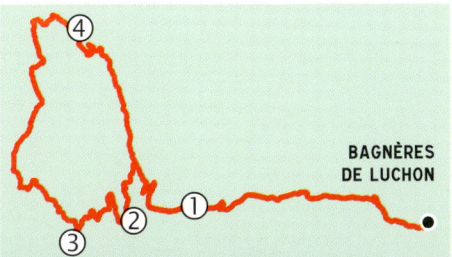

THE WILD AND WONDERFUL BALÈS

So quickly has the Port de Balès become established as a regular feature on the Tour de France itinerary that it's easy to forget that the road over the pass that lies just to the east of Mont Né had fallen into disrepair and was unfit for use until it was resurfaced in 2006. It featured on the Tour route the following season, and is best associated with "chaingate", the moment in the 2010 race when race leader Andy Schleck attacked his rivals, principally Alberto Contador, opening a gap, only to be immediately waylaid when his chain unshipped. As Schleck struggled with his bike, Contador and the rest flew, the Spaniard taking the yellow jersey. Should they have waited for the yellow jersey?

While the debate about whether Contador should have waited for the stricken yellow jersey instead of exploiting the mechanical breakdown will roll on and become one of the Tour's legendary stories, there's no doubt at all about the Balès's rightful place among the great Pyrenean passes. It's a hard test, and beautifully remote and scenic. The Tour has always come at it via its northern flank from Mauléon Barousse. Starting in Luchon, this means a nice, long, warm-up running down the Pique valley and into the Haute Garonne valley. Head north on the D125, a busy road but with a wide verge designed for bike use. Running very gently downwards, it makes for rapid progress. Just north of Cierp Gaud, most of the traffic filters away onto the N125 on the far bank of the Garonne.

Beyond Saléchan, take the D924 left to Mauléon Barousse. This smaller road quickly passes through Siradan, and here the route starts to climb for the first time, although with no severity. It will continue upwards, though, for almost the entirety of the next 30km. Following the course of a stream, the road winds through woodland initially, then enters open farmland, the twin summits of the Pic de Mont Las filling the view ahead.

At the T-junction in Mauléon Barousse, turn left and then, in a square a couple of hundred metres later, swing right onto the D925 to Luchon via the Balès. The initial half-dozen kilometres are a bucolic breeze, the route following the River Ferrère through Ferrère the village. Still rising gradually, the valley narrows, then opens out passing a cluster of holiday chalets. Just beyond, with a third of the ascent completed, the gradient kicks up more noticeably, and even more so when crossing from the left to the right bank of the river, although still not severely.

When the road cuts into and along a rock-face, the Balès's fiercer side starts to become apparent. With the river now lost way down in the forested valley below, the road takes its first big step upwards, gaining almost 150 metres in a kilometre and a half. There's a let-up, then another significant leap upwards coming into a run through the first two switchbacks. Once again, there's a lull after a kilometre at more than 10%. Above it, the road eases up through another series of hairpins, then come two kilometres at 10%.

In typically stepping Pyrenean fashion, the gradient eases again as the road negotiates a cleft cut through the rock and enters the wild upper part of the pass, almost free of trees. Weaving in and out of the contours of the mountainside, the final steeper section begins just before the 2km-to-the-summit sign. It was here that Schleck made his ill-fated attack, stomping away, only to collapse into his saddle as he lost his chain.

Rounding a large knoll and passing the sign announcing the final kilometre, the views up the bare flanks of the mountain and back down the valley are stunning. This is a

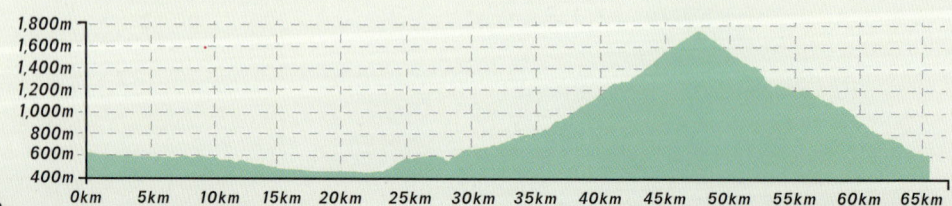

HAUTE GARONNE

The stunning upper section of the Port de Balès

wonderful natural arena for spectating. The summit, and a return to Haute Garonne from Hautes Pyrénées, arrives soon after, and what a glorious vantage point it is on a clear day.

The southern flank is not as steep, but long straights coupled with the openness of the terrain make it surprisingly quick, the road hurtling down the Oueil Valley through a string of villages, passing flower-filled meadows and pasture, barely wavering from its south-easterly course. A last steeper section drops to the junction with the D618 on the apex of a hairpin low down on the Peyresourde, where the helter-skelter rush into Luchon continues, the gradient only easing right on the edge of town.

Route in reverse

The southern side of the Balès is a little longer, but also a little easier. One of its principal difficulties lies in the fact the climb begins with less than a kilometre in the legs. I'd still recommend it, though, because it's quite different, more pastoral, but just as attractive. Why not compare the two sides with an out-and-back ride?

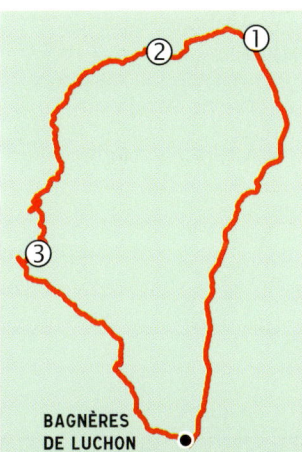

Distance: 65.7km
Elevation gain: 1,501m
Highest point: 1,755m
Est. moving time: 2.5-4.5hrs
Degree of difficulty: ●●●
Climbs: Port de Balès (1,755m)

Parcours

0km	Bagnères de Luchon
19km	D125/D825 ↑
22km	D825/D924 ← ①
28km	Mauléon Barousse ← then → on D925 ②
47.5km	Port de Balès ③
61km	D51/D618 ←
65.7km	Bagnères de Luchon

LUCHON'S TWIN PEAKS

Sitting in adjacent valleys to the south of Bagnères de Luchon, the climbs to Superbagnères and Hospice de France begin from the same junction in this corner of France that's tucked hard in against the border with Spain. Reaching this fork on the D125, it's hard to know which way to branch: left towards a refuge that's been a staging point for travellers since the Medieval era and was one of the first locations popularised for mountain pursuits during the mid-19th century; or right towards a ski resort established in the early 20th century and was a regular feature on the Tour de France route in the 1970s and 1980s, when Bernard Hinault, Greg LeMond and, on the last visit in 1989, Robert Millar were stage-winners here. So why not savour both?

The 6km approach to the fork from Luchon begins gently, then kicks up sharply as the valley narrows, before easing back down again and providing a couple of gentle kilometres to ponder the eternal question: left or right? Swayed by cycling history, tackling the bigger ascent with fresher legs and, decisively, a visibly less severe opening from the junction, Superbagnères gets the verdict.

The descent to cross the River Pique is extremely brief, the road kicking up immediately beyond it, entering the Lys Valley and following an undulating course for two kilometres, 2,700m peaks filling the view ahead. Three sweeping hairpins turn the road away from the river, and from here it's 8% average all the way to the ski station.

Rising through woodland, this is a typical access route for a big resort: wide, well surfaced and with plenty of space on the flattish switchbacks to accommodate coaches and other big vehicles. It's the "straights" between these bends that are the difficulty, some sections running at 10% for a good distance. This makes it hard to maintain a rhythm, which is precisely why pure climbers such as Millar and 1971 Superbagnères victor José Manuel Fuente who can quickly adjust to a change in pace have thrived here.

Sometimes climbs like this that are so obviously engineered to ease the progress of traffic can seem a little soulless, but Superbagnères avoids this, if only because the views are so magnificent once you come out of the trees a handful of kilometres from the top. The peaks are so close that you feel that you're going to end up among them.

The sight of the impressively imposing Grand Hôtel de Superbagnères, opened in 1922, signals the summit is little more than a kilometre away. This is one of the steepest stretches, but comes a little more easily knowing that the finish and a *chocolat chaud* is imminent. And what a finale it is, the Aneto, at 3,408m, the highest peak in the Pyrenees, visible on clear days along with the other 3,000m giants in the Maladeta massif. To the eastern side of the Grand Hôtel, there's a stunning view over Luchon and across the Peyresourde and Portillon passes and beyond.

Descending on ski station roads like this one is usually a pleasure because they're well maintained and broader than most mountain roads. The corners are so wide that it's possible to keep a decent amount of speed through them, and as a consequence the close to 360° right turn towards Hospice de France arrives quickly.

Although the closest neighbour to Superbagnères, it's very different, the road running directly south-west with just two or three hairpins on the way. After the first short rise, there's a flat section before the climbing gets serious. The next two kilometres through

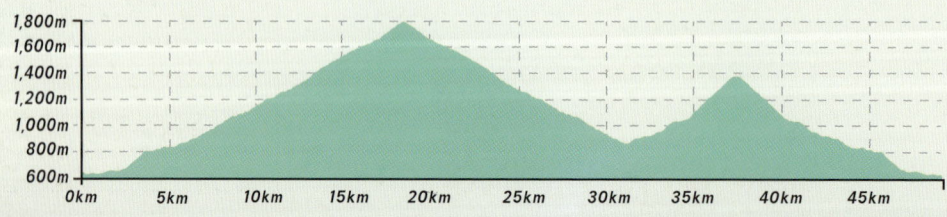

HAUTE GARONNE

Superbagnères ski station

pine forest are straightforward, but, beyond that, the final three are anything but. Averaging 11%, with many brief sections well above that, it's a hard slog to reach the very impressively renovated auberge, the starting point for numerous walks into the surrounding peaks. The 12km downhill run to Luchon begins very rapidly, but that initial rush soon eases to a breeze.

Route in reverse

I don't think tackling Hospice de France before Superbagnères changes much. You do get the steepest ramps out of the way sooner, but then have to take on the longer climb.

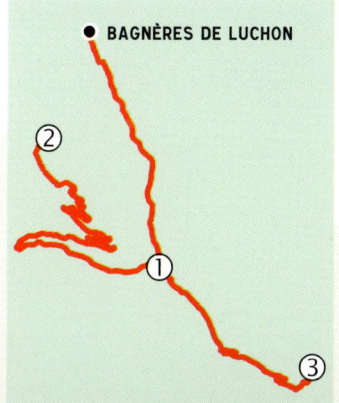

Distance: 49.2km
Elevation gain: 1,748m
Highest point: 1,800m
Est. moving time: 2.5-4.5hrs
Degree of difficulty: ●●●
Climbs: Superbagnères (1,800m), Hospice de France (1,385m)

Parcours

0km	Bagnères de Luchon
5.5km	D125/D46 ➡ ①
18.5km	Superbagnères ②
31.5km	D46/D125 ➡ ①
37.5km	Hospice de France ③
49.2km	Bagnères de Luchon

THE HAUTE GARONNE VALLEY

Starting in the Pique valley at Bagnères de Luchon, this route takes the sharp leap over the Portillon pass that's a regular feature on the Tour de France route to explore the top end of the Haute Garonne valley that gives this department its name. Then travelling north, it continues on roads that are well-trodden by *La Grande Boucle*, the big buckle, as the race has been dubbed, crossing the fierce western flank of the Col de Menté and the little but lovely Col des Ares on its way back to the spa town where it began.

The Col du Portillon has long been a vital route to the Val d'Aran in Catalonia, even for those on the Spanish side of the border. Prior to the construction of the Vielha Tunnel in 1948, their only access to the rest of Spain was via the 2,072m Port de la Bonaigua. As a consequence, the inhabitants of the Aran – hemmed in by the Maladeta massif to the west and south, the high border ridge of the Pyrenees to the north and the Bonaigua to the east – had closer links with Haute Garonne. These were not only geographic, but also linguistic, the local Aranés language having more in common with the Occitan long spoken in southern France. While the tunnel opened the Aran to the rest of Spain, this remote valley is still more easily reached via France.

Riding south from Luchon, the opening two kilometres are almost flat, while the next one ascends quite gently. This changes radically, though, when the road turns from a southerly to an easterly course, the gradient rearing to double figures and staying there for a kilometre and the first series of hairpins, which maintain the pressure. Relief arrives just above these bends on a long straight. This ends with a flick through a chicane, followed soon after by another double-digit ramp that's the prelude to two challenging kilometres, climbing through two sets of hairpins, the second ladder of bends arriving at the steepest kilometre, a close-to-12% grind that extends almost to the Franco-Spanish frontier, a solid stone post the only sign of the former customs point at the col.

The summit is set in dense pine forest, which generally shuts out what would otherwise be very spectacular views towards the highest peaks in the Pyrenean chain. By the time the trees do give way to a long and impressive view, coming into a series of hairpins, the Aneto and neighbouring summits are, unfortunately, hidden from view. Turn left below these bends, heading through the neat town of Bossòst and follow the rushing Garonne, just a few metres wide at this point, little more than 20km from its source on its 602km journey to Bordeaux. This N230 road can be busy, with lots of trucks taking advantage of the passage through to Spain and back, but progress is assisted by the gentle but consistent descent.

The route diverts briefly away from the main highway on the backroad through Fos, then rejoins it to reach Saint Béat. Bear left here on the D44 for a straight run back to Luchon, or head in the opposite direction on the same road onto the first slopes of the Col de Menté. While the other flank of this pass features two descents, there's no let-up coming at it from the west, the road rising for 10km at close to 9%. The incline is untypically consistent for a Pyrenean pass, the road running quite straight for its first half to reach the hairpin where Luis Ocaña crashed out of the 1971 Tour when in the yellow jersey. Above it, there are a dozen more switchbacks to reach the summit.

The road tumbles down a similar number of hairpins to Ger de Boutx, climbs briefly, drops

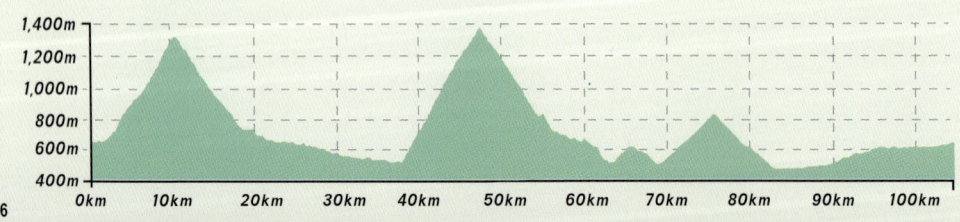

HAUTE GARONNE

Bossòst from the Portillon pass

again, then descends more sedately to the junction with the road that comes down from the Col de Portet d'Aspet. That's a testing diversion, but very worthwhile. The route swerves it, though, bearing left to weave through wonderful woodland via Juzet d'Izaut to reach the Col des Ares. This also has a steady grade, but little more than half the angle of the Menté, tree-covered all the way, the far side dropping just as gently to Antichan de Frontignes and back into the Haute Garonne valley.

The final 20km follow two rivers upstream, initially the Garonne as far as Chaum and then the Pique for the final few kilometres back to Luchon, arriving back in the attractive spa town on a backroad via Moustajon.

Route in reverse

It has pros and cons. I much prefer the eastern side of the Menté, to my mind one of the best climbs in the whole range. The Ares is equally enjoyable both ways and the same can be said for the Portillon. However, the ride up the N125/N230 from Saint Béat can be a chore if the traffic is heavy.

Distance: 105.1km
Elevation gain: 2,478m
Highest point: 1,349m
Est. moving time: 3.5-6hrs
Degree of difficulty: ●●●◐
Climbs: Col du Portillon (1,293m), Col de Menté (1,349m), Col des Ares (797m)

Parcours

0km	Bagnères de Luchon
1km	D125/D618a ➡
10km	Col du Portillon ①
18.5km	N141/N230 ⬅ to Bossòst ②
30km	➡ to Fos
32km	N125 ➡
38km	Saint Béat N125/D44 ⬅ ③
41.5km	D44/D125 ⬅
47.5km	Col de Menté ④
59km	D85/D618 ⬅
63.5km	D618/D5 ⬅ ⑤
75.5km	Col des Ares ⑥
86km	Chaum D618/D125 ➡ ⑦
100.5km	Antignac D125/D125C ➡
105.1km	Bagnères de Luchon

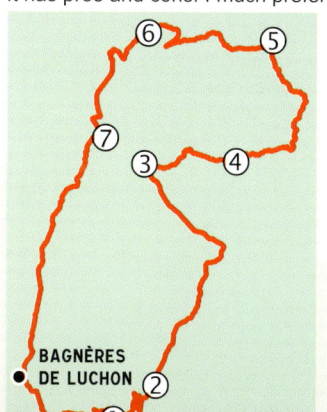

THE TOURMALET BOTH WAYS

This out-and-back route highlights an issue that's more prevalent when tackling the bigger passes in the Alps. Because these climbs tend to be in more remote regions, completing a circular route can mean an extremely long day in the saddle. While I've included a ride over the Tourmalet that starts and finishes in Bagnères de Bigorre (see page 150), this double ascent of this legendary Tour de France pass is around 30km shorter than that ride and also allows those who tackle it to give an immediate answer to the perennial question of which side is the toughest.

My take is that the toughest flank is whichever one you're on at the time, or even the side tackled second on this ride given the fatigue that's already been accumulated earlier in the day. My other observation is that the western ascent from Luz St Sauveur is more spectacular and therefore should be saved until last, which is why I've chosen to start in Ste Marie de Campan next to the statue of Eugène Christophe brandishing a newly fixed set of forks after the Frenchman had to carry his bike for 10km down the Tourmalet to the nearby forge to carry out that repair in the 1913 Tour.

It also has the advantage of starting more gently, with four initial kilometres that rise little more than 150m vertically before the gradient steepens beyond Gripp. As the road rises alongside the fast-flowing Adour de Gripp, veering away from the wider Adour valley (see page 154) that eventually leads up to the Col d'Aspin, the mountainsides start to close in. There are 13km remaining to the summit, the average close to 8.5% all the way, the road reaching that mark above Artigues going into an elongated hairpin where the apex points into the heart of the Arbizon massif.

Just beyond it an information board marks the approximate point where Christophe's forks failed in 1913, the resort of La Mongie coming into sight soon after.

The four kilometres before the ski station are the toughest on this side of the pass, the gradient sticking stubbornly around 10% as the road passes beneath a series of avalanche-protection shelters. La Mongie, the biggest skiing domain in the Pyrenees, is an eyesore, blighted by ugly 1970s blocks, a long way from the retreat for monks that was its original reason for being and from which it derives its name. Above it the terrain opens out, the road running between soaring peaks to the north and south, the 2724m Pic des Quatres Termes and surrounding pinnacles to the left, the 2872m Pic du Midi de Bigorre to the right, its eyrie-like observatory and weather station glinting in the sun on clear days.

The summit arrives via a series of hairpins. At the crest, there's a monument to long-time Tour de France director Jacques Goddet and a sculpture of Octave Lapize in lung-busting action, the Frenchman the first racer to reach the Tourmalet's summit in the 1910 Tour. Taken down each winter, the sculpture is replaced on the first Saturday in June, hundreds of cyclists riding up the pass that morning behind a truck carrying both the Lapize statue and a brass band.

The descent away from the summit is very fast to begin with, highlighting where the main difficulty lies when coming back up from Luz Saint Sauveur. It hurtles past Super Barèges, tiny compared to La Mongie, and into Barèges, the gradient easing on the final stretch into Luz, which has a lot more refuelling options than Ste Marie de Campan, providing another good reason for doing the double in this direction.

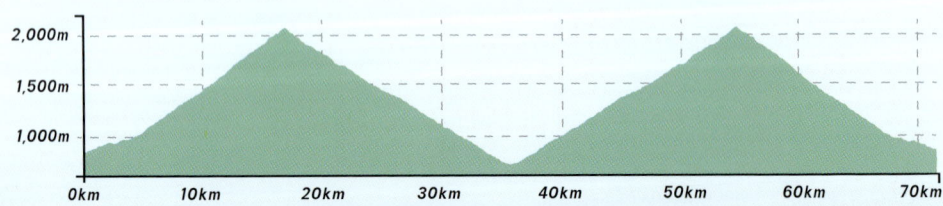

HAUTES PYRÉNÉES

Storm clouds over the western flank of the Tourmalet

The gradient is more consistent from the west, sticking at around 8%, the road much wider than it is on the eastern flank. Going into and through Barèges, it kicks up more sharply until it reaches the right turn to the original route to the pass, now the Voie Laurent Fignon, a one-way, bike-only route that splits away from the new road for 4.2km. Re-constructed after devastating floods washed away sections in 2013, the Fignon route is not as well maintained and a good deal steeper than the newer alternative through Super Barèges. With the steep final pitch up to the summit clearly visible and intimidatingly distant, there's a choice to be made: stay left and have it a little easier, or fork right and savour a bit of history that's completely car-free. The extent of your physical resources may be the deciding factor, but the Fignon way is worth exploring at some point.

The two roads merge with four kilometres to the summit. At close to 2,000m, these can be hard going, but the incredible views around the circus of peaks certainly should provide a spur, the Pic de Midi observatory much more evident and impressive from this flank. The road-painted names of cycling stars current and past may offer further motivation on this the Tour's most visited ascent.

The return to Ste Marie de Campan is fast as far as Artigues, but not too technical. Watch out, though, for livestock on the road, particularly in the avalanche shelters where sheep tend to gather in hot or inclement conditions – in other words, quite frequently. Below Artigues, the descent is straightforward, unless you fancy going full-on Eugène Christophe and shouldering your bike for 10km down to that forge.

Distance: 71.7km
Elevation gain: 2,707m
Highest point: 2,115m
Est. moving time: 3-5.5hrs
Degree of difficulty: ●●●●
Climbs: Col du Tourmalet (twice!)

Route in reverse

Just as good, the choice of direction being largely dependent on where you're travelling from.

Parcours

0km	Ste Marie de Campan
13km	La Mongie
17km	Col du Tourmalet ①
36km	Luz St Sauveur ②
43km	Barèges
45.6km	Voie Laurent Fignon ③
54.5km	Col du Tourmalet ①
71.2km	Ste Marie de Campan

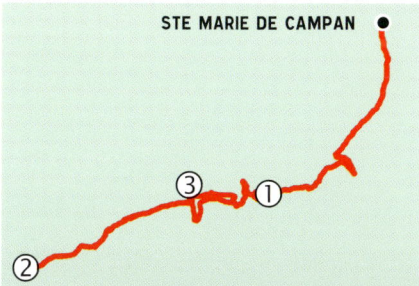

TOUR OF THE BIGORRE

Even the shortest circular routes over the Tourmalet come in at around 100km, the little variations between them depending on the roads taken through the low hills between Bagnères de Bigorre and Lourdes. My preferred option is not the shortest in terms of either distance or time, but it's arguably the most consistently attractive and light on traffic, cutting through the hills to the south of Lourdes in this southern part of the historic Bigorre region, which became part of the department of Hautes Pyrénées in 1790 as part of the administrative shake-up following the French Revolution.

From Bagnères de Bigorre, follow the main D935 road 3km north to Pouzac, turning left here onto the D26 towards Juncalas. This, the first of several lanes on which this route trundles westwards through the low foothills of the Pyrenees, soon enters an area of woodland and meadows, pretty hamlets and neatly-kept farms. Bear right at the first fork, climbing to a second one and going left to Neuilh, getting a first view south into the peaks, Hautacam among the closest.

At Neuilh, where the landscape opens up very impressively to the north, go right at a third fork towards Germ. It may not sound tempting, but it's well worth it, the road climbing briskly to reach a bracken-covered ridge with a fine view towards the Bigourdian capital of Tarbes and the plains to the north. Passing a right turn to a viewpoint and picnic area, the gradient eases a little for a few hundred metres, then picks up even more steeply, with a kilometre at 11%, to reach the Col de la Croix Blanche, from which the panorama is almost 360° and absolutely marvellous.

Descend from that high point to the edge of Germ, then cut back right towards Juncalas. This lane drops for 12km to Lugagnan, a few kilometres to the south of Lourdes. It's not too scarped initially, but it drops more sharply from kilometre two to four, haring down to a T-junction, where Juncalas to the left remains the goal. Go left again soon after at the Col de Lingous, the descent to Juncalas much more sedate, the road beyond there tracking the River Néez through Saint Créac to a T-junction on the D13, turning left here to head south (see page 168).

Stay with the D13 for 14km, passing the turn to Hautacam, going through Préchac and grazing the edge of Beaucens to merge with the main D913 road up this wide and fertile valley to a roundabout just south of Pierrefitte Nestalas, bearing left and keeping in a southerly direction into the Gorge de Luz (see page 164). Covering most of the 11km to Luz Saint Sauveur, this section is spectacular but can be busy, particularly at weekends and in high summer, because it's the main route towards the mountain circuses of Gavarnie and Troumouse, as well as into Luz Saint Sauveur and to the western side of the Tourmalet. The drama of the setting beats the drawbacks with the traffic every time, though.

Heading along the long straight into the centre of Luz Saint Sauveur, the slope starts to rise gently, the road sweeping left-handed, the gradient edging up a little more running alongside the rocky course of the Bastan. I find these initial kilometres a little dull. Like the river, the road has been reworked substantially in recent decades, and understandably so given the devastation caused by flash flooding. There is, though, a lack of romance, of Pyrenean character, the tightness of the valley and consequent lack of scenic distraction not helping either.

This changes, though, at Barèges, where the gradient gets more abrupt than steady-

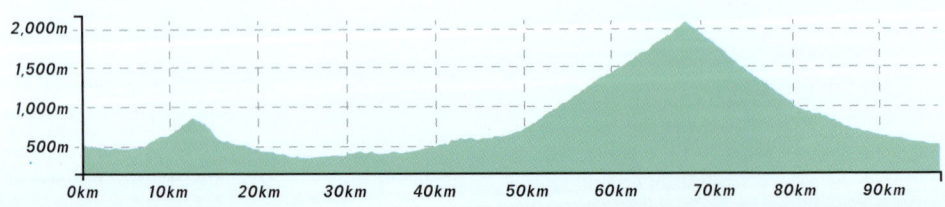

HAUTES PYRÉNÉES

Panorama from just above the Tourmalet pass

as-you-go 7.5%. The river and, as a result, the road start to meander and the open mountainsides and circus of peaks that characterise the upper half of the Tourmalet begin to emerge. The going is harder, but far less monotonous, and that unveiling continues on the new section of road the climb has followed since 2014 into Super Barèges after a devastating flood the year before washed out parts of what is now the Laurent Fignon cycle route.

The view is wonderful across to the old road and the mountains above it, the peaks on the northern edge of the Néouvielle massif peeping in from behind them as you climb. Although recently built, this section feels entirely Pyrenean, emblematic even, ascending into a glorious natural cathedral. Climbing through these final 8km to this famous pass, I always struggle but the same thought always emerges: this is why I ride. Even the final 10.5% kilometre to the pass can't dispel this. In fact, it's so majestic that it bolsters that belief.

The descent is fast but not overly technical, wandering livestock often the main concern. Sainte Marie de Campan arrives quickly, the road continuing to drop beyond it travelling north through Campan and back to Bagnères de Bigorre, a cycling rite of passage completed.

Route in reverse

The Tourmalet, and therefore most of the climbing, comes right at the start, which some may prefer. The 12km from Bagnères provide a good warm-up for it. Travel down the Gorge de Luz will be quicker and, therefore, there will be a little less exposure to that sometimes busy segment.

Distance: 97.6km
Elevation gain: 2,470m
Highest point: 2,115m
Est. moving time: 4-6.5hrs
Degree of difficulty: ●●●○
Climbs: Col de la Croix Blanche (906m), Col du Tourmalet (2,115m)

Parcours

0km	Bagnères de Bigorre
3km	Pouzac D935/D26 ←
7km	D26/D18 →
10km	D26/D18 ←
10.5km	Neuilh D26/D99 ←
12.5km	Col de la Croix Blanche ①
13km	Germ D99/D299 →
16.5km	D299/D26 ←
17km	D26/D7 ←
20.5km	Juncalas bear left on D26
24.5km	D26/D13 ← ②
36.5km	D13/D913 ←
39km	D913/D921 ← ③
50km	Luz St Sauveur D921/D918 ← ④
57km	Barèges
69km	Col du Tourmalet ⑤
85.5km	Ste Marie de Campan D918/D935 ← ⑥
97.6km	Bagnères de Bigorre

151

THE MAJESTIC COL DE PORTET

Showcased by the 2018 Tour de France, the Col de Portet has quickly joined the bucket list of Pyrenean climbs, a must-do for those who want to follow in the wheeltracks of Nairo Quintana, the winner that day. That stage was unusual, extending to just 65km between Luchon and the Portet, crossing the Peyresourde and Azet passes on the way. It's a stunning ride, but beyond the scope of most as an out-and-back option. This loop, though, gives a strong flavour of it.

It starts in Saint Lary Soulan, the attractive resort town in the Aure valley that sits between the Azet and Portet passes, taking the backroad to Vielle Aure and then north along the east bank of La Neste d'Aure. Bear right very briefly onto the main D929 to cross the river, veering left on the west bank to climb the hillside to Bazus Aure and Gouaux, continuing to rise to arrive in the pretty village of Lançon huddled around its striking Sainte Eulalie church (see page 152).

The road continues upwards to arrive at the Col de Lançon, descending from there through woodland to meet the D618, the main road up along the Louron valley, at Bordères Louron. Turn right onto it, ascending very modestly to Avajan, bearing right into this village and continuing for another 4km to Génos, at the foot of the Col d'Azet. This shortish pass was the 2018 Tour's final jump towards the Portet and is one of my favourites, with a lot packed in to its comparatively modest 7.4km length. It begins steeply, the first kilometre at 9%, then gets harder as it pinballs up the mountainside through 10 tightly spaced hairpins, reaching its easier second half coming out of the last of them, woodland giving way to open pasture at the same time, the views up and across the Louron absolutely majestic.

The summit panorama is even better, and well worth a pause for a few minutes to savour the 360° perspective. The descent away from it is quick, sweeping around a vast bowl initially, then scooting down to Azet, where the road narrows so much at a couple of points that you half-think you're riding down someone's driveway. The helter-skelter drop continues through Estensan, Sailhan and to the valley floor for the return to Saint Lary Soulan, continuing to Vignec to tackle the first sharp hairpin on the 16km ascent to the Portet.

It's the rudest of starts, the road rising at 10% to the next corner a kilometre and a half away. A plaque here marks the point where, in 1974, the 38-year-old Raymond Poulidor attacked Eddy Merckx and rode away to take a solo win at Pla d'Adet. The hard grind continues beyond it. Indeed, there's no noticeable easing of the slope until the village of Espiaube with its huge car parks for skiers, just short of halfway up.

Here, the road splits, the main route going left towards Pla d'Adet, the right fork continuing past more car parks to reach the turn to the Col de Portet, another 9km away. The gradient picks up, but not too much to begin with. Once the road reaches the first of 11 hairpins rising ladder-like up the rocky mountainside, the true difficulty of this climb emerges. The next three kilometres rise 300m, but with the gradient shifting almost all the time, from 20% to five and back again. Just be thankful that the road is well surfaced. Before the Tour's visit, it was very inconsistent, sections of decaying tarmac interspersed with long stretches of rubble and ballast where it was impossible to follow a straight line.

There's some relief in the two kilometres above these hairpins, and a chance to look

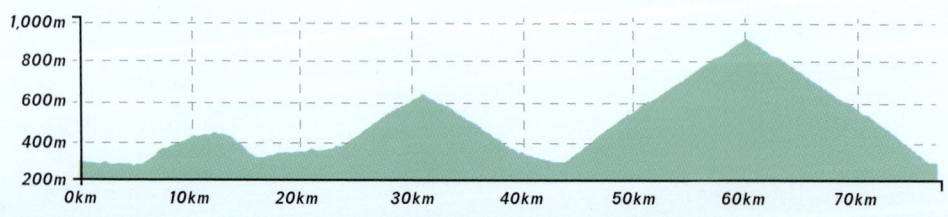

HAUTES PYRÉNÉES

Tightly coiled hairpins on the Col de Portet

ahead to the summit on the far side of the valley, its network of ski lifts surrounded by a ring of mountains. Another more abrupt pitch takes you above 2,000m, the final shift across to the summit including passage through a short, curving tunnel that's unlit, which is perhaps just as well because the smell inside makes it very clear that livestock frequently use it as a shelter. Returning to the light, the pass doesn't give itself up easily, its last kilometre almost 10%.

The staggering view from the highest point the Tour has ever reached in the French Pyrenees fully justifies what for most will be a slog. The Azet can be picked out across the Aure valley and, if it's clear, the Peyresourde beyond. In the other direction are the peaks at the eastern end of the Néouvielle massif, which overlook Lac d'Aumar and Lac de Cap de Long (see page 162). With rocks, sheep and cattle on the road, take the descent steadily, at least as far as Espiaube. Below that, on the wider and better surfaced road coming down from Piau Engaly, let rip. Recovery in Saint Lary is just a few minutes away.

Route in reverse

It comes down to the direction in which you want to tackle the Col d'Azet. They're quite different, but equally good. I liked the chance to get a good bite of the climbing done early on, but for a more Tour-like experience tackle the Azet and the Portet one after the other.

Distance: 77.4km
Elevation gain: 2,758m
Highest point: 2,215m
Est. moving time: 3-5hrs
Degree of difficulty: ●●●◐
Climbs: Col de Lançon (1,120m), Col d'Azet (1,580m), Col de Portet (2,215m)

Parcours

0km	Saint Lary Soulan D929
1km	D929 ←
1.5km	D929/D19 →
5km	D19/D929 →
	then D929/D25 ← ①
12.5km	Col de Lançon ②
16.5km	D618/D25 →
23km	D618/D25 → ③
24km	Génos D25/D225 →
31.5km	Col d'Azet ④
38.5km	Estensan D225/D25 ←
42km	D25/D929 →
	then D929/D19 ← ⑤
43.5km	Saint Lary Soulan D19/D223 ←
44km	Vignec D223/D123 →
51.5km	Espiaube D123/ unclassified to Col de Portet →
60.5km	Col de Portet ⑥
77.4km	Saint Lary Soulan

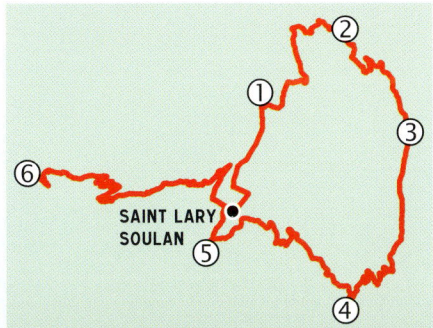

BEAUTIFUL AND ENDLESS MOUNTAIN VIEWS

Owner of the Col Collective cycle touring company, Mike Cotty has long made a business out of riding and leading trips in the high mountains, including the Pyrenees, where he's made his home. Reading my tweet for route suggestions when I was planning this book, he sent this one, describing it as one of his favourites thanks to its "beautiful and endless mountain views".

It commences in Sainte Marie de Campan, next to the statue of Eugène Christophe, who is immortalised brandishing the fork that he re-set in the village forge during the 1913 Tour de France having shouldered his bike for 10km down the Col du Tourmalet. That building, now a house, is a few hundred metres to the north of the village and is marked with a plaque. From the junction adjacent to Christophe's statue, head south on the D918 towards Arreau and the Aspin. The road bumps along through pasture and then woodland, the waters of the Adour de Payolle never far away. After half a dozen kilometres, it reaches Payolle, where the routes to the Hourquette d'Ancizan and Aspin diverge. Branch right over the river towards the former on the D113, crossing a cattle grid to enter wide-open grazing land that extends to the edge of Lac de Payolle, the turn towards the lake marking the point where the climb truly begins.

Rising through thickening woodland, the gradient remains quite comfortable, the road quiet and quite glorious, and even more so as it suddenly emerges from the trees and the first of those beautiful mountain views Mike highlighted appears, the ribbon of tarmac running through the middle of a bare-sided valley towards the high peaks of the Arbizon massif. A sharp turn arrives that leads up the hillside to a tree-enclosed crest, from which the road drops into the parallel valley for the final 3km to the summit.

There are strong hints of North Wales, the Lake District and Scotland in this landscape, no doubt because the abundant livestock keep the vegetation trimmed back to boulder-strewn grassland. This leaves the terrain so open that you're swivelling to take the whole magnificence in, pedalling now very much a subconscious action, to the extent that the summit of the Hourquette – believed to be derived from a Latin-turned-Gascon word for a pass – arrives almost by surprise, the Aure valley visible to the east and the Pic de Midi nosing above the mountain ridge to the west.

On the drop to the east it quickly becomes apparent why the Tour de France and other races tend to tackle it from that side. There are no false flats or short drops, it's a full-on downhill all the way, the gradient steepening significantly towards Guchen at the bottom. There are long views up the Aure towards Saint Lary Soulan in the final third, although you won't want to linger on them for long with the gradient at 9% and more. At the junction just above the valley floor, stay right towards Guchen and Saint Lary, and then go right again in Guchen on the D929. A little further on as this main road switches across the east bank of the Neste d'Aure, keep straight on the D19 on the west bank to reach Saint Lary, rejoining the D929 at the far end of this town, then almost immediately switching hard left on the D25 to climb the Col d'Azet.

Like the Hourquette, we're coming at this pass from its easier side, although that's where the comparisons end. The Azet's not hard to begin with, but is a stiff test above Sailhan, the gradient at 8-9% for 5km. Once again, though, it's the mountain views that hold your focus. Initially, it's the Zorro-like white scar on the hillside to the west that's

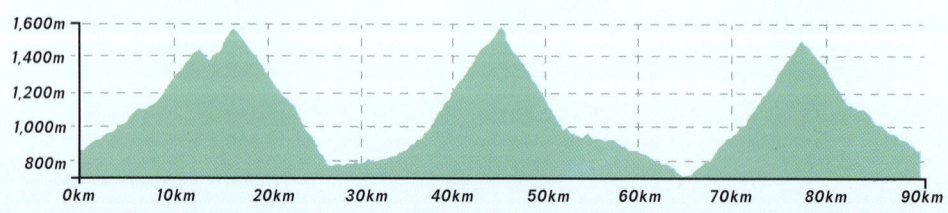

HAUTES PYRÉNÉES

the opening section of the climb to Pla d'Adet and the Col de Portet that stands out. Above the village of Azet, a staggering panorama unfolds, the resort of Pla d'Adet appearing and then a ring of peaks encircling it, before the angle changes again and the summits dividing the Aure and Louron valleys dominate. Higher still, on the final push to the Azet pass, this ensemble comes together in majestic fashion, and then combines with an equally arresting vista around the Louron valley when you roll up to the summit.

The road dives down to Génos (see page 162), the gradient at its steepest through a series of hairpins towards the bottom. Turn left in the village on the D25 heading north, this road soon merging with the D618, which descends steadily to the picturesque riverside town of Arreau. Go right on the D929 having crossed the river in the town centre, continuing north for a kilometre to reach the start of Aspin pass on the left.

Shorter and tougher than the western flank from Sainte Marie de Campan, it rises steadily through woodland, which soon recedes to reveal another impressive perspective, this time down the Aure valley, the Nistos massif to east and the rugged Baronnies region to the west. As on the Azet, the outlook keeps changing as you rise, the 3,000m-plus peaks along the Franco-Spanish border often clear as the road makes a long sweep beneath the Pic de Ger prior to the final two hairpins that step up towards the summit, the roadpaint left over from the most recent of more than six dozen crossings by the Tour very evident. This final section offers yet another breath-taking vista, best taken in a couple of hundred metres prior to the summit.

At the pass, there's another and much clearer view to the Pic de Midi before a rapid drop on longish straights back to Payolle to complete the three-col loop, the final 6km an easy return to Sainte Marie de Campan taken in the other direction earlier in the day.

Route in reverse

The climbing is a little harder, but not enough to put anyone off. This is definitely a circuit worth tackling in both directions because of the very different and equally impressive perspectives they offer.

View down the eastern side of the Aspin pass

Distance: 89.4km
Elevation gain: 2,606m
Highest point: 1,580m
Est. moving time: 3.5-5.5hrs
Degree of difficulty: ●●●◐
Climbs: Hourquette d'Ancizan (1,564m), Col d'Azet (1,580m), Col d'Aspin (1,489m)

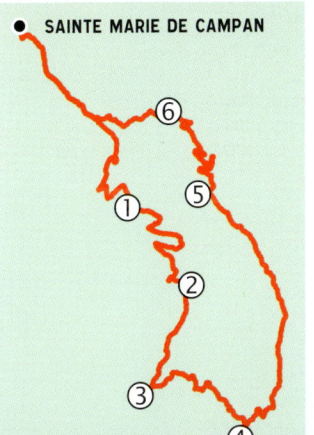

Parcours

0km	Sainte Marie de Campan
7km	Payolle D918/D113 ➡
16.5km	Hourquette d'Ancizan ①
25.5km	D113/D30 ➡
26km	D30/D113 ⬅
27km	Guchen D113/D929 ➡
28km	D929/D19 ➡ ②
33.5km	Saint Lary Soulan D929/D25 ⬅ ③
44.5km	Col d'Azet ④
51km	Génos D25 ⬅
55.5km	D25/D618 ⬅
64km	Arreau D618/D929 ➡ ⑤
65km	D929/D918 ⬅
76.5km	Col d'Aspin ⑥
89.4km	Sainte Marie de Campan

TOUR OF THE COMMINGES

Founded by the Romans in first century BC and established as a bishopric in the fifth century AD, the Comminges area in the Pyrenean foothills is often bypassed in the rush to get to the higher peaks and famous passes that lie to the south of it. It is, though, an area that merits exploration as this circuit is intended to demonstrate. It's not as rugged as the Baronnies further to the west, but like that secretive region it's a warren of undulating lanes, with, in this case, the addition of the equally overlooked ascent to the small cross-country ski station of Nistos-Cap Nestès.

Starting in the pretty village of La Barthe de Neste, head east on the D938 towards Montréjeau, running through agricultural land overlooked by those foothills, higher peaks peeping through at times. Encouraged by the prevailing wind and with the gradient slightly in your favour, progress should be smooth and serene. These roads are ideal for an easier day, particularly if the diversion to the tiny ski station above Nistos is bypassed.

Approaching Montréjeau, a wide swathe of mountainous terrain emerges across the pan-flat fields, stretching from the peaks of western Ariège at one o'clock to the Pic de Midi at five, the view underlining the spectacular benefits of rides outside the highlands. Keep straight through the centre of Montréjeau, following the signs to Luchon that lead down to a bridge over the Garonne and the start of a 40km loop through the Comminges.

Making initially for Cier de Rivière and then Barbazan, the terrain gets lumpier running into low and heavily wooded hills. Beyond Sauveterre de Comminges, the route climbs through a ravine to reach the Col Bouchet, continuing to rise through a series of pretty villages, Saint Pé d'Ardet the pick of them. At the early high point of Mont de Galié, where there are tantalising views of glowering peaks to the west, Nistos amidst them, a thrillingly twisting descent dives into and across the Garonne valley, where the route switches north to Bertren, then turns to run parallel to the Pyrenean foothills.

It skirts Saint Bertrand de Comminges, once the capital of this region, parts of its magnificent cathedral and cloisters dating from the 11th century and surrounded by a medieval village that has been garlanded as one of France's most beautiful. Standing proudly on a small hill above the plain around it, it's been dubbed the Pyrenean Mont Saint Michel. The road passing this historic town is very fetching too, alternating between farmland and woodland as it hurries westwards, passing the Grottes de Gargas, renowned for its hand-stencil cave paintings and engravings of prehistoric animals such as aurochs and mammoth.

At Aventignan there's a choice of routes: go right on the D26 to complete an 80km loop back to La Barthe de Neste or keep straight on to Nistos. The little-known climb is widely listed as being 24km long, but the opening dozen don't contribute much vertical gain. Rising gently through agricultural land interspersed with beautiful deciduous woods, the road tracks the River Nistes upstream through a string of farming villages. In the last of them, Gerlé, it swings left and sharply upwards.

The next 6km average 9% on what may be the most understated access road to a resort anywhere in the Pyrenees, often not much more than a car width across. Thick woods conceal the surrounding landscape, until, with the gradient dropping to threes and twos, the road emerges onto the bottom end of a ski run and reveals a view extending for an

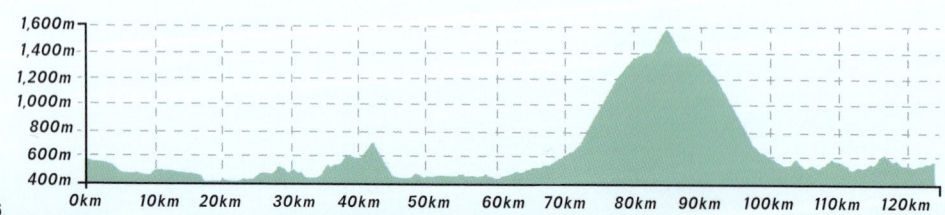

HAUTES PYRÉNÉES

Saint Bertrand de Comminges

immense distance across the flatlands of Hautes Pyrénées and Haute Garonne.

After contouring for another kilometre or so, the road re-emerges onto open mountainside, this time revealing the steep two-kilometre climb up to the summit that gives this portion of the route its odd profile, like a Pickelhaube, the distinctive 19th-century German military helmet. Pitching up at close to 9%, it winds into a large bowl, the "resort" at the top just a single building. Unfortunately, there's no jaw-dropping view to compensate for the effort expended on the climb, but the road from the valley is so scenic and serene that it hardly matters.

The return is by the same route until the D75 branches to the left just beyond the village of Nistos towards Bize, continuing north-west through rich green pasture to Montsérié, Montoussé and, from the centre of that village, back to La Barthe de Neste.

Route in reverse

As already stated, I always prefer to leave the main highlight of any ride till as late as possible. As always, though, I'm sure there are plenty of riders out there who will prefer to get the bigger part of the climbing behind them while they're still quite fresh, which would clearly be the case doing this circuit the other way around.

Distance: 118km
Elevation gain: 2,316m
Highest point: 1,592m
Est. moving time: 4.5-6.5hrs
Degree of difficulty: ●●●
Climbs: Col du Bouchet (608m), Nistos Cap Nestès (1,592m)

Parcours

0km	La Barthe de Neste D938
17km	Montréjeau D817/D825 → ①
18.5km	D825/D34 ←
20km	D34/D8B →
23.5km	Cire de Rivière D8B/D33L
27.5km	Barbazan D33L/D26 ←
31.5km	Garnère D26/D9 →
38km	Col Bouchet ②
39.5km	Saint Pé d'Ardet D9/D33B →
42km	Mont de Galié
46km	D33B/D825 → ③
49.5km	Castans D825/D26 ←
60.5km	Aventignan D26/D71 ← ④
85km	Nistos Cap Nestès ⑤
102.5km	D71/D75 ←
106km	Bize D75/D775 ← ⑥
108.5km	D775/D526 ←
111km	Montsérié D526/DD526A ←
112km	Montoussé D142
118km	La Barthe de Neste

157

TOUR OF THE BARONNIES

Lying to the south of a line between Bagnères de Bigorre and Lannemezan, the Baronnies is perfect for exploration by bike. Criss-crossed by streams and rivers, it's a maze of lanes that are continually meandering and incessantly undulating, and therefore not an area to venture into with the intention of getting anywhere fast. It's not by mistake that the main roads stick to its borders.

It's an area generally bypassed, but this route suggested by Reg and Sue Bettam, owners of the Le Closier bike B&B at La Barthe de Neste, aims to show that this warren of surprises merits a diversion, not least for the fine views into the Pyrenees from the string of cols on its southern edge. Commencing in Bagnères de Bigorre, a busy spa town long associated with cycling thanks to its proximity to the several famous passes and regular appearances on the Tour de France route, the first step is towards one of the highest of these passes, the Col des Palomières. Picking up the D84 on the eastern edge of Bagnères de Bigorre, this road heads south through woodland, climbing steadily for 4km to the pass, which is very open and offers an expansive panorama to the north towards Tarbes.

From this crest, this rollercoaster route drops into woodland, the road bordered by the rusty mulch of beech leaves. Head through Banios and towards Asque, this stretch is archetypally Baronnies, running through thick woodland one moment, out on a ridge with fine views the next, the road twisting so much that you're never quite sure what you're looking at. After a sharp drop into Asque, a quartet of tight hairpins lead up to the Couret d'Asque and a super view along the line of Pyrenean foothills to the east.

Continuing through the Baronnies labyrinth via Bulan and Laborde, the route reaches Esparros, the most renowned of around 400 limestone caves in the Baronnies, many of them linked by underwater tunnels. Inevitably, having descended into the village, the next step is upwards to reach a ridge that rises to the Col de Coupe, looking south over the Baronnies forest towards the 1,921m Signal de Bassia.

From this high point, the D26 drops sedately to the eastern edge of the Baronnies, the route then switching north to La Barthe de Neste. Pick up the D938 in the centre of this large and busy village, following it for 4km, then turning onto the Route des Baronnies to Tilhouse, the road soon reaching a crest, unveiling a magnificent panorama of the mountains that stretches for dozens of kilometres in both directions.

Unusually for this region, the road stays level and runs straight for a good while, allowing you to dwell on this vista until a dip leads back into the spider's web of lanes, first reaching Bourg de Bigorre and then Espieilh, the road climbing steeply through this village to merge with the D26, which wriggles and rolls almost all of the way back to Bagnères de Bigorre, mostly concealed within beautiful woodland but occasionally peeking above the trees to peer to the north. From Haut de la Côte – the top of the hill – turn left to drop back into Bagnères to complete a lovely, but sometimes dizzying, 65km loop.

Those who fancy a little more exploration of this area's back roads should go into Bagnères de Bigorre and pick up the main road north, the D935, following it until a left turn to Labassère. I stumbled across this attractive detour while searching for the Col du Couret, which, like the nearby Col de la Courade, looked intriguing on the map but needs a lot of work before it'll be suitable for

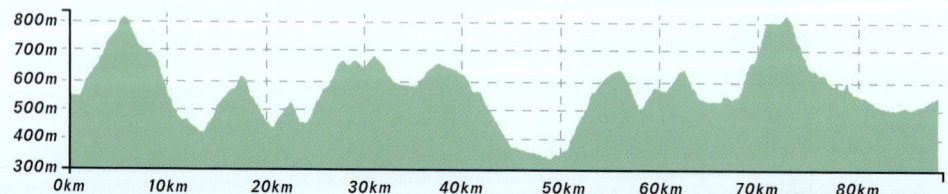

HAUTES PYRÉNÉES

In the heart of the Baronnies near Esparros

Distance: 88.9km
Elevation gain: 2,062m
Highest point: 1,417m
Est. moving time: 2.5-4.5hrs
Degree of difficulty: ●●●
Climbs: Col des Palomières (810m), Couret d'Asque (620m), Col de Coupe (720m), Col de Saoucède (835m)

road bikes again. Rising comfortably through open farmland, it steepens sharply towards the imposing church at Labassère, then eases back again to reach the Col de Saoucède.

Beyond the col, the road hurries down into Soulagnets. From here, track the River Oussouet downstream, the road and water never far apart until what has become the D26 sways right to Pouzac and from there back to Bagnères de Bigorre.

Route in reverse

Just as nice, no easier or harder. The loop over the Col Saoucède can once again be left until the end, or left out completely. Once in the Baronnies, there are numerous routes to choose from. It's an ideal place to wander without any clear destination, as it's never that far back to your start point.

Parcours

0km	Bagnères de Bigorre D938 and D84
5.5km	Col des Palomières ①
11km	Banios D84/D384 ➡
14km	Asque D384/D826 ➡
15.5km	Couret d'Asque D26 ②
17.5km	Bulan
22.5km	D26/D77 ➡ to Esparros
27km	Col de Coupe D26 ③
29.5km	D26/D929 ⬅
36km	La Barthe de Neste ④ D929/D938 ⬅
40km	D938/D82 ⬅
45.5km	D82/D14 ➡
49.5km	Bourg de Bigorre D14/D84 ⬅ ⑤
51km	D84/D684 ➡ to Espieilh
53km	D684/D26 ➡
63km	Haut de la Côte D26/D938 ⬅
64.5km	D938/D8 ➡ then ⬅ to D935 and ➡
66km	Bagnères de Bigorre D935/D88 ⬅
73.5km	Col de Saoucède ⑥
75.5km	Soulagnets D88/D18 ➡
82km	D18/D26
86km	Pouzac ⑦
88.9km	Bagnères de Bigorre

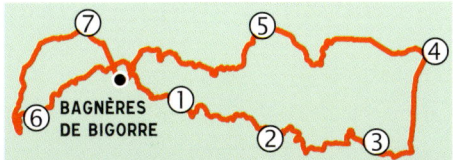

NÉOUVIELLE HIGH-RISE TRIPTYCH

From high up on the Col d'Azet, the mountains to the west of Saint Lary Soulan appear impenetrable, and as far as bikes are concerned they effectively are. The only way out of the bottom end of this valley is via the Aragnouet Bielsa tunnel into Spain, a route that's for motor vehicles only. There are, though, roads that are well worth exploring in this magnificent highland area, one to the ski station of Piau Engaly, which hosted a Tour de France stage finish in 1999, and another that accesses the stunning Cap de Long and Aumar mountain lakes that are just a few kilometres from the Col de Portet as the crow flies.

Like that spectacular cul-de-sac that first appeared on the Tour parcours in 2018, the path towards this trio of high points begins in Saint Lary Soulan. From the western end of this resort town, head in that same direction on the main valley road. The scenery is impressive from the off, tracking the River Neste d'Aure through a gorge and gaining altitude steadily. At Fabian, turn right towards the Néouvielle Natural Reserve, this a toll road for cars and other vehicles since 2019 but free to cyclists.

The first objective is Lake Orédon, where the road to Lakes Aumar and Cap de Long splits. Right away, it's a dramatic ride, the road often cut into the cliffs steepling up above the Neste de Couplan river. The gradient picks up as well, but it's not too fierce, holding to around 7% for 5km. Above the right turn onto the track that climbs to the Oule reservoir, it picks up a point, with regular sections nudging into double figures. At the same time, the road begins to clear the pine forest, switching through a string of hairpins, their outside edge protected by the squat and square concrete bollards that used to be so characteristic of the French Pyrenees but have been mostly filled in to become low walls that are more effective as barriers.

Above the pleasing curves of these half-dozen switchbacks, the road runs along a lofty ledge to reach a fork, the high side continuing for 3.5km to Lac de Cap de Long, while the low side travels for almost twice that distance to Lac d'Aumar, which is the first objective. Branching right, a kilometre-long drop leads out on the dam at the bottom end of Lac d'Orédon. Half-circling the lake, the road starts to climb, steadily to begin with, then very steeply into the toughest section on this route, with a kilometre ascending through hairpins at 10% and longish sections more acute than that.

The views that come with this rapid altitude gain are wonderful, extending along Orédon's blue waters to the Cap de Long road and into the Néouvielle massif. Approaching the southern edge of Lac d'Aumar, the angle of attack eases, reaching a false flat along the lake shore that just edges above 2,200m and enables contemplation of the circus of peaks to the north and west. A short descent leads into a car park between the Aubert and Aumar reservoirs and an orientation point detailing the panorama, some of the summits featured looking down onto the Col du Tourmalet on their northern side.

Return to the junction adjacent to Lac d'Orédon and turn hard right to climb steeply towards the Cap de Long reservoir, its high dam soon visible up to the right, dwarfed by towering pinnacles. Two tough kilometres lead to a flat section along a balcony with a jaw-dropping view across Lac d'Orédon. Following this short respite, the final kilometre rises sharply through a short ladder of hairpins amidst scree and boulder fields to arrive at the southern end of the dam and

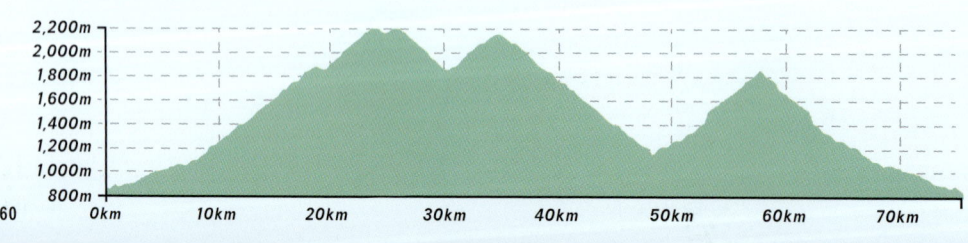

HAUTES PYRÉNÉES

The Cap de Long dam

what is indisputably one of the most wonderful vantage points a road cyclist will see in this region, Piau Engaly just a few kilometres away over the 2944m Pic Méchant to the south.

To reach the ski station, return again to the Orédon junction and continue down through the Couplan forest back to Fabian, turning right towards Spain. This 4km section through Aragnouet to the foot of the climb to the ski station is the steepest on the rise from Saint Lary Soulan. There's a brief respite as you bear right over a bridge towards Piau Engaly, but it's short-lived, the ascent close to 8% for the next 7k. High to the right, the soaring ridge sweeps up to the Méchant. More and loftier summits including the 3,173m Pic de Campbieil start to emerge as the road rises through hairpins, the resort also coming into sight. The angled façades of its buildings give it a space-age look that could be jarring but helps them to blend in to this marvellous landscape, best contemplated from the over-sized car park at the top that provides the almost obligatory finale.

After climbing above 2,000m on two occasions and clocking up more than 2,600m of vertical gain in 58km, the 20km descent to Saint Lary Soulan provides a gratifying reward to complete a staggeringly beautiful ride that should be on everyone's to-do list.

Route in reverse

There's no best way to tackle these three lovely climbs. An alternative route would be to ride them in increasing order of attractiveness, starting with Piau Engaly, then, in my opinion, Lac d'Aumar and, finally, Lac de Cap de Long.

Distance: 77.7km
Elevation gain: 2,618m
Highest point: 2,201m
Est. moving time: 3.5-5.5hrs
Degree of difficulty: ●●●●◐
Climbs: Lac d'Aumar (2,201m), Lac de Cap de Long (2,161m), Piau Engaly (1,870m)

Parcours

0km	Saint Lary Soulan
8.5km	Fabian D929/D118 ➡ ①
18.5km	D929/D177 ➡
24km	Lac d'Aumar ②
31km	D177/D929 ➡
34.5km	Lac de Cap de Long ③
48km	Fabian D929/D118 ➡ ①
51.5km	D118/D173 ➡
58.5km	Piau Engaly ④
65.5km	D118/D173 ⬅
77.7km	Saint Lary Soulan

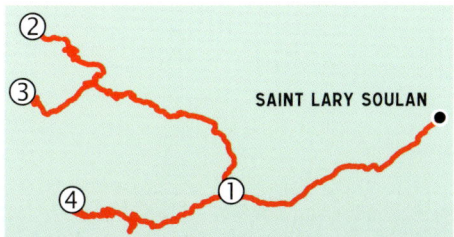

THE MAJESTIC CIRQUES OF GAVARNIE AND TROUMOUSE

Two of the most spectacular rides in this book back onto each other on opposite sides of the Franco-Spanish border. To the south is the route to Ordesa glacial valley in the Ordesa and Monte Perdido National Park (see page 174). To the north of this magnificent geological phenomenon are the equally impressive Cirque de Troumouse and Cirque de Gavarnie. Together they are listed by UNESCO as the Pyrenees Monte Perdido World Heritage Site.

All of these locations get extremely busy during holiday periods, particularly in mid-summer, but much of the hassle that results from this can be avoided by travelling to them by bike. With Luz Saint Sauveur as the base, this route features both of the French cirques, climbing to well above 2,000m at each end of an inverted capital Y, Gavarnie and the Pic de Tentes to the west, Troumouse to the east.

Setting out from the centre of Luz Saint Sauveur, head south on the D921 towards Gèdre. From the off, there's plenty to admire, the road rising at a comfortable rate up the Gorge de Saint Sauveur, soon passing the eastern end of the Pont Napoléon, the 2,031m Montagne de Coumély filling the view at the top end of the valley. Coming out of the pretty village of Gèdre, two very shallow switchbacks lead to a junction, Troumouse 15km away on the D922 to the left, Gavarnie 18km distant to the right. There's no best option on which way to fork first. In this case, it's left to Troumouse simply because it's not as well renowned as Gavarnie, one of Europe's great natural wonders.

Climbing more steeply, the road steps into what begins as a more rural setting, farms surrounded by lush pasture dotting the valley sides. Mighty peaks loom above, hinting at the drama to come. Quickly, the valley tightens and the landscape becomes more rugged, huge scree fields cascading down, the roadsides littered with piles of boulders approaching a right turn to the Lac des Gloriettes and the Cirque d'Estaubé, in between Troumouse and Gavarnie. Beyond the junction is a false flat, the respite well timed as the first sight of the cirque emerges dead ahead.

Passing the Chapelle de Héas a kilometre or so later, the gradient kicks up again, passing the *péage* where motor vehicles had to pay a toll to continue until the summer of 2019, when bigger car parks were opened higher up, shuttle buses now ferrying visitors the last 3km to the circus. Rising into the first of 14 hairpins above the chapel, the breath-taking scale of the glacial cirque starts to become apparent, every switchback revealing a little more of Troumouse's glory.

There's another brief lull at the Auberge du Maillet, where the shuttles begin their journey, the road dropping to cross a stream then rising again on its far side into the final 2.5km, averaging 9.5%. Through the last hairpins, the road straightens, and the astounding sweep of the circus is gloriously complete. Broader than Gavarnie, the ring of mountains soars to 3,000m and beyond, the 3,133m Pic de la Munia the pinnacle. In late spring and early summer, great waterfalls spill down from the snowy summits above, most dwindling away as the heat increases, each leaving a white scar on the cliffs.

Could Gavarnie be any more stunning? It doesn't take long to decide, the drop back down the Héas valley leading quickly to the junction above Gèdre and a left turn, this wider road winding up a wooded gorge, the incline modest for the initial 8km. The first sight of this more renowned circus arrives winding through the village of Gavarnie. It

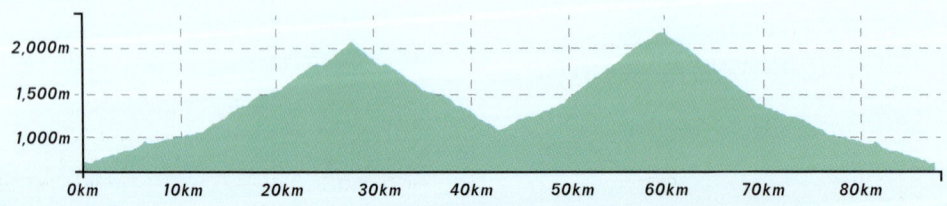

HAUTES PYRÉNÉES

The climb to the Col de Tentes

disappears as the route jags right over the river and starts to rise with more gusto through several hairpins. Initially, the imposing rock wall of the Ossoue valley to the south grabs attention. But as the road switches back southwards to run along a ledge hewn from a towering cliff, the eastern end of the Gavarnie raises the sense of anticipation.

There is, indeed, almost too much to absorb in this bare and rocky landscape – the sweeping bends below, long views to distant mountains, and the sudden appearance of the compact Gavarnie ski station. The circus, though, remains concealed for the most part, hidden behind the ridge on which the Col de Tentes sits. Then, with the gradient easing as the road arcs through upland meadows and limestone pavement, the unveiling gradually commences. There's a clutter of vehicles at the roadside and filling the car park at the col, but beyond them the panorama beggars belief. Even from a height of 2,200m, the peaks forming this cathedral of rock are forbiddingly impressive. There are very few ascents that serve up a reward on this magnitude. Indeed, when it comes to mountain views, this route is out on its own, one that should be on every rider's to-do list.

Route in reverse

I've based my plan of attack on the comparative renown of each of these tremendous natural arenas, but it's probably wiser to make a choice based on traffic. Gavarnie attracts bigger crowds, so heading that way in the early morning may be preferable, bearing in mind that the last 3km to Troumouse are, shuttles apart, traffic-free.

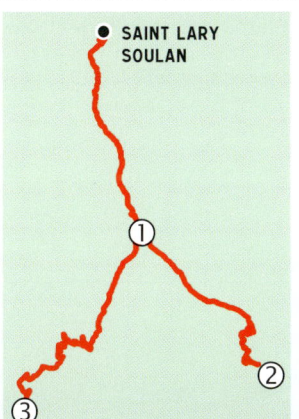

Distance: 90.3km
Elevation gain: 2,857m
Highest point: 2,208m
Est. moving time: 3.5-5.5hrs
Degree of difficulty: ●●●●◐
Climbs: Cirque de Troumouse (2,089m), Col de Tentes (2,208m)

Parcours

0km	Luz Saint Sauveur
12.5km	Gèdre D921/D922 ← ①
28km	Cirque de Troumouse ②
43km	Gèdre D922/D921 ← ①
60km	Col de Tentes ③
90.3km	Luz Saint Sauveur

TWO HAUTES PYRÉNÉES TOUR FAVOURITES

That the name Luz Ardiden has such resonance with me offers a clue to the period when I first became captivated by road racing. The Tour de France first visited in 1985, with Bernard Hinault in the yellow jersey, but struggling with facial injuries sustained in a crash and under pressure from his team-mate Greg LeMond. The Frenchman hung on to his lead, partly due to LeMond being refused permission at Luz Ardiden, and kept it to Paris.

It was the start of a close relationship between the Tour and this mountain that served up plenty more famous moments, not least Lance Armstrong's crash on its lower slopes in 2003 when his bars became entangled in the straps of a fan's bag. Armstrong remounted to win the stage, disappointing the many thousands of Basque fans bedecked in the orange of their hero Iban Mayo's Euskaltel team.

The classic route up to Luz Ardiden is via the Col du Tourmalet (see page 148), but I like this shorter option that also takes in the climb to Cauterets and, above it, the beautiful road to the Pont d'Espagne. Indeed, the fading glory of spa town Cauterets is the first objective from the route's start next to the church in the centre of bustling Argelès Gazost. After negotiating the one-way system, head south towards Pierrefitte Nestalas, which arrives quickly on a lovely section of flat valley road, ideal for leg-loosening. Bear right at the roundabout in the centre towards Cauterets, the road rising through a long switchback to enter a long, twisting gorge carved out by the Gave de Cauterets.

Stepping steeply up through neighbouring sets of hairpins, labelled the Côte de Cauterets when the Tour came this way in 2015, the road reaches a wider part of the valley, running straight into Cauterets at a far gentler angle, the conical Pic de Péguère dominating the view ahead. From the heart of the resort town, its grand buildings testament to its popularity and wealth as a thermal spa centre in the 19th century, follow the signs towards Pont d'Espagne, heading initially up a heavily wooded ravine to La Raillère, where the sulphurous thermal water often leaves a bad odour lingering in the air.

After circling the Griffons spa, the road climbs more steeply into a switchback ladder, entering dense pine forest, cascades tumbling through the trees. The appearance of these cataracts comes as the incline steepens to 10% for 2km, running all the way to the bottom end of the large car park at Pont d'Espagne. It's well worth continuing a little way up to the bridge that spans the confluence of the Gave de Gaube and Gave du Marcadau and once used to link France and Spain, waterfalls plunging into the ravine below it from two sides.

Return via the same roads to Pierrefitte Nestalas, going right here towards Luz Saint Sauveur, soon entering the Gorge de Luz that will be familiar to racing fans as a prelude to the ascent of the Tourmalet (see page 150). Extending most of the way to Luz, it's a lovely section of road, although it's a little disconcerting riding beneath the huge metal nets protecting it from rocks that occasionally tumble down from the cliffs above. At Luz Saint Sauveur stay on the D921 towards Gavarnie (see page 162), then bear right over the Gave de Gavarnie on the edge of Luz, switching around a hairpin to arrive at the right turn onto the climb.

At 13.5km long and with an average incline of 7.7%, it's got a similar profile to Tour's famous Alpine ascent of Alpe d'Huez, but this more southerly of the two ascents to "The

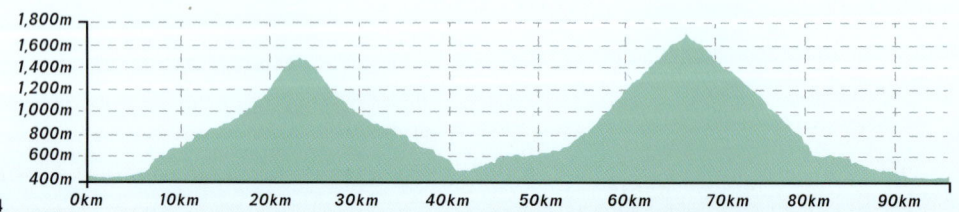

HAUTES PYRÉNÉES

Hairpins leading up to Luz Ardiden

Pyrenean Alpe d'Huez" begins less dauntingly, its opening 3km quite benign. Where this climb scores heavily over the Alpe is in looks. Rather than being an obvious and very impressive demonstration of mountain road engineering, the road to Luz Ardiden is more aesthetically considerate.

At Sazos, its complexion begins to alter, the angle sharpening a couple of points rising through woodland to Grust, then rearing up a little more with 3km above 9%. It eases thereafter, the views becoming more arresting after passing the turn to Viscos that will route back to the Luz valley. As the trees give way to steep grassy banks, the Pic de Midi can be picked out among the peaks to the east, while the curves of the hairpins below also draw the eye. In total, there are 25 switchbacks, a few more than Alpe d'Huez, the last one just before the ski station. Unfortunately, the main building at the summit spoils things, its glass and steel front utilitarian to say the least, although it is at least quite small. It is possible to ride a little higher, a service road continuing for a kilometre or so before turning to gravel, the view back across the ski station just before this making it well worth the effort.

Descend back 4km to reach the left turn to Viscos. This is much narrower than the main route to the resort. Although well surfaced for the most part, it should be taken with care. At Viscos, it does get a little wider, running into the two steepest kilometres back into the valley, arriving just above the Luz gorge and the gentle return to Argelès Gazost.

Distance: 94.4km
Elevation gain: 2,744m
Highest point: 1,718m
Est. moving time: 3.5-5.5hrs
Degree of difficulty: ●●●●
Climbs: Pont d'Espagne (1,463m), Luz Ardiden (1,718m)

Route in reverse

The only significant change would be the ascent to Luz Ardiden via Viscos, which is more reminiscent of Alpe d'Huez with two very tough opening kilometres. Although the Tour has always favoured the main road to the ski station, this narrower and more typically Pyrenean ascent is a variation well worth checking out.

Parcours

0km	Argelès Gazost
6.5km	Pierrefitte Nestalas D921/D920 ➡ ①
16.5km	Cauterets ②
22.5km	Pont d'Espagne ③
38.5km	Pierrefitte Nestalas ① D920/D921 ➡
51.5km	Luz Saint Sauveur D921/D12a ➡ ④
52km	D921/D12 ➡
65.5km	Luz Ardiden ⑤
69.5km	D12/unclassified to Viscos ⬅
79.5km	Viscos road/D921 ⬅
88km	Pierrefitte Nestalas
94.4km	Luz Saint Sauveur

TOUR OF VAL D'AZUN

One of the seven valleys in the Lavedan region to the south of Lourdes, the Val d'Azun is generally renowned among cyclists for the two ascents to the Col du Soulor, from the north via Ferrières and from the east via Argelès Gazost. This route features the first of these two climbs, but also highlights the variety of routes in this area, mostly on back roads that are often all but traffic-free.

It begins next to the church in Place du Foirail in the centre of Argelès Gazost, picking up the D918 towards Gez and branching right towards that village a few hundred metres later. Climbing quite steeply for a kilometre or so, the road rises through woods and pastureland, the incline easing as it approaches and passes through Gez. At the junction by the white cross coming out of the village, bear left and, soon after, swing right on Route des Bergons, this lane climbing more briskly again through stands of oak, beech and sweet chestnut. The gradient changes continually, dipping to 4%, jagging up to 12, the trees so dense in the Arragnat forest that the corridor of greenery becomes a dark tunnel.

While the gradient does relent, there's no break in the foliage, which is well worth bearing in mind on hot days. There's still an occasional steeper section, but nothing too challenging until just beyond the junction to the Col de Couraduque – this road, unfortunately, is in a very poor state of repair from this side and almost impassable. The last 2km to the Col de Spandelles average close to 10%, the incline often a good way above that figure as it rises up a corridor of bracken and pines. Approaching the crest, the trees fall back enough to allow tremendous views to the north and east.

The 10km descent off its western side to the D126 that ascends to the Col du Soulor is significantly steeper than the last 10km just climbed and should be tackled with care. As it runs down into farmland it is, though, much more open and attractive, tumbling through a lovely run of hairpins that will leave those who, like me, relish these tight twists and turns beaming with exhilaration. Below them, the road zips down more directly into the valley, where a left turn soon leads to Ferrières.

This village is essentially one long street that ends just as the ascent to the Soulor begins, a hairpin kicking up to the right and climbing steeply. For a short time, the road runs through dense woodland that closes off the view ahead. Then glimpses appear of the 2,050m Pic du Moulle de Jaout, and soon after towards the Col d'Aubisque and the 2,613m Pic de Ger. Above Arbéost, pasture replaces the woodland and the views becoming more extensive and quite glorious, opening out even more after negotiating a couple of tight left-hand bends.

The summit of the Soulor is now visible, as is the spectacular road cut into the almost sheer rock face between this pass and the Ausbisque. It's stupendous, almost enough to make you forget the gradient is still quite severe, although it slackens off steadily as the top of the pass nears. Turn adjacent to the café at the Soulor to descend to Arrens Marsous. It's straight and fast, a thriller for speed-lovers, but it's worth slowing at some point on the initial stretch to take in the vista across the peaks either side of the Arrens valley to the jagged pinnacles beyond them on the ridge to the west of Cauterets.

In Arrens Marsous, lively for a village so high up on a mountain pass, turn right in the direction of the Col des Bordères, branching left soon after to continue towards it. The

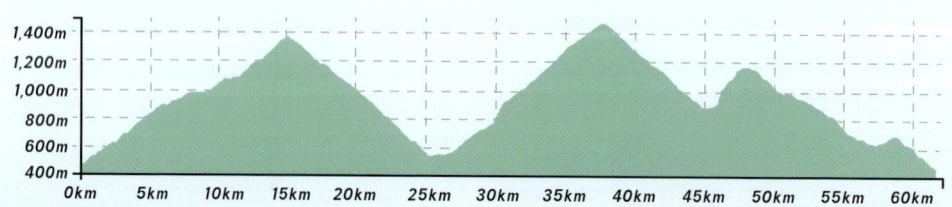

HAUTES PYRÉNÉES

The Ouzoum valley near Arbéost

Bordères is a short climb, but with teeth, initially running towards the rugged Pic du Midi d'Arrens before switching to the east to reach a crest enclosed by trees and leading into a descent with wonderful views into the massif on the far side of the Estaing valley, the fourth and final valley in the Val d'Azun, the other three, the Bergons, Ouzoum and Arrens, featuring earlier in the ride.

From Estaing, follow the Gave de Labat de Bun down this delightful valley towards Argelès Gazost, before branching away from it to reach Arras en Lavedan and rejoin the main road coming down from the Soulor for the final 3km back into Argelès Gazost.

Route in reverse

The Col de Spandelles is tougher from its western side, but this flank does have far better views and this is one good reason to tackle this circuit clockwise. In doing so, you'll also climb the Soulor by the route that the Tour most often takes.

Distance: 62km
Elevation gain: 2,261m
Highest point: 1,474m
Est. moving time: 2.5-4hrs
Degree of difficulty: ●●●◐
Climbs: Col de Spandelles (1,378m), Col du Soulor (1,474m), Col des Bordères (1,156m)

Parcours

0km	Argelès Gazost
0.5km	D918/D102 ➡
2.5km	Gez D102/unclassified ⬅ then ➡ on Route des Bergons
15km	Col de Spandelles ①
25.5km	unclassified/D126 ⬅ ②
38km	Col du Soulour D126/D918 ⬅ ③
45km	Arrens Marrous D918/D105 ➡ ④
46km	D105/D603
48km	Col des Bordères ⑤
50.5km	Estaing D603/D103 ⬅
55km	D103/D13 ➡
56.5km	D13/D103 ⬅
59km	Arras en Lavedan D103/D918 ➡
62km	Argelès Gazost

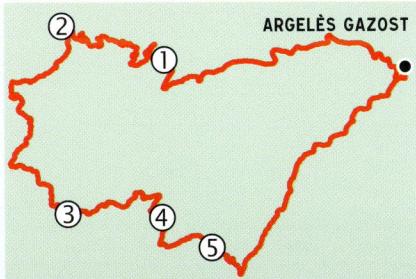

167

MOUNTAIN HIGHS AT ARGELÈS GAZOST

No visit to the Bigorre region encompassing Tarbes, Lourdes, Bagnères de Bigorre and the countryside around them could be complete without a trip up to Hautacam, the little ski station on the eastern heights above Argelès Gazost. The climb, which is actually to the Col de Tramassel, has a rather chequered Tour de France history. It first featured in 1994, but is best remembered for the two subsequent visits in 1996, when Bjarne Riis blasted away from his rivals to all but wrap up the title, and 2000, when a rampaging Lance Armstrong effectively did the same, although he lost out on the stage win to Javier Otxoa. Riis and Armstrong later admitted doping during their pomp, while Otxoa's fate was more tragic. His pro career was ended a few months later when he was hit by a car while training, his twin brother Ricardo dying in the same incident.

This circuit saves Hautacam till last, setting out westwards instead from Argelès Gazost for the Col du Soulor, a Tour regular, usually paired with passage over the Col d'Aubisque. From the centre of the Argelès Gazost, there's very little chance to warm up before the Soulor starts to climb seriously to reach Arras en Lavedan. Just take it steady and lap up the views over the Arrens valley. The next 9km are much more forgiving, the road barely deviating at all to reach the turn to Aucun, where a right turn leads to another small ski station at the Col de Couraduque. Beyond this village, the road flattens out completely through a wide valley to Arrens Marsous, where the ascent to Soulor begins in earnest, the average 8% for the remaining 7.5km, the steeper sections towards the summit.

This is a beautiful section of mountain road, rising through a regularly changing mix of woodland and pasture, a wonderful view along the Arrens valley peaks or up to 2,692m Grand Gabizos and the neighbouring summits never too long in coming. The final, very open kilometres to the pass are stunning, before switching right towards Ferrières at the crest. It's well worth stopping a kilometre or two into this descent to take in the view across a vast bowl to the Cirque du Litor Corniche, the spectacular road linking the Soulor to the Aubisque, before continuing the drop into the Ouzoum valley.

Travelling north from Ferrières, the D126 is a favourite of mine, a road that highlights why riding in the mountains isn't simply about bagging climbs and flashing down descents. Meandering alongside the busy waters of the Ouzoum through lush woodland, it's got a lovely peculiarity, the road splitting on three occasions, northward traffic on the east bank, southward on the west. Quiet and, in this direction, running slightly downhill, it's joyous. Emerging from the tight valley, it hurries through farmland to reach Prat. Turn right here towards Lestelle Bétharram.

This is the Route de Calvaire, the name stemming not from any particular difficulty, but because it heads towards the sanctuary of Lestelle Bétharram, where there is a 19th-century calvary route. This is another stunning stretch, running parallel to the mountains, the views into them magnificent, dappled woodland offering sanctuary of its own. Turn hard right here at Lestelle Bétharram onto the D937 towards Lourdes. The traffic can be heavy and fast-moving, increasingly so approaching Lourdes, so I prefer to avoid the pilgrimage centre by diving right after a few kilometres to Rieulhès. This lane's narrow, a little rough in places, but little-used and very pretty running through the Bois de Lourdes, the woods mainly beech.

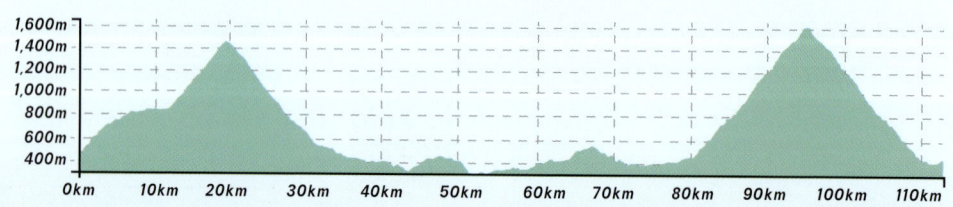

HAUTES PYRÉNÉES

Looking back down the climb to Hautacam

Reaching a T-junction adjacent to a campsite, turn right towards Ségus, continuing on to Ossen and Aspin en Lavedan. Beyond this village, cross the bridge over the D821 dual carriageway to pick D13 on the far side, travelling south for 8km, parallel to the highway but separated from it by crops and the River Ousse (see page 152). The climb to Hautacam starts right from it with a left turn off this road into Ayros Arbouix.

It's bucolic to begin with, the gradient not severe passing through meadows and the attractive village of Arbouix. Then it sweeps around a long bend and takes off, a kilometre at 10%, eases back for another three, then ramps up vigorously, the next half dozen kilometres at 9%, with long sections two and three points higher. That the panorama is fantastic may help distract from this grind, the peaks of the Arrens massif and towards the Soulor standing out. Approaching the summit, the gradient yielding a little, the views get more expansive. Then, after stepping up via the final hairpins, comes the Col de Tramassel, the little café at the summit a very welcome sight if it's open, but the close to 360° vista fully justifying the trip on its own. Compared to some summits, this one isn't especially high, but it surpasses most for drama.

Distance: 113.4km
Elevation gain: 3,273m
Highest point: 1,629m
Est. moving time: 4-6hrs
Degree of difficulty: ●●●●
Climbs: Col du Soulor (1,474m), Hautacam/Col de Tramassel (1,629m)

Route in reverse

Hautacam has to be the finale, but coming at it the other way with the Soulor directly before gives it a more epic feel and certainly makes the route more challenging.

Parcours

0km	Argelès Gazost D918
19.5km	Col du Soulor D918/D126 ➔ ①
31.5km	Ferrières
41.5km	Arthez d'Asson
43km	D126/D226 ➔ ②
51km	Lestelle Bétharram D226/D937 ➔ ③
57.5km	D937/D151 ➔
64km	D151/D13 ➔ ④
71km	Fork left and soon after take bridge across D821
80km	D13/D100 ⬅
95km	Hautacam/Col de Tramassel ⑤
113.4km	Argelès Gazost

THE TRANS-PYRENEAN BONE-BREAKER

Riding the Quebrantahuesos sportive, effectively the Spanish equivalent of the Étape du Tour, was one of my most memorable days ever on the bike. I got the opportunity thanks to the late Renny Stirling, Orbea's distributor in the UK, who set up the trip. Ultimately, all I had to do was pedal, and pedal, and then pedal some more. It was an epic day out both in distance and enjoyment, shared with 9,000 other cyclists. My only regret, after managing to crash going uphill and being racked with cramp in the final quarter, was finishing 17 seconds outside my nine-hour target.

I confess I wasn't as well prepared as I needed to be, but got around largely thanks to the advice I received just before the start from Orbea product manager Joseba Arizaga, who told me that the key was to ride well within myself until I reached the fearsome final four clicks on the Marie Blanque. According to Joseba, too many Quebrantahuesos participants go off too quickly, swept up by overenthusiasm and the high speeds of huge pelotons that form on the approach to the first difficulty, the Somport, where the sportive crosses into France. It proved sage counsel. If I'd gone off too quick, the immensely long Col du Pourtalet would have eaten me up.

The Quebrantahuesos begins in Sabiñánigo (the stress is on the second 'a'), a small town 50km north of Huesca and close to some of Spain's biggest Pyrenean resorts, including Panticosa and Formigal, which have both been summit finishes in the Vuelta a España. It hits out westwards along the Val Ancha, very much the wide valley its name indicates, running dead straight and parallel to A23 motorway, which sucks up much of the traffic. Stay with the N330/E7 when it fuses with the motorway approaching Jaca, following it to the north of the town and staying with it when it swings northwards towards France.

Running alongside the River Aragón, the N330 barely wavers as it makes for the border. This is one of the main routes between France and Spain in the central Pyrenees, so there can be quite a lot of heavy traffic. On the plus side, it's well surfaced, has a wide shoulder and isn't very steep until you reach the entrance to the 8.5km Somport tunnel that transports the main road and most of the vehicles beneath that pass. The roads split above Canfranc, the E7 disappearing into the rock, as the N330 forks right into the bizarre village of Canfranc Estación, once an international rail terminal with a huge and very grand station built in the early 20th century, which now lies empty after the rail link was closed following an accident on the French side in 1970.

Canfranc's name derives from the Latin Campus Franci, the field of foreigners, those travellers being pilgrims on a branch of El Camino de Santiago that crossed the Somport pass, its name also coming from Latin, summus portus signalling the top of the pass. The climb to it is steady, the gradient increasing a little beyond the tunnel while, at the same time, the views improve immensely. The buildings at the pass come into sight passing the ski station of Candanchú, the summit arriving soon after.

It's a rather soulless ascent compared to

The Somport pass

HUESCA

The top of the Pourtalet pass

most others in the range. The descent into France and Aspe Valley, however, is markedly different, the road twisting through tight bends, much narrower than before, the countryside less arid and almost luminous green thanks to the beech woods on either side. It's distinctly steeper too, dropping quite quickly to meet the road emerging on the French side of the Somport tunnel. Wider below this point and with a shoulder again, the road hurries on to Urdos, passing the imposing Fort de Portalet, built in the 19th century to protect France's Pyrenean border and briefly used in the months after the Second World War as a prison for Marshal Pétain, the head of the Vichy government, who was later found guilty of treason.

At a roundabout, stay right towards Accous to gain a brief respite from the N134, rejoining the main route beyond Bedous. The left turn towards the Col d'Ichère (see page 220) signals that the start of the Marie Blanque is not too distant, and it arrives just beyond a spectacular arched bridge carrying the railway over the main road and river. After swinging right again in Escot, the route is immediately very different. My principal memory of scaling this devilish little pass in the Quebrantahuesos is of those final 4k Joseba warned me about, climbing them in a huge pack of riders, the main sounds heavy breathing and the constant rush of the roadside river.

Winding down through thick woods, then reaching an open plateau, the descent then rattles through a string of twisting corners into Bielle in the wide bottom of the Ossau valley. Reaching the main D934 road, there are some cliffs off to the left, the Falaises aux Vautours, in this case bearded vultures, or *quebrantahuesos* in Spanish, so called because they drop dead animals from a height onto rocks in order to break their bones to access the marrow inside, the only bird species that specialises in feeding this way. They can often be seen soaring on thermals high above the valley, circling with not a flap of their almost three-metre wingspan.

After negotiating the narrow streets of Laruns, the D934 passes the left turn towards the Col d'Aubisque, continuing up the Ossau towards the Col du Pourtalet, no fewer than 29km away. There aren't any particularly savage ramps on this pass, it's simply the extent of it that makes it such a challenge, especially with 110km already in your legs. It commences dramatically, running through a tunnel to enter the narrow Gorge du Hourat. Above it lies Eaux Chaudes, its warm waters still used to treat rheumatoid complaints.

THE TRANS-PYRENEAN BONE-BREAKER

A Camino de Santiago marker on the Somport

It was just beyond here that I fell after clipping the wheel in front. I tumbled slowly into the roadside ditch, scrambling like an upturned beetle to get out, knees bleeding like a clumsy schoolboy. Even though the gradient rarely rises much beyond 6% above this point, it was a struggle, but what stood out was the sheer magnificence of the Pourtalet. In the heat, I was glad of the tree cover lower down, but soon enormous peaks could be seen through the canopy, including the towering Pic du Midi d'Ossau, which stands out tall (2,884m) and alone, its distinctive double peak visible from Pau, almost 60km away.

Above the dam at Fabrèges retaining the waters of the Gave d'Ossau, the route reaches more open terrain, the 2,716m Pic de Soques on the frontier dominating the view ahead. After passing beneath a series of avalanche-protection tunnels, there is a short run of hairpins and, beyond them, a beautiful view across the Cirque d'Anéou. The summit is close too. I received great applause as I stood on the pedals and appeared to sprint for the top, the spectators unaware that both of my legs had seized up with cramp and this was the only way I could now make progress. Even given that discomfort, the panorama at the top was quite something, undoubtedly one of the best in the range. I think I ate most of what was left at the feeding station while contemplating it.

The stores and restaurants just on the Spanish side of the pass are usually open and a good place to replenish your body and supplies before the long drop to Sabiñánigo, which contains one quite nasty final kick. On a good surface, the descent is straight and quite fast, at least if you want it to be. It shoots below the resort of Formigal (see page 176) and then runs along the ridge above the large Lanuza reservoir.

Below it and a longish tunnel, is the town of Escarrilla, and a little further on from this a left turn onto the A2606 heads in the direction of the town and, later, the resort of Panticosa. Take this road, although you might well soon be regretting you did. As it swings around to the south again, follow the right fork going downwards into El Pueyo de Jaca and continuing on a narrowish lane along the east bank of the huge Búbal reservoir. The views across the water to the Dolomitic outcrops of the Sierra de Limes are wonderful, but they're not the reason the Quebrantahuesos diverts onto this back road. That soon arrives, though, as the road starts to climb the Alto de Hoz de Jaca, two torturous kilometres on the steepest grades seen all day.

The section around the two mid-climb switchbacks is particularly gruesome, but it coughs you out on a balcony with views across the Búbal's turquoise waters towards the Limes massif. Even better, Hoz de Jaca itself and the top of the climb is not far away

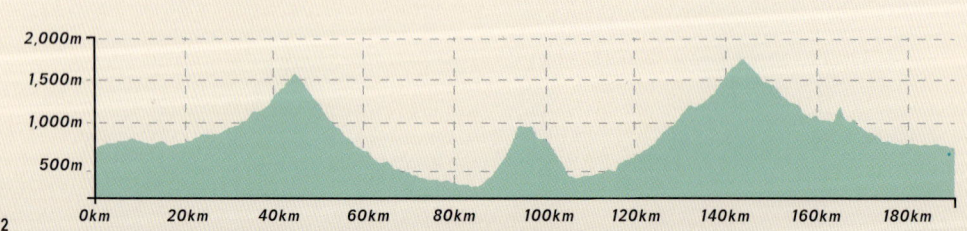

HUESCA

either. The road tumbles just as quickly back down to the edge of the reservoir to cross the dam that's responsible for the huge lake and pass through a dimly lit tunnel to rejoin the main road as it breezes down to Biescas and arrows on towards Sabiñánigo to complete a day out that is as tough as almost any Tour de France mountain stage.

Route in reverse

I'm very opposed to tackling it this way, as it removes a lot of the character from the route, primarily because you'd end up riding the comparatively unappealing section up and over the Somport towards the end. I'd be more tempted to ride up the Pourtalet, then return via Hoz de Jaca.

Hoz de Jaca

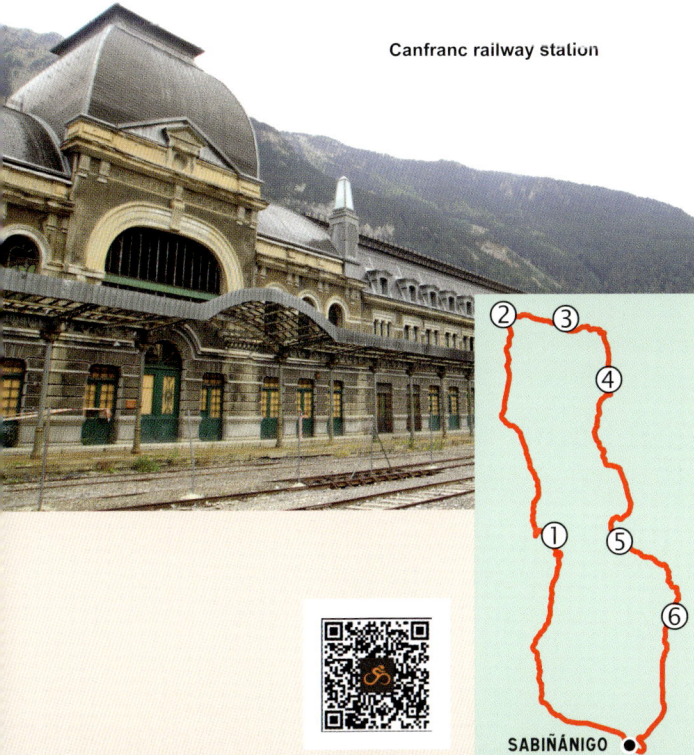

Canfranc railway station

Distancia: 190.5km
Elevation gain: 4,460m
Highest point: 1,794m
Est. moving time: 6-10hrs
Degree of difficulty: ●●●●●
Climbs: Puerto de Somport (1,640m), Col de Marie Blanque (1,035m), Col du Pourtalet (1,290m), Hoz de Jaca (1,272m)

Recorrido

0km	Sabiñánigo N330
36km	Canfranc Estación N330/N330a ➡
44.5km	Col du Somport N134 ①
72km	N134/D8234 ➡
77km	D8234/N134 ➡
84.5km	N134/D238 ➡ ②
85km	D238/D294 ➡
94.5km	Col de Marie Blanque ③
105.5km	Bielle D294/D3934 ➡
110km	D3934/D934 ➡
114km	Laruns ④
143.5km	Col du Pourtalet A136 ⑤
158.5km	A136/A2606 ⬅
159.5km	A2606/unclassified ➡
165km	Alto de Hoz de Jaca ⑥
167.5km	unclassified/A136 ⬅
190.5km	Sabiñánigo

173

THE WALLCREEPER AND ORDESA NATIONAL PARK

If you're looking for an easier option to the Quebrantahuesos, one solution is to tackle the shorter route that takes place on the same day as that epic sportive. It's dubbed the Treparriscos, or wallcreeper, the rock-climbing bird being a much smaller (and very distant) cousin to the bearded vulture that lends its name to the full-on version. The 80km loop is a decent day out, but becomes quite an extraordinary one by adding a short diversion at the halfway point to be awe-struck by one of the Pyrenees' natural wonders, the Ordesa and Monte Perdido National Park, a UNESCO World Heritage Site.

Starting, like the Quebrantahuesos, in Sabiñánigo, the ride begins by heading northwards up the Gállego valley on the N260 to Biescas, home town of former professional racer Fernando Escartín, who was third in the 1999 Tour de France and more recently became the race director of the Vuelta a España. Stay on the N260 as it skirts the northern edge of this town and start to climb towards Gavín. On the far side of this village, the gradient notches up a little to reach a long and unlit tunnel. Thankfully, it's straight so it's at least possible to see where you're meant to be heading, but lights are still advised, especially as there's another tunnel at the top of this pass, the Puerto de Cotefablo.

Returning to daylight, the road dips for a short while to reach Yésero, then starts upwards again for half a dozen kilometres. Running between stands of Scots pine, the gradient steadily increases, almost touching 9% just before the pass, the views extending all the while across the Serrablo massif to the south. The Cotefablo arrives just beyond the second tunnel, this one better lit, but again quite long.

Leaving the pass, the road glides down into the Broto valley to reach Broto itself, 13km later. Just before this little town, though, a left turn onto the A135 makes for Torla-Ordesa, a surprisingly busy town bearing in mind the lack of traffic seen so far. Glance ahead, though, and the reason for all this sudden activity becomes staggeringly apparent, precipitous cliffs soaring and, as the road continues northwards, running off to the west towards Monte Perdido, the third highest peak in the range. This Pyrenean Grand Canyon and cirque, which sits back-to-back with the equally astounding French cirques Gavarnie,

Ordesa

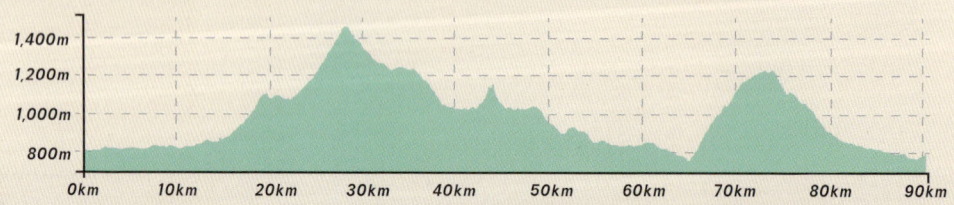

HUESCA

Torla, the gateway to the Monte Perdido and Ordesa National Park

Estaubé and Troumouse, is best explored on foot, but even so this little detour is undeniably worth the effort.

Back at the N260, the road wiggles down into Broto, an ideal refreshment stop, and strikes out southwards down the broad Ara valley. At the roundabout, go right in the direction of Sabiñanigo, still on the N260, this section of it little more than a decade old, beautifully surfaced and, for the most part, little used. It also has a wide shoulder, a bonus when climbing through a curving and well-lit tunnel. Soon after, there's a far longer one, 2.5km! There are two lanes on this the climbing side, but no shoulder, so lights are a must.

Above it, Puerto de Petralba soon arrives, heralding the beginning of 16 mostly coast-able kilometres back to Sabiñanigo.

Route in reverse

There are at least two good arguments for attempting it anti-clockwise. Firstly, you'll descend through the Petralba tunnel rather than climbing up it. Secondly, riding towards Broto, the views up the valley towards Ordesa are very impressive and largely missed if travelling the other way.

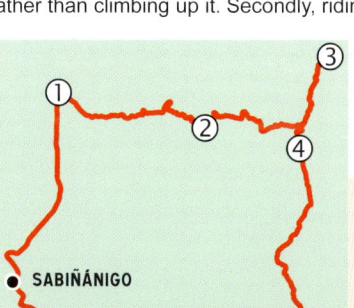

Distance: 90.5km
Elevation gain: 1,935m
Highest point: 1,423m
Est. moving time: 3-5hrs
Degree of difficulty: ●●◖
Climbs: Puerto de Cotefablo (1,423m), Puerto de Petralba (1,244m)

Recorrido

0km	Sabiñánigo N330 then N260
14.5km	Biescas ①
28km	Puerto de Cotefablo ②
39km	N260/D135 ←
44km	Ordesa ③
49km	D135/N260 ←
51.5km	Broto ④
64.5km	Roundabout →
73km	Puerto de Petralba ⑤
90.5km	Sabiñánigo

VUELTA FAVOURITES OLD AND NEW

The year I participated in the Quebrantahuesos, I stayed in a nice *pensión* in the village of Panticosa, a name that stood out because Bernard Hinault suffered one of his biggest and most surprising time trial defeats in the spa further up the valley during the 1983 Vuelta a España. In a test that ran 38km from Sabiñánigo to Balneario de Panticosa, the Frenchman, attempting to win Spain's national tour for the second time, finished in ninth place, two minutes and 13 seconds down on Spanish climber Marino Lejarreta. Although Hinault eventually managed to turn the race in his favour, the strain on his knees proved so much that he was unable to defend the Tour de France title a couple of months later.

This route revisits some of the roads on that test, as well as those where Chris Froome lost all hopes of victory in the 2016 Vuelta stage to Formigal, caught out by a coup enacted by Alberto Contador and Nairo Quintana. It gets under way in Biescas, tracking north on the A136 for half a dozen kilometres to the right turn towards Hoz de Jaca (see page 172), the village briefly visible on the hilltop to the left, above the Búbal reservoir. Dive through the dimly-illuminated tunnel and across the large dam and start to climb steeply.

Thanks to the Quebrantahuesos coming at this prickly little pass from the north, its southern side isn't as renowned, but is actually significantly more difficult because it flattens out after that first sharp ramp, and almost all of the climbing is done in the final 1.5km when the average is close to 10%. Passing a couple of waterfalls, the gradient hits double figures and stubbornly stays there, the final pitches before the village at 14 and 15%. A pause at the viewpoint just before the road tumbles away from the village is well earned after that rude haul.

Take care on this steep drop, especially on the initial balcony section, savour the spell down by the water with views across to the Limes massif to the west, then climb again through El Pueyo de Jaca to reach the right turn to Panticosa. Take the second turn at the roundabout just before the resort to pass above it and continue towards the spa higher up. The gradient remains quite benign for a couple more kilometres, then steps up considerably as the valley tightens and the road approaches two acute hairpins. It's not Hoz-steep and the deep gorge to the right provides a lovely distraction, but there's little let-up heading through another pair of hairpins and then into a third set, within which the road switches three times through an avalanche shelter. Beyond this, the gradient eases off, flattening out completely by the lake at the Ibón de los Baños, an attractive and still vibrant 19th-century spa town that's encircled by high peaks, its waters once said to provide a cure to liver complaints and herpes.

After descending back down to the main A136 road, turn right towards Escarrilla and climb up through a long tunnel to reach a right turn to Lanuza across a second dam. The view ahead on this reservoir-side lane is dominated by the Peña Foratata, a mesmerising mountain that locals claim has human form.

Weave upwards through Sallent de Gállego to pick up the back road into Formigal favoured by the Vuelta, continuing past the resort to a roundabout. Here there's a choice of routes. Swing left and downwards to follow the main route all the way back to Biescas, passing along the opposite side of both

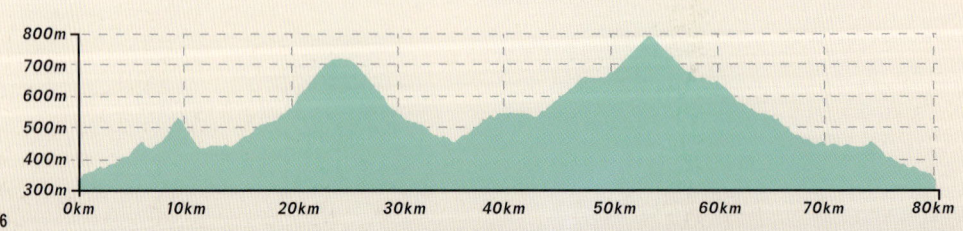

HUESCA

reservoirs. Or, for those who want more climbing, turn right and continue climbing steadily for a kilometre or so, then swing left, slipping past the barrier if it's down, and onto a rougher section of road that runs for 4km to reach a huge car park close to a number of ski lifts and runs, the gradient increasing to seven, eight and nine per cent before it plateaus.

The immediate surrounds, a large expanse of tarmac, are a little dismal in summer, but the views back down the valley and across the Pourtalet pass towards the peaks around the Pic de Midi d'Ossau make this cul-de-sac well worth the effort. From here, the return journey to Biescas is, bar a couple of small lumps, 27km of downhill. On hot days, don't leave it until too late in the afternoon as you might end up riding into a strong headwind all the way as warm air funnels up the pass from the plains below.

Peña Foratata overlooking Sallent de Gállego

Distance: 80.5km
Elevation gain: 2,202m
Highest point: 1,794m
Est. moving time: 3-5hrs
Degree of difficulty: ●●●◐
Climbs: Alto de Hoz de Jaca (1,272m), Balneario de Panticosa (1,630m), Aramon Formigal (1,794m)

Route in reverse

The main road climb towards the Pourtalet with the late diversion off to Aramón is steady, perhaps a little dull on the unchanging road, but very spectacular, particularly higher up. I wouldn't object to tackling it first, getting most of the climbing done early, then continuing on to the easier ascent to Panticosa.

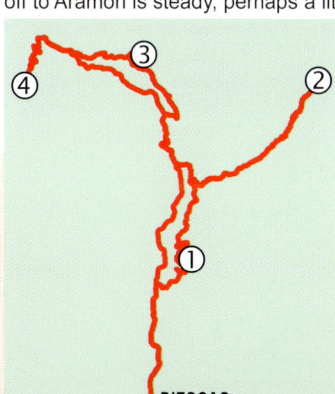

Recorrido

0km	Biescas
6.5km	A136/unclassified to Hoz de Jaca ➡
10km	Alto de Hoz de Jaca ①
15.5km	unclassified/A2606 ➡
25km	Balneario de Panticosa ②
35.5km	A2606/A136 ➡
39km	A136/unclassified Lanuza ➡
43.5km	Sallent de Gállego ③
48km	Formigal
48.5km	Roundabout/A136 ➡
50km	A136/unclassified ⬅
54km	Aramón Formigal parking/summit ④
58km	unclassified/A136 ➡
80.5km	Biescas

IN ANETO'S SHADOW

The region to the south of the Parque Natural Posets-Maladeta, where several of the highest peaks in the Pyrenees are located, is among the most problematic when it comes to finding circular routes. The area's ruggedness and remoteness are underlined by the almost complete absence of settlements that might be described as towns. Most of the villages are little more than hamlets and there are very few roads between them, surfaced ones at least. Yet the sheer magnificence of this terrain demands exploration, and this route endeavours to achieve that, venturing about as close as is possible to Aneto and Posets, the highest summits in the Pyrenean chain.

From the resort town of Benasque in the valley of the same name that runs into the heart of the Posets-Maladeta park, it starts to the south-west alongside the Linsoles reservoir. The shoulder's not wide on this main road, but traffic tends to be fairly light. Even though the route is moving away from the Pyrenees, the only real clue to this is the slightly downhill trajectory, immense massifs fill the view ahead until you enter the dramatic Ventamillo gorge, which becomes so narrow that the road is cut in beneath towering cliffs and, at the same time, juts out over the River Ésera. An unlit but relatively short tunnel signals the end of this spectacular defile, although the high cliffs continue to shepherd the road downstream, occasionally pressing in tightly.

The final squeeze through a second gorge brings the first brief period of climbing, the valley opening out beyond it to reach Campo. Beyond this village, turn left towards Torre La Ribera, the road rising very slightly and then with a touch more urgency to enter the Lierp valley, dominated on its northern side by the 2,492m Turbón. Once gained that altitude is, though, quickly lost on a steady descent that bottoms out at the turn towards Bonansa and Vielha.

It's here, with a third of the route already completed, that the climbing really begins, initially alongside the River Isábena. Unlike the Pre-Pyrenean terrain to the east, the landscape here looks more stereotypically Spanish, the topsoil stony, the greenness of the trees more evident in the dry, sun-bleached terrain. Gradually, the valley walls start to draw in until the only passage through is a longish, curving and unlit tunnel, three "windows" towards the top end allowing some light into the gloom. Beyond it is another wonderful gorge with five further tunnels, all but one much shorter than the first.

Above them, the gorge winds onwards, heading towards the first pass, the Alto de Bonansa. Switching east towards it – passing a smaller road that heads off westwards to Espés and bypasses the first two summits – the gradient rises but not too sharply until the road enters a man-made gully through the rock and another short tunnel, daylight at its far end revealing a lovely view down the valley just climbed. The Bonansa pass arrives a kilometre later.

The descent is only 6km long, but steep in places. Take particular care going through the short tunnel halfway down. Shooting down another gorge, it meets the N260. Turn left towards Castejón de Sos. Heavily wooded with deciduous trees and distinctly more verdant, the terrain looks different once again starting gently upwards to the Coll de Espina. Passing the turn to Noales, the gradient kicks up, running at 7% for most of the 6km to the crest, a few early ramps a good deal fiercer than that. It eases towards the top, but you might not notice that given the distraction of

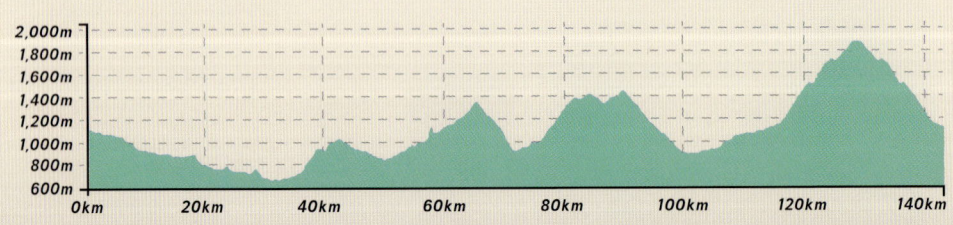

HUESCA

The climb above Cerler Ampriu

the phenomenal view towards the 3,000m peaks encircling the Aneto.

For the next 8km, the road bumps along to the Coll de Fadas, passing the shortcut in from Espés. Unfortunately, the view northwards stays hidden behind a ridge for most of this section, but there are glimpses of it on the wiggling 10km descent through the woods to Castejón de Sos, where the route rejoins the A139 just north of the Ventamillo gorge and returns to Benasque, 14km up the valley.

Continue past Benasque for a couple of kilometres to reach the foot of one of the Vuelta's classic summit finishes, the Alto del Ampriu, which overlooks the ski station of Aramón Cerler and features the toughest climbing all day, opening with 4km at 8% to reach the main resort at Cerler. The road flattens out running through it, then pitches up even more steeply entering a series of sweeping bends, one kilometre at 9%, the next at 10. With them comes the first glimpse of the highest Pyrenean peaks, which briefly disappear on a short downhill section, the prelude to the final 3km run to the Ampriu, which isn't as fierce as the two previous steps up and runs out into a vast car park with a wonderful view back to the Posets massif, the only slightly smaller neighbour to Aneto.

The return is a cinch, bar the brief bit of pedalling 3km down from the top. For those with anything left in their legs at the bottom, a right turn on the valley road does offer another 12km of riding to Llanos de Hospital de Benasque, once a hospital for walkers and now a hotel, sitting to the north of Maladeta and Aneto and the glaciers on and around them. Unfortunately, the valley is so deep that they aren't within sight, but it's still a lovely ride, and quite tough in the last few kilometres. For those who crave something more restorative, Benasque is a well-deserved 2km freewheel to the left.

Route in reverse

Turning left onto the N260 at Castejón on the way out does spread out the climbing a lot more. However, it also means riding up the narrow Ventamillo gorge, which is likely to make that stunning section less enjoyable, especially if there's lots of traffic.

Distance: 143.3km
Elevation gain: 3,109m
Highest point: 1,910m
Est. moving time: 5.5-10hrs
Degree of difficulty: ●●●●○
Climbs: Alto de Bonansa (1,380m), Coll de Espina (1,407m), Coll de Fadas (1,470m), Cerler Ampriu (1,910m)

Recorrido

0km	Benasque
13km	A139/N260 →
32km	Campo A139/HUV9601 ← ①
49.5km	HUV9601/A1605 ← ②
65km	Alto de Bonansa ③
71km	A1605/N260 ←
81km	Coll de Espina ④
89.5km	Coll de Fadas ⑤
100.5km	Castejón de Sos N260/A139 →
113km	Benasque
116km	A139/A2617 →
120km	Aramón Cerler
128km	Alto de Ampriu ⑥
143.3km	Benasque

HUESCA'S MINI GRAND CANYON

This is a shortish loop, but one that features one of the most unforgettable sections of road anywhere in the Pyrenees, running through the Añisclo canyon, a dozen kilometres or so north of Aínsa. In order to get warmed up for that treat, the route starts off to the east, over the bridge just upstream from the confluence of the Cinca and Ara rivers, the main road arrowing through a broad expanse of farmland as it leaves the town, then turning a few points to the north and onto a false flat leading up the Fueva Alta valley to Arró.

As the highway curves around this village, bear right following the sign to Los Molinos in order to cut across the main route to pick up the HF0106AA, which reads more like a battery code than a road number. This thin ribbon of tarmac running through gravelly terrain between low pines soon starts to climb, then drops into a valley where the trees are denser and more mature, the tarmac strip climbing again until it reaches a cluster of houses at Los Molinos.

Above here, the landscape changes, deciduous woods replacing the pine, pasture and fields of wheat and corn providing a softer look after the previous barrenness. The soaring limestone bluffs of the Serra Ferrera are a more striking, Spaghetti Western-like presence as the dusty road reaches its high point, presenting a fabulous view into the Ordesa and Monte Perdido National Park, the outcrops that form the Añisclo canyon at the southern end of it.

The subsequent descent reaches a T-junction on the edge of El Casal. Go left, still descending, but now more steeply and quickly to reach the twisting, paved streets of Laspuña, then continuing down to a T-junction on the A138. Turn left towards Aínsa and right less than a kilometre later, the road narrow and quite rough in places. During holiday periods it becomes one-way, the climb up the canyon only permitted from this direction.

The road rises steadily alongside the River Bellòs, its waters busy with bathers on hot days. This watercourse's erosive impact on the soluble limestone quickly becomes apparent, the river dropping from view in a steep-sided gully that deepens at almost the same rate that the road climbs, then reappearing further up where it runs over harder and more resistant stone, the pattern repeating over the next couple of kilometres. When a bridge carries the road across this second ravine, it's surprising how big the drop to the river is.

Now on the south bank, the road climbs into the main canyon on a narrow ledge, the rock wall above it steepening and, in some places, overhanging. The river has dropped even further away in the void just to the right, downstream from what soon becomes apparent is a substantial waterfall. It's impossible not to be astounded by the erosive effect the Bellòs has had over millions of years, producing a cleft that's not only extremely deep but also just a few metres wide.

On several occasions, it appears you're about to reach the upper end of the canyon, only for the next turn to reveal another extraordinary section of this 10km-long wonder. Rounding one bend a bridge crosses the river to the north bank and sends the road into a very dark, but quite short tunnel. Jumping back to the other side, it runs through another gloomy passage. The further it advances, the more wooded it is too, trees rooted on any tiny ledge or crack in the sheer rock walls.

Consecutive tunnels signal that this

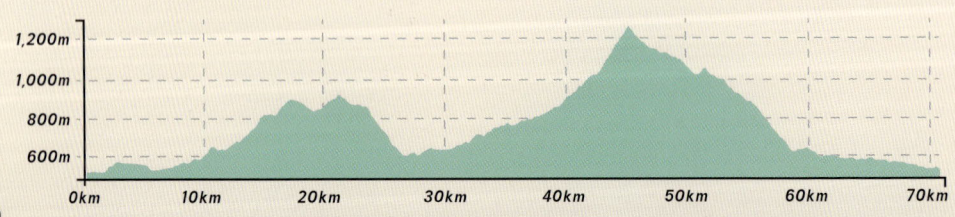

HUESCA

magical ride is nearly over. The canyon broadens to become a valley, the road widens a little as well, then climbs a little more steeply through some switchbacks, where it becomes apparent that the canyon isn't done at all, its course turning north to run deep into the national park, this section accessible on foot only. But there is still one more moment to savour. Turn left at the junction at the top end and climb what are, at 10%, by far the two steepest kilometres in the canyon section to reach the *mirador*. From this observation point the incredible tectonic and climactic forces that have shaped this extraordinary landscape can be more fully appreciated.

Another few hundred metres of ascent leads to the high point and the 26km return to Aínsa that is almost entirely downhill, the drop steady and often very attractive. Indeed, on many rides a road as impressive as this would be the highlight, the Ferrera massif filling the backdrop and well worth a view from the mirador above the final hairpins down into the valley, where the return for Aínsa is by 10 very straight and slightly downhill kilometres alongside the Cinca.

The ideal way to conclude this unforgettable ride is to venture into Aínsa's Plaza Mayor, a triangular and entirely fitting tribute to the beauty of stone, the cobbled, triangular "square" lined by buildings set over arched colonnades covering several cafes and restaurants, the Pyrenees peeping in from one corner.

Route in reverse

Riding the backroad below the Serra Ferrera would be an anti-climax after the Añisclo, but in busy holiday periods it would be well worth getting through the canyon as early as possible. Climbing from Puyarruego to the Añisclo *mirador* is a good ride in itself, but coming down the canyon from there is often not permitted.

Añisclo canyon

Distance: 71km
Elevation gain: 1,483m
Highest point: 1,267m
Est. moving time: 2.5-4hrs
Degree of difficulty: ●●
Climbs: Mirador de Añisclo (1,250m)

Recorrido

0km	Aínsa
9.5km	N260/HF0106AA ← ①
23.5km	El Casal HF0106AA/HUV6401 ← ②
27km	HUV6401/A138 ←
27.5km	A138/HU631 →
42.5km	HU631/unclassified to Escalona ← ③
44.5km	Mirador de Añisclo ④
59km	Puyarruego unclassified/HU631 →
60.5km	HU631/A138 →
71km	Aínsa

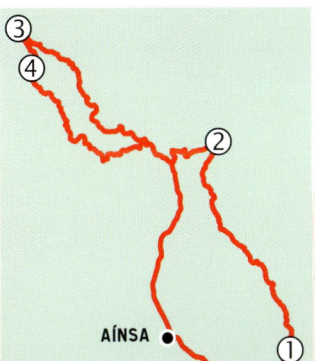

HIGH ROLLING AROUND JACA

Long an important crossroads for travellers, Jaca has been developed as a tourist destination over the last four decades. Lying 30km to the south of the ski stations of Candanchú and Astún, it has been Spain's applicant city to host the Winter Olympics on four occasions, losing out in the vote each time, most recently for the 2014 Games. It also has great cycling roads on all sides, as this route highlights, covering mainly back roads to the south, west and north of the ancient capital of Aragón.

Heading south from the centre of Jaca, pick up the A1205 towards Bernués and the San Juan de la Peña monastery. After dipping to the low point of the broad east-west valley, the road starts to climb towards the Puerto de Oroel, the peak from which it gets its name jagging upwards ahead. This is a comfortable ascent, a nice leg-warmer. After half a dozen kilometres, it tops out and leads into an even gentler descent through what is primarily pine forest to reach Bernués, mountains rippling into the distance and leaving you wondering whether there's ever any end to the uplands rolling across Spain.

The San Juan de la Peña monastery is the next objective, the road ascending moderately, much like the Oroel. The surface is good, traffic light. In short, it's perfect riding terrain. Rising onto a long ridge, the Pyrenees emerge too on its north side, their appearance prompting a lift in the incline, one that is, again, relatively easily dealt with. It runs through thick woodland to arrive at San Juan de la Peña's upper monastery, dating from the late 17th century, its proportions quite surprising given its remoteness. A twisting, steep but short descent leads to a much more astonishing discovery, though. The lower monastery, some of it dating from the 10th century and its greater part from the 12th, is built into the mountainside, almost like a wedge propping it up. Peña, it's worth noting, is Spanish for cliff, and this one is quite a glorious sight.

The descent continues more steadily, the views across the Aragón river plain to the Pyrenees wonderful on the initial section below the monastery. Keeping left towards Huesca at Santa Cruz de los Serós, the road breezes down through wheat and corn fields to meet the main road in the valley. Turn on it in the direction of Pamplona for an almost dead-straight 8km dash to Puente la Reina de Jaca, crossing the old bridge that gives this small town its name, bearing right on the far side for the Valle de Hecho.

Rising at a very shallow angle through farmland and passing an occasional vineyard, the road runs between low hills, tracing the course of the Aragón Subordán upstream, large peaks visible in the hazy distance. After 15km of almost imperceptible ascent, turn right in the direction of Jasa, the gradient edging up noticeably but still not especially challenging. As the summits in the Sierra de Bernera towards the French border start to appear in the distance, the road reaches a fork. Stay left to Aragüés del Puerto and, 10km beyond it, the Lizara mountain refuge nestled in the Bernera massif for some more testing climbing, or continue up into the pretty village of Jasa, its streets beautifully paved in the local style.

Extending to 12km, the climb to the refuge breaks down into quarters, the opening three quite straightforward, most of the height gained in the final one. Never much more than a couple of metres wide, the road runs through woods, but the next lovely view up to the Bernera range is never long in coming. It's blissful, even after a switchback to the

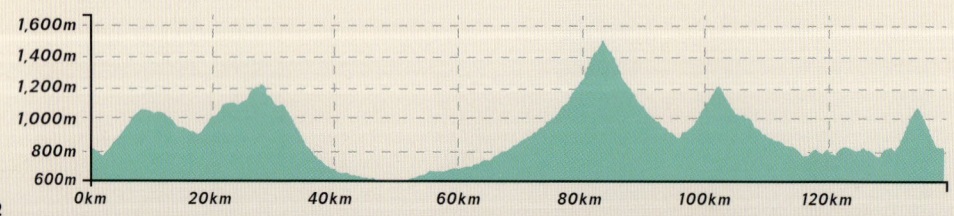

HUESCA

San Juan de la Peña monastery

left heralds the start of the steep inclines, with some short pitches into double figures, rising to the substantial and popular Lizara refuge, its mountain-ringed setting majestic.

After descending back through Aragüés del Puerto, swing left to Jasa, following signs towards Aísa, this road narrower and a touch steeper than it was before as it climbs into a heavily wooded valley. The higher it gets, the more it serpentines, the gradient increasing too. It tops out at a junction, the route going right and downwards to Aísa.

Follow the road around the eastern edge of the village, turning right on its bottom side towards Jaca, now descending the Aísa valley alongside the River Estarrún. As has been the case on much of this ride, this section is idyllic, with some little ups but mainly down, traffic negligible, the jagged peak of Oroel eventually signalling the way back to Jaca, where there's the possibility of one final diversion, to the Rapitán fort that overlooks the town from the north. Built in the 19th century to protect Spain's Pyrenean border, it's reached by a 3.3km road via 13 hairpins. A Vuelta a España finish in 2012, when Catalan pocket mountain rocket Joaquim Rodríguez won the stage, it has ramps up to 14% but averages a more modest eight. It's tree-lined to the summit, where a wonderful panorama is revealed across Jaca to Oroel and well beyond.

Route in reverse

It's just as nice a circuit with the climb to San Juan de la Peña and the Oroel as the finale. Wind direction may well be the deciding factor.

Distance: 139.3km
Elevation gain: 2,617m
Highest point: 1,523m
Est. moving time: 4.5-7hrs
Degree of difficulty: ●●●●
Climbs: Puerto de Oroel (1,080m), San Juan de la Peña (1,215m), Alto de Refugio de Lizaro (1,523m), Alto de Aísa (1,224m), Fuerte del Rapitán (1,080m)

Recorrido

0km	Jaca
0.5km	N240/A1205 ←
8km	Puerto de Oroel ①
17.5km	A1205/A1603 →
28km	San Juan de la Peña ②
40km	A1603/N240 ←
49km	Puente La Reina de Jaca N240/A176 → ③
65km	A176/A2605 →
71.5km	A2605/turn to Aragüés del Puerto ←
83.5km	Refugio de Lizara ④
95.5km	A2605 ← to Jasa
102km	Alto de Aísa ⑤
106km	Aísa A2605 → to Jaca
129.5km	Jaca
134.5km	Fuerte de Rapitán ⑥
139.3km	Jaca

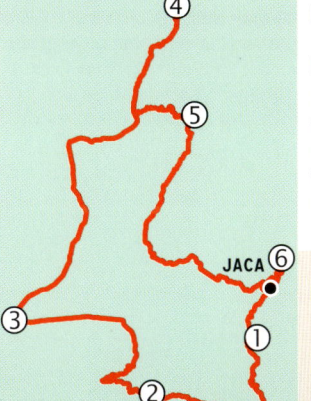

HUESCA'S BIG COUNTRY

One of Spain's least populated provinces, large areas of Huesca are beautifully remote. This route highlights this aspect as it explores the rugged countryside in the western part of the province, including a spectacular canyon deep in the Pyrenees that ends up within a few kilometres of the French border and a later one in the closing kilometres.

Its start point beneath Berdún encapsulates the out-of-the-way feel. Filling a bluff just to the north of the River Aragón, this village has a most photogenic setting, the Pyrenees providing the backdrop to the north, a vast plain running away into distant mountains to the south. It starts into the flatlands, following the main road towards Pamplona then turning to Fago, hills and high peaks filling the horizon beyond corn and wheat fields.

After passing through Villarreal de la Canal, the road begins to weave through low hills, the valley narrowing and crops giving way to low scrub and then woodland. The tendency is generally upwards too, although there are some dips among the gentle drags. But that progress remains difficult to judge until a tight hairpin that leads up to an observation point and, a 100m further on, a tunnel through a ridge, impressively craggy as it runs away to the east. The tunnel is very short and leads up to an even more outstanding viewing area from which it's far easier to see the erosive impact the stream somewhere in the gorge below has had on the limestone, a vertical gouge taken out of it over millennia.

A lovely section follows, initially high up on the edge of the gorge and then, after a brief descent, through a short gorge that leads into a wider valley and up to the village of Fago, where the cobbled streets appear to have seeped from the stone houses. Just above it, the road reaches a junction, the left fork continuing upwards to the Puerto de Matamachos and the Roncal valley (see page 186), while the route dips sharply right into Ansó.

Stay with the A176 as it skirts Ansó and runs down the valley for 2km, and then do so again as it swings left towards Hecho rather than branching right and straight back to Berdún, unless you want to shorten the ride. The road climbs through a short tunnel and continues to rise beyond it, the incline very moderate as it ascends to the Puerto de Ansó, then winds down to Hecho, the biggest town on this route, coming just before the halfway point.

Go left at the T-junction in the valley, heading through the town and towards the Parque Natural de los Valles Occidentales. A huge outcrop with brilliant white cliffs that is the gateway to the Western Valleys Park marks the route ahead. Above Siresa, a similar bluff comes into view opposite it, the road making for the gap between them. For a brief while, pine trees obscure the geological drama to come. Then, as you emerge from another short tunnel, a glorious surprise is revealed, the two protrusions standing sentinel at the entrance to a canyon, which you start to home in on.

As the outcrops squeeze together, the road is forced through another rock tunnel and onto a ledge deep in the gorge, the River Aragón Subordán in the gully below, rushing vigorously in late spring and early summer when nourished by snow melt. The canyon is heavily wooded in this the Oza forest, towering pines and maple competing for light in the narrow ravine, until the cliffs become so steep and close that there's room only for the road and river.

A wonderful final kilometre-long stretch of canyon ends in a broad, forested valley with

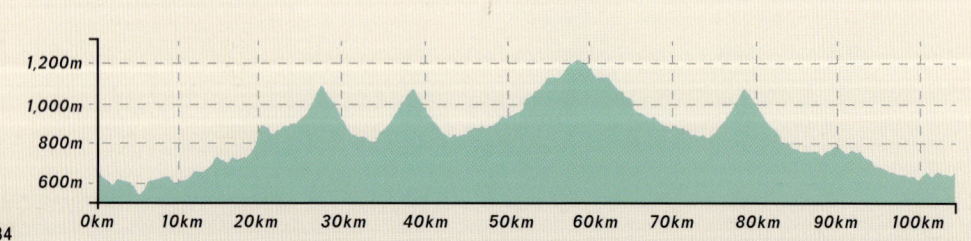

HUESCA

The village of Berdún

camp grounds and walking trails. The road surface begins to degenerate, the tarmac finally running out replaced by gravel as the trees thin. It is possible to continue a little further to see a little more of the surrounding peaks, but do so with care unless your bike is well equipped to cope with the rougher ride. If not, turn back and savour the journey back down the canyon and to Hecho, turning right just beyond the town to climb back over the hill and into the Ansó valley and the 20km return to Berdún on the A1602.

Little more than a lane, it's beautifully quiet as it traces the course of the River Veral downstream. There are a couple of little rises, but for the most part you can coast along, legs spinning easily, enjoying one final, quite lengthy and very impressive gorge, the Foz de Biniés, which ends just with a string of three rock tunnels above that village, overlooked by a well-preserved 14th-century castle. One last, short drag remains, the road returning to plain and making a bee-line for Berdún.

Route in reverse

Still a lovely ride, but one without the great climax provided by the Foz de Biniés canyon, which surely has to be left until last.

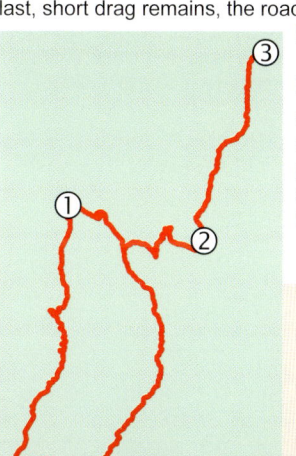

Distance: 104.3km
Elevation gain: 2,071m
Highest point: 1,234m
Est. moving time: 4-6hrs
Degree of difficulty: ●●●
Climbs: Alto de Vedao (1,095m), Puerto de Ansó (1,078m)

Recorrido

0km	Berdún
0.5km	N240 ➡
5km	N240/unclassified to Fago ➡
24km	Fago
27.5km	unclassified/A176 ➡ ①
31km	Ansó
33.5km	A176/A1602 ⬅
43km	Hecho A176/unclassified ⬅ ②
58.5km	Selva de Oza ③ (Oza forest)
74km	Hecho unclassified/A176 ➡ ②
83km	A176/A1602 ⬅
104.3km	Berdún

TOTAL TRANQUILLITY IN ARAGÓN

A tip of my hat to Iain Park for suggesting this route that starts in the Roncal Valley – which at its top end reaches the Col de la Pierre Saint Martin – and crosses from Navarra into the neighbouring province of Huesca to travel up the Ansó valley. It begins in the small town of Isaba, which has a typically Navarran look, its strong, solid, stone houses with the upper floor often rendered white clustered tightly together on narrow streets, their steeply sloping, red-tiled roofs hinting at the harshness of the winters this close to the high mountains.

There's surely no better start to a ride than a gentle descent on an almost empty and perfectly surfaced road, especially when there's always something to draw your eye. Roncal arrives quickly. Just to the south of the town, turn left onto the NA176, climbing for the first time, but the gradient only slight. For the next few kilometres the going is easy, passing through Garde, rising up a wooded valley, mainly of pine, but with ash and oak providing a lighter touch of green.

Finally, approaching a run of switchbacks and tight bends, the road climbs more decisively. For the first time there are longer views, initially of more pine-clad hills undulating into the distance, reinforcing the impression that you're a long way off the beaten track. Indeed, this is the fundamental beauty of so many of the roads on the Spanish side of the Pyrenees, particularly away from the population centres towards the coasts. They are extremely quiet and, partly as a result of that, are in very good nick. The names of the passes may be unfamiliar, but that makes them more rather less deserving of exploration.

The road continues to climb into the province of Huesca, part of the autonomous region of Aragón, reaching the Puerto de Matamachos. Soon after it begins to descend, turn hard left towards Ansó on the rougher and narrower A176. The town arrives quickly at the foot of a sweeping descent. You can either keep on past it to the roundabout below the town and then cut back to take the road north beneath Ansó, or divert into this attractive little town by a recycling point, climbing to the centre along cobbled streets. It's classed as one of Spain's most beautiful villages, and, located at around the halfway point, that surely makes it well worth a stop for a creamy *café con leche*.

Weaving northwards through its warren of streets will bring you out on the A1602 heading up the Ansó valley. Rising steadily, the scenery becomes more impressive, the road hugging the east bank of the rocky River Veral, passing through woods of alder, sycamore, maple and ash, and often cut into the rock face where the valley tightens. With the gradient remaining kind and traffic very intermittent, this is undoubtedly the type of climb that a rider at any level can enjoy.

Crossing the Veral, the road steepens, jumping from threes and fours to six per cent as towering cliffs and outcrops emerge above the greenery. These huge bluffs gradually encroach and start squeezing the road between them, then fall back to reveal a wider valley. Fork to the left coming into it towards Isaba, climbing away from the Veral to reach the top of the Alto de Zuriza at the Navarra sign.

It's now all downhill to Isaba, the drop as gentle as the climb has just been, and all the better for that because this hasn't been a ride to rush at any point. For some serious climbing, turn right towards the Col de la Pierre Saint Martin at the T-junction with the NA137. Otherwise, swing left towards Isaba, just three kilometres away. Time for a siesta!

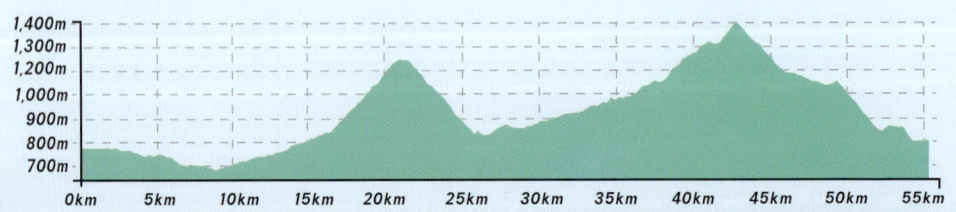

NAVARRA

Peña Ezcaurre in the Ansó valley

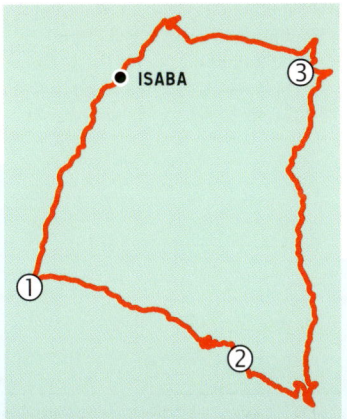

Route in reverse

The climb to the Zuriza's west side isn't quite as attractive, the road often running dead straight along a corridor of pines. Of course, this also means climbing from the off, although it's not very arduous.

Distance: 55.5km
Elevation gain: 1,164m
Highest point: 1,290m
Est. moving time: 2.5-4hrs
Degree of difficulty: ●◖
Climbs: Puerto de Matamachos (1,148m), Alto de Zuriza (1,290m)

Recorrido

0km	Isaba
8.5km	NA137/NA176 ← ①
21km	Puerto de Matamachos ②
26.5km	Ansó NA176/NA1602 ←
41.5km	NA1602/NA2000 ←
42.5km	Alto de Zuriza ③
52km	NA2000/NA137 ←
55.5km	Isaba

VUELTA A NAVARRA

Billed as a tour of Navarra, this route is more precisely a long circuit around the impenetrable – by road at least – Sierra de Areta, to the east of Pamplona, with the addition of the ascent of the marvellous Paso Tapia to finish. It gets under way on the riverside in the attractive town of Ochagavía, heading downstream with the Anduña to Escároz, 2km to the south, following the route of the 1996 Tour de France stage into Pamplona that was organised as a tribute to Navarran cycling great Miguel Induráin.

Just as that stage did, stay on the NA140 in Escároz as it turns right and westwards, climbing to the Alto de Jaurrieta, its gradient pegged to a modest 5.5% thanks to a series of looping hairpins that take the sting out of the hillside. The drop from the pass to the red roofs of Jaurrieta is a short one. Once past them, the road climbs again, this time to the Alto de Remendia, a little higher than its neighbour but a mere 2.5km long. As before, the descent from it is brief, the road taking off again, leaving dense woodland behind to reach a vast, open plateau, the high ridge of the Pyrenees easily picked out to the north on clear days.

This time the drop is more sustained, reaching Aribe on the River Irati. No sooner down, though, and you're climbing again, but only for 2.5km to reach a left turn and an almost uninterrupted descent over a dozen very impressive kilometres. Initially cutting through lush deciduous woodland, the road returns to the banks of the Irati below Olaldea, the highway and the river continuing together through Oroz Betelu and into the Iñarbe gorge, its natural impact slightly diminished by substantial engineering that's been undertaken, but striking nevertheless.

As the Irati continues south to feed the Itoiz reservoir, so enormous that it has induced seismic activity, the road shifts west, rising again to enter a 750m tunnel. It's lit, though not brightly, and has a shoulder, but lights are essential. There is a track – cement in some parts, gravel in others – that runs over the top of it and rejoins the main road on the far side. The diversion is 4km long, but it's the safest option for those without any lighting.

A handful of kilometres later, there's another tunnel, this one only a third the length of the first, but the use of lights is still advised – as before, there is an alternative route that goes off on a track to the right, but once again it's rough and a good deal longer. A few kilometres beyond it, turn right to Olaberri, this smaller road avoiding a longer third tunnel. This lane was probably the primary route down this valley once, but it's very much local traffic only now as it weaves and undulates through farmland, accommodating the terrain rather than ploughing straight through it.

Head towards Lumbier from Ecay de Lónguida, the road running along the northern side of the verdant Sierra de Gongolaz, the valley equally fertile, huge fields of cereal crops in every direction. At an altitude of 400m, this plateau is only half the height of most of Spain's Meseta Central, but has a very similar "big country" feel, the views long-ranging, the sky vast. From Lumbier, the route turns towards Navascués, running parallel to the Sierra de Leyre. Having steadily descended for most of the last 50km, it slowly begins to rise, initially to the Puerto de Iso. Most of that altitude gain is quickly lost, but once the road crosses the River Salazar at Puente de Bigüezal the next 50km are of steady ascent, culminating on the Paso Tapia.

The terrain gradually becomes more rugged, the valley narrowing, stands of pine

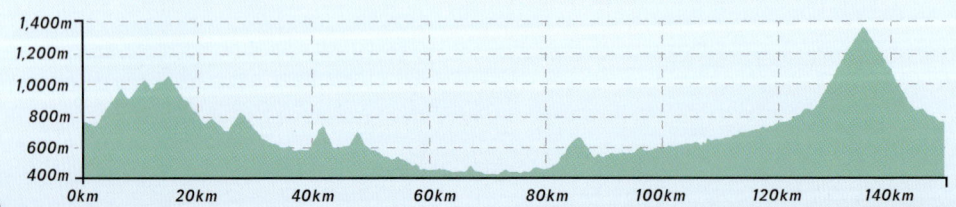

NAVARRA

replacing the crops. Beyond Escároz, rather than returning straight to Ochagavía, bear left following the sign to Irati. This marks the start of the Paso Tapia, although the opening 5km only make a modest vertical gain. They are very pretty, though, meandering through deciduous woodland, high summits occasionally peeking through the trees.

After this benign beginning, the road starts to weave a little more, the gradient picking up too, then taking off with more vigour, briefly reaching 10% in one pitch before settling down to between six and seven. Soon after, a sign announces the road is entering the Irati Forest, Europe's second largest mixed beech-pine forest after the Black Forest. Oddly, the landscape soon opens up and what views this results in as the road gains more height, stretching huge distances to the south and west across the terrain covered earlier, their magnificence enhanced by the colours of the beech, luminous green in late spring and summer, blazing reds and oranges in the autumn.

Beyond the last beech copse, the road runs beneath the ridge of the Sierra de Abodi to reach the Tapia pass, where the panorama is staggering. It's a tad disappointing that there's no clear view to the north, not even on the northern side of the pass, which drops for 9km through thick forest to Irati. But you can see the chain running away to the east and most of Navarra laid out before you, and that's quite a memory to carry back down to Ochagavía.

The Irati forest and massif from the Tapia pass

Distance: 149.4km
Elevation gain: 2,587m
Highest point: 1,340m
Est. moving time: 5.5-8hrs
Degree of difficulty: ●●●●
Climbs: Alto de Jaurrieta (977m), Alto de Remendia (1,040m), Puerto de Iso (670m), Paso Tapia (1,340m)

Route in reverse

Assuming the Tapia will still be tackled at the end, the deciding factor on direction of travel will be the wind. If it's the prevailing wind from the west or blowing from the north, you'll get most advantage following the route as described. If it's coming from the south and east, a clockwise approach should be easier.

Recorrido

0km	Ochagavía
2.5km	Escároz NA140/NA178 →
6.5km	Alto de Jaurrieta ①
10.5km	Alto de Remendia ②
25km	Aribe NA140/NA2030 ←
27.5km	NA140/NA2040 ← ③
44km	NA2040/NA1720 ←
52km	NA1720/NA2355 →
57km	Ecay de Lónguida ④
57.5km	NA1720/NA2379 →
58.5km	NA2379/NA150 ←
75.5km	Lumbier NA150/NA178 ← ⑤
85.5km	Puerto de Iso ⑥
119km	Escároz NA178/NA140 →
121km	Ochagavía NA140/NA2012 ←
135.5km	Paso Tapia ⑦
149.4km	Ochagavía

BASQUE COUNTRY BORDER HOPPING

Maps of the Pyrenees, and particularly those covering the Spanish side of the chain, are often unclear when it comes to indicating when a road is sealed and therefore passable on a road bike, which this route highlights particularly well. None of the three maps I have of Navarra indicate that the road running north from Aribe towards the French border is anything other than a track, but when riding to the Col d'Arnostéguy, just on the French side of the frontier, I noticed that the road from there towards Spain was surfaced and investigated further, with this route the result.

It begins in Aribe, which lies on the Irati river that flows down from the forest and massif of the same name, heading out of the village towards Orbaizeta. The road tracks the Irati upstream, initially through a narrow valley where the road is frequently cut into a cliff above the river. The river's quite placid at this point, and a gentle gradient reflects this.

Four kilometres north of Orbaizeta, the road steps up to the Real Fábrica de Armas, a munitions factory founded on the order of King Carlos III in the late 18th century to take advantage of the mining and metal smelting expertise that had long been associated with this area. A key strategic location, the factory was taken by French forces during the Battle of Orbaizeta in 1794 and continued to produce cannons and other armaments until its closure in 1884. It's interesting to note that similar factories were established at Eibar, in the heart of the País Vasco, where Orbea and BH were among the companies that produced gun barrels into the early 20th century, when they turned their production to bike tubing.

Beyond the church next to the ruined factory, the road narrows as its surface switches from tarmac to concrete slabs. This also heralds a chance in the gradient, which increases noticeably, dense beech woods pressing in on both sides. Much steeper sections follow, well into double figures, their imminence announced by the roadside stream rushing with more gusto. Thankfully, though, the road surface returns to tarmac once again, making it far easier to gain traction in what is often quite a damp environment.

As the incline begins to ease again, the road climbs out of the beech woods and into open pasture, bright yellow gorse standing out amidst the greenness. It reaches an initial summit, drops a few dozen metres and then trundles up to the border, cement returning for the last kilometre to the Col d'Orgambidé, flush on the frontier (see page 204). The view into the Pays Basque is already impressive, but after turning left and riding another 200m or so, the panorama is astounding.

Two steep kilometres follow through more beech woods, the first 10%, followed by another at nine. This is the toughest segment of the ride and above it the road starts to contour around open mountainsides at the top of the valley, reaching the Col d'Arnostéguy at its apex. This pass is remote but has great significance as the Camino de Santiago's crossing point from France into Spain.

Keeping an eye out for approaching pilgrims and grazing livestock, track around the other side of the valley until a sharp drop arrives at the left-hand turn to Arnéguy. Now off the Camino, you shouldn't have to worry about walkers as much, but there are still plenty of sharp drops and lots of sheep and cattle roaming, therefore caution is advised. The three kilometres below a second sign pointing left to Arnéguy, located at the Col Héganzo, get progressively steeper, the third averaging 12.5%. A gentler kilometre then

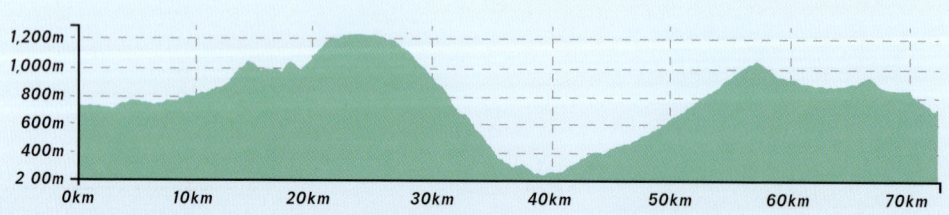

NAVARRA

Sunrise at the Col d'Orgambidé

leads into three more at 10%. Attention-grabbing views all the way down don't assist with concentrating on what's ahead. Further into the valley, there are some tight turns as well, the gradient finally relenting as the road starts to run alongside the Nive d'Arnéguy, the border between France on its east bank and Spain on the west.

At Arnéguy, branch left passing the French customs building and cross the river to enter Spain, arriving immediately at a T-junction. Go left here towards the Puerto de Ibañeta, otherwise known as the Roncesvalles pass. As highlighted on page 202, this is a beautiful road, but often busy with traffic, particularly in the villages lower down where the French buy cheap fuel and other goods. Another hazard is presented by the many El Camino pilgrims who opt for this lower route to reach the Ibañeta and, beyond it, the old Roncesvalles hospital, now a hostel. But these are minor gripes. This historic climb is well worth the effort as it incessantly snakes through glorious woodland, its gradient never more than 7.5%.

After passing the little chapel on the Ibañeta and sweeping down past the small but very grand collection of buildings at Roncesvalles, keep on through Burguete till the left turn towards Isaba, the road streaking south-east. It drops through Garralda, finally wiggling a little when it reaches the Irati river valley and returns to Aribe.

Route in reverse

This would certainly take the sting out of the descending, but makes the climbing a much more daunting proposition. But if you've got the gears and the legs to deal with sustained sections in double figures percentage-wise, the views – and the fact that you can focus on them – make this a good option.

Distance: 72.4km
Elevation gain: 1,790m
Highest point: 1,240m
Est. moving time: 2.5-4hrs
Degree of difficulty: ●●●
Climbs: Col d'Orgambidé (988m), Col d'Arnostéguy (1,236m), Puerto de Ibañeta (1,057m)

Recorrido

0km	Aribe NA2030
6km	Orbaizeta
14.5km	Col d'Orgambidé ← on D428 ①
23km	Col d'Arnostéguy ②
27.5km	D428/D128 ←
39km	Arnéguy D128/N135 ← ③
57km	Puerto de Ibañeta ④
63km	N135/NA140 ← ⑤
72.4km	Aribe

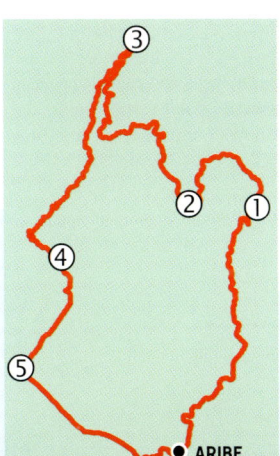

INSPIRED BY INDURÁIN

Renowned for the running of the bulls that takes place during the week-long San Fermín festival each July and for being a key staging point on the Camino de Santiago, Pamplona – and more precisely the suburb of Villava – is also the home town of five-time Tour de France champion Miguel Induráin. In 1996, the Tour paid tribute to Spain's greatest ever cyclist with a stage into Pamplona, where Induráin was widely expected to wrap up a sixth success. However, the immense 262km stage to Pamplona encapsulated the Spaniard's race as he struggled to stay with the pace of his principal rivals, the setback hastening his decision to retire just a few months later.

This ride is based on the shorter of the two route options in the sportive, La Induráin, that is held each year in homage to him soon after San Fermín. It commences in Villava and loops through the hills to the north and east of the city. Fittingly, it begins adjacent to the Polideportivo Hermanos Induráin – Miguel's younger brother Prudencio was also a pro, although far less illustrious in his achievements – on the Calle Fermín Tirapu in the centre of Villava. Follow Calle Bidaburua and Calle Andrezar and cross the River Ulzama heading for Huarte and Olatz, then head towards Aoiz.

The industrial clutter on the edge of the city quickly gives way to farmland, the road passing between large, rolling fields of wheat and corn as it heads eastwards, rising gradually for the first few kilometres, then gently losing that height over the next few. Overall, this isn't a tough route in terms of climbing, and my experience of riding hereabouts suggests that it's the elements rather than the terrain that determine the degree of difficulty. The summer heat can be withering and the wind unceasingly strong, the combination producing a hairdryer-like effect that can be immensely sapping. As a consequence, pick your route of attack carefully when venturing onto roads like these that are normally a breeze but can be hellish. I well remember one afternoon when a friend and I spent what seemed like hours trying to sit on each other's wheel in order to escape a head-on blast that sucked resources and motivation at the same unquenchable rate.

Turn left towards Olaberri coming into Ecay de Lónguida (see page 188), the road a narrow strip cutting through farmland, rising steadily for the most part to reach the NA1720. Turn left on this bigger road, holding a northerly course as it continues to climb, topping out in the 260m-long Nagore tunnel, where lights should be used. A short drop leads onto a flatter section, the road narrowing as it approaches the handful of houses that comprise Zandueta, beyond which it rises again through the verdant Arce valley towards the Mezkiritz.

This is a lovely section, the terrain becoming more wooded, huge beech trees and towering pines offering shelter on hot days. Turn left at the junction with the N135, which runs past Roncesvalles and over the Ibañeta pass into France (see page 202), to reach the large village of Espinal and, a kilometre or so further on, the Puerto de Mezkiritz, which is bisected by the Camino de Santiago. The descent away from the pass dives back and forth exhilaratingly, then takes a more direct line downwards, the Camino never far away. There's a lump or two on this mostly straight run into Erro, then a more sustained ascent leaving this town towards the pass of the same name, which is also bisected by the Camino and usually boasts a refreshments van that's ideally placed to take

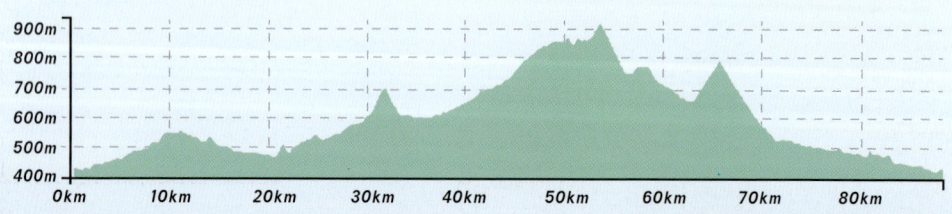

NAVARRA

Navarran beech forest near Erro

advantage of the busy crossing point.

Essentially, all of the day's climbing is now done, the N135 winding quickly down to Zubiri and then more gradually along the Esteribar valley to Pamplona, woodland slowly yielding to farmland and then to the industrial outskirts of the city. Turn right at Oloki following the signs to Pamplona on the PA30, going right again towards Huarte and back into the heart of Villava.

Route in reverse

Almost all of the climbing is in the first half, which some riders will prefer. However, as highlighted above, the key factor will be the wind. When making the choice on direction, try to ensure that you're not going to be riding into the teeth of it on the stretch between Pamplona and Aoiz.

Distance: 88.6km
Elevation gain: 1,200m
Highest point: 923m
Est. moving time: 3-4.5hrs
Degree of difficulty: ●●
Climbs: Alto de Mezkiritz (923m), Alto de Erro (795m)

Recorrido

0km	Villava
3km	Olatz ➡ NA8107
3.5km	NA8107/NA150 ➡
22.5km	Ecay de Lónguida NA150/NA2355 ⬅ ①
27.5km	NA2355/NA1720 ⬅
50km	NA1720/N135 ⬅ ②
53.5km	Puerto de Mezkiritz ③
62.5km	Erro
66km	Puerto de Erro ④
71.5km	Zubiri
84.5km	Oloki N135/PA30 ➡
85.5km	PA30/NA4200 ➡
88.6km	Villava

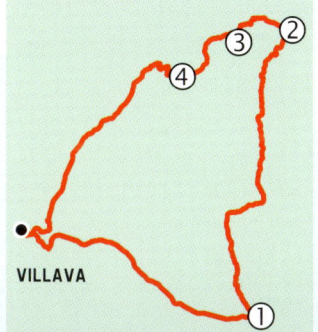

DOUBLY INSPIRED BY INDURÁIN

This loop can easily be joined with the other circuit inspired by the Induráin sportive (see page 192) to cover the same 180km course as the longer option available in that event. Simply take a right turn in Zubiri on the way back towards Pamplona from the Puerto de Erro for the full-on experience. Or, alternatively, tackle three passes instead of five on this route that runs north from Pamplona through rugged, remote and often stunning countryside to the small town of Irurita, returning via the equally impressive Puerto de Artesiaga.

Beginning adjacent to the Polideportivo Hermanos Induráin in Villava, head east from this suburb and then north to join the N135 as it tracks the River Arga upstream to Zubiri. Pass through this small town, staying with the Arga, the valley starting to narrow and the gradient picking up a tad too. The road meanders to Urtasun, where the long loop commences with a left turn towards Iragi and Olague via the Egozkue pass.

This is a beautiful climb, mostly through woodland. The initial ramp suggests a significant degree of difficulty, but it's actually quite benign as it snakes westwards, averaging a little less than 5.5%. Iragi lies two-thirds of the way up, its houses typically Basque, their white façades embroidered with sandstone and topped off with gently sloping red-tiled roofs, all huddled on a flat spot from which the road kicks up again for another 2km through shady trees to the pass.

Brief glimpses of long views to the north can be seen during the descent, which is a point or so steeper than the eastern side as it drops into the village of Egozkue. Beyond here, the slope eases significantly, the road trundling down into Anué valley to arrive in Olague. On the far side of this large village, the route joins the N121A highway that runs between Pamplona and the very busy border towns of Irún and Hendaye, and there's a good deal of HGV traffic on it. On the upside, the road is wide and features a long diversion to avoid two long tunnels that bore beneath the Belate pass, these underground sections improved in 2018 in order to ensure their use by goods vehicles.

After bearing right away from the main road and then diving underneath it, this smaller artery rears up for a few hundred metres, the gradient touching 11%, before settling down to climb at half that rate through the lustrous beech woods that are a feature of this region, providing a cool haven on hot days and luminous colour when it's gloomy. The final three kilometres to the Belate pass are a breeze, which is extended on the drop into the Baztán valley.

Soon after passing beneath a viaduct bearing the highway between the two tunnels, the route forks right towards Irurita, climbing again for a short while in the trees above the main road, before hitting out eastwards and away from it to enter rich pastureland with glorious views at every turn, the whites and reds of the Basque houses standing out in the verdant green patchwork of fields and meadows. The Baztán observation point, just above Zigaurre, is worth a brief stop for details on the surroundings. Beyond it, this marvellous backroad makes a final dip into the Baztán valley.

Lying just past halfway and at the foot of the final climb of the Artesiaga, Irurita is an ideal place for a break before heading south towards Eugi. As highlighted further on (see page 210), this is a peach of a road – very quiet, equally scenic, perfect for exploration on two wheels. Its 15.6km average 5%, but that latter figure conceals how difficult it is in

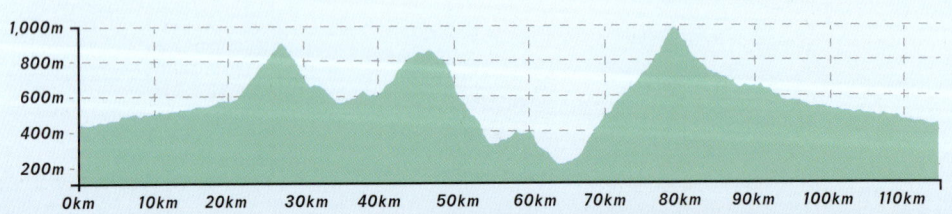

NAVARRA

parts, the first test arriving after 3km of what is effectively false flat, a short section at 12% coming on the heels of the pass open/closed indicator. But after this short grind, focus can return to the landscape, beech woods alternating with open segments looking across farmland and rolling hills. After a handful of kilometres allowing serene contemplation, the final 2km bring a series of double-digit ramps that ensure arrival at the summit for a magnificent panorama is well earned.

The drop away to the south is even more abrupt than the arrival from the north, but mirrors that flank in that these ramps only persist for a couple of kilometres. The road then eases downwards for 6km to a T-junction and on to the holiday village of Eugi on the edge of the eponymous reservoir. Urtasun lies just below the dam at the bottom end of the lake, with the return to Pamplona via the same route taken earlier in the day.

Route in reverse

The Induráin sportive tends to head north over the Artesiaga from Urtasun rather than tracking west over the Egozkue, and it's just as impressive. One of the beauties of riding in this region is the extensiveness of the road network and the many route options that are a consequence of this.

Irurita from the Baztán mirador

Distance: 116.7km
Elevation gain: 2,080m
Highest point: 996m
Est. moving time: 4.5-6.5hrs
Degree of difficulty: ●●●
Climbs: Alto de Egozkue (894m), Alto de Belate (847m), Puerto de Artesiaga (996m)

Recorrido

0km	Villava
3km	Huarte NA4200/PA30 ←
3.5km	PA30/NA135 →
17km	Zubiri NA135/NA138 ←
21.5km	NA138/NA2520 ←
27km	Alto de Egozkue ①
34.5km	Olague NA2520/NA8104 →
36km	NA8104/NA121A →
41.5km	NA121A/NA1210 →
47km	Alto de Belate ②
56.5km	NA1210/NA2540 →
69km	Irurita NA2540/NA1740 ③
81km	Puerto de Artesiaga ④
88km	NA1740/NA138 →
99km	Zubiri NA138/NA135 →
112.5km	N135/PA30 →
113.5km	PA30/NA4200 →
116.7km	Villava

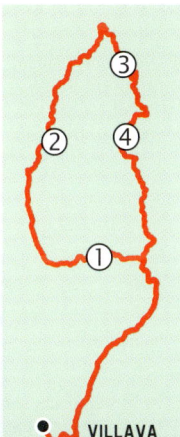

BASQUE RAMPS AND THE GORGEOUS GORRAMAKIL

As noted elsewhere, the Basque section of the Pyrenees is too often overlooked as a destination both by the major bike races and cycle tourists. This is odd given that the País Vasco is one of the heartlands of cycle sport and because of the quantity and variety of potential routes. This one, beginning in the Baztán valley, is a good example as it skirts the eastern side of the beautifully verdant Señorío de Bértiz national park and, later on, takes in the climb to the Pico Gorramakil, with wonderful 360° views from the summit.

Initially running south-west from Elizondo to Irurita and from there joining the main N121B road along the Valle del Baztán, the route turns northwards on the NA4453 next to a gravel works. Right from the off, this lane is stereotypically Basque. It's very narrow and extremely steep, well over 12% for a kilometre and a half as it scampers up through dense woodland. It's a savage start to the day's climbing, but the trees giving way to meadows signals a change to a much kinder degree of ascent with views to the south across the hills rolling towards Pamplona.

After switching direction regularly for 5km, the road reaches a crest and starts to travel due north, contouring around the mountainside beneath a rocky outcrop, Monte Legate, which is topped by a huge cross. To the west is the canopy of the Señorío de Bértiz park, a nature and wildlife sanctuary.

Passing Monte Legate, the road descends for a couple of kilometres, then kicks up again, the surface changing from asphalt to cement as it does so. Thankfully, given cement's treacherousness in the wet, the slab section with its slightly corrugated surface doesn't include any steep ramps up or down as it rises to a crest then trundles down into a dip beyond, tarmac returning for the short climbs up to the Collado de Edquisaroy. Soon after it passes a left turn to Etxalar (see page 222) and begins to climb again, approaching the Puerto de Otxondo from the east. For 4km it's a mixture of beauty and beasty, the former courtesy of the lengthy stands of beech that dapple the light on the road, the latter thanks to frequent double-digit pitches, the incline finally easing in the last few hundred metres to the main road rising from Elizondo to the Otxondo.

Go left here and climb for a few hundred metres to the pass and take the right turn towards Gorramendi. The road surface is far from perfect in places, but the views make this out-and-back ride to Gorramakil very worthwhile. To begin with, these are down the Baztán. With more altitude, though, long vistas emerge to the north. It's a bit like a mini version of the magnificently open passes close to Saint Jean Pied de Port, about 60km to the east. Running south for a distance, the road begins to climb again, almost encircling Monte Gorramendi, the views stupendous. Turning northwards for the final assault on the summit, the snowy peaks of the high Pyrenees appear to the east, those on the far side of Saint Jean amidst them.

Passing beneath the telecoms tower, some sections are very rough, gravel replacing tarmac in places or, worse still from the perspective of punctures, the top surface badly eroded and pitted. But I urge you to press on to the summit because the panorama it offers is absolutely extraordinary. The Gorramakil is higher than the surrounding mountains, so the stylish resorts of Saint Jean de Luz and Biarritz can be picked out on the Atlantic coast. To the east, the Ispéguy pass can be picked out. Beyond it, in the far distance, are some of the highest pinnacles in

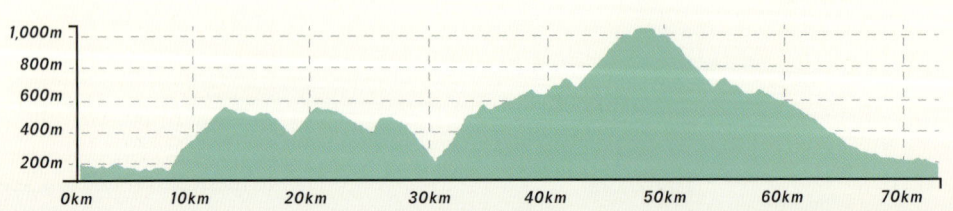

PAÍS VASCO

Etxalar

the Pyrenean chain.

Pick your way carefully back to the main road, turning left to glide down the Baztán on the straightest and smoothest stretch all day, ultimately following the course of the River Bidasoa back into Elizondo.

Route in reverse

This would mean the Gorramakil, the ride's outstanding highlight, would come early. At the end, the very steep descent on the Monte Legate road would need to be taken with great care.

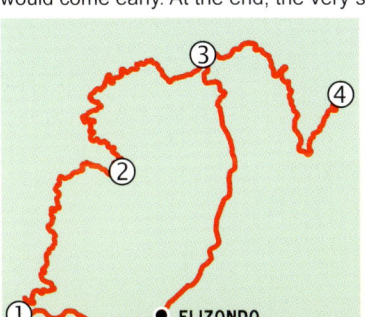

Distance: 72.8km
Elevation gain: 1,944m
Highest point: 1,090m
Est. moving time: 3-5hrs
Degree of difficulty: ●●●
Climbs: Collado de Edquisaroy (518m), Puerto de Otxondo (602m), Pico Gorramakil (1,090m)

Recorrido

0km	Elizondo NA8307
4.5km	Arraioz NA8307/N121B ←
7.5km	N121B/NA4453 → ①
26.5km	Collado de Edquisaroy ②
35km	NA4453/N121B ←
35.5km	Puerto de Otxondo ③ N121B/NA2655 →
47.5km	Pico Gorramakil ④
59.5km	NA2655/N121B ←
72km	Junction N121B/NA8307 ←
72.8km	Elizondo

A SAN SEBASTIÁN CLASSIC DAY OUT

The first big race after the Tour de France, the one-day Clásica San Sebastián is also one of the most attractive on the professional racing calendar. Starting beside the beach in the Basque city's stunning La Concha bay, this route includes the event's most renowned climb, the Alto de Jaizkibel, which rises high above the Bay of Biscay to the east of the city, looking out over the Atlantic and across towards the stylish resorts on the French Basque Country coast.

Heading east alongside La Concha, cross the River Urumea at the Puente de Santa Catalina and follow Ategorrieta Hiribidea and then José Elósegui Alkatea due east making for the suburb of Lezo. Long sections can be covered on bike paths, the handiest section one that runs parallel to the GI636. Go into Lezo, track around the centre and pick up the GI3440, with the Jaizkibel now signposted. Staying with this road as it forks to the right, the first ramps of the climb appear.

The change from the bustle of the city and, especially, from the industrial ugliness of the docks is instant and dramatic. The road lifts off through magnificent beech woods, climbing gently to start with and soon more steeply, rising quickly through a series of hairpins. Beyond them, the road plateaus, leaving the deciduous woodland behind, stands of pine now offering protection from the prevailing wind off the ocean. Higher up, these too disappear, giving unbroken views over the sea, back towards San Sebastián and along Spain's north coast.

The views are best a few hundred metres before and after the summit. At this latter point, you get a first glimpse eastwards into the Pyrenees. Continuing down, there is another impressive viewpoint adjacent to the Ermita Guadalupe, the foothills of the French Pyrenees standing out behind the frontier towns of Irún and Hendaye. These vistas become more extensive as the road breezes down to the edge of Hondarribia, a very picturesque and historic port located where the River Bidasoa reaches the sea.

Skirt the town on the ring road, pick up the N138 towards Irún, passing the airport, then the GI636 into Mendelu and Irún. Bear right in central Irún off this main route towards Artea, Meaka and the Peña de Aia. Within moments, this road passes beneath the motorway and quickly finds verdant countryside. Leaving Meaka, it begins to climb to the Puerto de Erlaitz, and abruptly too. Ascending a corridor of slender alder and then into beech woods, the gradient fluctuates either side of 10%. It eases entering a string of hairpins, then rears up much more sharply negotiating them. Above them, there's no let-up. Indeed, for a brief time it ramps up to 17%. It's no surprise, then, that this is another regular on the San Sebastián route.

The hard grind ends at a crest, the road still climbing but now very gently along a ridge with views alternating between the Atlantic on the right and the Pyrenees on the left. This southern flank of the Erlaitz is markedly different, the road stepping gently down for the most part, the terrain much more open, the panorama vast.

Go right at the T-junction with the GI2134, then left in Gurutze, this road briefly climbing very steeply, before starting to drop into San Sebastián. After diving beneath the motorway, it reaches the GI636, leading back down towards Lezo for the return journey to La Concha.

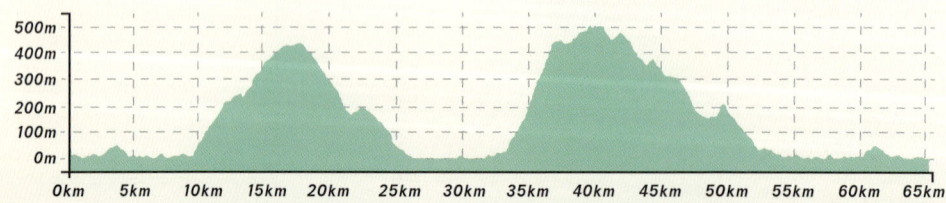

PAÍS VASCO

Towards San Sebastián from the Jaizkibel

Distance: 65.6km
Elevation gain: 1,513m
Highest point: 510m
Est. moving time: 2.5-4hrs
Degree of difficulty: ●●
Climbs: Alto de Jaizkibel (455m), Puerto de Erlaitz (501m)

Route in reverse

My only gripe would be that the Jaizkibel is tackled from the opposite side to San Sebastián's pro race. The counter to that is that the climbing is easier both on the Erlaitz and the Jaizkibel, and the finish off that final immense headland is more memorable.

Recorrido

0km	San Sebastián Head east on Ategorrieta Hiribidea, José Elósegui Alkatea and Pasaiako Portuko Zeharbidea
7km	GI636
7.5km	GI636/GI2638 ←
8.5km	Lezo GI2638/GI3440 ← ①
9.5km	GI3440 →
17.5km	Alto de Jaizkibel ②
26km	GI3440 →
27km	GI3440/N638 →
28.5km	N638/GI2134 ←
29km	Mendelu GI2134/GI636 ← ③
31km	Irún GI636/GI3454 →
37km	Puerto de Erlaitz ④
48.5km	GI3454/GI2134 →
48.5km	Gurutze GI2134/GI3632 → ⑤
53km	GI3632/GI636 ←
57km	Lezo ①
65.6km	San Sebastián

A TOUR OF EASTERN EUSKADI

The Itzulia, or Tour of the Basque Country, is one of my favourite races on the pro calendar. It generally boasts a strong field of stage race specialists, can count on the support of the fervent local fans and has a route that always seems to have been pieced together with the aim of including as many of the region's hills as possible, sometimes up to 10 during a single stage. Inspired by that final characteristic, this circuit inland from San Sebastián clocks up almost 3,500m of vertical gain but never crosses an altitude threshold of 700m. In short, it's typically and brutally Basque.

It gets under way in Hernani, one of San Sebastián's dormitory towns, lying to the south of the elegant port city, and heads off in the same direction towards Goizueta. Once beyond the factories on the edge of Hernani, the route enters glorious woodland bordering the River Urumea. Running just slightly uphill, the road is popular with local cyclists, the initial 30km stretch through Pagoaga and out to Goizueta ideal for a steady warm-up before climbing aboard the Basque rollercoaster that begins with the climb towards the Usoteguieta pass. It's rarely flat, but never too testing as it bumps south-east, always tracking the meandering course of the Urumea.

Beyond Goizueta, its attractive main street little more than a car's width across, the road starts to climb more consistently, passing old mine workings as the heavily wooded valley narrows. The gradient isn't fierce, occasionally touching 9%, but generally half that. The trees become sparser, signalling the Usoteguieta isn't too far ahead, the pass sitting at a T-junction on the NA170 with a surprisingly large hotel adjacent to it. Turn left towards Doneztebe, weaving eastwards through stands of pine and beech along a ridge, before gliding down through Ezkurra to reach a right turn to Saldías.

You can save yourself half a dozen kilometres by sticking with the main road here, but the diversion via Beintza and Labaien is well worth that little bit of extra distance. It commences with the steepest ramps of the ride so far, touching 14% to reach Saldías's spectacular perch. At the far end of this village, turn left towards Doneztebe, climbing more sedately to a high point with glorious views over a horseshoe of hills overlooking the Santesteban de Lerin valley. The road continues through the twin villages of Beintza and Labaien, then saunters down past Urrotz and into the patchwork of fields in the valley bottom to reach Doneztebe, close to half-distance and a good place to pause.

Head east on the NA1210, which plays cat and mouse with the N121A highway and the River Bidasoa to reach Oronoz, where you should continue this game by forking left on the NA8303. This does meet the main road, but acquaintance is very brief as the route turns immediately to the left onto the lane passing in front of the gravel works. As highlighted on page 196, it's venomously steep for a good way until it reaches open farmland with long views to the south, the gradient easing as it half-circles Monte Legate, the surface then changing from tarmac to concrete for six undulating kilometres. Soon after, go left towards Etxalar, the road rough in places, forking left soon after towards the same village.

The views are so impressive that a sedate pace remains almost obligatory until a sharp drop into Etxalar that should be taken very carefully. Turn left here, descending more comfortably on a perfect surface into the Bidasoa valley, running parallel to the river

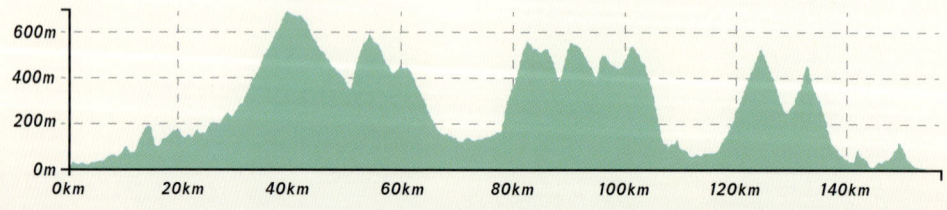

PAÍS VASCO

Saldias

Distance: 156km
Elevation gain: 3,437m
Highest point: 695m
Est. moving time: 6-9hrs
Degree of difficulty: ●●●●◐
Climbs: Puerto de Usoteguieta (695m), Puerto de Agiña (549m), Alto de Aritxulegi (439m)

and the N121A, crossing over this highway to meet the NA4000 towards Lesaka, where the final quarter of the ride begins.

First up is the Puerto de Agiña, an idyllic 8km ascent that eases through sweeping bends cut into thick woodland, the gentle gradient very welcome after earlier ramps. Nearing the summit, the road emerges onto open hillside and presents a majestic view that demands longer consideration from a short spur of concrete track at the pass. From the Agiña, there's a super 5km descent to the Endara reservoir, the road crossing the dam at the bottom of it and then climbing for 3.5km to the Aritxulegi pass, another leafy and uncomplicated ascent that culminates in an unlit tunnel linking the provinces of Navarra and Gipuzkoa (see page 224).

After a picturesque 8km descent there are two final hops, a small one to start with into Oiartzun (Elizalde) to meet the GI2134, the buzz of traffic a sign that the busy coastal strip is near, the second and larger one into Astigarraga, following signs for Hernani from there, close to 100 miles of Basque twists and rolls completed.

Recorrido

0km	Hernani to GI3410
25km	Goizueta
40km	Puerto de Usateguieta NA4150/NA170 ← ①
51km	NA170/NA4029 → to Saldías
64km	Urrotz
70.5km	Doneztebe NA4040/NA170 →
71km	NA170/NA1210 → ②
76km	Oronoz NA1210/NA8303 ←
78km	NA8303/N121A ← and immediately ← on NA4453 ③
98km	← to Etxalar
99.5km	← to Etxalar
108km	Etxalar unclassified/NA4400 ←
113.5km	NA4400/NA4000 ← to Lesaka ④
124.5km	Puerto de Agiña ⑤
133km	Alto de Aritxulegi ⑥
142km	Oiartzun GI3420/GI2134 ←
144.5km	Arragua GI2134/GI2132 ← ⑦
153km	Astigarraga
156km	Hernani

Route in reverse

Just as testing and equally enjoyable.

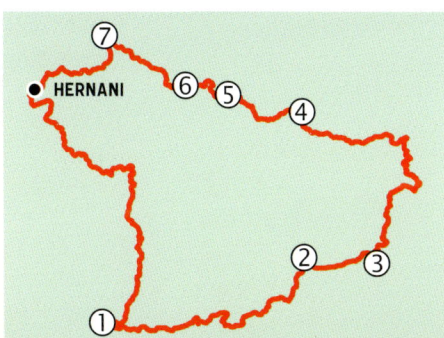

THROUGH THE RONCESVALLES PASS

This route encapsulates the beauty of both the French and Spanish parts of the Basque Country, crossing climbs that don't have particular significance within pro cycling but more than compensate for that thanks to their historical renown. Starting in the small but hugely attractive town of Saint Jean Pied de Port, which is overlooked by a 17th-century fortress that bears the impregnable imprint typical of Vauban, Louis XIV's illustrious military engineer, it initially heads west, climbing gently and then dropping into Saint Étienne de Baïgorry, the gateway to the beautiful Col d'Ispéguy (see page 212).

Although it's a wrench to swing south away from this cross-border route, the far longer climb to the Collado de Urkiaga is just as rewarding. Following the Nive des Aldudes river, it meanders for close to 20km to reach Aldudes. Beyond the town, with its solid white houses bedecked with red or green shutters that evoke the *ikurrina*, the Basque flag, fork right onto the D58, all the while heading towards Pamplona. Suddenly, the road rears up with some venom, easing briefly in Esnazu, then rising again, but less savagely, allowing the legs a chance to spin while taking in the long view from a ridge back down the valley you've all but climbed out of.

Moments later, a sign announces arrival in Spain, and the first building a usefully located store selling cheap (for the French) goods. The steady upward haul continues, but on a wider, better-surfaced road that winds through thick beech woods that glow an almost luminous green on bright days. There's a brief drop before the final step up to the Urkiaga pass and the start of a long, speedy but straightforward descent to the Arga valley, passing the ruins of the Eugi weapons factory and continuing on to the village of Eugi, a mini-lakeside resort that sits on the edge of a reservoir, its dam just a little further on.

At Saigots, Pamplona is only 20km away, but that's for another day (see page 192). Instead, turn towards France. The road climbs, and quite smartly on occasions, to reach the Erro pass, the Camino de Santiago pilgrimage route crossing it, a makeshift café in an old van usually open to serve the steady flow of walkers. The road plunges into Erro, then climbs once more, meeting the Camino again in dense woodland at the Mezkiritz

Camino de Santiago marker on the Ibañeta

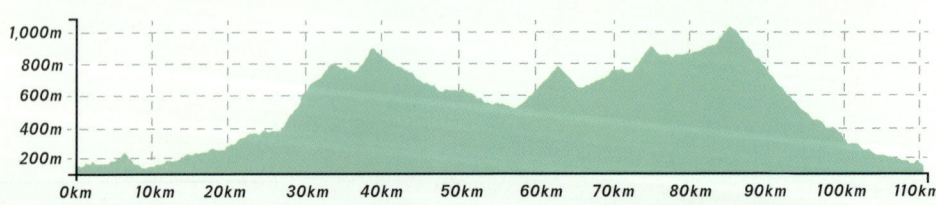

PYRÉNÉES ATLANTIQUES

pass.

After dropping from that high point through thick forest, the road turns 90 degrees left to head directly into and through Burguete, the large village overlooked by the mountains marking the border. Not far beyond it is the palatial hospital/dormitory for pilgrims at Roncesvalles. Built in the late 12th and early 13th century, the complex would host as many as 50,000 pilgrims during religious festivals in the Middle Ages, and remains an important stepping stone on the Camino as the first overnight halt after the challenging crossing of the Pyrenees.

A large switchback swings around it before climbing to the Ibañeta pass above, alongside it a tiny triangular chapel with a bell that pilgrims ring to announce safe passage over the mountains. It heralds the start of an exhilarating slalom extending to almost 30km back into Saint Jean Pied de Port. Heavily wooded and at times tightly hemmed in on both sides by cliffs, it's easy to understand why Basque tribes chose this renowned point to ambush Charlemagne's conquering army led by Roland in the eighth century. While it's often damp under the trees, this can be a beautifully shady haven in the summer, but keep an eye out for pilgrims walking up the pass, especially when conditions aren't great and many decide against the high-mountain route.

Chapel on the Ibañeta pass

Distance: 111.1km
Elevation gain: 2,158m
Highest point: 1,057m
Est. moving time: 3.5-6hrs
Degree of difficulty: ●●●
Climbs: Collado de Urkiaga (915m), Puerto de Erro (795m), Alto de Mezkiritz (923m), Puerto de Ibañeta (1,057m)

Route in reverse

Climbing the Roncesvaux pass, as it is known on the French side, is straightforward, but this tight and constantly weaving road can be busy, although the amount of traffic does drop off beyond the "duty-free" shops at Arnéguy. That brief annoyance apart, this option is equally impressive. See page 194 for a fuller description.

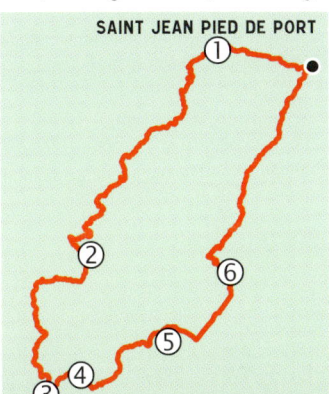

Parcours

0km	Saint Jean Pied de Port
1km	D918/D15 ←
9.5km	Saint Étienne de Baïgorry D15/D948 ← ①
26.5km	D948/D58 →
39km	Collado de Urkiaga NA138 ②
57.5km	Zubiri NA138/N135 ← ③
63km	Puerto de Erro ④
75km	Puerto de Mezkiritz ⑤
85km	Puerto de Ibañeta ⑥
103km	Arnéguy N135 becomes D933
111km	Saint Jean Pied de Port

THE PAYS BASQUE'S WILD FRONTIER

To adapt a famous phrase from the movie *Withnail and I*, this was a ride that I went on by mistake. Using the map on my phone as a guide, and therefore not seeing the length and seriousness of the climb that I was inexorably approaching, I ventured out late one afternoon looking for some gently rolling roads to warm me up for the daunting ascent of the Burdincurucheta and Bagargui the next day. It turned out to be almost as hard as that twin ascent, but utterly bewitching.

After climbing away from Saint Jean's fortifications, the road bobs in heartening fashion to Saint Michel and then follows the course of the Nive, which joins the Adour at Bayonne before emptying into the Bay of Biscay. Passing the covered fronton court at Estérençuby, the road continues on, a sign indicating the imminence of the Nive's source. The views in the valley are reminiscent of the Lake District or North Wales, with very few trees on the precipitous mountainsides and crumbling outcrops of well-weathered rock that are testament to its age.

Passing the left-turn that takes off at a severely steep angle on an alternative approach to the Bagargui that bypasses the fearsome Burdincurucheta but is no less formidable, the road continues on to the hotel and restaurant at the river's source. Just beyond it, what's already a narrow lane becomes even tighter and starts to climb more sharply, tracking one of the Nive's tributaries, the Orion. It rises quickly to reach the gate that closes the Orgambidé when it's impassable, then advances a little further to a small bridge over the river, where the gradient kicks up more abruptly, just below 10% for a kilometre, then above that mark for the next, coming out of the woods on the hairpin in between to reveal tantalising views towards the Bagargui.

Back among the trees on this most forgotten of back roads, the isolation of this route is almost frightening when the cloud starts to close in as it did when I rode up, dampening all sound, cutting off any indication of what might lay ahead and even what you've left behind. A vertiginous hairpin leads into a kilometre-long straight, then another hairpin and another straight, then a third.

Escape from this claustrophobic atmosphere arrives suddenly and spectacularly, the road climbing above the trees to give long views first to the east and soon after to the west. It's absolutely glorious, the ridge so lofty in what are the first significant peaks inland from the Atlantic that you feel like you're on top of the world, even at 988m, where this road meets one coming up from Orbaizeta in Spain (see page 194) at the Col d'Orgambidé.

Keeping one eye on the sheep that are abundant in what is now grassy pasture and the other on wonderful vistas that change with every curve, the road descends briefly then climbs again through pasture pocked with limestone pavement, evoking the Yorkshire Dales but on a high-rise scale. It sweeps around an immense bowl, the Col d'Arnostéguy at its apex.

A couple of easy kilometres on, the road briefly becomes the Camino de Santiago, the pilgrims trekking towards the highest point of their journey. On clear days, the Atlantic is visible from this high ridge that descends steadily to the Orisson refuge, behind which walkers camp out. From there it plummets helter-skelter into and through the hamlet of Huntto on a gradient that averages more than 12% for 4km and has pitches at 14 and 16, then concludes with a more sedate

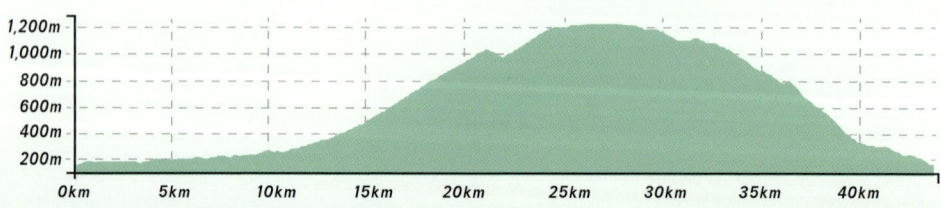

PYRÉNÉES ATLANTIQUES

The steep descent from the Arnostéguy pass to Saint Jean Pied de Port

roll into Saint Jean Pied de Port to conclude a short but quite unforgettable ride.

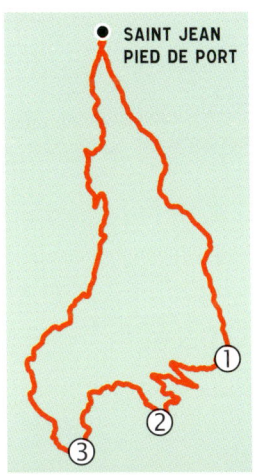

Route in reverse

Although both sides of the Arnostéguy are essentially the same length and gradient, that 4km section around Huntto makes the counter-clockwise option much more challenging. The flipside of that is that the descent back to Saint Jean is not as hairy.

Distance: 44km
Elevation gain: 1,281m
Highest point: 1,240m
Est. moving time: 1.5-3hrs
Degree of difficulty: ●●●◐
Climbs: Col d'Orgambidé (988m), Col d'Arnostéguy (1,236m)

Parcours

0km	Saint Jean Pied de Port D301
8km	Estérençuby
11.5km	D301/D428 ➔ ①
20km	Col d'Orgambidé ②
26km	Col d'Arnostéguy ③
44km	St Jean Pied de Port

STEEP WALLS AND RIDGEWAYS

This ride travels through terrain that, surprisingly, the Tour de France only ventures into on rare occasions. The climbs are very taxing, the descents very technical and the scenery absolutely stunning. Ideally, it should be done on a clear day when the spectacular views from the Iraty ridge can be fully appreciated.

After a short section on the main road out of Saint Jean Pied de Port, fork right into and through Saint Jean Le Vieux, quickly reaching tranquil back roads. The day's long loop begins just beyond Mendive at the junction of the D18 and D417. Continue on the former, rising gently through farmland, the Iraty valley gradually narrowing until a sign announcing 'Cols d'Iraty' heralds what quickly becomes a ferocious change in the incline.

A trio of cols lie ahead. The first is the Haltza, well named as pausing is something very much on the mind as the road averages close to 11% for 4km to reach it. There's little alternative but to take it slow and savour the landscape, one moment looking up the valley, the next back down it, as the road switches back and forth, before emerging suddenly onto what feels like a plateau at the Haltza as the gradient dials back to 5%. The best panorama is around the left-hand bend just beyond, looking up the road as it climbs the ridge towards the Burdincurucheta, and across the peaks rolling away to the west.

Leaving the woodlands behind, the road is now cut into a steep mountainside and you can't help but goggle at the wonderful vistas. The 5km between the Haltza and the Burdincurucheta are as good as any in the Pyrenees. Beyond the little iron cross that gives the Burdincurucheta its Basque name, the road plunges swiftly down to a mountain lake. Turn left here towards Larrau and the final pass in this troika, the Bagargui.

The ascent is now far easier, the route mainly in the trees, passing two big ponds, with walking/cross-country skiing trails heading off in all directions. The summit arrives at the second of two large developments. The view is impressive, but substantially better a kilometre or so below, where the Port de Larrau and Pic d'Orhy stand out as you look right down the spine of the Pyrenees, the Pic d'Anie above the resort of La Pierre St Martin also very apparent.

The descent to Larrau is initially narrow, steep and often quite rough because it's so exposed, so take it steady and savour the panoramas, the fields in the valley standing out like bright green eiderdowns laid down amidst the dark pine forest. After the little kick up into Larrau, bear left to follow the road alongside the Gave de Larrau/Saison as it rushes urgently down to the neat little town of Tardets-Sorholus, turning left here towards Ahusquy.

The next 5km run close to flat through farmland, until, almost beyond the village of Alçay, where the route starts to climb once again from a right turn signposted to Ahusquy and Mendive, the road winding a little confusingly through the houses before making for the hills. The gradient is fierce to begin with, almost 12% for a kilometre, then eases to nines for the next three. Narrow and bumpy, this is a track that isn't well beaten by anyone apart from local farmers and their wandering livestock. The rubbly, ancient landscape is quite different to the other side of the loop, but it's all the better for that.

A kilometre at 10% arrives at the Col d'Arangaitz, from which there's a short drop, the road then climbing more comfortably for 3km to reach a trident in the road at the Col Ibarburia, an information board on its left side detailing the host of peaks to the south. The

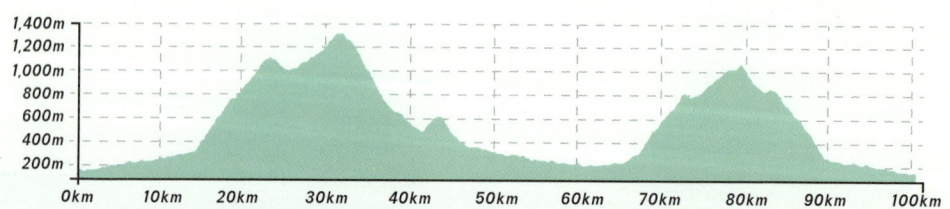

PYRÉNÉES ATLANTIQUES

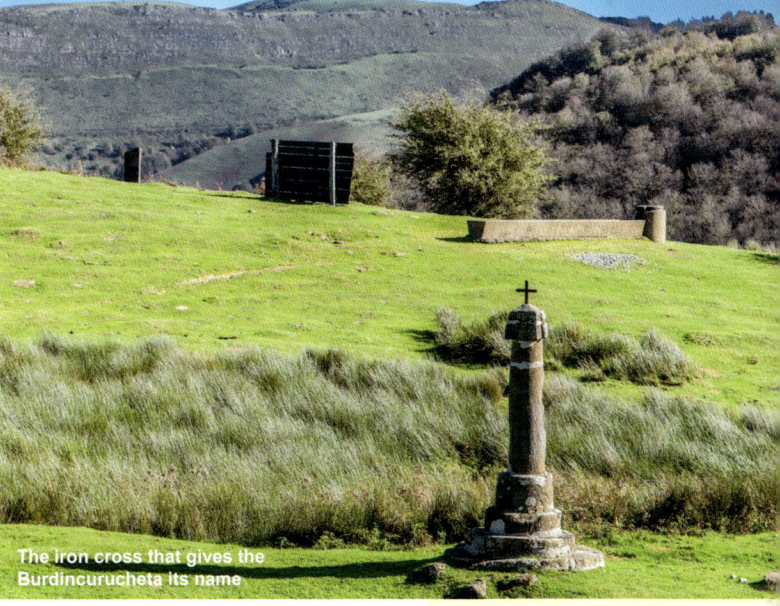

The iron cross that gives the Burdincurucheta its name

branch down to the left runs to the Col Burdin Olatze (see page 210), reached via a spectacular ridge that runs on to the Bagargui. Up to the right is the hamlet of Ahusquy, comprising just a solid-looking auberge and a couple of other buildings. Keep in between these two options, climbing the road cut into the bare mountainside where the views are marvellously wide-ranging and the sense of remoteness overwhelming.

Close to its high point at what is described in some places as the Col d'Ahusquy but is unmarked, there's a choice. Stick with the slightly wider road to the left, the D417, that is the more direct route to Mendive, or stay on the D117 for the longer option with more climbing. The beauty of the easier route, which soon begins to descend, and very quickly in parts too, is that you can see across to the cols you were climbing earlier in the day as you drop back to Mendive to join the valley road coasting into Saint Jean Pied de Port, which seems the ideal way to end a spectacular day.

Route in reverse

There's a good case to be made for tackling it in this direction because you'll be riding up the narrowest and least well surfaced sections rather than down them. There is, however, still no escaping lots of consistently steep sections if you do opt to go clockwise.

Distance: 100.8km
Elevation gain: 2,656m
Highest point: 1,327m
Est. moving time: 3.5-6hrs
Degree of difficulty: ●●●●
Climbs: Col de Burdincurucheta (1,135m), Col Bagargui (1,327m), Col d'Ahusquy (1,079m)

Parcours

0km	St Jean Pied de Port
3km	D933/D2933 ➡
4km	Saint Jean Le Vieux D2933/D18 ➡
11km	Mendive D18/D417 ➡
18.5km	Col d'Haltza
23km	Col de Burdincurucheta ①
25km	D18/D19 ⬅
31.5km	Col Bagargui ②
43km	Larrau D19/D26 ⬅
59.5km	D26/D918 ⬅
60.5km	Tardets-Sorholus D918/D247 ⬅ ③
65.5km	Alçay D247/D117 ➡
72.5km	Col d'Arangaitz ④
76.5km	Col Ibarburia ⑤
79.5km	Col d'Ahusquy D117/D417 ⬅ ⑥
90km	Mendive D417/D18 ➡
100.8km	Saint Jean Pied de Port

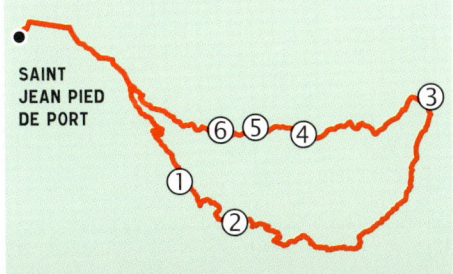

BREAK FOR THE BORDER

The profile suggests a rather crumpled Homburg, a wide brim leading into steep sides and, above them, a dimpled top. One of those sides is much more abrupt than the other, but I reckon that it offers the best route to the higher points of this hat-shaped route simply because I don't think my forearms could cope with the lactic burn that would be produced when braking on a descent that averages 12% for most of its 7km and often features ramps twice as abrupt.

From Saint Jean Pied de Port, follow the D301 (see page 204) towards and then through Estérençuby. After 11km, the road forks. Stay to the left, select a small gear and expect to spend a good deal of the next hour spinning it. Almost right away, it pitches up to 20%, then after 300m of grovel-inducing gradient, it drops to little more than four, setting the pattern for regular fluctuations all the steepling way to the Col d'Arthé, even including a short descent at one point early on.

The bends are coiled tight and quickly ascend onto open mountainside with long views that would provide considerable distraction if the incline weren't so rude, the climb towards the Orgambidé and the auberge at its foot easy to pick out if you do manage to drag your line of vision away from a point a few metres in front – and quite evidently above – your front wheel. The road is narrow and its surface often quite broken, further good reasons for going up it. Add in thick bracken and grazing sheep, and you could be riding up a renowned wall in the Yorkshire Dales or Moors, Park Rash or Rosedale Chimney perhaps, but this torment is three or four times more drawn-out than on those infamous ascents.

From the Arthé, there's a brief respite as the gradient relents, the road running along a ridge that one moment looks across to the Iraty cols and the next towards the Spanish border. In places, the mountainside falls away quite frighteningly from the edge of the road, and care should be taken if caught up here in mist or low cloud.

Reaching a pair of tightly coiled switchbacks, the gradient jags up again to find the top of the ridge, the road scrambling along it and towards a huge rock outcrop, then deviating at the last through boulders to its right-hand side and onto a more comfortable incline with a stupendous outlook to the south to arrive at the Col d'Arthaburu, the top of one side of the hat. Dive to the left at the fork here to slalom through a series of S bends and into half a dozen glorious kilometres through high-altitude moorland and a couple more through pine and beech woods, climbing towards the end to the Col de Sourzay.

Like the two previous cols, there's no obvious marker, just a remote farm, from which the route descends to meet the D18. You can go right here, but it's a dead end, the road dropping gently through the Iraty Forest to the Spanish border. It's a pleasant 10km round-trip, although always in amongst the trees within this huge pine and beech forest. Otherwise, go left to arrive at the junction between the Burdincurucheta and the Bagargui (see page 206), keeping straight on to climb to the former over two relatively benign kilometres.

Once up this short side of the Burdincurucheta, the descent back towards Saint Jean Pied de Port is fast. There are some long sections lower down that would be regarded as very steep on most mountains, but are comparatively tame compared to the drops you'd face doing this ride in the

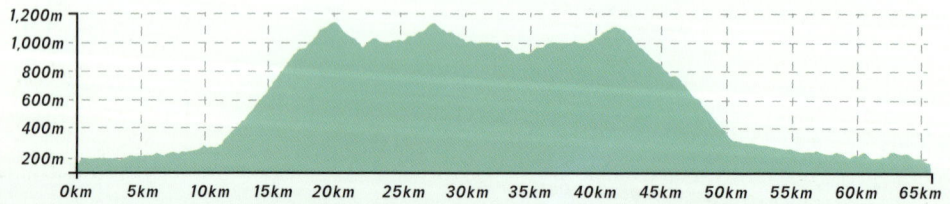

PYRÉNÉES ATLANTIQUES

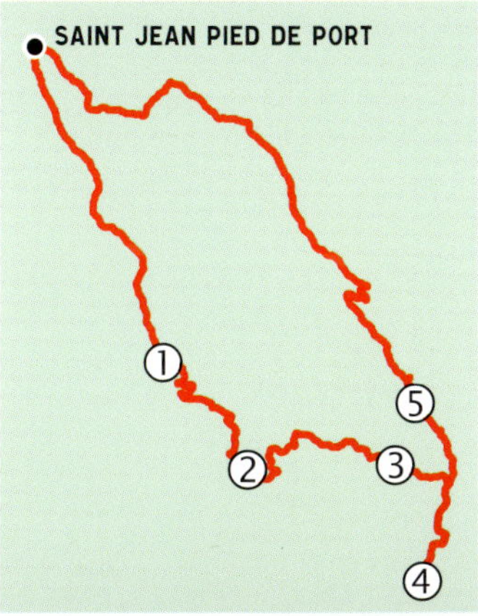

Wood pigeon shooting breaks above the Arthé pass

opposite direction. The road is wide, well surfaced and pretty quiet. The main distraction is likely to be the views, which on very clear days reach as far as the Atlantic.

Riding back along the valley towards Saint Jean, I couldn't help wondering why the Tour de France seldom passes this way, given the vogue for finding ever-steeper routes to test the pros. I can assume that they're too narrow to accommodate the race safely, as they rate highly in the challenge and spectacle they offer. They're certainly very well worth checking out.

Route in reverse

I'd advise against tackling this route in the opposite direction, not primarily because of the steepness of the descent back into the Saint Jean, but because its surface is poor in places and wandering livestock may also be a hazard.

Distance: 65.8km
Elevation gain: 1,800m
Highest point: 1,155m
Est. moving time: 2.5-4.5hrs
Degree of difficulty: ●●●●○
Climbs: Col d'Arthé (937m), Col d'Arthaburu (1,155m), Col de Sourzay (1,140m), Col de Burdincurucheta (1,135m)

Parcours

0km	Saint Jean Pied de Port
8km	Estérençuby
11km	D301/D428 ← ①
17.5km	Col d'Arthé
20km	Col d'Arthaburu ← ②
27.5km	Col de Sourzay ③
30km	Junction D301/D18 →
34.5km	Spanish border ④
39km	D18/D19 ←
41.5km	Col de Burdincurucheta ⑤
59km	D18/D118 ←
61km	Aincille D118/D401 →
65.8km	Saint Jean Pied de Port

AN HISTORIC COL AND A STUNNING RIDGE

The poor condition of some Pyrenean roads can often leave you wondering how long it has been since a repair crew spent time working on them. With that thought in mind, consider what the intrepid riders who first raced through the range back in the 1910 Tour de France were up against on routes that were sometimes little more than tracks used to move livestock. I mention this both because their fears should be remembered, but also because this route features a climb from that ground-breaking race, albeit one of the smaller ones. It also includes one of the most staggering sections of ridge riding in the whole range.

The historic climb features early in this ride that begins in Saint Jean Pied de Port and heads east to Saint Jean Le Vieux, carrying on through the village on the D120. Stick with this road, which climbs gradually through farmland to reach a low col, the Askonzabal – to confuse things the restaurant a couple of hundred metres up the lane above is called the Col de Gamia and I've both names applied to the col. There's then a drop to Ibarrolle followed by a right turn to Saint Just Ibarre, where the road climbs again, this time towards the Osquich, which featured on the epic 1910 Tour stage from Luchon to Bayonne that went over the Tourmalet and Aubisque for the first time. On that occasion, the racers were coming in the other direction.

The col arrives quickly and is unmissable thanks to an immense and rather functional-looking hotel and restaurant. What may seem odd is that the road continues to climb beyond it. Although col simply translates as "pass" and highlights a gap or a low point in a ridge, it often marks a point where two or more routes meet, so there may be several lower cols on the way towards a higher one.

In this case there's further confusion because this high point, 100 vertical metres above the original col, has over time become known as the Col d'Osquich.

After descending through lovely rural countryside to reach Musculdy and Ordiarp, the route turns south to Aussurucq on a country lane heading towards the high mountains. A little beyond the village, a sharp hairpin marks the start of a 12km climb, mostly through the Arbailles Forest. Ascending a steep corridor of woodland, the setting is markedly different to the more open landscapes throughout most of this region. It's a shady haven on hot days, dark and quite forbidding when the cloud's down.

Emerging from the trees at the Col d'Arangaitz (see page 206), the road keeps climbing up a shallow valley, its flanks bracken-covered, to emerge suddenly and spectacularly at the Col Ibarburia, just short of the hamlet of Ahusquy. Bear left and downwards, passing an observation point on the left, to follow the little-travelled but quite superb ridge road that runs south to the Col Bagargui. It's narrow and wonderfully scenic, the views initially south towards the Iraty ridge and west towards the coast.

The road bobs up and down until a series of hairpins signal two more abrupt kilometres of ascent at 9%. They lift the road above the treeline and onto the crest of a ridge from which the views extend in every direction. Following the contours for the most part, this extraordinary road cuts around the Pic des Escaliers, hugging the rockface closely on occasions, a photo opportunity at almost every twist and turn, then climbs again through woodland to emerge just shy of the eastern side of the summit of the Bagargui and the Iraty chalet village just beyond.

With the exception of the 2km ascent up

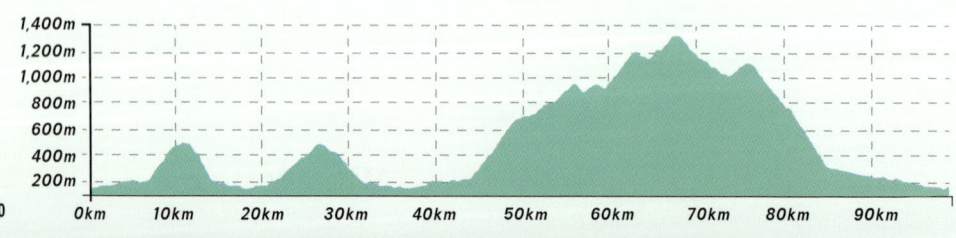

PYRÉNÉES ATLANTIQUES

Ridge road near the Ibarburia pass

Distance: 99.2km
Elevation gain: 2,417m
Highest point: 1,326m
Est. moving time: 3.5-6hrs
Degree of difficulty: ●●●◖
Climbs: Col d'Askonzabal (514m), Col d'Osquich (495m), Col Ibarburia (957m), Col Bagargui (1,327m), Col de Burdincurucheta (1,135m)

to the Col de Burdincurucheta (see page 208), which is not too hard, the 32km return to Saint Jean Pied de Port is downhill all the way. The first stretch to the junction where the Bagargui and Burdincurucheta roads meet runs through beautiful woodland and is quite benign. It's much steeper beyond that second col, particularly over the last 4km into the valley to return to Saint Jean Pied de Port via Mendive and Saint Jean le Vieux.

Route in reverse

Essentially it comes down to whether you want to do most of your climbing at the start of the day or at the end. Tackling it counter-clockwise, the climbing is perhaps a little tougher and there's more descending on small roads. It does end up crossing the Osquich in the same direction as the 1910 Tour.

Parcours	
0km	Saint Jean Pied de Port
3km	D933/D2933 ➡
4.5km	Saint Jean Le Vieux D2933/D120 ➡
11km	Col d'Askonzabal ①
18km	D120/D918 ➡
27km	Col d'Osquich ②
36km	D918/D147 ➡
52.5km	D147/D117 ➡
56km	Col Ibarburia D117/unclassified ⬅③
67.5km	Col Bagargui ④ unclassified/D19 ➡
73.5km	D19/D18 ➡
76km	Col de Burdincurucheta ⑤
95km	Saint Jean le Vieux D18/D2933 then D933
99.2km	Saint Jean Pied de Port

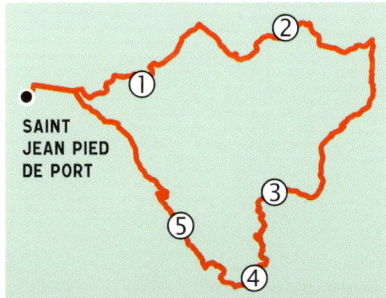

PAYS BASQUE AND EUSKADI

This ride over the border from the Pays Basque in France into Euskadi, as it's known by the Basques, in Spain makes that bridge via one of my favourite climbs, the Col d'Ispéguy, or to be more precise its eastern flank. It then features two more very attractive passes, neither of them particularly challenging, to complete a loop that a rider at any level should enjoy.

Heading west from Saint Jean Pied de Port, the first objective is Saint Étienne de Baïgorry, a little bump between the two providing a chance to get the legs and engine well warmed up. Weave through the pretty little town of Saint Étienne to pick up the D949, which continues westward and immediately begins to ascend towards the Ispéguy pass.

It's a short climb that thinks it's a big climb, with a whole lot packed into its eight kilometres. The road wanders through woodland initially, but it's when it emerges from the trees that it becomes spectacular. The road is cut into the bare mountainside, its meandering course offering long views up to the restaurant and shop at the summit and to the cluster of peaks across the valley. It's like a mini Tourmalet, grand and very impressive in spite of its small scale.

The descent from the pass is lovely too, a slalom through a series of switchbacks that send the road scurrying through rich farmland to meet the main road running along the Baztan valley, turning left. It's not especially busy and makes for quick progress alongside the River Bidasoa that forms the border between Spain and France downstream towards the Atlantic coast. After 5km, circle the roundabout to take a smaller road to the left into Elizondo and continue into Irurita, following signs in the town centre and just beyond towards Eugi.

This road usually features in the end-of-July sportive that bears the name and pays tribute to five-time Tour de France winner Miguel Induráin (see page 194) and it quickly becomes apparent why as it's beautifully tranquil. Barely rising to start with, it kicks up more sharply coming into a series of tight bends, although the gradient quickly settles again at around 6-7% passing through woods of beech, oak and chestnut. There are two or three steeper pitches in the final couple of kilometres before the 984m summit of the Puerto de Artesiaga, but nothing too exacting. All in all, it's a lovely climb, the view back down the valley towards Irurita from the summit quite wonderful.

The descent is much the same, a peaceful swoosh beneath a canopy of beech, oak and pine to meet the N138, coming up from Pamplona and heading for the Urkiaga pass and France. Turn left onto it and start heading back towards the border on another beech-lined road, climbing very gently indeed, the gradient never above 4% until the final kilometre. It passes the ruins of the Eugi royal munitions factory, once the centre of a village where 500 people lived, but captured and dismantled by French forces during the War of the Pyrenees in 1794.

Still cloaked by thick woodland, the road eases up to the Urkiaga pass, drops briefly, then rises gently to reach the frontier, a rather incongruous petrol station just before it essentially there to provide French drivers with comparatively cheap fuel. The view a little further on down the Aldudes valley is reminiscent and just as good as the one from the Artesiaga an hour or so before. The descent has a bit more punch, though, the road falling sharply through Esnazu to reach the village of Aldudes, from where it runs more steadily back to Saint Étienne de

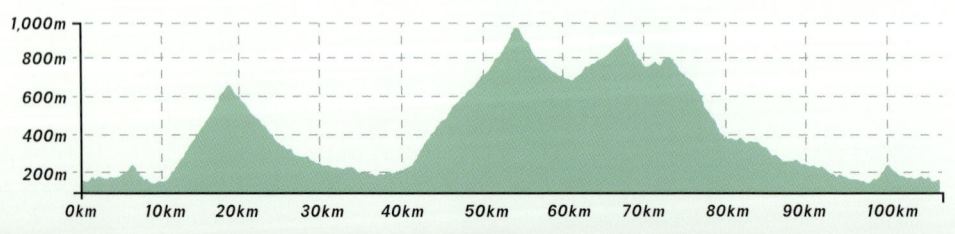

PYRÉNÉES ATLANTIQUES

Looking into France from the Ispéguy pass

Distance: 107km
Elevation gain: 2,187m
Highest point: 996m
Est. moving time: 3.5-6hrs
Degree of difficulty: ●●◐
Climbs: Col d'Ispéguy (672m), Puerto de Artesiaga (984m), Alto de Urkiaga (890m)

Baïgorry, the route then bumping on to Saint Jean Pied de Port.

Two border crossings, three very attractive and not too taxing passes and, for the most part, very little traffic – blissful!

Route in reverse

Just as nice, and with the added advantage of the Ispéguy coming towards the end, providing the perfect excuse for a decent coffee at the summit and the chance to fill your pockets with some Spanish goodies in the shop at the back that seems to stock everything.

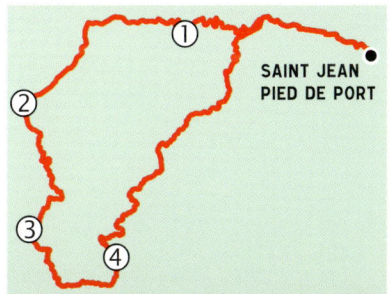

Parcours

0km	Saint Jean Pied de Port
1km	D918/D15 ←
9.5km	Saint Étienne de Baïgorry D15/D948 →
18.5km	Col d'Ispéguy NA2600 ①
30.5km	NA2600/N121B ←
35km	Elizondo N121B/NA8307 ←
38.5km	Irurita NA8307 ② /NA2540 ←
39km	NA2540/NA1740 ←
54.5km	Puerto de Artesiaga ③
61km	Junction NA1740/N138 ←
68km	Alto de Urkiaga ④
80.5km	Junction D58/D948 ←
97.5km	Saint Étienne de Baïgorry D948/D15 →
107km	Saint Jean Pied de Port

SHORT HAUL TO LA PIERRE SAINT MARTIN

Small, but thriving, I like Arette for its bike shop, which is a useful place to know in a relatively remote part of the Pyrenees, but, principally, for its gallery of local cycling stars affixed to the side of the sports hall. Among them are several famous names, including 1920s climbing sensation Victor Fontan, sprinting ace André Darrigade, two-time Paris-Roubaix winner Gilbert Duclos-Lassalle and Thibaut Pinot's loyal teammate Mathieu Ladagnous. What better place to start a ride than this?

The target is the ski station of La Pierre Saint Martin, where Chris Froome blew away his rivals in the 2015 Tour de France, setting up his second yellow jersey success. There are plenty of options for reaching this resort and the magnificent col above on the Franco-Spanish border, and this is perhaps the shortest loop for accessing the former, although that shouldn't be taken as an indication that it's easy.

Initially, the route heads in the opposite direction to the resort, running north-west to Lanne en Barétous. Just beyond, take the left turn onto the D632, La Pierre Saint Martin signposted as being 28km away. Heading south, the road tracks the aptly named River Vert through lush farmland, the gradient rising almost imperceptibly to Barlanès, then more noticeably beyond this hamlet.

At a sign announcing that the cross-country ski station of Issarbe is 11km distant, the gradient kicks up markedly, and will remain close to an average of 9% all the way to this first col. Swinging right over a small bridge, the road approaches its steepest section, rising through a dozen consecutive hairpins. Reaching the uppermost of these bends, long views emerge and the slope does start to ease a tad. Riding higher still, the vistas become very long-ranging to the north and west. Not far past the tiny and quite forlorn-looking ski station of Issarbe, the summit of this little-travelled but very testing col arrives.

After dropping 4km to the Col de Suscousse, continue straight across the junction to start the climb to the Col de Soudet. It lies just 4km away, but the pass doesn't arrive easily. After a first kilometre that's not too demanding, the angle on the next is close to twice as acute, the road clawing its way up through the pines. Above this progress is a little less demanding but there are still pitches well into double figures. Finally, the very last kilometre, the gradient relents a tad more, the trees giving way to open grassland, the views to the west glorious just before the col.

Turn right here onto the main road that climbs from Arette to La Pierre Saint Martin, which isn't the ugliest ski station in this range, but won't win many awards for beauty either. A cake and coffee aren't too hard to find, though. The top of the col is only a couple of kilometres and 100 vertical metres away, but that's for another ride (see page 216). Instead, head back to the D113 and begin the 23km descent to Arette.

To begin with, it's not severe. However, after passing the right turn onto the D441, the road drops away more sharply through a long

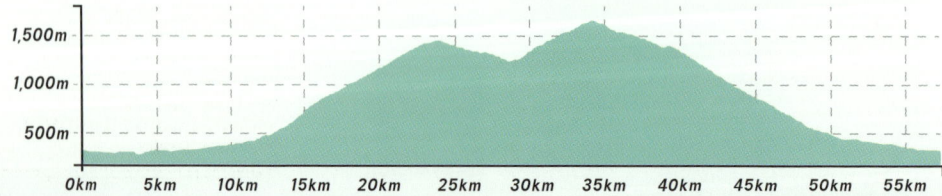

PYRÉNÉES ATLANTIQUES

series of hairpins. Thanks to the need to keep it open to traffic year-round, it is well surfaced and very broad. In short, you can really fly, sweeping back and forth in thrilling fashion, the fading roadpaint with names of the heroes of the 2015 Tour flashing beneath your wheels. A final 15% drop sends you dashing through the hamlet of La Mouline and into a far gentler section alongside Le Vert d'Arette back to the start.

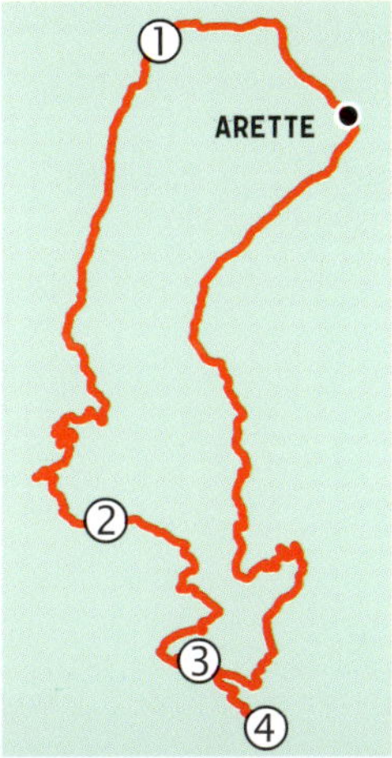

Route in reverse

Equally good, although the descent from the Col d'Issarbe is on a much smaller road that is not as well maintained as the main access route to La Pierre Saint Martin. Caution is advised.

Limestone pavement on the Col de Soudet

Distance: 57.5km
Elevation gain: 1,668m
Highest point: 1,650m
Est. moving time: 2.5-4hrs
Degree of difficulty: ●●●◖
Climbs: Col d'Issarbe (1,445mm), Col de Soudet (1,540m), La Pierre Saint Martin (1,650m)

Parcours

0km	Arette
5km	Lanne en Barétous
6km	D918/D632 ← ①
24km	Col d'Issarbe ②
28.5km	Col de Suscousse D632/D113 ←
31.5km	Col de Soudet D113/D132 → ③
34km	La Pierre Saint Martin ④
57.5km	Arette

LONG HAUL TO LA PIERRE SAINT MARTIN

This is a much beefier version of the short-haul ride to La Pierre Saint Martin (see page 214), taking in the Col de Soudet once again but run almost entirely on different roads and, on this occasion, pushing on beyond the resort to the magnificent col of the same name that lies four kilometres beyond the ski station.

It does head off in the same direction from Arette, but instead of swinging left towards the Col d'Issarbe, it keeps straight towards Montory, the valley road providing a perfect warm-up as it meanders between Pyrenean foothills. The easy start continues as the route starts to veer to a southerly course, initially on a lane that bumps across the shortest side of a triangle to join the D26 as it heads for Larrau and Sainte Engrâce, tracking the River Saison. The road climbs very gradually through Licq Athérey, the high peaks towards the Spanish border occasionally visible. At a mini-roundabout a couple of kilometres later, bear left towards Ste Engrâce and the Col de Soudet, the gradient picking up a touch more.

The top of the pass is 22km away, but almost half that is covered before the ascent of the Soudet properly begins. The road is cut into the cliff above the waters of the Uhaïtxa, a tributary of the Saison, winding very gradually up what is, to begin with, a tight valley. Passing the car park for the spectacular walk up the Kakuetta Gorge, where the walkways are often suspended over the turquoise waters of the river, the angle of incline nudges up a bit more, but it's still a breeze, a road that any level of rider can enjoy. At Calla, the valley opens out, the Col de La Pierre St Martin hidden behind the ridge up to the right.

Finally, in Ste Engrâce, its church once an important staging point on the Camino de Santiago route and still a draw for pilgrims, the gradient becomes more abrupt, a kilometre at 10% leading into a 500m stretch at 13, the road quickly scaling the very open northern flank of an otherwise heavily wooded valley. As it cuts through a short gorge, the road reaches some easier pitches, rising through forest, which dapples the sunlight, the steep cliffs providing short oases of cool on hot summer days. It arrives at a small plateau, with almost 7km remaining to the pass. Now the Soudet gets serious.

Those final kilometres average close to 9% with frequent ramps up to half as steep again. Approaching the Col de Suscousse, where the short option over the Issarbe arrives from the left, the trees and the gradient relent for a short while, but both return not too far beyond this junction. It's a grind until the final kilometre, where the trees fall back to reveal glorious views, although the slope remains quite rude almost to the pass.

To advance from the glorious to the truly spectacular, go right at the junction to climb, comparatively easily, for another 4km to the Col de La Pierre Saint Martin. The ski station arrives quickly, the panorama already expanding a long way across Pyrénées Atlantiques. Pause before the col to drink it in, then continue on to the high point to take in the view down into Spain, the road particularly striking as it weaves away to the south through scree fields and rocks.

The return to Arette begins with an 8km drop to the Col de Labays, where a right turn leads onto a much smaller road, which twists continually and is not a descent to rush, especially if it's wet or misty. Coming out of a sharp hairpin to the left, bear left towards Lourdios, entering a tunnel of green that also demands caution until the trees give way to pastureland. At Lourdios, there are three options. The shortest route to Arette is

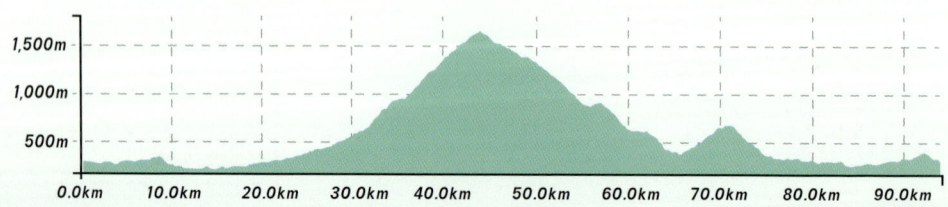

PYRÉNÉES ATLANTIQUES

Col de la Pierre Saint Martin

direct via the hump of the Col de Lie, the fastest is to continue alongside the river on the D241, but both would mean missing the little gem that is the Col d'Ichère, to the right on the D241.

It's short and very sweet, easier from this side, extending to just 4km at around 6%. On the eastern flank, the narrow road drops more quickly into the valley of the Gave d'Aspe, across which it has exceptional views. It arrives at the busy cross-border N134 highway. Turn left here for 10 quick kilometres, then left again on the D918 for a final and more leisurely 10 back to Arette, getting a final view of the mountains recently left behind from a little crest just before the town. It's the perfect way to end.

Distance: 98.4km
Elevation gain: 2,556m
Highest point: 1,760m
Est. moving time: 3.5-6hrs
Degree of difficulty: ●●●●
Climbs: Col de Soudet (1,540m), Col de La Pierre Saint Martin (1,760m), Col d'Ichère (680m)

Route in reverse

A lot of the climbing is through very thick woodland where there's little much to see beyond the road in front of you, but the descent of the Soudet is on a wider and better surfaced road. If you want views and aren't keen on technical descents, there's a strong argument for following the main route up and back down.

Parcours

0km	Arette
13km	D918/D726 ←
14.5km	D726/D26 ←
20.5km	D26/D113 ← ①
42km	Col de Soudet D113/D132 → ②
46km	Col de La Pierre Saint Martin ③
53.5km	Col de Labays D132/D441 → ④
61km	D441/D341 ←
69.5km	Lourdios Ichère D341/D241 →
74km	Col d'Ichère ⑤
79km	D241/N134 ←
88.5km	N134/D918 ← ⑥
98.4km	Arette

MY FIRST PYRENEAN CLIMB

This very long day out is a special ride for me as it features the first climb I ever conquered in the Pyrenees, the transborder crossing of the Port de Larrau. Riding into the range to watch the 1990 Tour de France, I still remember looking at huge birds of prey, most likely the bearded vultures or *quebrantahuesos* that give their name to Spain's most renowned sportive, as they circled way on thermals way above, thinking I'd never get that high. Three-quarters of an hour later, I was looking down on the birds as I approached the spectacular summit beneath the Pic d'Orhy and knew I'd found a new passion for the mountains.

It starts by taking the most direct route to the Col de La Pierre Saint Martin from Arette, heading south alongside the Vert d'Arette. The road rises from the off, but only gently for the first 9km, allowing you to warm up your climbing legs. The first steep ramp arrives just beyond La Mouline and there are plenty more over the next 9km as the road switches back and forth to reach the junction with the D441 at the Col de Labays. The average for that stretch is very close to 9%, and there are frequent ramps that are significantly fiercer as the road rises through thick forest. Keeping straight on at the Labays, the gradient easing considerably just beyond this col and remaining more comfortable up to the Col de Soudet, above which progress is a little more taxing for the 4km up to the Col de La Pierre Saint Martin.

The views dropping down from this high point are magnificent, and appreciation of them is assisted by the easiness of the gradient and the quality of the road. On the whole, the roads on the Spanish side of the range aren't as steep and are generally very well maintained. Why? A glance at the map reveals that there are far more towns and villages connected by high-mountain routes in France, while, in contrast, the Spanish side of the Pyrenees is all but deserted, the traffic very light on many of its roads.

Ten kilometres down from the col, and just before a ladder of seven switchbacks, there is an observation point next to a refuge and telecoms mast that's well worth a pause for the outstanding view it presents over the surrounding mountains and the lush green stripe of the Belagua valley cutting through them. The hairpins deliver a thrilling slalom to the valley floor, followed by a gentle glide down to Isaba. Just before entering this small town, which lies at around the halfway point and is a good place to pause and replenish, the route switches right towards Uztárroz. For the next 11km, the road rises gently through thick woods of, principally, oak and pine to the Alto de Laza, then drops to meet the NA2011, which leads back towards France.

These roads encapsulate riding in this remote area of Spain. The countryside is wonderful, the lack of traffic equally so. The gradients tend to be kinder too than on the other side of the frontier. The Larrau is a good demonstration of this – vicious on the French side, its Spanish flank is far more accommodating, a good place in fact to sample these mountains for the first time.

Winding up through pine, birch and beech woods, you don't get the impression initially that the border ridge of the Pyrenees is this road's ultimate destination because it's so benign. Seven kilometres up, it reaches open terrain and Orhy's pointed peak emerges. There's no obvious change in the grade, though, the incline consistent at 6-7%. After passing through a short tunnel, the summit quickly arrives, and what a panorama it presents, mountains rolling away for dozens

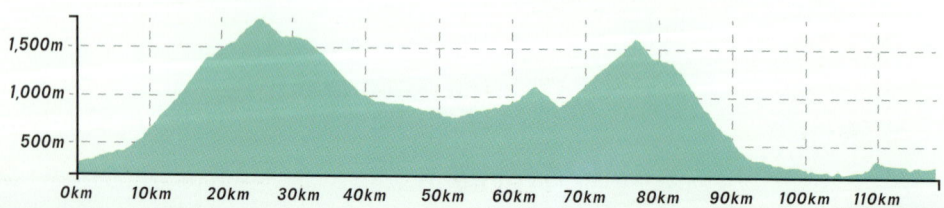

PYRÉNÉES ATLANTIQUES

Dropping back into France from the Larrau pass

of kilometres in every direction. Three decades on, I can still recall the feelings of exhilaration and wonder I experienced at this remote location.

I remember, too, the hurtling descent into France, the rattling of the overladen rack on my 10-speed Peugeot matched by the state of my nerves jangling, as both seemed to be coming apart. It's much more typically Pyrenean, the road narrow and sometimes rough, the gradient perpetually shifting, plateauing at one point, then running at 11% for half a dozen kilometres to plunge into Larrau (see page 206), before continuing in more sedate fashion, accompanying the Gave de Larrau and then the Saison to Laguinge Restoue, then shimmying right on the back road to join the D918 back to Arette.

Route in reverse

Essentially, the climbing is harder and the descending is easier. Extending to 15km, the Larrau averages 8% even though it includes a 2km plateau on the final approach to the summit. It is, in a word, brutal. In a similar way, though, the Spanish side of La Pierre Saint Martin is a lot more forgiving than the French equivalent.

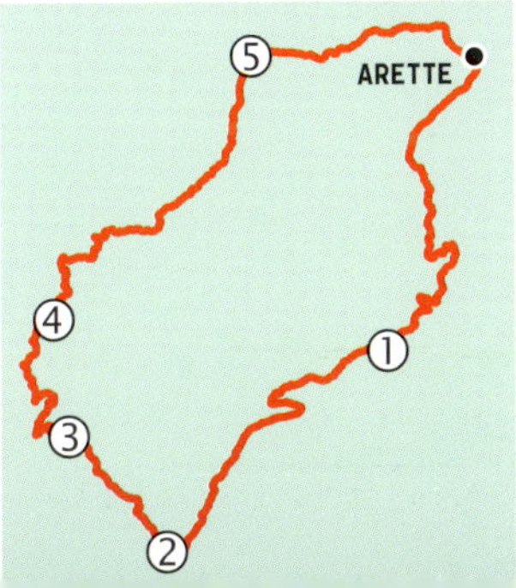

Distance: 118.4km
Elevation gain: 3,030m
Highest point: 1,760m
Est. moving time: 4-7hrs
Degree of difficulty: ●●●●○
Climbs: Col de La Pierre Saint Martin (1,760m), Alto de Laza (1,129m), Port de Larrau (1,573m)

Parcours

0km	Arette
25.5km	Col de La Pierre Saint Martin NA137 ①
51.5km	Isaba NA137/NA140 ➡ ②
63km	Alto de Laza ③
66.5km	NA140/NA2011 ➡
77km	Port de Larrau D26 ④
104km	D26/D726 ➡ ⑤
105km	D726/D918 ➡
118.4km	Arette

THE ARETTE, ASPE AND OSSAU VALLEYS

One element I always look for when poring over Michelin maps to seek out new rides are roads highlighted with a green edge that indicate they are scenic routes. Three-quarters of this sortie through the Arette, Aspe and Ossau valleys travel on roads classified in this way, including the crossing of one of the Tour de France's favourite Pyrenean passes, the deceptively difficult Col de Marie Blanque.

Outings like this one that avoid the higher passes are ideal for first-day acclimatisation, an easier option in the midst of some concerted col collecting, or for a day when the forecast isn't great and cloud is cloaking the peaks. Commencing in Arette, this ride follows the D918 for almost half its distance as it runs parallel to the Pyrenean ridge, running through woodland initially and then dropping into agricultural land, the foothills rising from the valley floor to the north, with the mountains to the south.

After a couple of kilometres when it merges with the busier N134 to reach Asasp, the D918 strikes out eastwards on its own right again in the direction of Arudy. It climbs into the green cloak of the Bois du Bager, reaching a little col, then tumbling downwards through bend after bend, before gaining that lost altitude again as it weaves into Arudy, which is located in the lower part of the Ossau valley that rises towards the Aubisque and Pourtalet passes.

At the junction with the D920, head towards Pau. This seems counter-intuitive as the city lies to the north and not to the south, but the routing is designed to keep traffic away from the centre of villages located in a triangle formed by this road and the main D934 that travels more quickly down this valley. These two routes merge at the second of two big roundabouts. Continue on the D934 for 3km before turning into Bielle on the D294, signposted towards the Marie Blanque.

Although similar in length, the two sides of this renowned pass are quite different. On this, the eastern flank, the road initially weaves up to and around Bilhères on the steepest sections of this pass. Above this village, there are long views across the Ossau valley, including the cliff-faces of the Falaise aux Vautours, home to the bearded vultures that can often be seen circling above these heights. Continuing to climb, the road emerges onto the Plateau de Bénou, a prime camping spot when the Tour is due over this pass but usually the preserve of wandering livestock. For a couple of kilometres, there's barely any altitude gain, then it kicks up through thick woodland, steeply for a short while, the gradient easing back towards the summit.

The western flank is far more direct and steep. After one switchback near the top, it bores down very quickly towards Escot, averaging more than 10% for the first half of the 9km drop, scooting down through the trees alongside the rushing waters of the Barescou. At the T-junction in Escot, turn left towards Oloron to follow the main road south for 5km to reach the foot of the Col d'Ichère (see page 216) on the right. It's essentially a mini version of the Marie Blanque that's all bends on its eastern side and far straighter on its western, the key difference being that it's much steeper from the east, averaging 9.5% for the 3km that ascend to the plateau on which the col sits.

I really like this little pass that's blessed with some big views, and it's followed by another in the same mould in the shape of the Col de Lie, which lies between Lourdios Ichère and Arette. Very narrow, with tufts of grass growing through its centre in places,

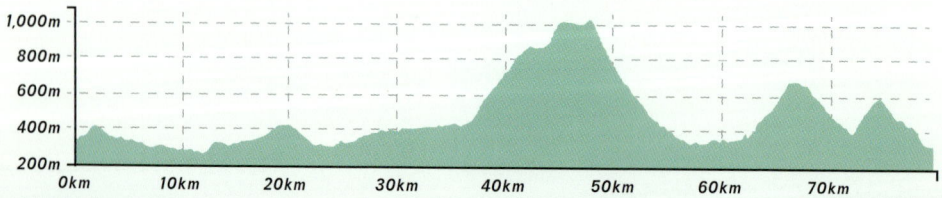

PYRÉNÉES ATLANTIQUES

Climbing out of the Ossau valley on the Marie Blanque

it's got a flavour of a country lane in northern England, complete with gorse and cattle who are quite sure that this is their domain. Within minutes of departing its summit, the road delivers you back to Arette, three valleys and three cols covered in just 80k.

Route in reverse

Almost all of the climbing comes in the opening 30km. The other significant difference is the degree of difficulty of the Marie Blanque. The final few kilometres of the ascent from Escot run at 10% for 4km and have ended the hopes of many Tour prospects, but are well worth tackling precisely for the test they present.

Distance: 80.0km
Elevation gain: 1,928m
Highest point: 1,035m
Est. moving time: 3-5hrs
Degree of difficulty: ●●◐
Climbs: Col de Marie Blanque (1,035m), Col d'Ichère (680m), Col de Lie (601m)

Parcours

0km	Arette
10km	D918/N134 ←
11.5km	Asasp N134/D918 → ①
31km	Arudy D918/D920 →
33.5km	D920/D934 →
36.5km	Bielle D934/D294 → ②
48km	Col de Marie Blanque ③
57km	Escot D294/D238 ←
57.5km	D238/N134 ← ④
62.5km	N134/D241 →
66.5km	Col d'Ichère ⑤
72km	Lourdios Ichère D241/D341 ←
74.5km	Col de Lie ⑥
80.0km	Arette

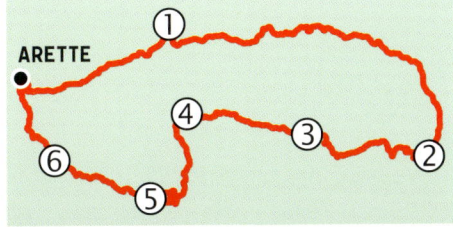

A SPICY CROSS-BORDER LOOP

Famed for its AOC red peppers that are sold in the town's market every Wednesday and the moderately hot spice that's made from them, Espelette put itself on the cycling map when it hosted the finale of the penultimate stage of the 2018 Tour de France, Britain's Geraint Thomas all but confirming his overall victory in that day's time trial. Its white-rendered houses adorned with shutters painted in the traditional Basque colours of dark green or maroon red affirm both its location and affiliation. This may be France, but it has its own very particular look and feel, much more akin to Euskadi across the border than its neighbouring regions to the north and east.

This ride offers a flavour of that, winding its way to the frontier, meandering across some of the first Pyrenean passes on the chain's long course east, before returning northwards to the Pays Basque, over a border that essentially doesn't exist in the minds of most locals.

From the Espelette's attractive centre, head south-west on the D918, then fork left onto the D20 just outside the town, heading in the opposite direction to the route of that 2018 time trial, climbing to the Col de Pinodieta, the lowest col in this book. Stay right on the D305 approaching Ainhoa, this road running through beautiful woodland to reach a T-junction. Head right here towards Sare, keeping left in the oddly-named village of Cherchebruit (Look for the Noise!) to reach Sare, bearing left coming into it towards the Col de Lizarrieta.

Now travelling south through fertile farmland, route-finding is a lot simpler and the traffic noticeably lighter. As the road starts to climb, it narrows, little more than a lane rising through birch woods. This region is criss-crossed by myriad roads of this type, linking tiny villages, bumping over short climbs, offering dozens of potential routes ideal for exploring by bike. I particularly like the ones that dart across a border that would once have been well policed but is now essentially reduced to no more than a snaking line on a map.

As the lane nears the frontier, it starts to weave relentlessly, gaining height through tiny and tight hairpins, before emerging from the trees onto the plateaued summit of the Col de Lizarrieta, where there are long views to the north and south.

Heading south into Navarra, the road is wider (and as a result better for descending) and lined by gorgeous beech trees. Initially it descends quite directly, then it slaloms wonderfully through endless twists and turns, the kind of descent that leaves you beaming with delight, particularly as the gradient is not that steep.

In the little maze of streets at Etxalar, follow signs for Zugarramurdi, climbing very steeply out of this heavily wooded valley. This is the most testing section, with ramps at up to 18% over what's often a rough surface on a road that appears to be going nowhere. It's as typically Basque as the village it's just left behind. Further up, as pine takes over from deciduous woodland, it emerges onto an exposed ridge, passing over an unnamed col, then dropping to a T-junction. Once again, follow the sign to Zugarramurdi, heading sharp left.

The route begins to head northwards, dipping sharply, climbing again to another unnamed col before tumbling sharply down a hillside on a well-surfaced stretch of road into Zugarramurdi, famed for occult activity and witch trials in the 17th century in the nearby Cuevas de Bruja – the Witch Caves. From the

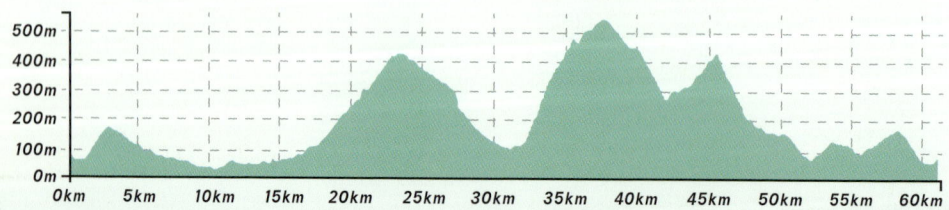

PYRÉNÉES ATLANTIQUES

Peppers drying in Espelette

central square, head towards Dantxarinea on the NA4401, which seems quite a highway after the narrow routes of the last 30-odd kilometres.

Turn left at the main road in Dantxarinea, bearing right soon after to pass the French customs building, continuing on to Ainhoa and soon after the route back into Espelette over the pimple that is the Pinodieta.

Route in reverse

It's probably easier to follow the route from Zugarramurdi through the thick woodland to Etxalar, but the very steep section down into that second village should be tackled with extreme caution as it has been poorly maintained. You'd miss that fabulous descent into Etxalar too.

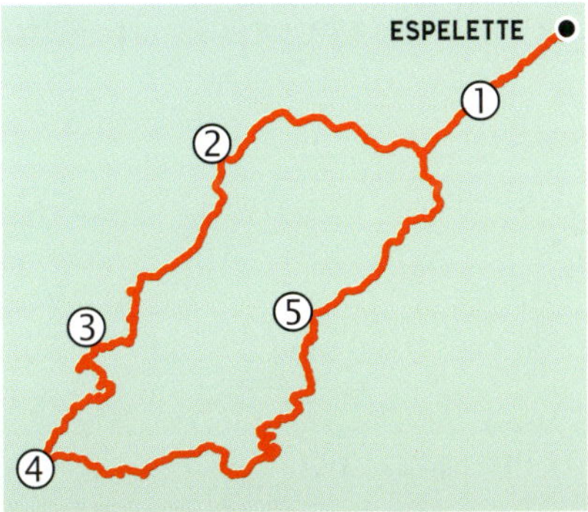

Distance: 62.9km
Elevation gain: 1,457m
Highest point: 546m
Est. moving time: 2-3.5hrs
Degree of difficulty: ●◐
Climbs: Col de Pinodieta (176m), Col de Lizarrieta (441m)

Parcours

0km	Espelette
1km	D918/D20 ←
3km	Col de Pinodieta ①
5.5km	D20/D305 →
8.5km	D305/D4 →
13km	Sare D4/D306 ← ②
25km	Col de Lizarrieta NA4400 ③
32.5km	Etxalar NA4400/ unclassified to Zugarramurdi ← ④
49.5km	Zugarramurdi NA4401 ⑤
53.5km	Dantxarinea NA4401/ N121B ←
54km	N121B/D20 →
60km	Col de Pinodieta
62.9km	Espelette

BACK COUNTRY BASQUE COUNTRY

With its principal focus on the mountains, this book doesn't provide many opportunities for riding by the sea. Indeed, due to heavy traffic during holiday periods on the Atlantic and Mediterranean coasts, most of the roads close to them are best avoided at these times. But I recommend this route that starts in elegant Saint Jean de Luz and heads along the Basque Corniche because it links very well into the routes over the Jaizkibel, just on the other side of the border, it lifts the lid on some stunning roads in the foothills of the Pyrenees, and because it highlights many of the best aspects of this region so well.

Heading south/south-west from Saint Jean de Luz, cross the River Nivelle and immediately take the D912 road running beside the marina towards the ocean. This quickly reaches the seafront and bobs up and down along the coast to reach Hendaye, once a haunt of Hemingway and now renowned in cycling circles as the Atlantic end of the Raid Pyrénéen, the end-to-end ride along the chain. Stick with the D912 through what is the last town in France, following the signs to Irún, which is reached via a bridge over the Bidasoa.

Head through Irún, heading towards San Sebastián and Oiartzun on the GI2134. This road dips under the motorway, weaves through some industrial lots, then starts to climb between green fields towards Gurutze. Go across the roundabout here, pass the road that comes down from the Puerto de Erlaitz (see page 198), and continue to Oiartzun, taking the left turn towards Lesaka soon after entering the town.

Beyond the village of Ergoien, the traffic, which has been gradually diminishing since departing Irún, all but dries up. Ascending gently through woodland, the beech glowing vibrantly from late spring, the gradient suddenly picks up, stretches of 2-3% followed by sections of eight and 10. The woodland gives way to bracken and gorse in a rockier landscape. An easing of the grade signals the approach of the Collado de Aritxulegi, the road running through a short and unlit tunnel at its summit, leaving the province of Guipuzcoa on its western end to enter Navarra on the eastern.

Dropping down through a stretch of woodland illuminated by the beech, the road reaches and then crosses the Endara reservoir, then starts to climb again through the trees. Radiantly green in summer, this road must be quite something in late autumn when the woods would be a mixture of yellows, reds and browns, especially when viewed from above on the Alto de Agiña, which lies just beyond them. Like the ascent, the descent off this, the ride's high point, is all sixes and sevens with regard to gradient, not too steep in other words. You won't want to rush it either, because the panorama is stunning, lines of hills running away into the distance.

Keep on through Lesaka to meet the N121 at a bridge over the Bidasoa. Turn left onto this main road for a couple of clicks, then bear right in Bera, turning right again towards France and the Lizuniaga pass in the middle of this bustling little town. This is the most benign of climbs, and all the more enjoyable for the relative lack of effort it demands as it edges up through another fine stretch of woodland. The border passes almost unnoticed, a stone at the roadside marking passage onto French soil for an undulating ride in Sare.

Coming into Sare, turn left towards Ascain, climbing once more, but only briefly to reach the Col de Saint Ignace, the starting point for

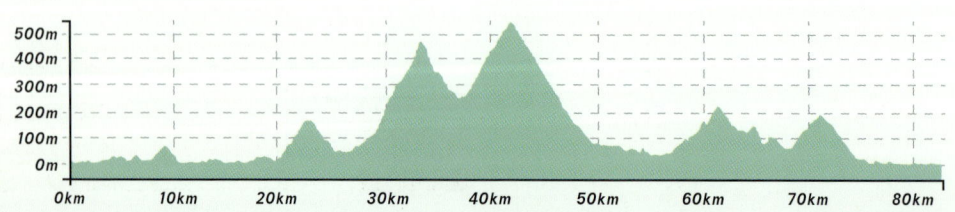

PYRÉNÉES ATLANTIQUES

The first Pyrenean foothills rising behind Hendaye

Distance: 82km
Elevation gain: 1,703m
Highest point: 550m
Est. moving time: 3.5-5.5hrs
Degree of difficulty: ●●
Climbs: Collado de Aritxulegi (439m), Alto de Agiña (550m), Collado de Lizuniaga (230m), Col de Saint Ignace (169m)

the Petit Train de la Rhune, a 4.2km, metre-gauge rack railway opened in the mid-1920s. One of the region's major tourist attractions, it hauls itself up to La Rhune's 909-metre summit at an average of 25%. Unfortunately for the Tour de France organisers, there's no parallel road access.

From there, the road drops quickly to Ascain. Go into the centre, taking the quieter back road on the left bank of the Nivelle towards Ciboure rather than the busier D918. At Ciboure, cross the Nivelle via the same bridge that led out of Saint Jean de Luz, heading for the beach and a rendezvous with an ice cream.

Route in reverse

Just as attractive. There's no obvious reason to favour one direction over the other.

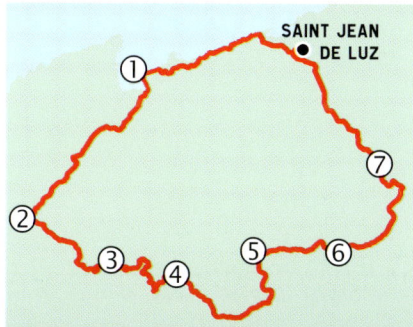

Parcours

0km	Saint Jean de Luz D810
0.5km	D810/D912 ➡
12.5km	Hendaye ①
15km	Irún bear right onto GI636
19km	GI2134 ⬅ towards Gurutze
19.5km	GI2134 ➡ towards Gurutze
22km	Gurutze
24.5km	Oiartzun GI2134/ GI3420 ⬅ ②
26.5km	Ergoien
33km	Collado de Aritxulegi NA4000 ③
41.5km	Alto de Agiña ④
50km	Lesaka
52km	NA4000/N121A ⬅
54.5km	N121A/Bera ➡
55.5km	Bera/NA4410 ➡ ⑤
61km	Collado de Lizuniaga ⑥
68km	Sare D406/D4
71km	Col de Saint Ignace ⑦
74.5km	Ascain D4/D504 ➡
81km	Ciboure ➡ onto D810
82km	Saint Jean de Luz

225

TOUR OF THE BASQUE COUNTRY

The first part of this long loop based on Saint Jean de Luz covers roads that are the launch-pad for popular variations of the west-to-east Raid Pyrénéen, notably the Col d'Ibardin, small in stature but far larger in renown thanks to being the first pass for many on this epic ocean-to-sea odyssey. It's deceptively difficult too, never venturing as high as even 500m, but still clocking up well over 2,000m of vertical gain, bumping along almost incessantly during its final two-thirds.

After crossing the Nivelle to reach Ciboure, stay on the busy D810 for a few hundred metres. At the commercial centre on the edge of town, a dedicated bike path separated from the road commences. This continues for the next few kilometres to a roundabout at Urrugne. Here, pick up the D4 towards the Col d'Ibardin and Ascain, which dips under the *autoroute*, traverses an industrial zone and then makes for open countryside. At Herboure, head straight on as the D4 right-angles left onto the narrower D404, which quickly starts to climb through woodland to reach the Ibardin, which sits right on the border with Spain.

Cresting this rather lovely little pass, drop quite sedately towards Bera (see page 224), going right, and staying on the NA1310, at the first junction, then following signs for Pamplona. The road leaving Bera soon merges with the main N121A highway between Irún and Pamplona. It's busy, often with lots of heavy traffic, but the shoulder's wide so that you can stay well out of the way. A brief diversion towards Lesaka and then back to the N121A is advised to avoid a tunnel. A kilometre later, fork right down the slip road to enter a leafy sanctuary on the NA4400 as it heads towards Etxalar.

Like so many roads in Navarra, this one is well surfaced, quiet and quite idyllic as it weaves gently upwards to Etxalar, steepening a little as it leaves this pretty village for the 8km climb of the Lizarrieta back into France. Never more than 8% and shaded by trees almost for its entirety, the climb is a haven on hot summer days and majestically colourful in the autumn, with long views emerging towards the top. On the French side, what is now the D406 is far narrower and has several blind corners that should be taken with caution, but it's just as idyllic as it skims down towards Sare.

Approaching Sare, branch right in the direction of Saint Pée sur Nivelle, staying on this road at Cherchebruit, then bearing left towards Ainhoa and then left again heading for Espelette over the Col de Pinodieta. Continue into Espelette and onwards into the attractive spa town of Cambo les Bains, following signs for Bas Cambo and the D410. Soon after dropping down to cross the River Nive, go right on the D420, which climbs to a ridge with long views in all directions. These vistas change as this road twists and rolls for half a dozen kilometres to meet the Route Impériale des Cimes.

Running for 25km between Bayonne and Hasparren, this strategically important route was taken by Napoleon's army during the Spanish War of Independence in the early 19th century as it marched towards Saint Jean Pied de Port and onward to Spain. It quickly becomes clear why the French followed this road, which doesn't ever climb very high but regularly offers clear vantage points over the surrounding countryside, as far as the coast to the west and the Pyrenees to the south.

Before it passes over the *autoroute* to reach St Pierre d'Irube and, soon after, Bayonne, it reaches a large roundabout. Go

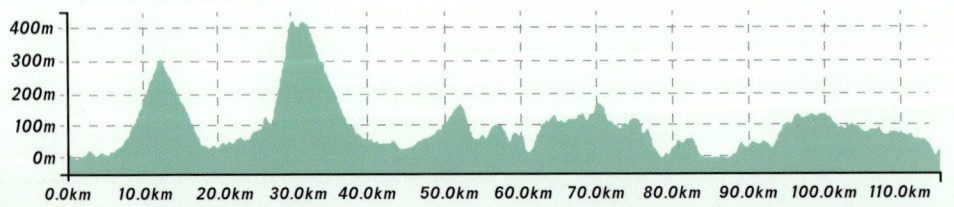

PYRÉNÉES ATLANTIQUES

Panorama over the hills above Etxalar

Distance: 113.8km
Elevation gain: 2,119m
Highest point: 441m
Est. moving time: 4.5-6.5hrs
Degree of difficulty: ●●●
Climbs: Col'Ibardin (317m), Col de Lizarrieta (441m), Col de Pinodieta (176m)

left towards and through Villefranque, this road running parallel to the Nive until it reaches Ustaritz. Track briefly towards the coast on the main D932, then, at another big roundabout, head due west towards Saint Pée sur Nivelle.

Stay on this road for 5km as it meanders through woodland to reach a T-junction, turning left here to continue through the trees towards Saint Pée. At the crossroads just before this village, there's a choice of routes. You can either go left into Saint Pée and from there follow the main D918 back into Saint Jean de Luz, or go across to reach the resort on quiet back lanes that bob across rolling hills and a short descent back into Saint Jean.

Route in reverse

Works just as well. The choice of direction largely comes down to whether you want to do the two most significant climbs early or late on.

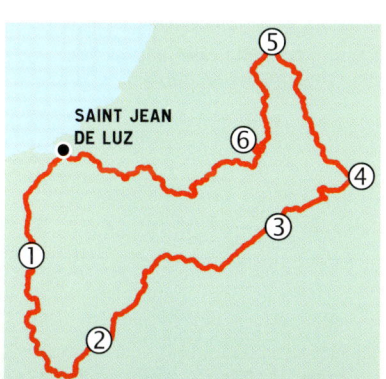

Parcours

0km	Saint Jean de Luz D810
4.5km	Urrugne D810/D4 ←
8.5km	Herboure D4/D404 →
12km	Col d'Ibardin NA1310 ①
17.5km	Bera → to N121A
24km	N121A/NA4400 fork → towards Etxalar
27km	Etxalar
30km	Puerto de Lizarrieta ② D306
41.5km	D306/D4 →
46km	D4/D305 ←
49km	D305/D20 ←
53.5km	D20/D918 ↑
55km	Espelette ③
60km	Cambo les Bains D918/D410 ↑
61km	D410/D420 ↑
65km	D420/D22 ← ④
79.5km	D22/D137 ← ⑤
90km	Ustaritz D137/D250 →
91km	D250/D932 →
91.5km	D932/D250 ← ⑥
97.5km	Junction D250/D3 ←
103.5km	D3/unclassified Miken Borda ↑
105.5km	Miken Borda/D855 →
106.5km	D855/unclassified ←
109km	unclassified/D307 →
115.9km	Saint Jean de Luz

GREEN AND PLEASANT BASQUE LANDS

I've got to know these roads during several stays in the Pays Basque, some of them quite short when working on the Tour de France and the Vuelta al País Vasco, others longer when drawn back on family holidays to this beautiful region. This route highlights why I've enjoyed spending time in the Basque Country, encompassing countryside that one moment evokes the green, rolling hills of southern England, but within a few kilometres stirs memories of the stark and stunning ruggedness of North Wales or the Lake District.

Commencing in Espelette, it leads off to the south-west, hopping over the Col de Pinodieta to Ainhoa and its wonderfully Basque main street, the houses rendered white with wooden doors and shutters in either dark red or green. It reaches the Spanish border at Dantxarinea, which hosted the finish of a 2019 Vuelta stage won to huge local acclaim by Basque rider Mikel Iturria. The pros were travelling in the opposite direction that day, coming down the 10km drop off the Puerto de Otxondo.

This is a steady climb, barely touching 4% for 3km, then fluctuating either side of six for the next half dozen. It rises through huge, sweeping bends where there are long-ranging views on several open sections, before concluding with another kilometre through thick woods to the summit, adjacent to the turn to the Pico Gorramakil (see page 196). The descent off it is almost a mirror image in terms of profile, dropping steadily into the Valle del Baztán.

Turn left at the crossroads in Ordoqui, heading towards the Col d'Ispéguy, scene of a battle between French Republican troops and Spanish and French royalist forces during the War of the Pyrenees in 1794, the larger Republican brigade driving their rivals from the ridge and back down this side of the pass into Spain. The road arrows through farmland, gaining a little bit of altitude but not enough to force most seasoned riders out of the big ring for half a dozen kilometres. On bright days, the range of greens, from the darkness of the oaks to the fading colour of newly cut hay meadows, is gorgeously striking.

The ease of the gradient allows you to draw in the splendour of this valley, sections of six, seven and eight per cent only arriving once the road is wiggling upwards to the summit, by which point marvellous views help to suppress any thought of this being a struggle. The arrival at the col underlines what a gem this comparatively small pass is. Order a *café con leche* at the restaurant astride the border and soak in the view into both countries, with those into France particularly fine.

The difference in the landscape on the French side is immediately striking. The Ispéguy's eastern flank is more rugged, bare rock and bracken dominating. As mentioned elsewhere (see page 214), this side of the pass has a "big climb" feel to it, with stretches that wouldn't look out of place on the Port de Balès or even the Tourmalet. It's a good deal steeper too, averaging more than 6% with sections towards the bottom at 10. It makes you want to hurry, but watch out for the more technical sections lower down.

At Saint Étienne de Baïgorry, a pretty town that's ideal for a lunch stop, pick up the D948 in the direction of Saint Martin d'Arrossa. After bumping alongside the Nive de Aldudes, the road and this little river merge with a bigger highway and waterway at Ossès. Turn left onto the D918, on the banks of the Nive, staying on this busy route for just a kilometre before swinging right towards Irissarry.

It's this final stretch of this route that has

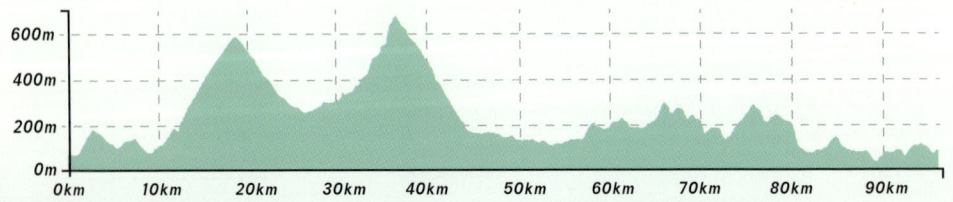

PYRÉNÉES ATLANTIQUES

a touch of southern England about it. The farms and villages may look unmistakeably Basque, but the oaks and beech and patchwork of fields set in low, rolling hills will make many Brits feel quite at home. At Irissarry, turn left for 18 rollercoaster kilometres to Hasparren.

Looking for another option to this direct route into Hasparren, I noticed the smaller D152 running a little to the west and highlighted in green on the Michelin map, indicating a scenic route, and I reckon it's worth the diversion. It's reached via the D452 to Mendionde, where you turn into and continue through the square onto the quite narrow and tree-lined lane that dips, weaves and, finally, dives into beautiful Hasparren, a vibrant town with the Église de Saint Jean Baptiste at its hub. Rejoin the D22 here, heading for Cambo les Bains and, not far beyond, Espelette.

Route in reverse

I love the French side of the Ispéguy so, given the choice, I'd probably opt for this clockwise direction. Essentially, though, it comes down to whether you want to do the bigger climbs early in the ride or late on.

Ainhoa

Distance: 98km
Elevation gain: 2,081m
Highest point: 672m
Est. moving time: 3.5-5.5hrs
Degree of difficulty: ●●●
Climbs: Col de Pinodieta (176m), Puerto de Otxondo (602m), Col d'Ispéguy (672m)

Parcours

0km	Espelette
1km	Junction D918/D20 ←
3km	Col de Pinodieta
6km	Ainhoa
9km	Dantxarinea N121B
18.5km	Puerto de Otxondo ①
26.5km	N121B/NA2600 ←
38km	Col d'Ispéguy D949 ②
46.5km	Saint Étienne de Baïgorry D949/D948 ←
54.5km	Ossès D948/D918 ←
55.5km	D918/D8 → ③
63km	Irissarry D8/D22 ← ④
73km	D22/D452 ← and merge with D252 ⑤
75.5km	Mendionde D252/D152 →
82.5km	Hasparren Junction D152/D22 ← ⑥
85km	D22/10 ←
92km	Cambo les Bains D10/D918 ←
98km	Espelette

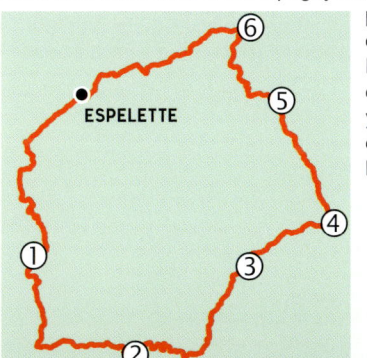

THE MAGNIFICENT AUBISQUE AND SOULOR

This is one of the classic Pyrenean rides, featuring two legendary Tour de France ascents, the Aubisque and Soulor, and some of the most stunning scenery in the range, including the spine-tingling balcony Cirque du Litor section between these two passes.

It begins in Arudy, where the usual choice would be to head south up the Ossau valley on the main road, the D934. It doesn't tend to be that busy, but even so I still prefer the lane that runs parallel to it on the other side of the Gave d'Ossau, initially accessed via Louvie Juzon. Running through the small villages of Castet, Béon and Aste Béon, I like this road principally because it's so quiet, but it also gives an idea of what the larger road would probably have looked like a few decades back before it was substantially widened. At Béost, where the 2,613m Pic de Ger is already drawing the eye ahead, you have a choice of continuing straight on to climb through Assouste to Eaux Bonnes, or to cut across onto the main road into Laruns in order to tackle the classic route up the Aubisque in its entirety.

If opting for the latter, as indicated here, weave through Laruns and around a long sweeping bend that reaches a junction, the Pourtalet 29km away to the right, the Aubisque an 18km climb to the left. It begins gently, barely making any vertical gain at all through two large and lazy hairpins, then easing up to the well named spa of Eaux Bonnes, once grand, but now very faded indeed. The road goes up one side of the elongated main square, turns to come halfway down the other side, then switches right to climb again, now with more determination as it rises away from Eaux Bonnes through a narrow ravine above the rushing waters of the Valentin.

As the valley begins to widen, the road crosses the river to the other side of it, then steps up through a couple of hairpins to enter the second, much more challenging, half of the Aubisque. Above two avalanche protection shelters, this col's beauty becomes more apparent too, the comb-like crest of the Ger and the pointed pinnacle of the Pêne Médaa standing out approaching another shelter, just below the ski station of Gourette. Above here, the road narrows a little and shifts to a northerly course, climbing through lovely woodland initially, then reaching open mountainside where the panorama across the valley to a circus of high peaks including the Ger is breath-taking. When they disappear behind a ridge, the view opens out gloriously to the west and north, the summit arriving soon after, its café blessed with an extraordinary 360° view.

The descent continues in the same astonishing manner, looking over the Cirque du Litor, a vertiginous, south-facing rock wall that derives its names from the Occitan word for avalanche. The road switches down to run on a balcony cut into the face of these cliffs, the abyss to the left quite terrifyingly close in places, a plaque at one point marking where Dutchman Wim van Est went over the edge when leading the 1951 Tour. He fell dozens of metres, but survived and was hauled out by a rope fashioned from innertubes that had been tied together.

Thankfully, the angle of descent eases considerably through this section, enabling you to steal glances across at the road on the other side of this cavernous valley that this route will soon follow away from the Soulor and to a huge array of peaks beyond. There are two tunnels through the rock lower down, the second one leading into the short climb up to the Soulor pass, where there's another

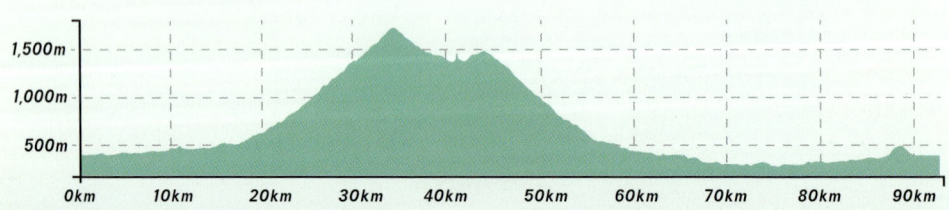

PYRÉNÉES ATLANTIQUES

Looking over the Col d'Aubisque to the Massif du Ger

café with a view to die for.

As already highlighted (see page 168), the descent from the Soulor towards Ferrières is consistently steep, fast and picturesque. At least a couple of stops are recommended to get another perspective on the height and drama of the Cirque du Litor and the incredible engineering feat that is the road that runs through it. At Ferrierès, the gradient lessens considerably following the Ouzoum downstream on one of my favourite sections of valley road.

Approaching Asson, turn left towards Bruges Capbis Mifaget, this another attractive road, mainly through flat and open farmland and running parallel to the mountains, the vistas very impressive still. There's one last brief rise just before Louvie Juzon, followed by the short return from there to Arudy to complete one of the most scenic circuits in the Pyrenees.

Route in reverse

Just as good because of the different perspective it offers on some astonishing mountain scenery. The Soulor isn't as high as the Aubisque, but its northern flank is just as tough a climb. I prefer the upward route around the Cirque du Litor, too, simply because it allows you more time to take in this almost incomparable section of road.

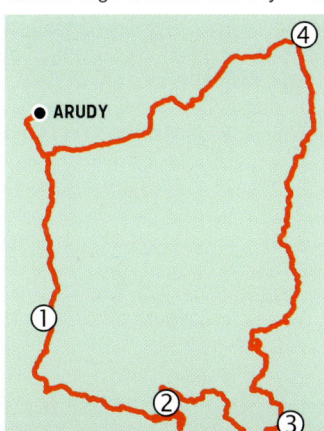

Distance: 93.2km
Elevation gain: 2,091m
Highest point: 1,709m
Est. moving time: 3-4.5hrs
Degree of difficulty: ●●●◖
Climbs: Col d'Aubisque (1,709m), Col de Soulor (1,474m)

Parcours

0km	Arudy to D3920
2.5km	Louvie Juzon D3920/D35 ←
3km	D25/D240 →
14km	Béost D240/D240E →
14.5km	D240E/D934 ← ①
17km	D934/D918 ←
34km	Col d'Aubisque ②
43.5km	Col du Soulor D918/D126 ← ③
72.5km	Asson D126/D35 ← ④
90km	D35/D3920 →
92.7km	Arudy

IN THE SHADOW OF PIC D'ORHY

As mentioned elsewhere (see page 218), the Larrau was the first Pyrenean pass I ever climbed up back in 1990 on the way to watch that year's Tour de France. I came up it from the Spanish side, a wonderful memory that still stays with me. I don't remember the descent off it in quite the same way, though. It was cold at the top, cloud was closing in and I couldn't see much, just a few hundred metres ahead, but it was enough to realise that the French side was a whole lot harder than the Spanish. It's only much more recently that I've become fully aware of how much more challenging this climb is. It's so monstrously steep that it's astonishing that it's only featured on the Tour route a couple of times, the last occasion in 2007.

Those who love a steep ramp are in for a treat with this route as I've paired the Larrau with its near-neighbour, the Col de Bagargui, another pass that's been criminally overlooked by the Tour. Starting in the village of Larrau, this pass is the first objective, the first move towards it downwards to the Gave de Larrau, the road tracking this river and then a stream that runs into it upstream through thick beech woods in a narrow and damp valley.

A dramatic change comes at a switchback that crosses this stream, the road entering open terrain. Above a second hairpin, the gradient starts to alter too, beginning a 5km haul averaging 11%, the middle three a degree higher than that. The landscape is wonderfully dramatic, the pointed peak of the Pic d'Orhy above the Port de Larrau standing out in a wide sweep of summits. The road is in good shape too, making the Tour's reluctance to head this way even harder to understand.

A little beyond an odd section where the two sides of the road split for a couple of hundred metres, the incline relents, the last hairpin turning the road northwards and in doing so presenting a breath-taking vista back down the valley to Larrau and to dozens of distant peaks. The top of the pass arrives soon after, the route switching right just before it, the road unmarked but just as outstanding as the Bagargui in the views it delivers. Running for 11km to the hamlet of Ahusquy, most of this stretch follows a high ridge, usually on one side or the other of it, but sometimes, and absolutely gloriously, atop it as it circles around the Pic des Escaliers. Although it undulates a good deal, it loses 400 metres travelling in this direction from the Bagargui, once or twice through steep pitches, but mainly at a gradual rate that makes it easy to savour the setting.

The route reaches a junction at the Col d'Ibarburia, turning right to descend for 16km to Tardets Sorholus, the first segment not too rude, but the road a good deal steeper after bearing right at the Col d'Arangaitz, the surface often damp in this forested section. It drops rapidly into Alçay, then levels out in farmland extending all the way to Tardets. Turning right here, there's little change in the incline as the road tracks the Saison upstream, the going easy for most of the return to Larrau, the Gave de Larrau taking over from the Saison as the rushing roadside accompaniment.

Passing the Auberge Logibar, with 3km to Larrau, a very long pitch at 10% heralds 10km averaging just a point below that. It's a grind up to Larrau and the little plateau where the route got under way, the frantic energy of the Gave de Larrau emphasising the abruptness of the gradient. Above the village, the road rises into woodland, the gradient erratic, 12%

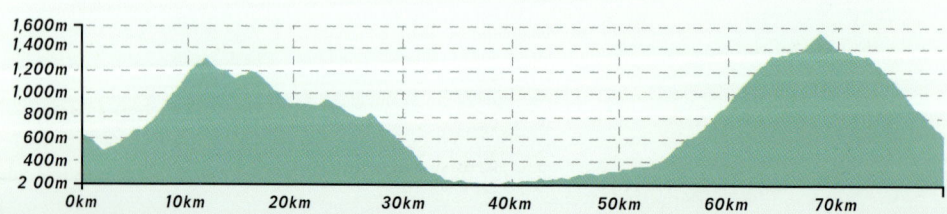

PYRÉNÉES ATLANTIQUES

Looking towards the Larrau pass on the Spanish side

one moment, six the next, making it hard to maintain a steady tempo. Then it settles down to a more regular rate of ascent, emulating the Bagargui with 5km at 11%.

Tall trees make it very hard to avoid focusing on the incline for most of that relentless stretch. When they do disappear, there's distraction aplenty, an elbow in the pass presenting expansive views across the terrain covered earlier and, for the first time, a close view of the Pic d'Orhy. The outlook gets more magnificent arriving at the Col d'Erroimendy, the start of a 2.5km plateau, the landscape wild and weathered. It leads into the final 1,500 metres up to the border, at more than 10% of course. With the Orhy almost within touching distance behind you, the panorama is to the south into Spain and along the chain to the east.

The return to Larrau is an adrenalin rush of however much speed you want to allow yourself. The road's in better condition than when I dropped down it in 1990, teeth and bike rack rattling, finishing the day a little shaken but hugely stirred. The Larrau is that good.

Route in reverse
It's a lot easier all the way to the foot of the Larrau, but the descent into the village off the Bagargui is quite something too.

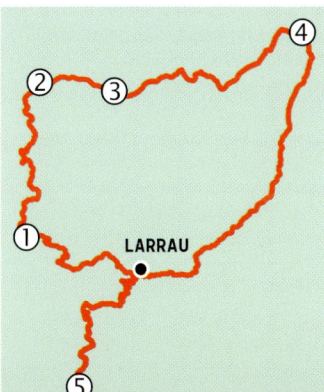

Distance: 80.0km
Elevation gain: 2,627m
Highest point: 1,578m
Est. moving time: 3.5-6hrs
Degree of difficulty: ●●●●◐
Climbs: Col Bagargui (1,327m), Col Ibarburia (957m), Port de Larrau (1,578m)

Parcours

0km	Larrau D19
11.5km	Col de Bagargui D19/unclassified ➡ ①
22.5km	Col Ibarburia unclassified/D117 ➡ ②
26km	D117/D47 ➡ ③
33.5km	Alçay D117/D247 ⬅
39km	Tardets Sorholus D247/D918 ➡ ④
40km	D918/D26 ➡
56.5km	Larrau D26/D19 ⬅
68.5km	Port de Larrau ⑤
80km	Larrau

233

RAID PYRÉNÉEN

There was only ever one way to finish this book, and that was by drawing up an end-to-end route, my own Raid Pyrénéen. The original Raid was conceived by Maurice Bugard in 1912, but the two world wars scuppered his plans to see the project through. As a consequence, it wasn't until June 1950 that Paul Mathis and Lily Betbeder completed the first officially recorded Raid. Over the subsequent seven decades, almost 10,000 riders have completed the Raid following the regulations laid down by the Cyclo Club Béarnais in Pau, the most important being that they start at Hendaye on the Atlantic and finish at Cerbère on the Mediterranean (or vice versa) and have to finish within 100 hours if they are following the original Randonneur route, which most do. This option based on Bugard's original idea is 720km long, crosses 18 cols and racks up 11,000m of vertical gain.

The CCB subsequently pieced together a second Raid route, the Touriste, which is 800km long, traverses no fewer than 28 cols and clocks up 18,000m of vertical gain, for which the time limit is 10 days. This is the one I prefer, largely because it follows the chain's spine more closely, but also as a result of the fact that some of the roads taken by the Randonneur aren't conducive to enjoyable bike riding any longer – the N20 from Tarascon to the Col de Puymorens is one that springs to mind. However, although I do like this route, I suspect I'm like most other riders in thinking that my dream Raid is even better. In fact, I can go further than that and state with certainty that it's better, because it takes in many of my favourite Pyrenean ascents. Here's how it shapes up…

Like official Raids, mine can be tackled in either direction, though I've sketched it out from west to east, by far the preferred option according to the CCB stats, with 90% of Raiders setting off from Hendaye. After the traditional dip of the rear wheel in the waters of the Bay of Biscay, the first col is the Saint Ignace (see page 226). It's not easy to piece together a trans-Pyrenean route that is truly that in as much as it crosses from France to Spain and back again, but the two ends do offer that opportunity. In this case, rather than heading east across the Pays Basque, this route turns south into Navarra to traverse the Puerto de Otxondo (see page 196), subsequently turning east again to return to France via the Col d'Ispéguy (see page 230), included particularly with its beautiful western flank in mind for those travelling in that direction and nearing the end of their trek.

I'm not going to specify where to break for the night, but I'd need a very big reason to head through Saint Jean Pied de Port without pausing for a meal in one of its many good restaurants and a slow amble through its beautiful and historic streets. All the better, too, to prepare for what lies ahead in the shape of the Burdincurucheta-Bagargui double (see page 214), the ramps on the former quite savage in parts, the ridge between them absolutely spectacular, the drop from the latter thrilling. The pairing also works just as well in the other direction.

After the descent to Larrau, where the temptation to divert over the eponymous pass is strong (see page 232), the route descends with the Gave de Larrau, then switches south-east towards Sainte Engrâce and the Col du Soudet (see page 216). This is a spectacular road from the off, the valley tight, the river close, the views impressive. In many ways, the Soudet approaches my ideal of the perfect climb. Of course, the parameters for that ascent also include having some very testing sections, and the Soudet isn't short of those either, especially in its final sections when there's a kilometre at 11.5% and ramps up to 14 and 15. The finale is wonderful, and I'd be very tempted to divert to La Pierre Saint Martin, a couple of kilometres up

Saint Jean Pied de Port

the road, and the col (see page 212) above it to push the wow factor to the maximum.

Sweeping down to the Col de Labays for the right turn that eventually runs all the way down to Arette, the next col is a much smaller one, the Ichère, only 680m high but a little gem that hops into the Aspe valley and towards the Col de Marie Blanque (see page 218), again not too high, but still fulfilling many of the criteria I'd lay down for climbing nirvana, its final 4km savage from this western side. This was also the first place I saw the Tour de France, back in 1990, the memory that stands out the throng of fans in the high meadows on the eastern side they came up that year and spooked cattle rampaging across spectators' tents, thankfully unoccupied.

Now in the Ossau valley, the next run of passes is predictable, but almost essential to any Raid, beginning with the Aubisque (see page 228). It's historic, spectacular and relentlessly tough over its final 7km. In the midst of researching this book, I bumped into ride leader, sportive supremo, film-maker and king of the cols Mike Cotty in Sainte Marie de Campan at the foot of the Tourmalet and asked him what his favourite ride would be. He picked this side of the Aubisque for its drama, including the spine-tingling and nerve-jangling balcony section through the Cirque du Litor on the eastern flank towards the Col du Soulor. Anyone who's ridden it would surely agree it's unforgettable.

After the long descent from the Soulor to Argelès Gazost, my mind would be trying to tempt me into another diversion, this time to Col de Tramassel (see page 168), better known for the Hautacam ski station that sits atop this summit with a sensational panorama, but my legs would no doubt be encouraging southwards through the Gorge de Luz to the most celebrated Pyrenean climb of them all, the Col du Tourmalet (see page 148). While there's really no clear answer to the debate about which side of this famous pass is the most difficult, the question of which is the most attractive is pretty clear-cut. The western side undoubtedly is, even more so since the re-routing of the road following a flash flood in 2013 that has resulted in a long section of the old road being set aside for bike use only, the Voie Laurent Fignon named in tribute to the two-time Tour winner who had a touring business in Bagnères de Bigorre.

After descending through La Mongie and into the Campan valley, the next up would normally be the Aspin. Although this route starts towards this traditional Tour de France route either to or from the Tourmalet and Peyresourde, it branches southwards instead to cross the Hourquette d'Ancizan (see page

154), a personal favourite because of its looks and views. It also enables an easier link with the Col d'Azet (see page 154), which is very open on this western side and offers amazing vistas across to the Col de Portet, where the Tour ventured for the first time in 2018, and to the towering pinnacles at the top end of the Vallée d'Aure. From the top, there's a clear view to the next high point, the Col de Peyresourde (see page 140).

I'm not keen on the eastern flank of this pass. The road is too steady in its incline, too wide, too well engineered to fit with my idea of what a true Pyrenean ascent should be. From Loudenvielle on the west, though, it is a little more in keeping with what I appreciate on a climb in this range, even though the lack of hairpins is a black mark against it. Much better, however, is the Col de Menté (see page 138), which comes next. Although I do prefer the eastern flank of this one too – it is, in a number of ways, the archetypal Pyrenean climb, complete with a spirit-sapping descent – there's plenty to relish as you rise from Saint Béat. It's consistently hard, averaging close to 9% for 10km, presents some fine views and isn't short of switchbacks, the second of which has legendary significance too as it's where Luis Ocaña crashed during a freakishly intense mountain storm when leading the 1971 Tour. As the Spaniard tried to get back to his feet, Joop Zoetemelk hurtled into him, leaving Ocaña with injuries that forced him to abandon the race.

The descent – including what is in this direction a climb – leads to another pass often associated with a Tour crash, the Col de Portet d'Aspet (see page 138). Although quite short, this side of the pass on the border between the departments of Haute Garonne and Ariège is unrelentingly steep. It soon reaches the point where, during the 1995 Tour, Fabio Casartelli fell with a number of other riders as they were descending from the top of the Portet d'Aspet, the Italian sustaining head wounds that tragically cost him his life. The white marble memorial to Casartelli is beautiful, moving and thought-provoking, those feelings heightened by the utter tranquillity of its location in thick woodland on what has always been a backroad.

The next pass links two of my favourite little towns, Castillon en Couserans and Seix. I didn't know the Col de la Core (see page 108) before researching this book, but it was love at first sight. Cut into a soaring cliff at one exceptional point, it provides stunning views up to the flat-topped peak of Mont Valier, its shape so distinctive when looking at the Pyrenees on the approach from Toulouse. The eastern side is super too.

The most direct way to Tarascon from Seix is via the Agnes and Lers passes, a hard but attractive ride. Instead, though, my Raid takes a longer course onto my home roads, reaching Massat via the leafy, little climb of the Col de Saraillé (see page 98). Continuing east, the route starts up the wiggling Col de Port, then switches left and skywards halfway up to scale the Mur de Péguère (see page 84). Three kilometres at 12%, it's monstrous, best to be avoided most of the time, but has taken on legendary status since being introduced to the Tour and, more importantly, allows me to ride through my home village, Saint Pierre de Rivière.

At Foix, the route turns south, almost reaches Tarascon, but diverts onto the Route des Corniches road just before this town to climb onto the heights above the Ariège valley and avoid the busy N20. The views from this road as it contours towards the Col de Marmare and then the Col du Chioula (see page 102) are wonderful. Beyond the Chioula, the descent leads into the Port de Pailhères (see page 114), one of my favourite

climbs anywhere when tackled from the east. Running up a narrow valley from the ski station of Ascou, the final 6km from the resort are a full-on grind. It's not particularly attractive, at least not until the summit and a panorama that's among the best in the chain.

After hopping over the Garavel, the next pass, the Jau (see page 76), is another favourite, but, like the Pailhères, I prefer it from the eastern side, from which the Mediterranean is visible on clear days. The Jau's summit is notable because it marks a switch in climate zones, from the damper and more typically highland Pyrenees to the Midi, where it's drier, the landscape bleached in the summer, the wind always likely to be gusting fiercely, especially nearer the coast.

Raids typically pass just to the south of Perpignan when heading for or leaving the finish point at Cerbère, but the roads in this corner of French Catalonia can be extremely busy, especially in holiday season, so rather than head east from Prades this route jumps from the Têt valley to the Tech via the very picturesque Col Palomère (see page 20). At Céret, the issues with traffic re-emerge but there's an opportunity for another hop to avoid it, via the Coll de Manrella (see page 28), where thousands of refugees and many members of the Republican government escaped from Franco's forces at the end of the Spanish Civil War, a monument marking this event at the summit, which is reached via a couple of kilometres of gravel road.

After dropping into Catalunya, the route cuts to the east to Espolla to climb for the final time, to the Coll de Banyuls (see page 28), the road back into France resurfaced in 2018 and dropping into Banyuls sur Mer and, a few kilometres to the south, to the beach at Cerbère and the ceremonial dipping of the front wheel in the Med.

Cirque du Litor

Autumn colours in the Ariège

Distance: 830km
Elevation gain: 22,128m
Highest point: 2,115m
Est. moving time: 5-10 days
Climbs: 25 cols

Route in reverse

I've chosen several of these passes because the climbs from the east stand out, among them the Jau, Pailhères, Menté, Azet, Hourquette and Bagargui.

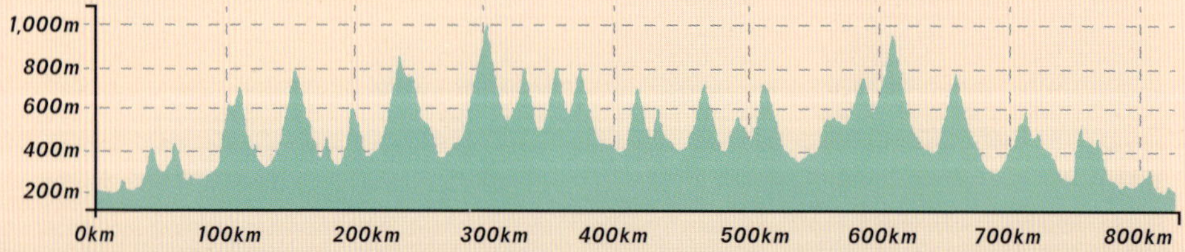

Parcours

22km	Saint Ignace
44.5km	Otxondo
63km	Ispéguy
104km	Burdincurucheta
112km	Bagargui
156km	Soudet
180km	Ichère
200km	Marie Blanque
235km	Aubisque
246km	Soulor
303km	Tourmalet
332km	Hourquette d'Ancizan
357km	Azet
375km	Peyresourde
418.5km	Menté
433km	Portet d'Aspet
468.5km	Core
493.5km	Saraillé
514km	Péguère
568km	Marmare
589.5km	Chioula
612km	Pailhères
661km	Jau
714km	Palomère
770km	Manrella
810km	Banyuls

INDEX OF CLIMBS

Note: Start locations in italics

Agiña 200, 224
Agnes 98, 100, 110
Ahusquy............................. 206
Aínsa 180
Aísa 182
Alzen 96
Amélie les Bains............ 24, 26
Andorra la Vella.......... 118, 120
Añisclo 180
Ansó 184
Arcalís 120
Ares (Pyrénées Orientales) 38
Ares (Haute Garonne) 138, 146
Arette......... 214, 216, 218, 220
Argelès Gazost.. 164, 166, 168
Aribe 190
Arinsal................................ 122
Aritxulegi 200, 224
Arnostéguy 190, 204
Arques 74
Artesiaga 194, 212
Arthaburu........................... 208
Arthé 208
Arudy 230
Askonzabal 210
Aspin 154
Aubisque.................... 230, 234
Aussières 72, 76
Auzines................................ 18
Ax les Thermes.....92, 102, 114
Ax 3 Domaines 102
Axat 66, 76, 78
Aychides 62, 78
Azet 140, 152, 154, 234

Babourade............................ 64
*Bagnères de Luchon 140,
.... 142, 144*
Bagnères de Bigorre.. 150, 158
Bagargui 206, 210, 232, 234
Balès................................. 142
Banyuls 28, 32, 234
Banyuls sur Mer.................. 32
La Barthe de Neste............ 156
Basseta............................. 132
Bataille 36
Bedos 74
Beixalis 122
Belate 194
Belitres 32
Benasque 178
Berdún 184
Beret 134
Berga................... 54, 56, 59
Biescas 176
Bóixols 128

Bonaigua 134
Bonansa 178
Bordères 166
Botella............................... 122
Bouchet 154
Bouillouses 12
Brousse 22, 26
Burdincurucheta 206, 208,
.... 210, 234

Cabus 122
Calvaire 114
Camperie................... 72, 76
Camporiol 40
Camprodon....................... 40
Canes 42, 46
Canillo 122
Cantó 130
Carcanières 78
Carrera 40
Catchadégué 108
Céret........................... 22, 30
Cerler 178
Chioula 92, 102, 234
Coll de Nargó............ 124, 128
Collfred 42
Collioure 28
Comella 118
Comte 124
Core 90, 108, 234
Cortals Encamp 120
Cotefablo 174
Coudons 62
Couiza 68
Coume Mourère 14
Coupe............................. 158
Couret d'Asque158
Coustouges 26
Creu 10
Creueta 48, 52
Croix Blanche 150
Croix Dessus 8
Croix des Morts 64
Crouzette 82

Dona 36

Edquisaroy........................ 196
Egozkue............................ 194
Elizondo............................ 196
Encamp 116
Engolasters 120
Envalira 116
Enviny 136
Erlaitz............................... 198
Erro 192, 202

Espelette.................. 222, 228
Espina.............................. 178
Espinas 68

Fadas................................ 178
Fage 70
Faidella 128
Foix........ 80, 82, 84, 86, 88, 96
Font Romeu....................... 14
Fontcouverte...................... 34
Força Réal 36
Formigal........................... 176
Formiguères 10
Formiguères (Station)........ 10
Fourches 74
Fourtou 20, 34
Frare 32
Fuerte del Rapitán 182
Fumanya..................... 56, 59

Gallina 118
Garavel 78
Gavarnie 162
Gorramakil 196
Goulier Neige 104
Grau de Maury..................... 8
Grès 8
Guilhem 8
Guzet Neige......................110

Hautacam 168
Hernani 200
Hospice de France 144
Hourquette d'Ancizan 154, 234
Hoz de Jaca............. 168, 176

Ibañeta...................... 190, 202
Ibarburia 210, 232
Ibardin.............................. 226
Ichère............... 216, 220, 234
Ille sur Têt.......................... 36
Isaba 186
Iso................................... 188
Ispéguy 212, 228, 234
Issarbe 214

Jaca 182
Jaizkibel........................... 198
Jau 76, 234
Jaurrieta 188
Josa 56
Jou................... 46, 54, 124
Jouet......................... 54, 56

Lac d'Aumar 160
Lac de Cap de Long 160

239

Lançon 140, 152
Larrau 218, 232
Larrau 232
Larrieu 104
Latrape 100, 110
Lauze 80
Laza 218
Legrillou 96
Lers 84, 98
Lie 220
Linas 70
Lizarrieta 222, 226
Lizuniaga 224
Llauro 20, 22
Lli 26, 28, 234
Llo 14
Llose 10, 12
Lordat 94, 102
Loubière 74
Luz Ardiden 164
Luz Saint Sauveur 162

Manrella 26, 234
Mantet 16
Marie Blanque ... 168, 220, 234
Marmare 92, 102, 234
Mas 72
Matamachos 186
Maury 8
Menté 138, 146, 234
Meranges 50
Merolla 48
Mezkiritz 192, 202
Mine de Batère 24
La Molina 52
Mont Louis 12
Monts d'Olmes 86
Montségur 86
Moulis 78

Nistos Cap Nestès 154

Ochagavía 188
Olot 42, 44
Ordino 120, 122
Orgambidé 190, 204
Oroel 182
Osquich 210
Otxondo 196, 228, 234
Ouillat 30

Pailhères 66, 114, 234
Pal 52
Palomère 20, 234
Palomières 158
Panticosa 176
Paradis 74
Pause 112

Péguère 82, 84, 88, 96, 100, 234
Pera 40
Perafita 32
Perche 14
Perthus 30
Petralba 174
Peyresourde 140, 234
Piau Engaly 160
La Pierre Saint Martin 214, 216, 218
Pinodieta 222, 226, 228
Pinodieta
Pla de Beret 134
Pla des Peyres 88
Plateau de Beille 94
Pont d'Espagne 164
Port (Ariège) 88, 98
Port (Barcelona) 56
Port Ainé 136
Portech 108
Portel (Aude) 62
Portel (Ariège) 82, 100
Portet 152
Portet d'Aspet 106, 138, 234
Portillon 146
Pourtalet 168
Pradeilles 14
Pradel 66, 92
Pradell 59
Prades 16, 18
Prat d'Albis 88
Prats de Mollo 38
Puigcerdà 50, 52
Puymorens 114, 116

Quillan 62, 64, 70, 72
Quillane 114

Rabassa 118
Rasos de Peguera 59
Redoulade 70
Refugio de Lizara 182
Remendia 188
Rennes le Château 68
Ripoll 46, 48
Rocacorba 44
Roque Jalère 18, 76
Roquefixade 80, 86
Route des Crêtes 28

Sabiñánigo 168, 174
Saint Béat 138
Saint Eusèbe 16
Saint Girons 90, 106, 108
Saint Ignace 224, 234
Saint Jean de Luz 224, 226
Saint Jean Pied de Port 202, 204, 206, 208, 210, 212

Saint Lary Soulan 152, 160
Saint Louis 72
Sainte Marguerite 34
Sainte Marie de Campan.. 148, 154
San Juan de la Peña 182
San Sebastián 198
Saoucède 158
Saraillé 90, 98, 234
Seille 38
Seix 110, 112
Sentigosa 46
Sept Frères 62, 92
Serra 28
Serra Seca 124
La Seu d'Urgell.. 126, 130, 132
Somport 168
Sort 136
Soudet 214, 216, 234
Soulcem 104
Soulombrie 94
Soulor 166, 168, 230, 234
Sourzay 208
Spandelles 166
Superbagnères 144

Tapia 188
Tarascon sur Ariège 94, 98, 104
Termes 74
Tentes 162
Thuir 34
Toses 48, 50
Tougnets 64
Tourmalet 148, 150, 234
Tramassel 168
Trava 126
Tribi 8
Troumouse 162

Urkiaga 202, 212
Uscla 96
Usoteguieta 200

Valmigère 68, 74
Vallter 2000 40
Vedao 184
Vielha 134
Villava 192, 194
Vinça 20

Xatard 20

Zuriza 186